Consociational Democracy

Political Accommodation in Segmented Societies

Edited and with Original Essays by

Kenneth D. McRae

The Carleton Library No. 79

McClelland and Stewart Limited

THE CARLETON LIBRARY
A series of Canadian reprints and new
collections of source material relating
to Canada, issued under the editorial
supervision of the Institute of Canadian
Studies of Carleton University, Ottawa.

DIRECTOR OF THE INSTITUTE
Davidson Dunton

GENERAL EDITOR
Michael Gnarowski

EXECUTIVE EDITOR
James H. Marsh

The Canadian Publishers
McClelland and Stewart Limited
25 Hollinger Road, Toronto 374

Printed and bound in Canada

CONTENTS

1979(Ⅱ-1898)754

PART FOUR:

PREFACE

This book represents a by-product of a larger study of linguistic pluralism in several societies that has been in progress for several years. If the present study has any precise inspiration it originates not so much from anything read in the literature as from living temporarily in Belgium and Switzerland during 1969-70 and becoming modestly acquainted with the political process of those two countries at first hand. For a Canadian it was a novel experience to observe political systems that emphasize the *continuous* adjustment of sharply diversified and clearly articulated interests. If the results of this adjustment seem somewhat nebulous and inconclusive from a distance, what stands out on closer acquaintance is the relatively high level of responsiveness of the process itself. One soon senses that in these countries, as compared to the more familiar Anglo-American model, the major parties and interest groups are continuously and formally involved in policy discussion and decision-making.

The experience of living in Belgium and Switzerland reinforced for me two personal convictions that had been growing since the early 1960's. The first is that the political traditions of Western democracies are highly diversified and the significance of any particular country's political system is not a function of its size or population. Those who set out in the 1970's to reflect upon or borrow from the political traditions of the West may well find that the experience of some of the smaller and lesser known democracies is most worthy of attention and most relevant to their situation. The second conviction is that Canadians, whatever their other advantages and providential blessings, do not possess, as they often assume, the best political system in the world. There is evidence that unquestioning acceptance of Anglo-American norms in the Canadian political system has not served Canada well, and that closer study might suggest modifications that would make that system more responsive to Canada's diversified social structure. Many Canadians have envisioned a political system that would fashion a more integrated Canadian society; the real problem is to find one that will reflect and support its continuing diversity.

In the 1960's that problem became more urgent. Many Canadians, French-speaking and English-speaking alike, concluded that the Canadian federation was doomed and that French and English Canadians would go their separate ways through the political independence of Quebec. I do not accept the need for such a solution. I do accept that it is imperative to explore, with urgency, imagination, and willingness to innovate, just how that federation may be continued and adapted so as to accommodate and reconcile forces that are threatening to tear it apart.

The readings in this volume have been chosen with several modest but distinct objectives in view: to indicate how the successful accommodation of serious political cleavages in certain countries has given rise to the concept of consociational democracy in the recent literature of political science; to identify and analyze the main approaches to the consociational theme in its broader sense; to illustrate more fully the European settings in which consociational political systems have arisen; to consider how far the consociational model may be useful in understanding the Canadian political system; and to raise for further discussion the question of using the consociational model normatively or prescriptively, in Canada and elsewhere, as a criterion for evaluating the past performance of political systems and shaping their future development. This book has no precise solutions for the present crisis in Canadian federalism. It offers, at the most, a first small guidepost for a journey that may prove long and arduous, a journey whose end lies far out of sight.

In preparing this volume I have had encouragement and assistance from many sources, and I should like to express my thanks in some small measure here: to the Canada Council for a Leave Fellowship in 1969-70 and to Carleton University for the sabbatical leave that gave me a first-hand glimpse of consociational politics; to the organizers of the 1972 Quebec Round Table on Multilingual Political Systems, jointly sponsored by the International Political Science Association and the International Centre for Research on Bilingualism, for the opportunity to explore the theme in detail; and to the Board of Directors of the International Centre for Research on Bilingualism at Laval University for allowing republication in this collection of my own two papers, which are to appear in the Round Table proceedings in slightly different form. The original drafts of these two papers have been much improved as a result of comments and friendly criticism by Val Lorwin, John Meisel, Jean Laponce, William Mackey, and Albert Verdoodt. I have also benefited from discussions about consociationalism with two of our doctoral candidates at Carleton, Ilja Scholten and Jim McAllister. In the many and diverse tasks of preparing the volume as a whole I have had generous assistance from my wife and from my secretary, Mrs. Maureen Sayers.

A final note of thanks must go to the authors and original publishers of the other contributions to the volume for their prompt cooperation in meeting a tight publication deadline, and particularly to Gerhard Lehmbruch and Val Lorwin for allowing papers already well known and widely cited to be printed for the first time in this collection.

Ottawa,
August 1973.

PART I
INTRODUCTION

Kenneth D. McRae

THREE APPROACHES TO CONSOCIATIONAL DEMOCRACY

In the 1950's, when the study of politics shifted from a traditional concern with formal institutions to an interest in the political process, the classification of Western-style democratic regimes looked deceptively simple. The earliest typologies tended to contrast stable two-party systems based on alternating majority governments with more volatile multi-party systems based on fluctuating ministerial coalitions. Most developed countries of the West seemed to fit one or other of these categories. The first was exemplified in the United States, the United Kingdom, and – with a few apparently negligible aberrations – the countries of the Old Commonwealth. The second category covered, broadly speaking, the countries of Continental Europe – France, Italy, Germany, and the other European democracies. When it was noted that some of the smaller countries did not empirically bear out the apparent correlation between ministerial stability and the number of significant parties in the legislature, there was a tendency to dismiss these examples as deviant cases, or as an intermediate category combining characteristics of the other two.[1] Besides, these smaller countries remained virtual *terrae incognitae* to most political scientists and as such did not unduly disturb the symmetry of theory. Finally, since the study of politics in the developing world was just getting under way, there was more interest in testing theoretical models against the emergent political systems of the Third World.

The 1960's brought an increased sophistication in the development of models and a wider range of questions for analysis. The stability of regimes was differentiated from ministerial stability. Political integration and nation building, questions of burning concern to developing countries, were studied in the older Western societies as well. There was a growing realization that the major powers of the West were not the only possible models for the developing world. The United States may have been the first new nation, but was its pattern of social and political development the most relevant one for those emancipated more recently? By this time the Third World had been developing some distinctive political patterns of its own, and this innovation in turn stimulated a closer look at variations in the political experience of the West. Specifically, the political processes of the long neglected smaller democracies of Western Europe attracted a share of this increased attention. By the late 1960's the result was a rapidly growing literature on these countries which has important impli-

---

[1] A well known example is G. A. Almond, "Comparative Political Systems," *Journal of Politics*, Vol. 18 (1956), 391-409.

cations both for theory formation and for possible application in other parts of the world.

My concern in this book is not with the smaller European democracies in general, but with certain patterns of social structure and political behavior that have been exemplified most sharply in the Netherlands, Belgium, Austria and Switzerland. All four of these countries have been characterized by substantial cleavages in social structure in addition to those arising from socio-economic differences, cleavages founded on broad ideological or religious foundations. In general their political parties and voluntary associations – and to a degree even their formal governmental institutions – have been structured so as to acknowledge and reinforce these cleavages. They have all tended towards multi-party systems in which no single party can dominate the legislature. Nevertheless all four countries have been able to develop stable, effective governments commanding the support of a broad sector of the legislature. All four have successfully accommodated a degree of social and ideological cleavage that elsewhere has reduced multi-party systems to paralysis and chronic instability. The apparent paradox of strong social fragmentation combined with political efficiency and stability has led a number of writers to consider these four countries—along with certain others that are sometimes linked with them—as a separate category in the typology of democracies.

Before proceeding further we should note that a rather varied terminology has been applied to these patterns and processes. Val Lorwin has used the term *segmented pluralism,* and the term is also used by other writers.[2] The term "segmented" here is used to distinguish it from the more familiar pluralism of American political literature, founded on overlapping and cross-cutting memberships; others have tried to make the same distinction by using the term *vertical pluralism.*[3] Perhaps more widely known is the expression *consociational democracy* which Arend Lijphart has proposed as a third alternative to the centripetal (homogeneous and stable) and the centrifugal (fragmented and unstable) types

---

[2] V. R. Lorwin, "Segmented Pluralism," *Comparative Politics,* Vol. 3 (1971), 141-175 [below, 33-69]; G. Lehmbruch, "Segmented Pluralism and Political Strategies in Continental Europe: Internal and External Conditions of 'Concordant Democracy'" (Paper presented at the Torino Round Table of the International Political Science Association, 1969).

[3] See the special issue of *Social Compass* on "Vertical pluralism," Vol. 9, Nos. 1-2 (1962).

developed by earlier theorists.[4] Gerhard Lehmbruch uses the term *"concordant" democracy*, or *Konkordanzdemokratie*, which emphasizes how elite decisions are reached by mutual agreement rather than by majority rule.[5] Still another term is *Proporzdemokratie* or "proportional" democracy, which calls attention to the balanced distribution of appointments and patronage amongst the coalition partners.[6] In turn, *Proporz* in the strict sense is a variable concept and must be distinguished from systems which lean towards a fixed equality (*Parität*). Some other terms are found in relation to specific countries. Lijphart's longer study of the Netherlands is described as a *politics of accommodation*,[7] and Bluhm refers to the reconstruction of the Austrian political system after the Second World War as a *contractarian democracy*.[8]

While I propose to use *consociational democracy* or *consociationalism* as the most convenient generic terms for the phenomena that we shall examine, these variations in terminology are nevertheless important. Far from being simply exchangeable synonyms, they have different overtones and resonances. They call attention to the fact that different analysts have emphasized different aspects of the political systems of the countries concerned, and in this way they constitute a first step towards more systematic distinctions.

[4] A. Lijphart, "Typologies of Democratic Systems", *Comparative Political Studies*, Vol. 1 (1968), 17-35, and "Consociational Democracy", *World Politics*, Vol. 21 (1969), 207-225 [below, 70-89]; H. Daalder, "On Building Consociational Nations: the Cases of the Netherlands and Switzerland," *International Social Science Journal*, Vol. 23 (1971), 355-370 [below, 107-124] and "The Consociational Democracy Theme: a Review Article," *World Politics* (forthcoming); R. P. Stiefbold, "Elite-Mass Opinion Structure and Communication Flow in a Consociational Democracy (Austria)" (Paper presented to the Annual Meeting of the American Political Science Association, Chicago, 1968).

[5] G. Lehmbruch, "Konkordanzdemokratie im politischen System der Schweiz: Ein Literaturbericht," *Politische Vierteljahresschrift*, Vol. 9 (1968), 443-459, and also his "Segmented Pluralism and Political Strategies in Continental Europe."

[6] G. Lehmbruch, *Proporzdemokratie: Politisches System und politische Kultur in der Schweiz und in Österreich* (Tübingen, 1967); J. Steiner, "Majorz und Proporz", *Politische Vierteljahresschrift*, Vol. 11 (1970), 139-146.

[7] A. Lijphart, *The Politics of Accommodation: Pluralism and Democracy in the Netherlands* (Berkeley and Los Angeles, 1968).

[8] W. T. Bluhm, "Nation-Building: The Case of Austria," *Polity*, Vol. 1 (1968), 149-177, and also his "Political Integration, Cultural Integration and Economic Development" (Paper presented to the Eighth World Congress of the International Political Science Association, Munich, 1970).

To state the central issue as briefly as possible, the existing literature suggests that consociationalism has been approached from three principal standpoints:

1) As a pattern of social structure, emphasizing the degree of religious, ideological, cultural or linguistic segmentation in the society itself;

2) As a pattern of elite behavior and mass-elite relationships, emphasizing the processes of decision-making and conflict regulation;

3) As an underlying characteristic of the political culture arising from historical circumstances that may antedate the period of mass politics.

Of course in any given situation none of these elements will be found in total isolation. The combination will vary from country to country, and in the literature to date the emphasis has also varied from one author to another. However it seems both possible and useful for analytical purposes to isolate the structural, the behavioral-attitudinal, and the historical-traditional components of consociationalism and to examine them separately. One can then assess the relative importance of each component in those countries that are generally considered to have consociational political systems. When this has been done it should be possible to identify and analyse aspects of consociationalism in countries where it is only imperfectly realized and also to consider it in the context of other kinds of social cleavage than the religious-ideological dimension that constitutes its usual setting in Europe.

Consociationalism as segmented social structure. The first approach to consociationalism, which is perhaps best exemplified in the work of Lorwin, is to see it as a function of the structure of social cleavage. The more completely a society is segmented around a single cleavage line, the more it is an appropriate site for the development of consociational politics. But this outcome is not a certainty, only a possibility. The hallmark of this approach is to begin from institutionalized cleavage structures and then observe to what extent elements of cohesion and cooperation actually emerge in the political system. As Lorwin has expressed it:

> Lijphart's definition is put in terms of the "overarching cooperation at the elite level with the deliberate aim of counteracting disintegrating tendencies in the system" ("Typologies," p. 21). I should rather define the system in terms of the bases of party formation and voluntary association and leave open the question of elite cooperation and outcomes. Not building effective elite cooperation into the definition makes one more likely to examine the conditions

which induce, and those which inhibit or frustrate, such cooperation.[9]

In the four European cases that we shall examine, the primary cleavage is religious and ideological. The development of mass politics in the Catholic or partially Catholic democracies of Western Europe has led typically to a tripartite division of social organization and a corresponding structure of major political parties, comprising in general terms a Roman Catholic, a secular liberal and a socialist sector. These three categories apply fairly directly to Austria and Belgium, and also with minor variations to Switzerland (where the farmers have a fourth significant party and corresponding interest groups) and to the Netherlands (where Calvinism has developed its own social sector and its own religiously oriented parties). In other settings segmentation can run along other cleavage lines, such as language, race, caste, or social class. But the requirement for segmented pluralism would seem to be that the cleavage in question should be sufficiently intense and durable to give members of the respective groups a distinctive and persistent outlook or cultural orientation that is different from that of other sectors, a *raison d'être* for maintaining organized segmentation. In some countries the linguistic-cultural dimension fulfils this condition. In two of the countries being examined here, Switzerland and Belgium, linguistic-cultural cleavage is also important, but it remained secondary to religious-ideological cleavage during the formative period of political parties and interest groups in the nineteenth century.

In this view of consociationalism, then, the respective segments each maintain their own distinctive generalized view of life, and this outlook serves as a rallying point for preserving segmentation in an organizational sense. Lorwin describes these cultural segments in a broad general sense by the terms *familles spirituelles* or *Weltanschauungsgruppen*[10], and this is also the term most frequently applied in Belgium, but there are local variations. In the Netherlands the segments are better known as *zuilen*, or "pillars," and their study by sociologists antedates the literature focussing explicitly on consociational politics by at least a decade.[11] The sociological process is *verzuiling*, or "pillarization," which has overtones of both segmentation and integration, of

[9] "Segmented Pluralism," 144, note 5 [below, 36-37, note 5].
[10] *Ibid.*, 141 [below, 33].
[11] J. P. Kruijt, "The Influence of Denominationalism on Social Life and Organizational Patterns," *Archives de Sociologie des Religions,* No. 8 (1959), 105-11 [below, 128-136], and cf. his *Verzuiling* (2nd ed., Zaandijk, 1959).

both separation of the columns and support for overarching structures at the top. From the Netherlands this concept has spread, with nuances, into Belgium and Germany (*Versäulung*). In Austria the image changes sharply: the *Lager* of the First Republic became armed camps in the literal sense, but they have succeeded in working out a politics of accommodation in the Second. Nevertheless the terminology and to some extent the imagery remain.

The extent to which segmentation can be carried in a consociational system can be quite startling to an observer raised in a more integrative setting. It is possible for a person to pass most of his life among persons and associations of his own persuasion from the moment of his birth in a denominational hospital to his burial in a denominational cemetery. Along the way he may be educated in confessional schools, attend a denominational university, be hired by an employer of his own persuasion, join a denominational trade union, buy provisions at a denominational cooperative, and patronize tradesmen of his own political persuasion only. His associational activities, whether for music, sports, youth groups, charitable works, or whatever, may be similarly organized by his own segment, and his leisure time spent by preference with friends who share his beliefs. He will read denominational books and a denominational press;[12] in extreme cases he may even watch only denominationally produced television programmes. And he will vote for a political party that makes a strong case for segment solidarity as a defence against opposing philosophies.

Of course in the real world no segmented system is completely compartmentalized. One pillar may be ideologically purer and structurally more complete than another. Under conditions of increasing urbanization all pillars are likely to suffer some attrition as cross-pressures increase, and Dutch sociologists also speak of the reverse process of *ontzuiling*, or dismantling of the pillars.[13] In the 1960's the ideological foundations of segmented pluralism appeared to be weakening in all countries, but even where this

---

[12] It seems to be no coincidence that in the Netherlands and Switzerland the opinion press has been more successful than elsewhere in resisting the advance of the information press, though even in these countries it has been slowly losing ground. Cf. L. F. Tijmstra and A. Gaspart, "La diffusion des opinions dans la presse: les exemples hollandais et suisses," *Gazette*, Vol. 4 (1958), 165-178.

[13] J. P. Kruijt and W. Goddijn, "Verzuiling en ontzuiling als sociologisch proces," in A.N.J. den Hollander *et al*, eds., *Drift en koers: Een halve eeuw sociale verandering in Nederland* (3rd ed., Assen, 1968), 227-263, translated into French as "Cloisonnement et décloisonnement culturels comme processus sociologiques," *Social Compass*, Vol. 9 (1962), 63-107.

was most marked there remained nevertheless a formidable residue in the structure of parties and interest groups. These in turn are in the hands of elites having a personal stake in the preservation of these structures, and to the extent that ideological quiescence endangers their position they can in many instances remobilize their followers by an appeal to the dangers of dismantling the barriers.[14]

Consociationalism as a pattern of elite behavior. The second approach to consociationalism is perhaps most directly associated with the work of Lijphart, and somewhat less directly with that of Lehmbruch. The most vital area of concern here is the capacity and good will of the elites. As Lijphart says, "the essential characteristic of consociational democracy is not so much any particular institutional arrangement as overarching cooperation at the elite level with the deliberate aim of counteracting disintegrative tendencies in the system."[15] The particular ways of operationalizing the cooperation are not of great importance, and will depend upon historical, geographical and other factors surrounding the structure of cleavages. In a later article Lijphart identified three of the six possible outcomes of conflict among subcultures as developed by Dahl – mutual veto, autonomy, or proportional representation – as jointly characterizing solutions of a consociational type while the others – repression, separation, and assimilation – do not.[16]

The concept of overarching cooperation for Lijphart has four requirements which must be fulfilled if consociational democracy is to be successful. The elites must first of all be able to recognize the dangers of fragmentation; secondly, they must have some commitment to maintaining the system; thirdly, they must be able to transcend subcultural cleavages at the elite level to work with the elites of other subcultures; and lastly, they must have the ability to forge appropriate solutions that will accommodate the divergent interests and demands of the subcultures.[17] According to this approach, much will clearly depend on the ability, mutual good will, and allegiance of the elites; the role of leadership is crucial. On the other hand, the process of accommodation may be facilitated, as Lehmbruch notes,[18] by the fact that any legislature

---

[14] Lehmbruch, "Segmented Pluralism and Political Strategies," 6-7.

[15] "Typologies of Democratic Systems," 21.

[16] A. Lijphart, "Cultural Diversity and Theories of Political Integration", *Canadian Journal of Political Science*, Vol. 4 (1971), 10.

[17] "Typologies of Democratic Systems," 22-23; "Consociational Democracy," 216 [below, 79].

[18] G. Lehmbruch, "Strukturen ideologischer Konflikte bei Parteienwettbewerb", *Politische Vierteljahresschrift*, Vol. 10 (1969), 305.

is itself a powerful agent for socializing its members into a cooperative pattern, a "consensual subsystem" with respect to one another, and the same argument can probably be made for other organs of institutionalized cooperation among the subcultures.

Beyond these prerequisites, certain other factors may be observed to be conducive though not necessarily essential to the establishment or continuance of consociational politics among the elites. Lijphart singles out the existence of external threats, a balance of power among the subcultures, and a relatively low total load on the system as a whole, as favorable conditions. He also mentions distinct lines of cleavage between subcultures and internal political cohesion of the subcultures as important, while popular acceptance of government by elite cartel is also helpful.[19] Lehmbruch develops a similar but somewhat more extended list, drawing distinctions between internal and external conditions, as well as between generating and sustaining conditions.[20] However most of the factors listed by both authors seem to be not so much necessary conditions as empirically observed characteristics of the countries concerned that have facilitated the development of appropriate elite attitudes and behavior. Both mention as important the previous establishment of consociational patterns, but for Lijphart the time factor is important only in that after a certain point "inter-elite cooperation becomes habitual" and "consociational norms become more firmly established."[21]

The first approach that we have examined, that is, consociationalism as segmented social structure, is bound to the notion of long-lasting subcultural cleavages by its very definition. In this second approach the existence of significant subcultural fragmentation is the main reason for establishing a consociational pattern of elite behavior, but one may then question the necessity for the continuance of distinctive lines of cleavage. Lijphart does not make the continuance of distinctive cleavage structures a formal requirement, but he considers that it facilitates the work of the elites by minimizing tensions among subcultures at the mass level, maintaining the political cohesion of the subcultures and hence their support for agreements reached by their leadership, and also by articulating adequately the interests of the subcultures.[22] Lehmbruch, on the other hand, suggests that the concordant or consociational pattern of conflict management "may become so firmly established that it remains essentially the same even if the

[19] "Typologies of Democratic Systems," 25-30; "Consociational Democracy," 217-222 [below, 80-85].

[20] "Segmented Pluralism and Political Strategies," especially 3-7.

[21] "Consociational Democracy," 216-217 [below, 80].

[22] Ibid., 219-221 [below, 82-85].

matter of conflicts changes. . . . If our hypothesis is correct this would mean that continued existence of fundamental cleavages is not an absolute condition of the persistence of this pattern."[23] We may tentatively conclude that, in this view of consociationalism, a political system will function best when there is a clearly defined cleavage structure to articulate subcultural interests and provide clear channels for elite-mass relationships, but this need not be the *same* cleavage structure that first gave rise to the need for an accommodative pattern. Once the consociational pattern of elite behavior is well established, it may be adapted to accommodate new lines of persistent cleavage as well as other areas of more transient disagreement over policy.

What stands out most strongly in this second approach to consociationalism – especially as presented by Lijphart – is its emphasis on a pattern of learned behavior. The necessary conditions are few; success rests on the learning capacity of a relatively small group of leaders. The historical setting and geographical environment are relatively unimportant because of the "possibility of transnational diffusion of knowledge."[24] Or, as he has said earlier:

> Deep, mutually reinforcing social cleavages do not form an insuperable obstacle to viable democracy. The crucial factor in the establishment and preservation of democratic norms and democratic stability is the quality of leadership. The politics of accommodation opens up the possibility of viable democracy even where the social conditions appear unpromising. For those committed to the democratic creed, this is an optimistic and happy conclusion.[25]

The attractiveness of this second view of consociationalism, so heavily founded on the rational capacity of the elites, is that it promises to be so easily exportable to other countries.

Consociationalism as an underlying characteristic of the political tradition. A third approach to consociationalism, which is perhaps the most elusive and difficult to define, is suggested in the work of Lehmbruch and has been restated more cogently by Daalder with reference to the cases of Switzerland and the Netherlands. In this view, it is the existence of older patterns of elite

---

[23] G. Lehmbruch, "A Non-Competitive Pattern of Conflict Management in Liberal Democracies: The Case of Switzerland, Austria and Lebanon" (Paper presented to the Seventh World Congress of the International Political Science Association, Brussels, 1967), 6 [below, 94].

[24] "Cultural Diversity," 13.

[25] *The Politics of Accommodation*, 211.

cooperation in the pre-modern period that paves the way for a politics of accommodation in an age of mass politics: "In sum, ancient pluralism has facilitated the development of a stable, legitimate and consistently pluralist modern society."[26] Or, as he has expressed it elsewhere: "Older elite styles eased the transition to mass politics and made for a tradition in which the principle of proportionality led to a de-emphasis of the majority principle in favor of a pluralist autonomy of all subgroups in the society."[27]

The crucial factor in this third view of consociationalism is the pattern of the historical political tradition. On this point the four countries that we are examining reveal certain variations which can best be examined on an individual basis later on, but they also have one important common characteristic. All four lay at one period or another within the boundaries of the Holy Roman Empire, and all four escaped in varying degrees the long, gradual centralization of authority that was characteristic of France, Spain, England, Scotland and other national monarchies from the twelfth to the sixteenth centuries. Further, all four felt to a greater or lesser degree the impact of the Thirty Years' War and the religious settlement of the Treaty of Westphalia. Lehmbruch notes that the Treaty provided explicitly for resolving differences between the Protestant and Catholic members of the Empire by mutual agreement rather than by majority vote: *sola amicabilis compositio lites dirimat non attenta votorum pluralitate.*[28]

One of the most interesting illustrations of this Imperial heritage may be seen and analyzed in a setting where it is no longer the undisputed political norm, contemporary West Germany. The early years of the Federal Republic appeared to have established a competitive party system, and public attitudes towards *Proporzdemokratie* on the Austrian model seemed generally unfavorable. Yet the formation of a Christian Democratic-Social Democratic coalition in 1966, Lehmbruch notes, was an occasion for calling attention to the fact that

> large sectors of the political system preserve traditions of proportional participation which date back to a situation when alternative government was a notion alien to German political thought.

[26] Daalder, "On Building Consociational Nations," 361 [below, 114].

[27] H. Daalder, "Cabinets and Party Systems in ten European Democracies," *Acta Politica,* Vol. 6 (1971), 299-300. He explores the theme more broadly in his "Parties, Elites, and Political Development in Western Europe," in J. La Palombara and M. Weiner, eds., *Political Parties and Political Development* (Princeton, 1966), 43-77.

[28] *Proporzdemokratie,* 7-8.

Pointing out that the concept of *Proporz* is prominent in local government executives, federal parliamentary committees, in the Federal Constitutional Court, the supervisory boards of the broadcasting media, and in other agencies, he goes on to suggest that in West Germany such institutional arrangements

> can be regarded as an older stratum of political culture in which party co-operation is viewed as a condition of impartial, hence just and rational decision-making, which has only recently been partially overlaid by a stratum constituted of the above mentioned trends towards alternative government. On the whole, the political system of West Germany may be characterized as a mixed system which combines elements of party competition and majority rule with elements of proportional division of influence and of bargaining, and its *Proporz* segments keep alive political attitudes which may regain preponderance on the level of national policy-making too.[29]

Since both the second and third approaches to consociationalism focus upon elite accommodation, it becomes important to clarify the difference between them. In the second approach elite cooperation is seen as a pattern of learned behavior, a deliberate response to the disintegrative perils of segmentation; in the third approach elite cooperation is a longstanding characteristic of the political system, a factor which itself helps to moderate tensions as mass party formation develops along pluralist lines. The difference is not simply a matter of timing, but of causal relationships. Daalder suggests that elite behavior should not be viewed solely as a dependent variable, but that "the élite culture is in itself a most important independent variable which may go far to determine how cleavages are handled in a political society . . ."[30]

The distinction between these second and third approaches becomes of the utmost significance when we consider how far the consociational model may be appropriate in other settings. Lijphart argues that the behavior of elites can be restructured through imitation of foreign examples.[31] Daalder insists on the long-run tradition of elite accommodation – at least in the Dutch and Swiss cases – as an independent component of political culture. Nevertheless, he suggests that the consociational model may still be relevant for some developing nations if they can recognize their older pluralist traditions as useful foundations to build upon

---

[29] G. Lehmbruch, "The Ambiguous Coalition in West Germany", *Government and Opposition*, Vol. 3 (1968), 181-204.
[30] "On Building Consociational Nations," 368 [below, 122].
[31] "Cultural Diversity," 13-14.

rather than obstacles to be overcome as nation building proceeds.[32] But the question may then be posed as to whether consociationalism has any place in societies where older traditions of pluralism and elite accommodation are weak or substantially absent, a question that becomes relevant when we consider the case of Canada in Part IV below.

THEORETICAL APPROACHES AND SPECIFIC APPLICATIONS: THE FOUR "CLASSIC" CASES.

From the recent literature on comparative politics we have identified and outlined three distinct approaches to consociational democracy. It is clear that different authors have approached the concept in different ways, but are they describing different phenomena in different countries? To explore this possibility we shall review very briefly the four "classic" cases of consociationalism among developed Western democracies, namely the Netherlands, Austria, Belgium, and Switzerland, in order to estimate how far each of the three approaches applies in each specific case.

The object of this exercise is both to understand more clearly how the political systems of these four countries have functioned during certain stages of their development and also to test certain theoretical propositions advanced in the consociational literature in a variety of actual political settings. In doing so we shall be doubly selective. In the first place certain other countries that have been identified by some authors as consociational systems, such as Lebanon, Cyprus, Luxembourg, Colombia, Uruguay, and Malaysia, will not be examined here. Secondly, we shall be interested primarily in those aspects of theory that relate to the three major approaches outlined above. As the readings and bibliography later on will show, the literature on consociationalism, recent as it is, yields a variety of further theoretical insights and hypotheses that cannot be followed up in detail within the limits of this book.

The Netherlands. From the standpoint of social segmentation, the phenomenon of *verzuiling* has been examined in a number of studies.[33] Historically, there have been three main *zuilen* or blocs in Dutch society, Catholic, Calvinist, and secular. The secular *zuil* is further divided into socialist and liberal ideological groups, each with its own major political party, and some authors also treat fundamentalist and latitudinarian Calvinists and their respec-

---

[32] "On Building Consociational Nations," 368.

[33] Kruijt, "The Influence of Denominationalism" [see below, 128-136] and also his *Verzuiling;* Lijphart, *The Politics of Accommodation;* Lorwin, "Segmented Pluralism," [see below, 33-69].

tive political parties, the Anti-Revolutionary Party and the Christian Historical Union, as separate blocs. According to the criteria used, therefore, one can view Dutch society in terms of three, or four, or five main blocs.[34] Lorwin attempts to estimate the intensity and completeness of religious-ideological segmentation among the blocs by establishing a table for some 15 sectors of social activity – education, the mass media, socio-economic organizations, leisure, and the political realm – and for the Netherlands he finds high or at least medium levels of segmentation for all sectors examined.[35] Even the electronic media show segmentation in that the broadcasting systems developed through a highly unusual system of five private societies, each having its own ideological outlook, its own paid memberships, and its own share of programming time.[36]

Various empirical studies show that the degree of segmentation is particularly high – in some organizational sectors up to 90 per cent – in the Catholic and Calvinist blocs while the liberal and socialist segments of the secular bloc are somewhat more open to cross-memberships and cross-pressures. There are strikingly high correlations between religious affiliation and party preference.[37] It is important to note, however, that the three main Dutch *zuilen* (including both Socialists and Liberals for this purpose in one secular bloc) show similar patterns of status and income distribution, so that class cleavage cross-cuts bloc or *zuil* cleavage almost perfectly and constitutes a factor reducing interbloc tensions.[38] Other cleavages have been negligible in recent decades; linguistic diversity (between Dutch and Frisian) has never become politicized. On balance, then, until the force of segmentation began to show signs of weakening in the later 1960's, Dutch society was highly segmented along a single cleavage dimension into three major blocs of roughly comparable socio-economic status.

[34] J. Goudsblom, *Dutch Society* (New York, 1967), 31-32, 124-125.
[35] "Segmented Pluralism," 155 [below, 48].
[36] J. De Boer and P. Cameron, "Dutch Radio: the Third Way", *Journalism Quarterly*, Vol. 32 (1955), 62-69; A. J. Heidenheimer, "Elite Responses to Ontzuiling: Reels within Wheels in Dutch Broadcasting Politics" (Paper presented to the Eighth World Congress of the International Political Science Association, Munich, 1970).
[37] Lijphart, *The Politics of Accommodation*, ch. 2; H. Daalder, "The Netherlands: Opposition in a Segmented Society," in R. A. Dahl, ed., *Political Oppositions in Western Democracies* (New Haven, 1966), 214-216.
[38] Lijphart, *The Politics of Accommodation*, 88-93, and see also his "Cleavages in Consociational Democracies: a four-country comparison" (Paper presented at the Symposium on Comparative Analysis of Highly Industrialized Societies, Bellagio, 1971), 18-20.

One can point to a pattern of innovative elite responses to emerging political cleavage. The 1870's and 1880's witnessed the beginnings of modern mass parties among both Calvinists and Catholics as these groups began to challenge the supremacy of the more secular, higher-status, liberal-oriented ruling elite. There followed a series of governmental alternations between religious coalitions and Liberal ministries, with increasing polarization over the questions of religious schools and the suffrage. In 1913 the Ministry of Cort van der Linden undertook to resolve the issue by appointing two special parliamentary commissions with equal representation from all seven of the parliamentary political parties. By 1917, against an international background of extreme external danger, parliament had accepted the commissions' recommendations and sanctioned constitutional changes that became basic features of the Dutch political system and models of *Proporzdemokratie*: all schools, public and religious alike, were to receive state aid proportionate to enrolment, and the franchise question was resolved by adopting manhood suffrage and proportional representation. The Pacificatie of 1917 did not resolve all inter-party issues, but it set a precedent for negotiated accommodation which tended in time to become the norm.[39]

This pattern of modern parliamentary development, however, should be set against the more distant background evoked by Daalder.[40] Situated on the periphery of the Empire and at the delta of the Rhine, the Low Countries developed vigorous trading patterns and wealthy mercantile cities at an early date. No single centre predominated, and the political tradition became one of particularism, corporate liberties, and a notable absence of centralized authority beyond a certain predominance accorded to the *stadholders* and the Province of Holland to represent the Dutch Republic on the international scene. The nineteenth century brought greater administrative centralization and a more conscious period of nation building, but this resulted in transferring differences among the emerging mass movements from the local to the national political arena. In this setting the religious issue and particularly the role of the churches and the state in education dominated all other cleavages during the formative period of mass political parties, and with the addition of a socialist party in the 1890's the party structure reached the same general dimensions that it maintained into the 1960's.

On balance, the case of the Netherlands is inconclusive in that it clearly exemplifies all three aspects of consociationalism. Persistent segmentation along distinct cleavage lines and articulated

[39] Lijphart, *The Politics of Accommodation*, 104-112.
[40] "On Building Consociational Nations," [below, 107-124].

in distinctive parties was strongly evident from the 1890's to the 1960's. The elites were able to meet this challenge by accommodationist policies, particularly after the Pacification of 1917. But could they have done so in the absence of the extensive tradition of pluralism in the Dutch Republic? This question remains hypothetical and cannot be answered explicitly in the setting of the Netherlands alone.

Austria. The First Republic of 1918 was born in trauma, a German-speaking remnant of the shattered Habsburg Empire, with no sense of constituting a separate nation. Its principal political parties were inherited from the Habsburg period, but this period had no experience of ministerial responsibility to Parliament, and the rising ethnic aspirations that ultimately led to breakdown gave rise to a multiplicity of parties with cleavages running along both ethnic and class lines. After the departure of the other ethnic groups the main political blocs remaining in the truncated German-Austrian territory were the Catholic Conservatives, the Social Democrats, and secular, middle-class liberal nationalists, the latter group being the weakest of the three after being cut off from its strongest base among the Sudeten Germans. These three blocs had become organized and institutionalized subcultures prior to the birth of the Republic in 1918, and the First Republic (like the Second) was the product of "a *contrat social*, a state-founding treaty between the political parties representing the classes of the German-Austrian people."[41]

The existence of institutionalized segmentation among the three subcultures has been generally recognized in the literature. Diamant, who describes the three *Lager* in some detail, considers that of the socialists to have been the most complete and homogeneous.[42] Lorwin, analyzing by sectors of activity, finds high to medium segmentation in all sectors and a total profile only slightly lower than that of the Netherlands.[43] But there are also some interesting differences. In Austria subcultural segmentation was reinforced by geographic regions – a "Red" Vienna and a "Black" hinterland – and also by class and economic interests, with the result that interbloc rivalries tended to set industrial workers against farm interests, industrial centres against the countryside, socialists against bourgeois, as well as secularists against

[41] Otto Bauer, quoted in P. Pulzer, "The Legitimizing Role of Political Parties: the Second Austrian Republic", *Government and Opposition*, Vol. 4 (1969), 332 [below, 165].
[42] A. Diamant, *Austrian Catholics and the First Republic* (Princeton, 1960), 73-74 [below, 150-151].
[43] "Segmented Pluralism," 155 [below, 48].

practising Catholics. Furthermore, the image of contending *Lager* was no mere figure of speech. After the breakdown of a short-lived coalition between Catholics and Socialists in 1920 the political atmosphere became one of growing hostility and mistrust. Segmentation reached its logical conclusion in the formation of private armies, and continuous paramilitary strife after 1927 between the socialist *Schutzbund* and the Catholic *Heimwehr* paved the way for the overthrow of the democratic regime in 1934 and annexation by Nazi Germany in 1938.[44]

The Second Republic inherited the same three cleavage blocs, though the nationalist bloc had lost ground through its wartime connections with Nazism. While the pattern of politics changed dramatically after 1945, organized segmentation has persisted. Engelmann notes that while *ideological* differences have subsided, *psychological* separation (in the form of *Lagermentalität*) continues.[45] In trying to analyse this phenomenon Stiefbold has found that polarization remains most pronounced among the middle-level political elites, though his conclusions have been questioned by Bluhm.[46] Whatever the variations in political and ideological climate, however, the broader conclusion must be that institutional segmentation was high in the First Republic and has remained high in the early decades of the Second.

In terms of deliberate elite adjustments to segmented pluralism the Second Republic is a classic case. Those who revived the Austrian political parties after 1945 inherited virtually the same cleavage structures that had destroyed the First Republic, and they faced the additional constraints of Allied occupation. Nevertheless they succeeded in overcoming a most unpromising heritage. The essential feature of their solution was a grand coalition of Catholics and Socialists which lasted through six elections to 1966. This coalition rested upon a contractarian base, the terms of which were established in 1947 and renegotiated after each election and even published on each occasion from 1956 onwards. A system of *Proporz* in the distribution of ministries and patronage went a long way towards correcting the underrepresentation of the Socialists in the public sector. The function of opposition was preserved not only by the small parties outside the coalition

[44] F. C. Engelmann, "Austria: the Pooling of Opposition," in R. A. Dahl, ed., *Political Oppositions in Western Democracies* (New Haven, 1966), 264-265.

[45] *Ibid.*, 267-268.

[46] Stiefbold, "Elite-Mass Opinion Structure"; Bluhm, "Political Integration," 38. For an empirical study in one community, see G. B. Powell, Jr., *Social Fragmentation and Political Hostility: An Austrian Case Study* (Stanford, 1970).

but to some extent also by a unique practice of *Bereichsopposition* in which each coalition partner acted as a critic of the departments dominated by the other. The details of the Austrian coalition system are interesting, but they need not be elaborated here. The important thing to be stressed is that the two coalition partners, each one hostile to the other in ideology but yoked together by massive mistrust of the other's role in governing, succeeded through cooperation in developing a stable parliamentary system that was not substantially weakened when the grand coalition ended in 1966. For the first time in Austrian history the parliamentary regime itself was adequately legitimized.

Finally, what is the role of older elements of the political culture in facilitating this successful cooperation? Imperial Austria had shared fully in the tradition of the Holy Roman Empire, and after 1867 it had developed its own institutions of *Ausgleich* and *Junktim* that enabled the highly fragmented society of the Dual Monarchy to find a precarious and complex *modus vivendi* for half a century. Nevertheless one must conclude that these traditional elements were not decisive, for otherwise they would also have been significant, or at least visible, during the First Republic. Even if we grant that the political conditions were somewhat more propitious for stability in 1945 than they were in 1918 owing to foreign military occupation and a diminished allegiance to Germany after the Nazi period, the Austrian case is perhaps the clearest example of consociationalism as an innovative pattern of elite cooperation that develops in response to a major challenge.

Belgium. Religious-ideological segmentation is highly developed in Belgium; in terms of organizational completeness, Lorwin finds more sectors highly segmented in Belgium than in any of the other countries he examines.[47] At the same time this dimension of segmentation is less complicated than the case of the Netherlands in having a classic tripartite Catholic-Liberal-Socialist base. The Catholic sector, as Lorwin notes, is the most highly and fully organized, the Liberal sector the least.[48] The central feature of this structural cleavage is of course the political parties themselves. The issue of church and state gave rise to the Catholic and Liberal parties, and the emergence of the Socialist party as a significant parliamentary force in the 1890's completed a pattern which has persisted strongly ever since.

[47] "Segmented Pluralism," 155 [below, 48].
[48] V. R. Lorwin, "Conflict and Compromise in Belgian Politics" (Paper presented to the Annual Meeting of the American Political Science Association, Washington, 1965), 28-30 [cf. below, 202-203].

The religious-ideological dimension, however, is not the only major line of cleavage in Belgian politics. For more than a century there has been a growing linguistic-cultural polarization around the struggle for equality between the country's two major languages. Beginning predominantly in the literary and cultural realm, the Flemish movement remained relatively little politicized until major expansions of the suffrage in 1893 and 1919 enfranchised the Flemish masses and called attention to the economic underdevelopment of the Flemish provinces. The first Flemish nationalist members were elected to parliament in 1919, and the period since 1945 has seen the emergence of "linguistic" splinter parties among both major language groups, culminating in the 1971 election when they won 45 of the 212 seats in the lower house. The emergence of political parties appealing to one linguistic group only has put some severe strains on the traditional parties, whose linguistic wings find themselves under pressure to articulate linguistic and regional demands against the other wing of their own party in order to avoid losing even a larger share of the electorate. There has been a corresponding growth in linguistically based voluntary associations, especially ones oriented towards culture, leisure, or sports, and existing associations have been reorganized to provide increased autonomy for their linguistic sections.

The outlook for associational segmentation in Belgium is difficult to predict. Though the three traditional blocs have suffered from these linguistic cross-pressures, organizational persistence remains relatively strong. The development of new institutional channels for the expression of regional cultural autonomy and economic decentralization has been too recent to assess its long-run impact on social segmentation and party alignment. For the future any one of the following seems possible: (1) linguistic segmentation might continue to develop until it becomes dominant, or (2) with linguistic pacification through new institutional arrangements the traditional religious-ideological cleavage might reassert itself with renewed force, or (3) both the linguistic and the religious-ideological cleavage dimensions might continue to co-exist and compete with each other for a considerable period.

In terms of elite responses to the challenge of segmentation, the Belgian experience seems to be one of several evolutionary stages over a considerable time rather than a major crisis followed by a far-reaching pacification. There is an early precedent for a politics of accommodation at the dawn of Belgian independence, when Catholics and Liberals joined together in a "union of the oppositions" in 1827 to resist the anti-Catholic and pro-Netherlandic policies of King William I. The Unionist alliance not only achieved independence but guided the young state through its early diplomatic difficulties until 1847. There followed a succession of single-party governments, but the advent of a socialist movement and of organized mass parties late in the century was soon followed by proportional representation in Parliament. As Lorwin notes significantly:

> In conceding proportional representation, in 1899, the Catholic government preserved the unitary state, the national character of the three parties, and the system of segmented pluralism. Thenceforth, in almost all phases of public life at all levels, the proportional representation of the three "traditional parties" and of all recognized interests tended to become the rule. Flemish linguistic interests were not yet among those traditional interests; the system of segmented pluralism did not recognize them.[49]

Similarly since 1919 all ministries have been coalition ministries except during the Catholic party's temporary majority in rather special circumstances from 1950 to 1954. Most coalitions have been two-party alliances, but tripartite ministries have emerged at certain critical periods.[50]

If the accommodationist style has developed rather gradually, certain episodes may nevertheless be singled out for mention. In 1935 the three major parties closed ranks in the Van Zeeland ministry to carry out a program of major economic reform and also to meet the challenge of the rightist anti-democratic Rexist movement, which captured 11 per cent of the vote in the 1936 election. In 1958 they came together again to negotiate an end to the second *guerre scolaire* which raged in the 1950's. The text of the Schools Pact, a formal agreement between the three parties signed by 13 party representatives, bears a striking resemblance to an international treaty.[51] Finally the search for a solution to linguistic problems in the later 1960's was participated in by all six parliamentary parties, while the constitutional changes necessary to give effect to the new regime of cultural autonomy were assured of the necessary two-thirds majority by the support of the three traditional parties.

There is, to be sure, a noticeable difference in tone between religious-ideological argument and linguistic argument in Belgium.

[49] V. R. Lorwin, "Linguistic Pluralism and Political Tension in Modern Belgium", *Canadian Journal of History*, Vol. 5 (1970), 9.

[50] J. Meynaud, J. Ladrière, and F. Perin, *La décision politique en Belgique: le pouvoir et les groupes* (Paris, 1965), 66-67.

[51] *Ibid.*, 170-176.

Religious-ideological debate may be sharp, even hostile, but the differences are long established, understood, accepted, and tolerated, if not always treated with respect. Linguistic differences are bitter, intolerant, and reveal little reciprocal understanding. At the mass level, the feeling of being an endangered or a disadvantaged minority is strong on both sides. These feelings, however, developed during a period when linguistic interests were very imperfectly articulated by the parliamentary parties, and they may diminish if the new machinery for institutional accommodation of cultural autonomy provides the needed outlet. On balance, party elites in Belgium have striven in the 1960's to accommodate linguistic tensions deliberately as they did in earlier times to reconcile religious and ideological diversity, and if it is too soon to evaluate their success, there can be no question as to the effort that has been made.

If the Belgian pattern of elite accommodation has developed gradually, building upon the earlier collaboration that won Belgian independence, how is this pattern related to the older political tradition of the Low Countries? On this point we encounter a complexity appropriate to Belgium's position as a crossroads of several cultures. The territorial components of modern Belgium all shared, in greater or lesser degree, in the heritage of the Holy Roman Empire, but this tradition was interspersed and overlaid with a series of dynastic and imperialistic ventures, Burgundian, Spanish, Austrian, French, and Dutch, that left somewhat conflicting imprints of foreign rule and centralization. At a time when the Northern Netherlands was a dynamic commercial power on the world stage, the Southern provinces were undergoing two centuries of economic and intellectual stagnation. While the Prince-Bishopric of Liège was echoing the Paris revolution of 1789, the provinces under Austrian rule were resisting the reforms of Joseph II in defence of ancient privileges. While an older conservative, pluralist tradition thus existed, the architects of the independent Belgium of 1830 turned away from it and built on different foundations. On the whole, therefore, the older political tradition is ambiguous, and its very diversity makes its influence on the modern political culture difficult to assess.

Switzerland. Lorwin estimates Switzerland to be the least highly segmented of the countries that he examines,[52] but the main point to be underlined is that organized segmentation along any one cleavage line is low not because cleavages are weak but because they are multi-dimensional and cross-cutting.[53] As in the other

---

[52] "Segmented Pluralism," 155 [below, 48].

[53] Lijphart, "Cleavages in Consociational Democracies," 18-20.

three countries the usual religious-ideological cleavage was historically the most important, and it became the basis for the formation of the major political parties. The ideological roots of the split between Radicals and Catholics may be traced back to the Reformation, and with the development of the Socialist Party and the Farmers' Party in the twentieth century the roster of major parties became complete.

However this party structure is superimposed upon a political system which is also characterized by significant linguistic and regional cleavages. Linguistic diversity, which was characteristic particularly of the subject territories of the Old Confederation, assumed greater importance after the Napoleonic Mediation, and was effectively accommodated in the federal Constitution of 1848. It has never been significantly politicized at the federal level, except for a brief period prior to and during the First World War. What we might call "regional segmentation" arises from the intense geographic particularism of Swiss society; the cantons and communes are vital elements of the political system, and many issues are mediated there which might be more intractable at the national level. As Daalder has noted, because of multiple cleavages "accommodationist practices [in Switzerland] are diffused among many more sites and arenas than in the Netherlands," and conversely, "partly due to the much greater role of regional factors, Swiss political culture is more highly fragmented than Dutch political culture."[54]

Some discussions of conflict resolution in Swiss politics rely heavily on structural factors to explain the success of the Swiss in mediating conflict. One of the best examples is that of Mayer, who suggests that

> the Swiss "miracle" of unity in diversity rests upon a peculiar equilibrium of cross-cutting cultural divisions which is historically unique and cannot be duplicated under different conditions. Interestingly, and largely unknown to the outside world, Switzerland itself furnishes proof that if the divisions between the linguistic and religious groups do not overlap but coincide the result is conflict instead of harmony.[55]

He then goes on to examine certain structural conditions which in modern Swiss history have created overlapping loyalties and neutralized cleavages: these include (1) the cross-cutting of linguistic and religious boundaries; (2) the cross-cutting of linguistic and

---

[54] "On Building Consociational Nations," 366 [below, 120].

[55] K. B. Mayer, "The Jura Problem: Ethnic Conflict in Switzerland," *Social Research*, Vol. 35 (1968), 707.

cantonal boundaries; (3) the cross-cutting of economic differences and linguistic boundaries; (4) the relative demographic stability of the linguistic groups despite differences in fertility, mortality and internal migration patterns.

Where these conditions are lacking, as in the northern part of the Bernese Jura, where religious and linguistic cleavages are mutually reinforcing within the same canton, conflict can occur even in the Swiss setting, and in historical perspective the French-speaking Catholic population of the Jura was caught up religiously in the *Kulturkampf* in the 1870's and linguistically in the pan-German movement prior to 1914. Mayer concludes that "even in Switzerland cultural coexistence requires specific structural underpinnings. When these are missing ethnic conflicts become as intractable there as elsewhere."[56]

Mayer's emphasis on the structure of cleavages is interesting because it suggests that to some degree at least certain structural factors are a necessary condition of consociational democracy. By itself, however, this seems insufficient. It does not explain, for example, why the Austro-Hungarian Empire, with a similarly complex structure of overlapping linguistic, religious, and class cleavages, was so unsuccessful. Besides, Mayer, whose primary concern is the linguistic and cultural dimension, pays little attention to religious-ideological differences as expressed in the party system and the political process, although in addition to structural factors he does note certain "informal practices" and attitudes in the political and bureaucratic realm tending towards a politics of linguistic *Proporz*.[57]

The pattern of elite accommodation in Switzerland is probably well known, at least in its general outlines. At the executive level the Federal Council is composed of members of all four major parties according to a fixed formula which changes only at rather infrequent intervals. Since 1959 the proportion has been two Radicals, two Conservatives, two Socialists, and one member from the Farmers' Party. But there are also firm conventions for regional representation (which must include Zurich, Bern and Vaud) and for linguistic representation (which calls for over-representation of the smaller linguistic groups). Similar conventions apply to parliamentary committees, the bureaucracy, and the Federal Tribunal. Moreover, as Girod has shown, the same patterns of multi-party executives may be found in virtually all of the

[56] *Ibid.*, 741, and see also K. B. Mayer, "Migration, Cultural Tensions, and Foreign Relations: Switzerland", *Journal of Conflict Resolution*, Vol. 11 (1967), 139-152.

[57] "The Jura Problem," 720.

cantons, including some rural cantons with relatively homogeneous populations in which one party has a clear legislative majority.[58]

There is, however, an important question of timing to be noted. The pattern of elite accommodation through multi-party executives did not develop in response to a specific integration crisis, but rather it was institutionalized gradually and completed rather recently. As Girod notes:

> Nearly half a century lapsed after the Sonderbund War before a member of the Catholic-Conservative party became a member of the Federal Government and 25 years passed between the Strike of 1918 and the election of the first Socialist federal councillor . . . Many other examples could be quoted to show that the "all-parties government" is not at all inherent to the Swiss regime as such, but a construction of the last period of history.[59]

The pattern of deliberate elite accommodation of diversity is highly visible in contemporary Swiss politics, but to understand its development we must begin considerably further back. Traditions of compromise lie deep in Swiss history. Before the Reformation a dangerous gulf between rural and urban cantons had been resolved in 1481 through the mediation of Nicholas of Flüe, an enigmatic and symbolic figure whose role has been evoked many times in later crises. The Reformation and its aftermath left the cantons sharply divided on religious lines; only gradually, and with periodic setbacks, did there emerge a principle of parity of Protestant and Catholic cantons analogous to that of the Empire.[60] When the Confederation and some individual cantons acquired various neighbouring territories by conquest or treaty from the sixteenth century onwards, their own traditions of local autonomy were extended to the newly acquired lands, and linguistic and religious diversity were accommodated to the point that when these territories were "liberated" by the Napoleonic armies in 1798, most of them chose to remain within the enlarged Confederation as full cantons.

The liberal revolution of the 1830's brought new strains which culminated in the Sonderbund War of 1847. Yet such was the

---

[58] R. Girod, "Geography of the Swiss Party System", in E. Allardt and Y. Littunen, eds., Cleavages, Ideologies, and Party Systems (Transactions of the Westermarck Society, 10, Helsinki, 1964), 137-143 [below, 211-217].

[59] Ibid., 146 [cf. below, 219].

[60] Lehmbruch, "A Non-Competitive Pattern," 5 [below, 93] and also his Proporzdemokratie, 15-16.

spirit of accommodation that after a brief but decisive campaign both sides sat down together to produce a new federal constitution which came into force less than a year after the outbreak of hostilities. Perhaps the outlook of this period is best expressed in the words of Numa Droz: "Presque toutes nos lois sont, plus que dans d'autres pays, le résultat de transactions entre les partis, les régions, les races."[61] The date here is significant, for Droz is speaking in 1885, before the age of mass politics, at a time when the Radicals still monopolized all seven seats on the Federal Council.

We may conclude that in Switzerland recent patterns of elite behavior are subsumed within a well established political tradition. The mechanisms of accommodation – multi-party executives, proportional representation, decentralization, over-representation of minorities – are sequels and consequences of political patterns developed in earlier times. Unlike the Austrian case, the political tradition of Switzerland is, as Lehmbruch notes, "historically homogeneous."[62] Unlike the Belgian case, where the secondary cleavage on linguistic lines was not recognized and accommodated on account of its relatively late arrival on the political stage, all major social cleavages in Switzerland are of relatively long standing and have been accommodated more or less continuously as the political system developed.

From this brief consideration of the four "classic" cases of consociationalism we may now attempt a limited cross-national assessment of the three approaches outlined at the beginning. The problem is to assess the importance or significance of each of the approaches in each of the cases, and a first, rather tentative attempt to scale these dimensions is given in Table 1. There seems to be no automatic relationship between the first of these dimensions and the other two; extensive social segmentation may be neither a necessary nor a sufficient condition for consociational politics, but it may well be a facilitating condition, for reasons that we have noted above.[63] Further, while the dimension of elite behavior is rated high in all four cases, this may be misleading without some qualification. In the Dutch and Swiss cases these ratings may simply represent linkages with older traditions of pluralism, whereas the Austrian case suggests significant innovation and the Belgian example seems more ambiguous. This rudimentary cross-national comparison could of course be carried much further. In particular one could explore the implications of

---

[61] Quoted in Lehmbruch, *Proporzdemokratie*, 19.
[62] *Ibid.*, 51.
[63] See above, p. 9.

the mutual cross-cutting of various cleavages one against the other.[64] To do this, however, would go somewhat beyond the primary purpose of this book, which is concerned basically with those cleavages that have been comprehensively incorporated into social structures and reflected in the political process.

These four "classic" cases of consociational democracy are all examples of countries that have overcome the divisive potentialities of deep and lasting social segmentation through a politics of accommodation. During the period in question each has kept anti-system parties to low levels and each has attained a satisfactory level of regime stability. But in all four cases the primary dimension of cleavage, at least in the formal structural sense, has been religious and ideological, reflecting broad cleavage lines that are common to much of Western Europe. The question then arises as to whether the concept of consociationalism may be relevant for countries where some other primary axis of cleavage has become politicized.

Lorwin emphasizes the voluntary nature of segmented pluralism and suggests that "the availability of individual alternatives distinguishes the politics of segmented pluralism from those based on the cleavages of caste, communalism, race, or even language."[65] But this view raises two questions. First, given the logic of comprehensive segmentation with minimal cross-pressures in the consociational model, are voluntary interbloc transfers of allegiance likely to take place as long as the level of segmentation and even hostility remains high? Secondly, and more fundamentally, is the principle of individual freedom of choice a necessary condition – or even a facilitating condition – for segmented pluralism? If not, the apparent distinction between religious-ideological cleavage and other forms of cleavage may be less fundamental than Lorwin appears to suggest. This issue is an important one, for if the experience of the successful consociational democracies in mediating deep and lasting religious and ideological cleavages can be shown to be relevant to societies where divisions of similar intensity run along ethnic or cultural or linguistic lines, then that experience may be important for a very substantial part of the contemporary world.

[64] The measurement and comparison of cross-cutting cleavages in the consociational democracies is being currently (1973) investigated by Lijphart. See his "Cleavages in Consociational Democracies" and also his "Linguistic Fragmentation and Other Dimensions of Cleavage: a Comparison of Belgium, Canada, and Switzerland" (Paper presented at the Ninth World Congress of the International Political Science Association, Montreal, August 1973).

[65] "Segmented Pluralism," 143 [below, 35].

Table 1. Degree of importance of three elements of consociationalism in four "classic" cases.

Element	Netherlands	Austria	Belgium	Switzerland
1. Organized segmentation in social structure (on religious-ideological dimension)	High	High	High (but increasingly cross-cut by language)	Medium (extensively cross-cut by language and region)
2. Deliberate efforts by elites to mediate cleavages (with crisis periods noted)	High (1913–1917)	High (post-1945)	High (1827–31 and many times since)	High (1847–48 on religion; 1914–18 on language)
3. Strength of pluralism in older political tradition.	High	Low	Medium	High

PART II
THEORETICAL AND COMPARATIVE
PERSPECTIVES

The five articles in this section have been selected to illustrate the three approaches to consociationalism already discussed in Part I, but they also touch on other themes of the consociational literature. Val Lorwin, whose article "Segmented Pluralism" dates from 1969 in its original version, concentrates upon the fragmented social structures that form a base for consociational politics in the four European cases that we have examined. More important, he directs attention to the question of measuring and comparing the extent and intensity of segmentation, providing some rough benchmarks which will be used later for comparisons with Canada.[1] Beyond these central concerns he also traces the historical development of segmentation in the political mobilization of the workers in the late nineteenth century and finally touches on the dynamics of segmented political systems by examining the interplay of factors of continuity and change.

Arend Lijphart's "Consociational Democracy" (1969) is a reworking of some parts of his earlier paper "Typologies of Democratic Systems", the original version of which was presented at the Brussels Congress of the International Political Science Association in 1967. Both articles draw attention to the inadequacy of prevailing classifications of political systems and stress the existence of a separate category of democracy that is both fragmented and stable. More than any other author, Lijphart has underlined the role of political elites in counteracting the dangers of social fragmentation by deliberate negotiated accommodation of divergent interests at the summit of the political system. This central emphasis on elite behavior and its possibilities of emulation in other settings, together with the simple clarity of his model, have combined to make Lijphart's work perhaps the most widely known among the consociational literature.

Gerhard Lehmbruch's "A Non-Competitive Pattern of Conflict Management in Liberal Democracies", like Lijphart's earlier paper, was written for the 1967 Brussels Congress of the International Political Science Association. In it he also seeks to define a third category of democracies beyond the competitive and the bureaucratic models that he finds exemplified by the Anglo-American and Franco-German traditions respectively. Like Lijphart, Lehmbruch also describes a process of conflict regulation that works by negotiated agreement and compromise, but while Lijphart stresses the conscious efforts of the elites in making such a system work, Lehmbruch points to the importance of historical tradition in shaping the norms of conflict regulation. In Austria, Switzerland, and Lebanon, specific historical circum-

[1] See below, 245-247.

stances gave rise to certain patterns of elite behavior which were then transmitted as norms through political socialization. Although some of Lehmbruch's later work focuses on the specific internal and external conditions that generate and sustain consociational politics,[2] the 1967 paper tends to explain modern patterns of conflict regulation by tracing elite political culture to its historical antecedents.

Jürg Steiner's article "The Principles of Majority and Proportionality" first appeared in German under the title "Majorz und Proporz" in 1970. The version printed here is a translation, with slightly reduced footnotes, by Geoffrey Hosking. From the standpoint of political decision-making, Steiner views the majority principle and the proportionality principle as opposite ends of a continuum the profile of which will emerge only after systematic study of individual political systems. For this purpose he develops some preliminary hypotheses concerning the effect on the decision-making process of the size of polity, the degree and dimensions of segmentation, and the force of societal norms, and also concerning the influence of this decision-making process on other political variables. Though the starting point is his own work on Switzerland, Steiner's aim is to develop some of the propositions in the early consociational literature to the point where they might be incorporated into empirical political theory in a more general sense.

Hans Daalder's "On Building Consociational Nations: the Cases of the Netherlands and Switzerland", first published in 1971, was written for the UNESCO Meeting of Experts on the Problems of State Formation and Nation Building (August 1970) and has also been published in the two-volume work that followed from that conference.[3] It constitutes perhaps the most explicit argument to date of the influence of older political traditions upon modern patterns of elite accommodation and conflict regulation. Where Lijphart stresses the conscious and deliberate efforts of elites to overcome the effects of fragmentation, Daalder strongly emphasizes the role of older pluralist traditions in shaping a political culture which prevents social fragmentation from running to political extremes.

The chronology of the articles in this section deserves special notice. All five were written between 1967 and 1970; the two earliest were both presented at the Brussels Congress of the International Political Science Association. Though most of the

---

[2] See the Select Bibliography below.

[3] S. N. Eisenstadt and S. Rokkan, eds., *Building States and Nations: Models, Analyses and Data Across Three Worlds* (2 vols., Beverly Hills: Sage Publications, 1973).

*ingredients for consociationalism can be discerned in earlier liter-
ature, these ingredients do not seem to come together as an
explicit insight into comparative politics theory until the later
1960's. It is interesting that Lijphart and Lehmbruch, working
simultaneously but primarily on different countries (Lijphart on
the Netherlands, Lehmbruch on Austria and Switzerland) arrived
at models that have some striking similarities, in spite of diverging
views as to how political systems of this type may arise. On the
other hand, Lijphart and Daalder can look at the same political
system and differ substantially as to the crucial variables and
sequence of development.*

*In longer perspective the five articles in this section may well
be viewed as belonging to the formative phase of consociationalism. The later 1960's gave rise to the consociational model as a
distinct category of democracy which differed in important ways
from preceding classifications. This significant theoretical insight
was accompanied by a considerable discussion of the origins,
limiting conditions, political processes, and potential transferabil-
ity of consociational politics, much of which remains unresolved
in 1973. It seems likely that in the next stage these insights and
propositions will give rise to more detailed empirical research, a
tendency already visible in some of the longer studies that have
already appeared.[4] In the long run one may expect that these
early hypotheses, tested and reformulated in case studies, will be
refined and developed more fully and integrated into the study of
comparative politics.*

---

[4] See the Select Bibliography below, especially the full-length studies
by Lijphart, Steiner, Powell, and Presthus.

SEGMENTED PLURALISM: IDEOLOGICAL CLEAVAGES AND POLITICAL COHESION IN THE SMALLER EUROPEAN DEMOCRACIES*

Val R. Lorwin

Source: V. R. Lorwin, "Segmented Pluralism: Ideological Cleavages and Political Cohesion in the Smaller European Democracies," *Comparative Politics*, Vol. 3, No. 2 (January 1971), 141-175. Reprinted by permission of *Comparative Politics* and the author, who has reviewed and slightly revised the text for this volume.

In an era of political and scholarly concern with national integration, segmented pluralism serves as one historic model of the attempt to reconcile religious and ideological diversity with civic cohesion. Segmented pluralism is the organization of social movements, educational and communications systems, voluntary associations, and political parties along the lines of religious and ideological cleavages. It is pluralist in its recognition of diversity of religious, socioeconomic, and political affiliations; it is "segmented" in its institutionalization of most other forms of association along the lines of politico-religious cleavages.

A social or cultural organization is "segmented" if it is composed chiefly of, and directed by, members of one of several churches or *Weltanschauungsgruppen* (or *familles spirituelles*). I distinguish segmented organization from what I shall call functional organization. In functional organizations people associate only in terms of a specific economic or social purpose. Thus, a trade union organized solely on lines of skill or industry or employer unit is a functional organization, while a Catholic or Protestant or Socialist trade union is a segmented organization. A Boy Scout or Girl Scout troop organized only by age or locality is functional; but a Catholic or Protestant or Socialist Scout troop is segmented.

These terms are meant to be neutral (and, of course, they are unrelated to debates about functional analysis). Neither "func-

* This is an entirely revised version of a paper originally presented at the International Political Science Association Round Table on Comparative Politics at Turin, September 9-14, 1969. For generous support of my research and that of my colleagues on the International Study of the Politics of the Smaller European Democracies, I thank the Ford Foundation, the Social Science Research Council, the John Simon Guggenheim Memorial Foundation, the Rockefeller Constitutional Democracy Program, the Graduate School of the University of Oregon, and the Center for Advanced Study in the Behavioral Sciences. I am deeply and happily indebted to many individuals; I hope to thank them – however inadequately – in a forthcoming book.

tional" nor "segmented" implies any judgment as to the effectiveness of an organization in relation to the needs or desires of its
constituency or of the society. A functional organization may
evoke as much solidarity as a segmented one; a segmented organization may be as ready to compromise differences as a functional
one.

A political system is one of segmented pluralism when its
cleavages have produced competing networks of schools, communications media, interest groups, leisure time associations, and
political parties along segmented lines, of both religious and antireligious nature. The phenomenon will be understood more clearly
with the aid of a metaphor which I owe to those Dutch sociologists
who first analyzed the phenomenon of segmented pluralism,
although contemporary observers had commented on it in Belgium
and elsewhere for generations. The Dutch sociologists' greatest contribution has been to identify and measure what they call *verzuiling*
in their own country. This neologism refers both to the historical
process of the development of segmented organization and to the
condition of segmented pluralism.[1]

A *zuil* is a pillar. In the Dutch figure of speech, each of the
nation's ideological groups is a "pillar," standing vertical and
separate on its own base of religious or secular ideology. Each
has its own party, socio-economic associations, press, leisure time
groups, radio and television broadcasting chain, and – in the case
of Catholicism and two major forms of Calvinist Protestantism –
its churches, parish leagues, and schools.

The Dutch first spoke of *verzuiling* soon after World War II,
using the word in a positive sense to refer to the integrating role
of the *zuilen*. They saw the pillars as sustaining an overarching
unity above the diversity of the nation's social and political structure. But many of them came increasingly to look upon the
ideological blocs not only as sustaining pillars but also – to change

[1] See, for example, the witty volume of J. P. Kruijt and others,
Verzuiling, (2d ed., Zaandijk, 1959); J. P. Kruijt, "The Influence of
Denominationalism on Social Life and Organizational Patterns,"
Archives de sociologie des religions, Vol. 4, No. 8 (July-December
1959), 105-11; J. P. Kruijt and W. Goddijn, "Verzuiling en ontzuil-
ing als sociologisch proces," in A. N. J. Den Hollander et al., eds.
Drift en Koers: Een halve eeuw sociale verandering in Nederland (2d
ed., Assen, 1962), pp. 227-63; Johan Goudsblom, *Dutch Society*
(New York, 1967); Hans Daalder, "The Netherlands: Opposition in
a Segmented Society," in Robert A. Dahl, ed., *Political Oppositions
in Western Democracies* (New Haven, 1966), pp. 188-236; and
Arend Lijphart, *The Politics of Accommodation: Pluralism and
Democracy in the Netherlands* (Berkeley and Los Angeles, 1968).

the metaphor – as compartments separating groups of people from each other except at levels of elite relationships. Many, therefore, advocated *ontzuiling* or the breaking down of these institutionalized compartments; some even described the onset of a process of *ontzuiling*. Belgians, especially those of Dutch (Flemish) speech, took up the discussion in the light of conditions in their own country.[2]

Among the ways in which societies have organized and divided themselves, segmented pluralism approaches the lower limit of rigidity if we take the visibility of group identification and the possibility of individual choice in membership and marriage as indicators. At the upper limit of rigidity in the contemporary world are the ascriptive inequalities of caste and of polycommunalism; the stigmata of communal membership have high salience, and individual choice within the system is practically nil. In societies of voluntary, rather than enforced, pluralism, language identifies and separates people and may limit occupational choice. In areas of language contacts, while individuals may move out of the language groups into which they were born, the costs of change are usually so high by the time people are old enough to exercise choice that what choices they make are likely to be for their children rather than for themselves.

Segmented pluralism depends on self-definition, and the possibility of individual choice was at the origin of the system. In practice there may be high costs, in social pressure or individual trauma, of change; but in principle the individual can change at almost any time – definitively and entirely, or momentarily and partially, by simply reading an opposition paper or splitting his vote. The availability of individual alternatives distinguishes the politics of segmented pluralism from those based on the cleavages of caste, communalism, race, or even language.

The segmented pluralism I am discussing is, of course, not that of the stratified plural societies of Southeast Asia or the Caribbean which John S. Furnivall, M. G. Smith, and others have analyzed. I refer to the voluntary groups which function at various levels between the individual or primary group and the state,

---

[2] See especially Kruijt and Goddijn, and Arend Lijphart, "Kentering in de Nederlandse Politiek," *Acta Politica*, Vol. 4, No. 3 (April 1969), 231-47. *Cf.* Belgian discussion in B. J. De Clercq, *Kritiek van de Verzuiling* (Lier, 1968), Jan De Meyer, "Verzuiling en doorbraak in de hedendaagse politiek" (Address delivered at European Study and Information Center, Brussels, 3 April 1967), numerous articles in *De Maand*, and L. Huyse, *Die Niet-Aanwezige Staatsburger* (Antwerp, 1969), and *Passiviteit, Pacificatie en Verzuiling in de Belgische Politiek* (Antwerp, 1970).

and to the solidarities and conflicts of such groups in the national integration[3] of comparatively open Western societies.

Segmented pluralism has been prominent in the social mobilization and the structuring of political conflict and compromise in the Netherlands, Belgium, Luxembourg, Switzerland, and Austria,[4] and it is with these five countries that this article will deal. In none of these societies except Austria has segmentation approached completeness. If it had, interest-group and political life might have become too stifling, and perhaps even explosive. We are dealing with relatively, not completely, segmented polities. In other democracies, notably France, Italy, and Germany, there has been considerable segmentation, but that has not been the dominant characteristic of their political systems. In England and the United States, there has been much less, although there is a significant amount of unavowed religious segmentation in the United States. Paradoxically, just as segmented pluralism has apparently passed its high point of development in several countries, it is beginning to receive attention in the literature of comparative politics.[5]

[3] On the concept of national integration, see the nuanced and sensible introductory remarks in Aristide R. Zolberg, "Patterns of National Integration," *Journal of Modern African Studies,* Vol. 5, No. 4 (1967), 449-52.

[4] I am not discussing Northern Ireland, which is neither state nor nation, and which has not created a system of segmented pluralism out of its fierce religious loyalties and hostilities. For an excellent survey, see Richard Rose, *Governing without Consensus: An Irish Perspective* (London, 1971). As I am discussing only modern and democratic states, I do not take up Lebanon.

[5] Arend Lijphart has written of "consociational democracy" and Gerhard Lehmbruch of "Konkordanzdemokratie" and "Proporzdemokratie," by which they have characterized systems and arrangements based on what I have called segmented pluralism: Lijphart, "Typologies of Democratic Systems," *Comparative Political Studies,* Vol. 1, (April 1968), 3-44, and "Consociational Democracy," *World Politics,* Vol. 21, (January 1969), 207-25; Gerhard Lehmbruch, *Proporzdemokratie: Politische System und politische Kultur in der Schweiz und in Oesterreich* (Tuebingen, 1967), and "A Noncompetitive Pattern of Conflict Management in Liberal Democracies: The Case of Switzerland, Austria, and Lebanon" (Paper given at the International Political Science Association's Seventh World Congress, Brussels, 1967).

Lijphart's definition is put in terms of the "overarching cooperation at the elite level with the deliberate aim of counteracting disintegrating tendencies in the system" ("Typologies," p. 21). I should rather define the system in terms of the bases of party formation and voluntary association and leave open the question of elite coopera-

"HUNGER IS NEITHER CATHOLIC NOR PROTESTANT"

When, in the nineteenth century, European workers, peasants, and lower-middle-class elements began to organize for representation of their group interests, they had the choice of three basic frameworks: that of an existing framework of religious organization, the "functional" framework of socioeconomic interests alone, or that offered by some form of the new doctrines and organization of socialism. Politically, the most important organizations were to be those of peasants and of workers, the latter being the more important, because they were a growing class, more dynamic and more open to conflicting appeals.

"The future belongs to the class which knows how to create its own institutions," proclaimed Emile Vandervelde, but he was a Socialist, writing in the springtime of the workers' awakening to the struggle for social and political emancipation. In Belgium, Switzerland, Luxembourg, Austria, and the Netherlands, workers created their own institutions as Socialists or Catholics or, in some cases, as Protestants. The Socialists generally took the lead. Christian unions, cooperatives, and friendly societies paid Socialist vice the tribute of virtuous imitation, and some trade unions were even blessed with the characterization "anti-Socialist" in their names. Among the peasants and lower middle class, Catholics and Protestants were in the lead.

The Socialists, to be sure, would have embraced all workers in their organizations. However, in the countries I am discussing – as distinct from Scandinavia and Britain – the Socialists' antireligious

---

tion and outcomes. Not building effective elite cooperation into the definition makes one more likely to examine the conditions which induce, and those which inhibit or frustrate, such cooperation.

For other suggestions of somewhat similar terminology, see Michael Fogarty on "vertical or ideological pluralism," in *Christian Democracy in Europe, 1820-1953* (London, 1957), p. 42; Joseph Gusfield, on "superimposed segregation," in "Mass Society and Extremist Politics," *American Sociological Review*, Vol. 27 (February 1962), 29, and Juerg Steiner on "Conflict Resolution and Democratic Stability in Subculturally Segmented Political Systems," *Res Publica*, Vol. 11, No. 4 (1969), 775-98, and his *Gewaltlose Politik und kulturelle Vielfalt: Hypothesen entwickelt am Beispiel der Schweiz* (Bern, 1970).

Ralf Dahrendorf speaks of *"Versaeulung"* in *Gesellschaft und Demokratie in Deutschland* (Munich, 1965), pp. 134-44, 302-4, and 436-38, but in a looser and broader sense than do the Dutch. His English version, *Society and Democracy in Germany* (New York, 1967), pp. 116-18 and 276, gives only a small part of the original discussion. He has kept the literal sense of the Dutch *verzuiling* with "pillarization."

tone tended to repel Christian workers, and they ridiculed the idea of political neutrality, as Swiss Socialists did that of an *Arbeiterbund* "whose head would be red while its tail was black."[6] Attempts at political neutrality likewise incurred the suspicions of ecclesiastical authorities. Clerical and anti-clerical intolerance fed on each other, but they also promoted organization and counterorganization among workers. If the division of class forces weakened, the rivalry and emulation of traditional religion and the new secular religion of socialism stimulated organization. Even Vandervelde predicted, in his native Belgium as early as the year of *Rerum Novarum,* that "the more rapid the progress of socialism, the more importance will the movement of Christian Democracy take on."[7]

In the countries of mixed religions, the Catholic-Protestant cleavage also shaped the new social movements.[8] "Hunger is neither Catholic nor Protestant," indignantly declared a Swiss Catholic deputy.[9] Nonetheless, Swiss and Dutch churches long sought to ensure that the organization against hunger would be Catholic or Protestant. They discouraged their faithful, not only from joining Socialist or even functional organizations, but also from forming joint Catholic-Protestant organizations.

A unidimensional political cleavage on ideological grounds was possible only as long as a happy few had the political terrain to themselves. That model may be seen with classical clarity (even more sharply than in Britain) in Belgium's Liberal-Catholic two-party system from the 1830s to the 1880s. But in the age of mass politics class cleavages had to be expressed within or between parties. Thus, it was a combination of religious-ideological and class alignments that structured the political life and the voluntary associations of the segmented pluralist nations. Religious politics narrowly won out over class politics in the hierarchy of cleavages in the Netherlands; moreover, while the Catholic party cut across class lines, the two Calvinist parties represented differences not only in religious temperament, but also between lower-class and bourgeois followings.

In the overlapping between religious and social alignments during the era of universal equal manhood suffrage after World

[6] R. Ruffieux, "La Suisse," in S. H. Scholl, ed. *150 Ans de Mouvement Ouvrier Chrétien en Europe de l'Ouest, 1789-1939* (Brussels, 1966), 462.

[7] Emile Vandervelde, *Enquête sur les Associations Professionnelles d'artisans et ouvriers en Belgique,* 2 vols. (Brussels, 1891), II:54.

[8] On these and other cleavages, see Stein Rokkan, *Citizens, Elections, Parties* (New York and Oslo, 1970).

[9] Quoted by R. Ruffieux, "La Suisse," p. 462.

War I, among the five countries I have mentioned only interwar Austria experienced class conflict as intense as religious-ideological conflict in determining the tone of politics. As Richard Rose and Derek Urwin have recently shown,[10] there is not a single instance of a democratic polity with a uni-dimensional party cleavage on class or economic lines. The nine-teenth century politico-religious ideological alignments segmented later voluntary associations, the press, and, in some countries, education. Modified but not displaced by class alignments, they occupied much of the political space of the countries I am dis-cussing, making it difficult for new political formations to enter the scene.

Brevity makes it necessary for me to force the distinctions between religious-ideological and class alignments. Anticlericalism was a major component of the new socialism, and the defense of established class interests was a major concern of most leaders of the confessional parties. The Liberals were generally allied with the latter in the defense of property interests, while fighting them on the terrain of the *Kulturkampf*. The outspoken, very conserva-tive leader of the Belgian Catholic party declared to his Liberal opponents in 1878, "We and you cannot admit that there is a social question to be resolved, we cannot admit the regulation of labor conditions, because then we should have no defense against the worker asking us, in the name of the suffering of his family, for work and for bread."[11]

Despite the conservatism of most Christian party leaders and most prelates, the religiously oriented organizations helped to reconcile peasants' and workers' traditional loyalties with the new voluntary associations and political action of an era of social mobilization. Among workers and the lower middle classes, and especially among peasants, many were unwilling and often unable to organize unless they could do so within old frameworks. Seg-mented organizations mediated between religious hierarchies and the disadvantaged social groups, asserting new rights by new forms of collective action. Religiously oriented peasants' leagues and labor organizations joined, at first in a subordinate capacity, in political action with the dominant classes of their coreligionists. In the multilingual states, the Socialist, Liberal, and Christian

---

[10] Richard Rose and Derek Urwin, "Social Cohesion, Political Parties, and Strains in Regimes," *Comparative Political Studies*, Vol. 2 (April 1969), 7-67.

[11] Charles Woeste, House of Representatives, 20 February 1878, *Annales parlementaires*, p. 408. Cited by B. S. Chlepner, *Cent ans d'histoire sociale en Belgique* (Brussels, 1956), 65.

segmented organizations united their members across the frontiers of language.

In the long run, the combination of confessional and anticonfessional organizations enabled the lower strata of the population to achieve a higher rate of social and political organization than, say, the United States. (Scandinavia shows high rates of organization, too – but in a religiously homogeneous society.) In the countries of segmented pluralism it is not true, as E. E. Schattschneider has said of the United States, that "in the pluralist heaven, the heavenly chorus sings with a strong upper-class accent."[12]

The moderation of early Christian social organizations helped to keep the demands of newly mobilizing groups at levels easily manageable – perhaps too manageable – for the system. Of course, all these states had political parties and administrative institutions of a sort which put them in a different category from the new states about whose premature social mobilization Samuel P. Huntington has warned.[13] The caution of many of the early Christian organizations, inspired by their own weakness, deference, and prelates' restraints, was such that it often sacrificed social justice for social peace. Some early joint Protestant-Catholic labor groups in the Netherlands and Switzerland were more militant, but they were dissolved by their churches' opposition.

The specialization of function achieved by Belgian Catholic, Dutch Catholic, and Dutch Protestant organizations gradually lent a greater realism to social and economic attitudes and programs aggregated by their blocs. Ultimately, the cohabitation of clashing social movements within the Christian blocs made their elites aware of the utility, or at least of the inevitability, of the tensions of conflicting group interests. This heterogeneity gave those blocs a liveliness often lacking in the more socially homogeneous Socialist bloc after its "heroic period."

CONDITIONS FOR THE EMERGENCE OF SEGMENTED PLURALISM

Some of the conditions for the emergence of segmented organizations were among the more general conditions for the emergence of political democracy. In addition, there had to be at least two *Weltanschauungsgruppen* of relatively numerous followings, with some geographical concentration of each, and, in some areas,

[12] E. E. Schattschneider, *The Semi-sovereign People* (New York, 1960), 35. See also Charles Perrow, "The Sociological Perspective and Political Pluralism," *Social Research*, Vol. 31 (Winter 1964), 411-22.

[13] Samuel P. Huntington, "Political Development and Political Decay," *World Politics*, Vol. 17 (April 1965), 386-430.

Table 1   National Religions and Extent of Segmented Pluralism,*
Western Democracies, about 1905-65

National Religions	Extent of Segmented Pluralism		
	High	Medium	Low
Catholic	Austria Belgium Luxembourg	France Italy	Ireland†
Catholic and Protestant	Netherlands	Germany Switzerland United States	Great Britain
Protestant			Denmark Finland Iceland Norway Sweden

* Segmented pluralism defined, as in text, only in terms of religious-
  ideological cleavages and organization.

† Refers only to what is now the Irish Republic.

contact with members of another group. As Table 1 shows,
segmentation has been highest in several Catholic countries and
in one of mixed religion. In all the countries of *verzuiling*, a
national or, as in Switzerland, cantonal Catholic or Protestant
church was challenged by other faiths and by anticonfessional
Liberal and, later and more powerfully among the masses, Socialist groups.

With industrialization, urbanization, and geographic mobility (in these small countries, sometimes only by daily or weekly
commuting), the churches became concerned about risks to the
faith of the masses. If isolation could no longer protect the
faithful from exposure to influences corrosive of their faith, special institutions had to encapsulate them. In areas relatively
untouched by migrations and changes in social structure, traditional hierarchies and values might remain unchallenged. No segmented social organization was necessary in these places, and a
single party could monopolize political representation. A classic
case is the Swiss half-canton of Appenzell Inner Rhoden.[14] In
other, often less picturesque, rural areas and small towns of

[14] Roger Girod, "Geography of the Swiss Party System," in E. Allardt
and Y. Littunen, eds. *Cleavages, Ideologies, and Party Systems* (Helsinki, 1964), pp. 137-38.

traditional Catholic or Protestant life, similar situations have endured.

Another condition of segmented organization was that the elites from different social classes of the same faith have enough communication and mutual trust to encourage cooperation in a lasting political organization. (These were lacking most of the time among French and Italian Catholics because of social distance and because of disputes about the legitimacy of the regimes.) The protection or advancement of a church's schools and, to a lesser extent, its welfare activities, produced enough long-term solidarity across class lines for political organization for a long time.

SMALLNESS OF STATES

Is another condition of segmented pluralism the state's smallness of population and power? If so, what have been the intervening variables between smallness and viability of such a system? Is the critical variable to be found in the international system? Is it the lack of a foreign policy "load" on the political systems of small states?

Under certain conditions, external demands in small or large nations make for solidarity against outside threats; in others they cause increased discord. The historic experience varies among nations, and from period to period and sometimes from issue to issue within the same nation; it depends somewhat on whether external demands press along the lines of existing cleavages within the state. In the 1830s and early 1840s, foreign threats to the very existence of the new Belgian state united Liberals and Catholics in a period of "unionism" which consolidated the kingdom's survival; but the threats were not along the lines of internal cleavages. In Austria the First Republic was torn apart by external pressures following the fault lines of the new state's precarious political structure; however, the Second Republic found viability in surmounting external demands, which no longer followed internal "fault lines." Switzerland has long been sensitive to threats of intervention from the big powers; the Nazi menace encouraged a lasting peace between labor and employer organizations, and the belated admission of the Socialist party to the federal executive. In Belgium, each world war deepened national integration above class lines, but exacerbated linguistic and regional conflict.

Given the character of the international system in this century, and of the larger neighbors of each of the segmented pluralist nations, the reduction of external demands (by all except interwar Austria) represents a considerable feat of political management. It would be unkind to the great powers to compare the effectiveness of their foreign policies with those of the smaller democratic states in the first half of this century. Factors of location aside, segmented pluralism has not made these small European democracies any more vulnerable to external threats, or less capable of formulating policies of survival, than the unsegmented small states. If World War I somewhat divided the Swiss, it was along lines of language, not ideology. The Nazi threat united them across lines of ideology, social class, and language.

Despite all the professions of socialist internationalism and the discipline of international Catholicism, international ties did not determine the relations of blocs to each other. We may see an exception in the international strength of corporatist currents which helped divide each of the segmented states, but also divided their Catholic communities. Catholic corporatism between the wars owed much to Pope Pius XI's tolerance of this reactionary and gaseous doctrine expounded in Italy, and to his pleas to restructure modern society along the lines of a "mitigated corporatist state."[15] But in the one state where corporatism seemed momentarily to carry the day, its success was due to Mussolini's meddling in Austrian politics, and not to the Pontiff's eloquence or to international Catholic ties.

Size has helped the segmented pluralist (and other small) democracies in one essential respect. Not being possessed, in the age of industrialism, of the means of international aggression, none of them has cherished illusions about its international role. This sort of realism has reduced the external demands on them. It has had the futher effect, in the segmented pluralist states, of making the system more receptive to the admission of Socialist and Catholic parties, which, in the larger states of Germany and France, offended the hypernationalism of political leaders and powerful domestic groups. *Ceteris paribus,* the smaller the state, the easier it is to recognize solidarity in diversity.

It is, of course, possible to cherish a myth of the mission of a national state even in a country without pretensions to international grandeur. In not one of our five smaller democracies does such a myth exist, however. The Swiss cantons ceased to be expansionist when, with the Reformation, the existence of religious differences was accepted. (The continued strength of Swiss communal and cantonal political life continues to be a marvel of

[15] The phrase is that of the distinguished Catholic historian, Msgr. A. Simon, in the course of a sympathetic appraisal of the work of Pope Pius XI, in "Le Vatican," in S. H. Scholl, *150 Ans,* p. 42. On Catholic corporatism, see also Paul Vignaux, *Traditionalisme et syndicalisme: Essai d'histoire sociale (1884-1941)* (New York, 1943).

the age of the national state.) Even colonial power, though its sins were grievous, sinned abroad rather than at home. It did not create illusions of state power, either within the Netherlands, whose old empire gave it some influence in extra-European affairs, or within Belgium, which briefly held such vast domain.

QUALITIES OF SEGMENTED PLURALIST STATES

The postwar politics of the five states show a number of common characteristics. To be sure, many of these qualities are not unique to them, but are common to other democracies as well. In each of the five states, as in any modern political entity of any size, there is a unique configuration of qualities, but one cannot dwell on these here.

All the states except Austria have long traditions of municipal and provincial or cantonal liberties and initiatives. While provincial autonomy disappeared in the Low Countries with the French Revolution, neither the modern Netherlands nor Belgium has become anything like a Jacobin state; in both, localism remains a significant dimension of political life, despite the unitary state. (Luxembourg, of course, is only city-state size.) In all the states under discussion there are strong linkages between local and national politics. There is, therefore, none of the myth of the state which has overshadowed diversity within modern Germany or – in a less virulent form – in France.

Even though only Switzerland and Austria have formal federal structures, in the 1960s Belgium moved toward a federalism in cultural, social, and party life, for which its political leaders are still seeking governmental institutions. But federalism offers a different sort of pluralism than does *verzuiling*; it recognizes diversity in territorial space, although that diversity may correspond – as to a considerable extent in Switzerland – with religious and linguistic diversity. Segmented pluralism calls for representation of diversity within the same space, as well as for ties of voluntary association between members of competing blocs across internal boundaries. Proportional representation is its logical political counterpart. All the five countries have multiparty systems (with Austria coming nearest to a two-party system), and the proportional representation characteristic of continental democracies, which in the larger states has aroused the indignation of so many English-language writers.

With multiparty systems, coalition government has, of course, been the usual practice. The exception has been an occasional single-party majority government in Belgium and Austria; there has been no recourse to minority government (à la Denmark) or to extraparliamentary cabinets. Coalitions have most often assembled more than the minimum required parliamentary support, and the numerically strongest party has generally been a partner even in coalitions among three parties. The segmented pluralist nations have come to place greater weight on joint decision making and mutuality of rights and obligations than upon majority decisions and majority-minority alternations of power (which are, moreover, often unattainable in multiparty systems). The principle of *amicabilis compositio* – in the suggestive formula of the Peace of Westphalia recalled by Juerg Steiner – has come to prevail in much of political and socioeconomic life.

Switzerland has informally institutionalized unique systems of legislative-executive relations at cantonal and national levels. These include an executive *Kollegialprinzip*[16] which goes far beyond normal coalition practice in its inclusiveness, stability, and capacity for compromise – though not in its learning capacity, Steiner argues. The principles of "all-parties government" (Roger Girod's term exaggerates only slightly) were first developed in a number of communes and cantons before becoming the unwritten rule of the confederation. No canton with a four- or five-party coalition has ever gone back to a two- or three-party coalition.[17]

Austria, Switzerland, and Belgium have carried proportionality into the civil service and the staffing of public corporations, as well as the agencies of administrative pluralism. The Swiss and Belgian systems naturally include recognition of language and regional or cantonal diversity in addition to religious-ideological bloc representation. The Austrian *Proporz* is most clearly party-determined; the Swiss practice is the least formal.

The Belgian situation, aside from its very thorny linguistic conflict, which is at least regulated by law, requires the most subtle adjustments between uncodified principles and uneasy practice. The Belgian parties practice a sort of *Proporz*, which takes account not only of the individual's party or associated trade union affiliation, but also of his identification as a practising Catholic or freethinker. Ritual calls for each new government to proclaim its devotion to a merit system and its intent to do away with political appointments and (more important these days) pro-

---

[16] Erich Gruner, *Die Parteien in der Schweiz* (Bern, 1969), p. 24.

[17] For Steiner's views, "Nonviolent Conflict Resolution in Democratic Systems: Switzerland," *Journal of Conflict Resolution*, Vol. 13 (September 1969), 295-303. For the "système de gouvernement de tous les partis," R. Girod, "Le Système des partis en Suisse," *Revue française de science politique*, Vol. 14 (December 1964), 1130. See also François Masnata, *Le parti socialiste et la tradition démocratique en Suisse* (Paris, 1963) and Christopher Hughes, *The Parliament of Switzerland* (London, 1962).

motions. But it insists that the balance within the public service reflect the divisions within public opinion. Therefore, each government moves first to reestablish a hypothetical equilibrium upset only by the regrettable partisanship of its predecessors. An unavowed and constantly shifting *Proporz* in favor of the parties of the governing coalition prevails; but governments *à la recherche des équilibres perdus* do not dismiss people in order to restore balance, although they may sidetrack them from decision making.

EXTENT OF SEGMENTATION

Table 2 offers some gross comparisons of the degrees of penetration into different social milieux by the various ideological blocs about 1950-1960, when the systems of segmented pluralism attained their highest development. Table 3 offers some equally gross comparisons of the degrees of segmentation by spheres of politically relevant activity in the same period. As these tables indicate, segmentation has been more extensive in the lower social strata.

Workers and farmers have been much more inclined than employers and members of the liberal professions to act through segmented organizations. Liberal, Catholic, and Protestant employers have very largely surmounted religious differences in order to work through neutral employer associations, leaving the Catholic or Protestant-oriented associations to serve as study groups. The most important segmented employer associations, those of the Netherlands, cooperated earlier and at first more effectively with each other than did the segmented labor unions.[18] The fullest data on association memberships by socioeconomic categories come from the Netherlands. There, as in the United States, association memberships as a whole rise with advances in socioeconomic status. However, the contrary holds true for membership in segmented associations; it is high among workers and low among employers.[19]

[18] John Windmuller, *Labor Relations in the Netherlands* (Ithaca, 1969).

[19] Netherlands Central Statistical Bureau, *Vrije-tijdsbesteding in Nederland, 1962-1963, Deel 7, Verenigingsleven, zomer 1963* (Hilversum, 1965), p. 47.

For data in Tables 2 and 3, I have relied on the results of elections to official or semiofficial representative bodies (the chambers of labor, agriculture, and commerce in Austria; the elections to works councils and health and safety committees in Belgium), the membership data of various voluntary associations and some survey research (notably in the Netherlands and Austria), and on the research and scholarly "guesstimates" of my colleagues in the International Study of the Politics of the Smaller European Democracies,

Table 2   Extent of Penetration by Ideological Blocs into Occupational Milieux, about 1950-1960

Social Milieu	Austria				Belgium				Netherlands					Switzerland				
	CA	SO	CO	LR	CA	SO	CO	LR	CA	SO	CO	LR	PR*	CA	SO	CO	LR	PR
Manual Workers	3	1	3	4	2	2	3	3	2	2	4		2	3	1	3	3	3
White-collar Employees	2	2	4	3	2	2	3	3	3	2			2	3	2		2	3
Farmers	1	3		4	1			3	2				2	2			2	2
Farm Laborers	1	2			1	2			2	2			2					
Small Business	1	3	3	3	1	3	2	2	2	2			2	2	2		1	3
Employers	1	3	3	2	1		2	2	2	3			2	2	2		1	2
Liberal Professions	2	2	2	2	1	2		2	2	2			2	2	3		2	2

NOTE: Ideological Bloc – CA = Catholic; SO = Socialist; CO = Communist; LR = Liberal-Radical; PR = Protestant.

Strength of bloc organization in milieu: 1 = majority support; 2 = extensive support, between about 15 and 49 percent; 3 = significant minority, between about 5 and 14 percent; 4 = some support, but less than 5 percent.

* Includes both Protestant blocs (Hervormd and Gereformeerd).

Sources: See note 19.

Table 3 Extent of Segmented Pluralism, by Sphere of Activity, about 1950-1960

	Austria	Belgium	Luxembourg	Netherlands	Switzerland
Education					
Primary		H	(1)*	H	M
Secondary	M	H	(2)*	H	M
Higher	M	H	(3)**	M	L
Mass Media					
Press	H	M	H	M	M
Electronic	M			H	
Socioeconomic Organization					
Labor	H	H	H	H	H
Farmers	H	H		H	M
Small Business	M	H		H	
Employers	M	L		M	L
Liberal Professions	M	M		M	
Health Care	M	H		H	H
Consumers	H	H			L
Leisure Activities	H	H		M	M
Politics and Government					
Religion-Party Ties	H	H	H	H	M
Bureaucracy	H	H			H

Note: Degree of segmented pluralism H = High; M = Medium; L = Low.

* 1, 2 = State schools under clerical influence; **3 = No university.

Sources: See note 19

Some of these class differences in the degree of segmented activity reflect the wider range of social and communications skills in the higher-status occupations and the wider networks of personal relationships made possible by education and economic means. They also reflect historic differences in approaches by religious authorities to the faithful of different classes as they sought to inoculate or encapsulate them against contaminating contacts. The poverty of social relations experienced by most

---

on which see Val R. Lorwin, "Historians and Other Social Scientists: The Comparative Analysis of Nation-Building in Western Societies," in Stein Rokkan, ed. *Comparative Research across Cultures and Nations* (Paris, 1968), esp. pp. 111-14.

peasants, workers, and lower middle-class elements made possible a concept of "total" organization for them which one can hardly imagine proposed to a modern upper-class constituency. This is the concept stated in the 1950s by the chaplain of the Belgian Catholic Workers' Movement: "A triple idea governs the structure of our great Christian labor organization: that of totality, of complexity, and of unity.... Our movement must embrace the whole person of the worker, the whole of the worker's life, the whole family of the worker, all workers' needs, and the whole working class. We want the working man and woman, youth and adult, in coming into our movement, to find everything there."[20] Peasant leagues achieved as much for Catholic peasants. Abraham Kuyper, who organized in the Netherlands the mass movement of fundamentalist Calvinists against the bourgeois leaders of the latitudinarian Dutch Reformed church, proclaimed, "There is no sphere where Christ does not say, 'Mine!' "[21]

Nor was it only the religiously oriented leaders who tried to organize an all-embracing framework for the lives of workers. Lacking only the equivalents of the parish and parochial schools, the Socialists sought similar ends. The Belgian Workers' party proposed "to take the whole man at every age of his life and in all the manifestations of his existence."[22] The greatest density and intensity of such organization – and the greatest cultural emancipation – were those achieved between the wars among the workers of "Red Vienna."[23]

RELATIONS AMONG THE BLOCS

In each country, each bloc eventually had to recognize that no one bloc or even coalition could have a tranquil or durable national (or, in Switzerland, cantonal) majority on any decision which threatened the *raison d'être* for another bloc's political organization, notably, the relations between state and schools. Also, as in every political democracy, the dominant social and economic groups came to recognize the need for sharing power in the regulation of the labor market and distribution of the national product with the industrial and political representatives of the working classes. In the segmented pluralist polities, that meant recognizing the legitimacy of the competing segmented organizations of workers rather than attempting to play off one segmented

[20] Msgr. A Brys, *Comment est conçu et organisé le Mouvement Ouvrier Chrétien en Belgique* (Brussels, n.d.), 10.

[21] Quoted in Kruijt, *Verzuiling,* 14.

[22] Emile Vandervelde, *La Cinquantenaire du Parti Ouvrier Belge* (Brussels, 1935), 324.

[23] Charles A. Gulick, *Austria from Habsburg to Hitler,* 2 vols. (Berkeley and Los Angeles, 1948).

organization against another. Socialist organizations had to accept the legitimacy of organizations formed on denominational lines within the social class which the Socialists claimed for their own on grounds of ideology and of historical primacy in the field. Working-class elites had to achieve enough unity in economic and political bargaining to prevent pluralism from keeping them too weak to represent their constituents adequately.

The full acceptance by contending blocs of the legitimacy of their rivals at every level was slow in coming, and it has prevailed for only a short time. In Switzerland, with its curious mixture of egalitarianism and stratification, traditionalism and capacity for compromise, the Socialist party got a seat on the federal executive only a generation ago, and it did not get two seats, in accordance with its share of the national vote, until 1959. (It was possible for the Socialists to wait with some confidence, since they had been sitting on communal and cantonal executives since the 1930s.) In every nation the mutual acceptance of the legitimacy of social, especially labor, organizations of opposing ideologies dates chiefly from World War II.

There is a tension between the fixity of segmentation and the options of pluralism. Faithful clienteles and hereditary voters exist in an atmosphere of voluntary associational and electoral competition. A host of socializing agencies, beginning with the family, and networks of social services transmit bloc attitudes and attachments from generation to generation. But some margin of uncertainty and fear of competition, which were at the base of the system's establishment, remain necessary, in another day and another spirit, to make the system viable. Bloc members can have the advantages of pluralism only if they feel, and their elites know, that they may exercise some freedom of choice in association membership and voting. Such possibilities help keep leaders responsible to the needs of their rank and file. Of course, too much uncertainty may lead to competitive bidding and overbidding by leaders of mass organizations; nonetheless, segmented labor organizations in the smaller European democracies have shown more sense of the public interest and more civic responsibility since World War II than the functional organizations of the United States or Britain.

Comparison of the extent and effectiveness of participation in segmented and in functional organizations is one of the many aspects of our problem which still calls for systematic research. The pluralism due to segmentation has, on the whole, made for more, rather than for less, participation in voluntary associations. All other things being equal, the more pluralism in an area of socioeconomic association, the larger the number of posts to fill at all levels. Two building trades unions have twice as many presidencies and secretaryships, and almost twice as many executive board positions, as a single building trades union for the same territory. They will furnish more union representatives to public regulatory bodies and to collective bargaining commissions than a single union. Pluralism creates more pluralism. In what may be a wholesome form of Parkinson's law, competition of organizations for places on the various elected bodies of labor representation and protection creates a need for candidates, some of whom are already activists; but thousands more become active only because of the contested elections. The usual proportional representation gives even the organization of a foreordained minority position the incentive to compete in a unit where it does not hope to win.

On the other hand, a high ratio of participation to membership among people low in organizational experience and formal training will, at least initially, lower the quality of representation. Responsibility may develop competence, but only if the initial disparity between skills and responsibilities is not too great and not too suddenly manifest to participants and critical observers. Demands far in excess of competence discourage participation and frustrate its aims. In all these countries, even little Luxembourg, the workings of segmented pluralism in some spheres have been so complicated as to give the masses the impression that the system could work only by a concentration of decisions at top levels. Hence there arose a peculiar blend of democracy and elite decision making shrouded in confidentiality, of "leadership and passivity."[24]

Benefits have their costs, and those of segmented pluralist diversity include waste and *immobilisme*. The duplication of facilities and services is more uneconomical in small countries than in large, and less justified by a need to prevent organizational leviathans. One should rate diversity ahead of efficiency where there is competition of ideals and opinions. Competition in the age of the welfare state, however, is often based not on meaningful differentiation of services but on the natural pursuit of institutional growth: for example, the competition for students between public and Catholic school systems in Belgium, or the competition of health care systems for numbers of enrollees.

More damaging than waste is *immobilisme*. Voluntary organizations or the state may fail to take desirable action because of mutual veto powers held by the segmented organizations, or because of lack of the public resources to accomplish in all of the

---

[24] Hans Daalder, *Leiding en Lijdelijkheid* (Assen, 1964); also his essay in Dahl, *Political Oppositions,* and the work of Lijphart, Juerg Steiner, and Huyse.

recognized institutions what there are resources to accomplish in only one of them. The block on innovation by mutual veto comes with greater force from segmented organizations than in other forms of pluralism, because the differentiation of organization is tied to the values of religious and political choice.

AUSTRIA INFELIX

If we do not restrict discussion to current regimes, we may examine the conditions under which segmented pluralism has failed and succeeded within the same country. With the same formal institutions between the wars and after World War II, Austria is the best example of discontinuities in the history of segmented pluralism. The First Republic presents a limiting case of unmanageable conflict; the Second Republic presents a limiting case in conflict management which goes to the point of depriving politics of much of its meaning.

The Austrian state was a creation of the victorious enemy; in 1919 the Allies were naturally unwilling to see Germany aggrandized by the *Anschluss* supported by the Austrian parties and people. The German-speaking remnant of the Hapsburg Empire had little sense of national identity or national goals and no accepted national symbols. Schoolbooks did not even perform their normal socialization functions, but led youngsters to understand that they were part of an ideal Germany.[25] Loyalties ran to the ideological blocs and their parties, which had their own symbols and their own armed forces. The bitterness of party struggle weakened the state, whose weakness in turn gave more scope for party struggle. Unable to enforce law or order on the parties, Austria was a state characterized by "a strong tendency toward non-existence," a *Staat wider Willen.*[26]

From the three "camps" or *Lager* of prewar days, society and politics became polarized when the smallest and least widely organized of the three, the German Nationals, threw much of their support to the "Blacks" against the "Reds." Class and geographical alignments deepened those of religion and ideology: Catholic businessmen, artisans, and farmers versus Socialist workers; rural areas versus industrial cities; the Black hinterland versus the Red capital. The Catholic bloc lacked the sort of labor or left wing that was giving such blocs some balance and some progres-

---

[25] I am indebted to Kurt Steiner for this information, which is based on research for his *Politics in Austria* (Boston, 1972).

[26] R. Lorenz, *Der Staat wider Willen* (Vienna, 1938), quoted by H. P. Secher, "Coalition Government: The Case of the Second Austrian Republic," *American Political Science Review*, Vol. 52, (September 1958), 791

sive impetus in other countries. Its elites, including the prelates, treated the workers as inferior and dependent – and actually or potentially subversive. Not even papal pronouncements were proof against this attitude; *Quadragesimo Anno* in 1931, despite its corporatist emphasis, was all but suppressed in Austria.[27]

The Austrian Socialists were a classic case of reformists whose revolutionary language confused their followers and alarmed their antagonists. *Suaviter in re, fortiter in modo* might have been the motto of the party. Committed to political democracy, despite all the subtleties of "Austro-Marxism," the Socialists nevertheless employed a vocabulary of class struggle – notably in the famous Linz program of 1926 – to keep their left wing within the party. Unity was the opium of the party activists. "It is a hundred times better to go the wrong way united," argued Otto Bauer, "for errors can be corrected, than to split in search of the right way."[28] But Socialist unity in the face of potential Communist competition or left-wing dissatisfaction was bought at the expense of whatever chances there were of a minimum of national unity.

Foreign pressures accentuated internal divisions. Mussolini's open and covert interventions encouraged the Catholic *Lager* in its mortal combat with the Socialist camp. Much feebler was the pressure of international Communism, but its influence helped make the Socialists more revolutionary in rhetoric, and more reluctant to reach compromises. Unlike the other states of segmented pluralism, Austria had no tradition of smallness of size and the use of balance-of-power considerations among powerful states to preserve its own independence; to be sure, the shortsightedness of the democracies gave it little opportunity in that direction.

THE SECOND AUSTRIAN REPUBLIC: PLURALISM AFFIRMED
The spirit of paradox bids us learn from history that people never learn from history. That is not so; sometimes they learn, and sometimes they learn too much. Leaders and masses of the two Austrian blocs learned many lessons in the late 1930s and the 1940s. There was the lesson of the civil war: politics must never come to that again. There were the lessons of dictatorship: Mussolini's brutality and corruption, and the greater horrors of Hitlerism and Stalinism sensitized Catholics and Socialists against all

[27] Alfred Diamant, *Austrian Catholics and the First Republic* (Princeton, 1960), ch. 5.
[28] *Parteitag, 1927*, p. 128, quoted by Gulick, *Austria from Habsburg*, I: 694. Cf. Norbert Leser, "Austro-Marxism: A Reappraisal," *Journal of Contemporary History*, Vol. I (1966), 117-33, and his *Zwischen Reformismus und Bolschewismus: Der Austro-Marxismus als Theorie und Praxis* (Vienna, 1968).

dictatorship. There was the lesson of the concentration camps: there many Catholics and Socialists learned to know and esteem each other as human beings and as political colleagues and to stress the values that united them, including even the national independence of Austria.

The four-power occupation and the Soviet presence placed a premium on concerted efforts by the two parties to end the occupation and lessen the threat of Soviet intervention. The needs of postwar reconstruction directed energies toward concrete tasks bringing into play shared interests rather than incompatible ideologies. In principle, the new structure of the Catholic party gave manual workers and white-collar employees equality with businessmen and farmers. The Socialists no longer felt concern over possible Communist competition on their left, as a result of collective memories of the Soviet behavior on entering Vienna and of the Soviet occupation of Eastern Austria; the failure of the Communists' *Putsch* in 1950 firmly sealed them off from power.

Class and geographical polarization declined, with the nation's further industrialization and changes in social structure, and with the development by both parties of more diversified territorial and social constituencies. The Catholics gained strength among workers, notably in Vienna. The Socialists gained in other classes, and outside Vienna and the industrial cities. As Walter Simon found, "it became more and more frequent that a peasant was a Socialist and a worker an anti-Socialist."[29]

The issues of clericalism and anticlericalism subsided. The bishops gave up endorsement of political candidates, and affirmed the ideal of "a free church in a free society." The Socialists, like their German brethren, moved beyond old antireligious positions. Other old issues had lost their thrust and counterthrust. With the widespread and widely accepted postwar nationalization of Austrian industry, further nationalizing ceased to be a vital issue. With the Western orientation of the big parties, international pressures now unified, rather than tore apart, the small state.

When the Republic was reconstituted by Allied action, there was no *koalitionsfaehig* minor party. Socialists and Catholics entered upon a "grand coalition" which was to last two decades. This extraordinary arrangement included the *Proporz* for the allocation of many of the places in public services and in nationalized enterprises.[30] After the coalition broke up in 1966, its

---

[29] Walter B. Simon, "Politische Ethik und politische Struktur," *Koelner Zeitschrift fuer Soziologie und Sozialpsychologie*, Vol 11, No. 3 (1959), 450. See also Kurt Shell, *The Transformation of Austrian Socialism* (New York, 1962).

[30] Frederick C. Engelmann, "Austria: The Pooling of Opposition," in Dahl, *Political Oppositions*, 260-83; *Proporz* is defined on pp. 265 and 274; Otto Kirchheimer, "The Waning of Opposition in Parlia-

successors – first a Catholic, then a Socialist, cabinet – continued the *Proporz*.

Was there any meaning left in the drama of segmented pluralism in the postwar atmosphere of leadership accommodation and mass passivity? There was, even beyond the *Bereichsopposition* by which each coalition partner was free to criticize the management of the areas under its partner's direction. The doctrines of the two blocs had lost most of their intensity and much of their significance to the actors, but attitudes of identification with each bloc and negative associations with the other bloc lived on. Since the Catholic and Socialist camps had somewhat diversified their social and geographic bases, the competition within social groups and within geographic areas might eventually be keener.

Within each camp, moreover, there remained a middle-level political elite, living much among its own people, and with an interest, as Rodney Stiefbold has shown, in maintaining the consciousness of political difference amidst the homogenizing effects of the coalition and its aftermath.[31] Organized labor was united in a single trade union federation, but its Socialist majority permitted a unique recognition of the international ties of segmented pluralism: the affiliation of the Catholic minority with the International Confederation of Christian Trade Unions, and of the Communist minority with the World Federation of Trade Unions.

Many of the restraints on partisanship had been lifted with the conclusion of common tasks, the end of the occupation, and changes in the international environment. Time had removed many of those who could recall the civil war or the concentration camps. The tasks of reconstruction had been concluded, to make way for Austria's own *Wirtschaftswunder*. Cold war pressures for unity had dwindled, despite the grim reminders of Hungary in 1956 and Czechoslovakia in 1968.

The partisanship that revived had neither the ideological character nor the virulence of the partisanship of the 1920s and 1930s, and it accepted both state and regime. Its stakes were lower and the penalties for defeat were limited. In the *Wirtschaftswunder* there was more for all groups, room for movement and accommodation, and toleration for what unkind observers called refined or less refined forms of corruption. Issues were bargainable and

---

mentary Regimes," *Social Research*, Vol. 24 (Summer 1957), 127-56, reprinted in his *Politics, Law, and Social Change* (New York, 1969), 292-318.

[31] Rodney Stiefbold, "Elite-Mass Opinion Structure and Communication Flow in a Consociational Democracy: Austria" (Paper given at the Annual Meeting of the American Political Science Association, September 1968).

apparently soluble, as they had not often been under the impoverished First Republic. The chief changes were in the nature of the state, its international setting, and the collective actors, even after the individual actors who had learned so much had departed from the scene. The Socialist bloc of the Second Republic is not the Socialist *Lager* of the First Republic; the People's party bloc of today is not the Christian Social *Lager* of a harsh and passionate yesterday.

THE DECLINE OF SEGMENTED PLURALISM

The height and the decline of institutions, as of doctrines, often come hard upon each other. For a time there is movement in both directions. Did Parliament's repeal of the Corn Laws in 1846 usher in the "age of laissez-faire" in Britain? Perhaps, but the same Parliament, only a year later, carried state intervention a long step forward by the Ten-Hours Act.

The 1950s saw the apogee of the system of segmented pluralism. During those years, two events marked turning points in two countries. One was the *Mandement* (Pastoral Letter) of 1954[32] in which the Dutch episcopate reiterated and amplified its old attempts to safeguard Catholics from the corrosive effects of modernization, liberalism, and socialism. Recalling the imperatives of unity and separateness in political and social action, the *Mandement* threatened workers who joined the Socialist-led unions with denial of the sacraments. Oddly enough, of Catholics in the Labor party (successor to the prewar Socialist party) it demanded no more than an examination of conscience. Coming from the most conservative section of the church, the *Mandement* turned out to be a last look backward. Many Catholics, notably among the intellectuals, attacked its spirit of isolationism and defensiveness and narrow clericalism. Catholic and Socialist union leaders did not cease the cooperation which had made possible the nation's postwar recovery. In 1965 the bishops formally retracted the ban on Catholic membership in the Socialist-led unions.[33]

The Belgian school pact of 1958 was a very different sort of turning point. In it the leaders of the three traditional ideological parties compromised the outstanding issues of the school fight that had embroiled them intermittently for a century.[34] Although

---

[32] *De Katholiek in het openbare leven van deze tijd. Bisschoplijk Mandement van 1954* (Zeist, 1954).

[33] Windmuller, *Labor Relations*, pp. 121-26.

[34] See "Le Pacte scolaire," in Jean Meynaud, Jean Ladrière, and François Perin, eds. *La Décision politique en Belgique* (Paris, 1965), 150-76.

the pact was negotiated only for a twelve-year period (and was still under renegotiation in 1970), its implementation quickly convinced Belgians that its principles had become permanent national policy. The pact ended the sharp conflict of the 1950s over the levels and conditions of state aid to the Catholic secondary schools – an aid already granted at primary school and university levels – and established a general *modus vivendi*, with mutual recognition of the legitimacy of both public and Catholic schools.

The pact immediately reduced the church's intervention in elections and the support by Catholic social organizations for the Christian Social party, for it removed the strongest argument for separate Catholic political action and for Catholic political unity. The managers of the Christian Social party could soon experience the pertinence of Oscar Wilde's and Bernard Shaw's principle that there are only two tragedies in life – not getting what you want, and getting what you want.

The systems of segmented pluralism have reached, and begun to retreat from, their maximum development. The structures and attitudes of segmented pluralism will no doubt persist a long time, but the dynamic has gone from the principle. Paradoxically, the system looks as if it may last longest where it once had the worst results, i.e., in Austria. Where it was first and most successful, the Netherlands – in part because of its successes there – it has decomposed most.

Why, beyond the obvious (but easily ignored) certainty that systems change, should we now see a weakening of segmented pluralism? If the reasons vary from country to country, among ideological blocs, and among social organizations and parties within the blocs, we may nevertheless note some general bases for *ontzuiling*. (To identify the disintegration of systems of segmented pluralism, I shall use the Dutch *ontzuiling*, because there is no English word or even phrase as crisp and, once defined – as it is on page 35 – as clear.)

Ontzuiling is possible because the ideological blocs have succeeded in their defensive missions, while their offensive missions have ground to a halt. The denominational blocs have won state support for their schools and welfare activities. They have not arrested the long-term trends of secularization, but they have prevented the forcible secularizers from having their way. The Liberal and Socialist blocs, on the other hand, have prevented the churches from dominating the state. They have not secularized all education, far from it, but they have affirmed the state's role in education. Where once there rang the shouts of "Ecrasez l'infâme!" and the countershouts of "Deliver us, O Lord, from schools without God and teachers without faith," there are not only truce here and peace there, but signs of a tolerance which may lead to new forms of educational pluralism.

The last clash of offensive missions was probably the Belgian school fight of the 1950s. An age has passed since the Liberal and Socialist parties formed, in 1954, a national government coalition "for a generation" to carry out an active public school policy that would permanently reduce the recruitment of a Catholic electorate out of the Catholic secondary schools. That "generation" and that coalition lasted the four years of a single legislature, at the end of which (with elections unsuccessful for the coalition) the Liberals and Socialists joined the Catholics in writing the school pact.

In different historical settings, different results flow from similar actions. The Dutch *Pacificatie* of 1917, with its school pact, was followed by rapid development of the denominational schools and bloc organizations, unions, and parties. The patterns of education and organization had been formed, but the Catholic and fundamentalist Calvinist and Socialist organizations had not yet carried the social emancipation of their followers as far as they could. The Dutch social movements and political parties needed a generation to develop through segmented structures before those structures would appear to many of their elites as confining rather than liberating; so the Dutch pact took four decades to begin to produce its consequences of *ontzuiling*. The Belgian school pact came, in a later phase of social and political development, near the height, rather than the beginning, of mass membership. It took less than a decade to elicit comparable consequences.

Changing technology has sharply cut the proportions of purely intra-bloc communications in several ways. In the first generations of social mobilization, most forms of communication were segregated by origin and by self-selection of audiences: religious services or Socialist meetings, voluntary gatherings, demonstrations and mass meetings, petitions and pamphlets, and the party press. But electronic media finally defied effective segmentation. At first, with radio, the Dutch blocs found a way to practice *apartheid* with equality, under a unique government scheme for the sharing out of broadcasting time among the blocs. The Dutch carried this principle over into television, but here the medium was too potent for *apartheid* to work, especially since the more expensive facilities were not available for competing programs at the same hours. It was futile to expect most people not to watch programs indiscriminately. Although programs have occasionally shocked viewers of other blocs, the general effect on the masses, who did not normally share social life with members of other blocs, has been to weaken old stereotypes and enhance understanding of other groups. Since television programs brought intrabloc as well as interbloc conflicts into the living rooms of the ordinarily deferential Dutch citizens, they eroded some of the simplified self-images of the segmented society.[35]

In newspaper publishing, rising costs of production and distribution have made it difficult for ideological blocs to compete with neutral, or ostensibly neutral, publishers of heavily capitalized, ideologically uninhibited papers. No doubt many of the segmented socioeconomic movements could assess themselves enough to support better papers, even though the parties themselves do not have the means. But the movements have not, for the most part, cared to risk the sums needed, and many party and bloc papers have declined in quality and appeal, some to the point of disappearance or amalgamation. (This is not surprising in small countries, when even in Britain the Labour party has been incapable of supporting a daily newspaper at all worthy of its size or mission.)

Among the elites of the four nations caught up in the war, contacts in exile helped to erode the sharpness of old antipathies while affirming the best of traditional values. Postwar social and economic controls, the great extension of collective bargaining, and the various forms of partial national planning and interest-group consultation have multiplied elite contacts with members of rival bloc organizations, with members of government, parliament, and bureaucracy, and with economic bargaining partners. These contacts have, on the whole, tended to replace stereotypes of members of other blocs with more realistic and more differentiated images, diminishing political distance between elites and between parties. These changed perceptions among elites have been self-reinforcing. The most obvious consequences have been Socialist-Christian political coalitions and labor movement cooperation. While party coalitions have been dissolved and re-formed, the labor union understandings have continued and deepened.

The changing nature of the provision of social insurance and welfare services has been another element of *ontzuiling*. The state has rendered general and obligatory the unemployment compensation and health care insurance provided originally by trade unions and friendly societies. The segmented organizations may still administer the benefits, but under legislation and regulation which make for a more or less uniform professionalization of personnel and bureaucratization of services.

With success, the business element of any social organization, functional or segmented, grows at the expense of the element of

35 Arnold J. Heidenheimer, "Elite Responses to Ontzuiling: Reels within Wheels in Dutch Broadcasting Politics" (Paper delivered at the Eighth World Congress of Political Science, Munich, 1970).

emancipating movement. Among the segmented organizations, this unavoidable asymmetry of growth blurs the distinctions which were the reasons for creating separate organizations. There is nothing so like a Socialist union's unemployment compensation office as a Catholic union's unemployment compensation office. The labor organizations have difficulty finding issues that might differentiate those of one bloc from those of another.[36] The success which has built them into the structures of the welfare state has cost them their original particularistic appeals.

Youth had shown disaffection from the ideological blocs well before the turmoil of the late 1960s. Even among young people attracted by the heart of the Christian or liberal or socialist message, many have tended to reject the structures to which the message has given rise. Youth are easily put off by the complex and emotionally unsatisfying compromises of the systems of segmented pluralism. Discontent has ranged from that of unideological sports club members (sports are the least segmented field of voluntary association activity) to that of students with a thirst for the absolute – ecumenical, ideological, nationalist, or libertarian.

Young Flemish Catholics led an antiepiscopal movement which successfully defied the Belgian bishops who had refused to turn the bilingual University of Louvain into an exclusively Flemish institution. Many went on to question the necessity of separate Catholic educational institutions. In the Netherlands, surveys showed that, with religious practice held constant, younger voters gave less support to the confessional parties than did older voters, and that when students deviated from their fathers' party choices, it was to turn away from the confessional parties.[37]

THE CHRISTIAN BLOCS

Ontzuiling in the Catholic blocs was under way long before the second Vatican Council. One trend has been that of the increasing autonomy of lay organization among the once most dependent social categories: workers, farmers, women. The Austrian Christian Workers' movement could no longer be called "the movement of the vicars."[38] Yet until the late 1960s the Dutch

[36] For example, Pierre Aragno, "La Division artificielle des salariés suisses," *Revue syndicale suisse*, Vol. 55 (September 1963), 241-48.

[37] The two Dutch surveys are: (1) Attwood Statistics, cited by Arend Lijphart in draft paper for forthcoming volume edited by Richard Rose, Electoral Behavior: A Comparative Handbook (New York: Free Press, forthcoming), and (2) C. J. Lammers. "Deconfessionalisering en radicalisering bij studenten?" *Acta Politica*, Vol. 3 (January 1968), 149-61.

[38] L. Reichhold, "Austria," in S. H. Scholl, *150 Ans*, p. 111.

bishops insisted on maintaining diocesan workers' leagues, under their own direction, to the confusion of the more modern, autonomous organizations of the Catholic trade unions.[39]

The lay organizations have been able to recruit their own leadership, thanks to the general rise in literacy, to preparation for public service in youth movements, workers' education, and training institutes (Catholic or public), and to the accumulation of experience in groups once dominated by clerics or members of the higher social strata. With increasing autonomy and lay leadership, the Catholic organizations have shown an increasing willingness to work with neutral or rival-bloc organizations. They have gained self-confidence in this work from the observation that neither Socialists nor, *a fortiori* in these countries, Communists were likely to absorb or displace the Christian social organizations.

The failure of ecclesiastical organizations to Christianize the governments or the peoples (or, in some cases, the churches) has not discouraged lay initiatives in the social and political field; on the contrary, it has evoked more action by Catholic and Protestant organizations and individuals. The individuals have shown an increasing readiness to work outside of specifically Christian milieux, and often in organizations with a historical background of hostility to Christianity. An increasing number of people, notably elites, especially the young, show a desire to "go out among the others, with the others," rather than to serve, or bear witness, or simply defend their group interests in specifically Christian organizations.

Those who have put the issue of the appropriate milieu for Christian temporal action on the simple level of conversions have had to meet the argument put forward by a distinguished Catholic scholar and public servant, that "to the extent that Catholic institutions realize their aim, they risk constructing around Catholics a sort of fortress which preserves them from dangers from without and from dechristianization. But to that very extent, they isolate them from the nonbelievers and assure the latter against any possible risk of Christian contagion."[40] Even where their faith is nominally that of the vast majority, some thoughtful Catholics have not hesitated to speak of a Catholic "ghetto" to describe the dangers of isolation from their fellow men by the pervasive complex of parish leagues, schools, myriad voluntary associations, and political party; for intensity of communication

---

[39] Windmuller, *Labor Relations*, pp. 37, 59, 127-28.
[40] André Molitor, quoted in *Informations Catholiques Internationales* (1 June 1958), p. 16.

among some has been purchased at the price of communication with others.

Critics of segmented pluralism argue that the complex of confessional social and political organizations tends to diminish the spiritual character of the church and hamper its true mission. What once appeared to be the organizational means to a Christian life in society risk becoming ends in themselves. Overorganization may have greater dangers for religious life than underorganization. Associations taking in every aspect of social life but employment (and often that, too) envelop the masses in a "sociological Christianity" likely to foster a religious practice of social conformity rather than personal devotion. At the expense of the aims of the lay apostolate, they risk inducing in the elites an excessive concern with the organizational and instrumental. "Confessionally oriented structures and institutions have rendered and still render great services," said André Molitor, "but their existence risks arousing in us a spirit of power and of domination hardly in keeping with the message of the Beatitudes."[41]

To the confessional party, such a comment applies with special force. As Dutch Catholics who could not accept their bishops' antisocialist pastoral letter of 1954 said, "Political power has been a wall between the church and the soul of the people."[42] The danger to religion (and to the church) was all the greater where Catholicism was the dominant faith of the land; for the church and the Catholic party were likely to identify with the interests of property holders as well as with the temptations of political power.[43]

If, in partisan politics, the churches became less active, individual Christians might be more active than ever. For at least among the elites, in a period when ecclesiastical and political party establishments were put in question, there was a deepening appreciation of the validity of politics as an individual human concern. Catholic and Protestant churchmen and laymen reexamined their relations to denominational parties. Many Catholics had long anticipated the second Vatican Council's abandonment of the old commandment of the political separateness and political unity of the faithful. North of the Alps, at least, as a Jesuit sociologist has remarked, "the question of whether parties should be formed on a confessional basis or on a purely socioeconomic basis has lost

[41] Ibid.

[42] Quoted in A. J. Arntz, "Les Catholiques hollandais dans la nation," Vie Intellectuelle, Vol. 26 (October 1955), 150.

[43] See for example Msgr. A. Simon, Le Parti Catholique Belge, 1830-1945 (Brussels, 1958), esp. chs. 5 and 6.

the character of a question of principle."[44] Political action need not be taken through a confessional party; Catholics could legitimately differ about the most appropriate form of political action.

The lifting of constraints on the citizen may free the institution as well. The Catholic hierarchy's disentanglement from its partisan role in national politics may turn out to be comparable to the loss of the temporal states of the papacy a century ago. What the church then considered a catastrophe turned out to be an inestimable boon, since it freed the popes from the petty responsibilities of rule over a small band of Italian territory for the ampler performance of a universal spiritual role. Now most Catholics see the church's change of role in a happier light than that of the papacy of 1870. The Austrian bishops put it in these terms in 1952, "Today the church has no emperor and no government, no party, no class, no cannon, and no capital behind her. . . . And thus the church goes out from a dying age to meet a new epoch of social development."[45]

The Socialist blocs show a profound *aggiornamento*, too. The church and confessional organizations have ceased to be their chief negative reference groups; or, where they have retained that primacy, the intensity of feeling has subsided among Socialist elites and masses. Some of the reasons are common to the confessional groups as well, notably contacts during the war under perils and for a cause which made for solidarity. An Italian Socialist, sheltered in the Vatican cellars while the departing Nazis searched above for him, is reported to have said to a Catholic and a Communist sharing his hiding place: "Twenty years of my life wasted in anticlerical activities!" The greater social and political progressivism of the Christian blocs made it no longer possible to tag Christian unions as "yellow." The postwar emphasis on planning, rather than on nationalization or the class struggle, called for extensive consultation and an "ecumenical" approach to the representatives of all legitimate group interests, religiously oriented or not. Pragmatism induces pragmatism. The diminishing salience of the confessional quality and of the clerical presence in their rivals' organizations induced a "de-confessionalization" of Socialist doctrine and rhetoric. As religion itself seemed less relevant to Christians, the attack on religion was less relevant – and

[44] H. Hoefnagels, *L'Eglise et la société prométhéenne: problèmes de sociologie religieuse* (Paris, 1966), p. 85.

[45] Quoted by William T. Bluhm, "Political Integration, Cultural Integration, and Economic Development: Their Relationship in the Nation-Building Experience of Republican Austria" (Paper read at Eighth World Congress of Political Science, Munich, 1970), p. 20.

politically less attractive to Socialist leaders, in terms of either electoral appeal or of membership response in their own organizations. There was a positive element too, in a new conception of the "socialist man" – or rather, in the disappearance of the old conception of *homo socialisticus*, the man for whom socialism was an all-embracing (and anticonfessional) vision of life. "There is not, and cannot be, a Socialist *credo*," wrote the Swiss Socialist Jeanne Hersch. "This absence of *credo* is not an impoverishment of man but an appeal to a liberty which transcends any political discipline; it implies also that there is no socialist *mystique* ... because socialism does not address itself to the whole man.... Hence, all incompatibility between socialism, on the one hand, and religions and churches on the other hand, disappears. No socialist *credo* stands opposed to their *credo*."[46] Nor was hers merely the view of an internationally-minded philosopher. The Dutch Labor party, a new creation on a largely Socialist base, insisted that it was "simply the meeting place of those who agree on a progressive political program. The collaboration of these people is valuable only if they have strong principles, rooted in a philosophy of life which they must seek outside the labor movement. It is expected that each member of the party will be a Catholic, a Protestant, or a 'humanist,' and will behave and wish to be treated accordingly."[47] In 1958, the Austrian party, although affirming the rest of its seventy-year socialist heritage, wooed Christians with these words: "Socialism and Christianity, the religion of love of one's neighbor, are entirely compatible. There can be no conflict between a Socialism which is based on ethical convictions and the religious communities, so long as the latter avoid using the machinery of the state for the attainment of denominational demands."[48]

The inability of the political system to cope effectively with pressing problems is yet another cause for change. In only one country of the five, however, has any issue become so compelling as to shake the parties of segmented pluralism: the language issue in Belgium.[49] Once the school pact had removed an essential

---

[46] Jeanne Hersch, *Idéologies et réalité* (Paris, 1956), pp. 159-60.

[47] Quoted in Fogarty, *Christian Democracy*, p. 384.

[48] *The New Programme of Austrian Socialism, adopted at the Conference of the Austrian Socialist Party, 14 May 1958* (Vienna, 1958), pp. 6-7.

[49] "La crise de l'unité belge," in Jean Meynaud et al., eds. *La Décision*, pp. 89-149: George A. Kelly, "Belgium: New Nationalism in an Old World," *Comparative Politics*, Vol. 1 (April 1969), 343-65, and Val R. Lorwin, "Linguistic Pluralism and Political Tensions in Modern Belgium," *Canadian Journal of History*, Vol. 5 (March

cement of the Christian Social party's national structure, the old Flemish-French-speaking cleavage threatened that structure and the party's very existence. Similar, but milder, tremors shook the Socialist party and labor unions. The third of the traditional ideological parties, the Liberal party, reorganized itself in 1961, and ostentatiously renounced its century-old anticlericalism. Its initial success as a "catchall party" of the center and center right increased pressures for "deconfessionalization" within the Christian Social and Socialist parties. Its success also showed how much *ontzuiling* depended not only on long-term social and political trends, but on determinations by party leaders that *ontzuiling* would pay off.

The segmented pluralist systems have reached maturity too recently for us to have much evidence yet for any theory of *ontzuiling*. But it seems that disarray within one ideological bloc tends, as one would expect, to encourage disarray within rival blocs. The hostility, or at least the perception of hostility, of other blocs is a source of intrabloc solidarity; the decline of another bloc diminishes the perception of hostility and of threat. With a blurring of the image of unity of the others comes a blurring of the self-image.

At this period in the development of segmented pluralism a sort of "domino effect" comes into play within a bloc. If bloc organization weakens in one area of public life, it tends to weaken in other areas. As strength transmitted strength, weakness or disaffection transmits weakness. If the schools do not need the party, their supporters are freer not to support the party. If trade unions, cooperatives, and friendly societies do not find the party necessary, they will pay fewer of its bills and those of the party press, and they will do less to recruit political personnel and voters for the party. If party and church-oriented student and other youth movements fall off, as they are doing,[50] potential leaders will be less likely to start out on a party-oriented *cursus honorum*.

FACTORS OF CONTINUITY

After looking at some of the factors of change, one must return to the factors of continuity and adjustment within existing political systems. If *verzuiling* originally was not inevitable, but rather

---

1970), 1-23, and an expanded and revised version thereof in Joshua Fishman, ed. *Advances in the Sociology of Language*, vol. II (Paris and The Hague, 1972), pp. 386-412.

[50] Frank A. Pinner, "Tradition and Transgression: Western European Students in the Postwar World," *Daedalus* (Winter 1968), 150.

the result of a series of historical choices, so *ontzuiling* is not inevitable now. Modern social and political organizations have great powers of survival with the help of inertia. It took the combined holocaust of the Nazi revolution and war to raze the segmented structure of German trade unionism. Organizations built on ideologies may endure long after the ideologies have lost most of their dynamism. The bloc organizations continue to perform functions to which the state and their members and voters have become accustomed, however much the distinctiveness of the competing organizations has faded.

These organizations have been recognized and subsidized in the public or quasi-public authorities administering education, communications, social insurance and health care, and regulation of the labor market. Religious affiliations may even provide the basis for allocation to individuals of desiderata in short supply, as with the Dutch government's allocation of land reclaimed from the *Zuider Zee*.[51] The Belgian school pact delegates the continuing interpretation of its terms to representatives of the three political parties which negotiated the pact.

The socioeconomic and cultural organizations associated with the blocs carry on a great deal of political socialization, some in close relationship with primary groups. They play an important role in the recruitment of political personnel; moreover, by offering defeated candidates a relatively painless retreat back to sponsoring organizations, they diminish the risks of political engagement for activists from the lower classes. Union and friendly society pluralism offer something of an option in societies in which, despite political democracy and consumer satisfactions, the elements of choice for workers are very restricted; even the small Catholic and the small Protestant labor movements of Switzerland offer elements of such choice to some Swiss workers. To be sure, highly developed cooperation among segmented organizations in many fields deprives them of much of the rationale for separateness. At the same time, however, by diminishing the frictions of competition, it removes much of the pressure that might come for unification.

Attitudes, which persist after ideologies wane, are conditioned by milieux and traditions which are still largely separate and often uncomprehending of each other. "Political clienteles in Austria are still so strongly structured," Klaus Liepelt argues from a new comparative analysis of survey data, "that a significant upheaval

---

[51] A. K. Constandse, "Acquaintanceships of Farmers in a Newly Colonized Area," *Social Compass*, Vol. 6, No. 2 (1959), 69.

in their behavior is practically impossible."[52] Perceptions and attitudes are based on issues formulated to a large extent by the segmented organizations and the messages which their elites and their *Lumpenelites* emit to their own people, as well as to those of other blocs. A left-wing Catholic writes in despair about the religious news in a Brussels Socialist daily, "Reading *Le Peuple*, one never has the impression that there may be Catholics who might also be Socialist. Every year I have to go to seek comfort from my friends in the Dutch Labor party."[53] But most people do not have friends in another bloc in another land.

Intermarriage is one indicator of bloc isolation or openness. In the Netherlands, where *ontzuiling* has been most conspicuous, we nevertheless find that intermarriages have declined, rather than increased. Between 1947 and 1960, bloc intermarriage declined, and intramarriage increased, in each of the three major religious groups, as well as among those categorized as of "other" religions or no religion.[54]

Attitudes born of past conflicts may condition present conflicts that express themselves in other terms. In the multidimensional pluralism of Switzerland, the limiting case – the only "separatist" movement – is that of the autonomists in the *Jura Bernois*, in the Catholic uplands of the French-speaking district of the overwhelmingly Protestant and German-speaking canton of Bern. The autonomists pose their demands in terms of linguistic rights; but memories of a bygone religious discrimination are perhaps more important (if unconscious) sources of resentment than the present (and apparently undisputed) rights of the French language and culture in this northwest corner of the Confederation.[55]

Inertia and lags in perception pose the old questions of the relationships between belief-systems and institutions. The inherited structures of segmentation are related to a religious-ideological pluralism which nobody among elites or masses, except a very small extreme left, would repudiate. "But the difficulty is," as Jean Ladrière has said, "that people cannot seriously

[52] Klaus Liepelt, "Esquisse d'une typologie des électeurs allemands et autrichiens," *Revue française de sociologie*, Vol. 9 (January-March 1968), 28-29.

[53] "La Chronique religieuse du *Peuple*: II," *La Relève*, Vol. 21 (10 July 1965).

[54] Lijphart, *The Politics*, pp. 189-91.

[55] Kurt B. Mayer, "The Jura Problem: Ethnic Conflict in Switzerland," *Social Research*, Vol. 35 (Winter 1968), 736-38, analyzes the voting in the 1959 popular initiative which provided a crucial test of autonomist sentiment.

conceive of such a philosophical pluralism without a certain institutional base. If the present base does not seem capable of constituting a lasting level of stabilization, it will be necessary to find other institutional forms of pluralism."[56] These other forms will be related to the segmented pluralism which their leaders and members seek to transcend or transform.

People can usually learn more from the failures of political systems than from their successes; the export of political prescription has always been less effective than the import of political warning. There are, however, both successes and failures in the experiences of the segmented pluralist nations which have interest for anyone concerned with the relationships between ideologies and organizations, between old loyalties and modern associational needs, and between cross-cutting and reinforcing cleavages, in the processes of national integration.

As Sir Arthur Lewis has recently recalled, the Anglo-American experience (real or fancied) does not afford appropriate models to the leaders of plural societies of the Third World.[57] For such societies, the "segmented integration"[58] of some European democracies is of interest – an interest quickened by their being, like most African states, small in population and international power. In developed (sometimes quaintly called "fully developed") societies, too, we may ponder the observation of a Swiss political scientist that "national unity must always be reconstituted."[59] Recalling that some segmentation has characterized all democratic polities, it is encouraging to know that scholars are contemplating and doing a great deal more than this modest intermediate report has attempted in the comparative study of structures and processes of group solidarity and hostility and their relations to "national unity," the protection of diversity, and the management of political conflict in the countries I have discussed and in other countries.[60]

[56] Jean Ladrière, in J. Meynaud et al., eds. La Décision politique, p. 32.
[57] W. Arthur Lewis, Politics in West Africa (London, 1965), ch. 3.
[58] The phrase is that of Goudsblom, Dutch Society, p. 124.
[59] Erich Gruner, "Le Fonctionnement du Système Représentatif dans la Confédération Suisse" (Paper read at Seventh World Congress of Political Science, Brussels, 1967).
[60] For discussion of some types of needed studies, see, inter alia, Sidney Verba, "Some Dilemmas in Comparative Research," World Politics, Vol. 20 (October 1967); Peter H. Merkl, "Political Cleavage and Party Systems," World Politics, Vol. 21 (April 1969), 476; Rokkan, Citizens, pp. 42-43, 69-70, and 138-40; Liepelt,

For a historic moment, the systems of segmented pluralism have embodied a remarkable equilibrium in a number of small democracies. The number is not large, but then the number of democracies is not very large. The equilibrium will not have lasted long, but then – despite what historians may say – history abhors an equilibrium.

"Esquisse," 32; and the articles by Joseph LaPalombara, Harold D. Lasswell, Guenter Lewy, Roy C. Macridis and Dankwart A. Rustow, in *Comparative Politics*, Vol. 1 (October 1968). For a systematic approach to some problems of definition, measurement, and formulation of theory: Douglas W. Rae and Michael Taylor, *The Analysis of Political Cleavages* (New Haven, 1970).

CONSOCIATIONAL DEMOCRACY*

Arend Lijphart

Source: Arend Lijphart, "Consociational Democracy," *World Politics*, Vol. 21, No. 2 (copyright © 1969 by Princeton University Press); pp. 207-225. Reprinted by permission of Princeton University Press and the author.

TYPES OF WESTERN DEMOCRATIC SYSTEMS

In Gabriel A. Almond's famous typology of political systems, first expounded in 1956, he distinguishes three types of Western democratic systems: Anglo-American political systems (exemplified by Britain and the United States), Continental European political systems (France, Germany, and Italy), and a third category consisting of the Scandinavian and Low Countries. The third type is not given a distinct label and is not described in detail; Almond merely states that the countries belonging to this type "combine some of the features of the Continental European and the Anglo-American" political systems, and "stand somewhere in between the Continental pattern and the Anglo-American."[1] Almond's threefold typology has been highly influential in the comparative analysis of democratic politics, although, like any provocative and insightful idea, it has also been criticized. This research note will discuss the concept of "consociational democracy" in a constructive attempt to refine and elaborate Almond's typology of democracies.

The typology derives its theoretical significance from the relationship it establishes between political culture and social structure on the one hand and political stability on the other hand. The Anglo-American systems have a "homogeneous, secular political culture" and a "highly differentiated" role structure, in which governmental agencies, parties, interest groups, and the communication media have specialized functions and are autonomous, although interdependent. In contrast, the Continental European democracies are characterized by a "fragmentation of

* This note represents an intermediate stage of a research project concerning political stability in democratic systems. An earlier and briefer discussion of the concept of consociational democracy, in the context of a critical analysis of the utility of typologies in comparative politics, appeared in the author's "Typologies of Democratic Systems," *Comparative Political Studies*, I (April 1968), 3-44. The author is indebted to the Institute of International Studies, Berkeley, for financial support.

[1] Gabriel A. Almond, "Comparative Political Systems," *Journal of Politics*, Vol. 18 (August 1956), 392-93, 405.

political culture" with separate "political sub-cultures." Their roles "are embedded in the sub-cultures and tend to constitute separate sub-systems of roles."[2] The terms "Anglo-American" and "Continental European" are used for convenience only and do not imply that geographical location is an additional criterion distinguishing the two types of democratic systems. This point deserves special emphasis, because some of Almond's critics have misinterpreted it. For instance, Arthur L. Kalleberg states that the two types "are based on criteria of geographic location and area," and that "Almond does not come out and specify that these *are* his criteria of classification; we have to infer them from the titles and descriptions he gives of each of his groups of states."[3] Actually, Almond does indicate clearly what his criteria are, and he also specifically rejects the criterion of geography or region as irrelevant, because it is not based "on the properties of the political systems."[4]

Political culture and social structure are empirically related to political stability. The Anglo-American democracies display a high degree of stability and effectiveness. The Continental European systems, on the other hand, tend to be unstable; they are characterized by political immobilism, which is "a consequence of the [fragmented] condition of the political culture." Furthermore, there is the "ever-present threat of what is often called the 'Caesaristic' breakthrough" and even the danger of a lapse into totalitarianism as a result of this immobilism.[5]

The theoretical basis of Almond's typology is the "overlapping memberships" proposition formulated by the group theorists Arthur F. Bentley and David B. Truman and the very similar "crosscutting cleavages" proposition of Seymour Martin Lipset. These propositions state that the psychological cross-pressures resulting from membership in different groups with diverse inter-

---

[2] *Ibid.*, 398-99, 405-07 (italics omitted).

[3] Kalleberg, "The Logic of Comparison: A Methodological Note on the Comparative Study of Political Systems," *World Politics*, Vol. 19 (October 1966), 73-74. Hans Daalder's critical question "Why should France, Germany, and Italy be more 'continental,' than Holland, or Switzerland, or more 'European' than Britain?" seems to be based on a similar erroneous interpretation: see his "Parties, Elites, and Political Developments in Western Europe," in Joseph LaPalombara and Myron Weiner, eds., *Political Parties and Political Development* (Princeton, 1966), 43n.

[4] Almond, 392. There is also no reason, therefore, to call the exclusion of Scandinavia and the Low Countries from the "Continental European" systems an "artificial qualifier," as Kalleberg does, 74.

[5] Almond, 408.

ests and outlooks lead to moderate attitudes. These groups may be formally organized groups or merely unorganized, categoric, and, in Truman's terminology, "potential" groups. Cross-pressures operate not only at the mass but also at the elite level: the leaders of social groups with heterogeneous and overlapping memberships will tend to find it necessary to adopt moderate positions. When, on the other hand, a society is divided by sharp cleavages with no or very few overlapping memberships and loyalties – in other words, when the political culture is deeply fragmented – the pressures toward moderate middle-of-the-road attitudes are absent. Political stability depends on moderation and, therefore, also on overlapping memberships. Truman states this proposition as follows: "In the long run a complex society may experience revolution, degeneration, and decay. If it maintains its stability, however, it may do so in large measure because of the fact of multiple memberships."[6] Bentley calls compromise "the very process itself of the criss-cross groups in action."[7] And Lipset argues that "the chances for stable democracy are enhanced to the extent that groups and individuals have a number of crosscutting, politically relevant affiliations."[8] Sometimes Almond himself explicitly adopts the terminology of these propositions: for instance, he describes the French Fourth Republic as being divided into "three main ideological families or subcultures," which means that the people of France were "exposed to few of the kinds of 'cross-pressures' that moderate [their] rigid political attitudes," while, on the other hand, he characterizes the United States and Britain as having an "overlapping pattern" of membership.[9]

In his later writings, Almond maintains both the threefold typology of Western democracies and the criteria on which it is based, although the terms that he uses vary considerably. In an article published in 1963, for instance, he distinguishes between "stable democracies" and "immobilist democracies." The latter are characterized by "fragmentation, both in a cultural and structural sense" and by the absence of "consensus on governmental

[6] David B. Truman, *The Governmental Process: Political Interests and Public Opinion* (New York, 1951), 508, 511.

[7] Arthur F. Bentley, *The Process of Government: A Study of Social Pressures*, 4th ed. (Evanston, 1955), 208.

[8] Seymour Martin Lipset, *Political Man: The Social Bases of Politics* (Garden City, 1960), 88-89.

[9] Almond and G. Bingham Powell, Jr., *Comparative Politics: A Developmental Approach* (Boston, 1966), 122, 263; Almond and Sidney Verba, *The Civic Culture: Political Attitudes and Democracy in Five Nations* (Princeton, 1963), 134.

structure and process" (i.e. the Continental European systems). The former group is divided into two sub-classes: one includes Great Britain, the United States, and the Old Commonwealth democracies (i.e. the Anglo-American systems), and the other "the stable multi-party democracies of the European continent – the Scandinavian and Low Countries and Switzerland."[10] And in *Comparative Politics: A Developmental Approach*, published in 1966, a distinction is drawn between modern democratic systems with "high subsystem autonomy" (the Anglo-American democracies) and those with "limited subsystem autonomy" and fragmentation of political culture (the Continental European democracies). The third type is not included in this classification.[11]

In what respects are Switzerland, Scandinavia, and the Low Countries "in between" the Anglo-American and Continental European democracies? Here, too, Almond consistently uses the two criteria of role structure and political culture. A differentiated role structure (or a high degree of subsystem autonomy) is related to the performance of the political aggregation function in a society. The best aggregators are parties in two-party systems like the Anglo-American democracies, but the larger the number and the smaller the size of the parties in a system, the less effectively the aggregation function will be performed; in the Continental European multi-party systems only a minimum of aggregation takes place. The "working multi-party systems" of the Scandinavian and Low Countries differ from the French-Italian "crisis" systems in that some, though not all, of their parties are "broadly aggregative." Almond gives the Scandinavian Socialist parties and the Belgian Catholic and Socialist parties as examples.[12] This criterion does not distinguish adequately between the two types of democracies, however: if one calls the Belgian Catholic party broadly aggregative, the Italian Christian Democrats surely also have to be regarded as such. On the other hand, none of the Dutch and Swiss parties can be called broadly aggregative.

[10] "Political Systems and Political Change," *American Behavioral Scientist*, Vol. 6 (June 1963), 9-10.

[11] Almond and Powell, 259 (italics omitted).

[12] Almond, rapporteur, "A Comparative Study of Interest Groups and the Political Process," *American Political Science Review*, 52 (March 1958), 275-77; Almond, "A Functional Approach to Comparative Politics," in Almond and James S. Coleman, eds., *The Politics of the Developing Areas* (Princeton, 1960), 42-43. See also Göran G. Lindahl, "Gabriel A. Almond's funktionella kategorier: En kritik," *Statsvetenskaplig Tidskrift*, No. 4 (1967), 263-72; and Constance E. van der Maesen and G. H. Scholten, "De functionele benadering van G. A. Almond bij het vergelijken van politieke stelsels," *Acta Politica*, 1 (1965-66), 220-26.

Instead of using the extent of aggregation performed by political parties as the operational indicator of the degree of subsystem autonomy, it is more satisfactory to examine the system's role structure directly. Like the Anglo-American countries, the Scandinavian states have a high degree of subsystem autonomy. But one finds a severely limited subsystem autonomy and considerable interpenetration of parties, interest groups, and the media of communication in the Low Countries, Switzerland, and also in Austria. In fact, subsystem autonomy is at least as limited in these countries as in the Continental European systems. According to the criterion of role structure, therefore, one arrives at a dichotomous rather than a threefold typology: the Scandinavian states must be grouped with the Anglo-American systems, and the other "in-between" states with the Continental European systems.

The application of the second criterion – political culture – leads to a similar result. Almond writes that the political culture in the Scandinavian and Low Countries is "more homogeneous and fusional of secular and traditional elements" than that in the Continental European systems.[13] This is clearly true for the Scandinavian countries, which are, in fact, quite homogeneous and do not differ significantly from the homogeneous Anglo-American systems. But again, the other "in-between" countries are at least as fragmented into political subcultures – the *familles spirituelles* of Belgium and Luxembourg, the *zuilen* of the Netherlands, and the *Lager* of Austria – as the Continental European states. Therefore, on the basis of the two criteria of political culture and role structure, the Western democracies can be satisfactorily classified into two broad but clearly bounded categories: (1) the Anglo-American, Old Commonwealth, and Scandinavian states; (2) the other European democracies, including France, Italy, Weimar Germany, the Low Countries, Austria, and Switzerland.

FRAGMENTED BUT STABLE DEMOCRACIES

The second category of the above twofold typology is too broad, however, because it includes both highly stable systems (e.g., Switzerland and Holland) and highly unstable ones (e.g., Weimar Germany and the French Third and Fourth Republics). The political stability of a system can apparently not be predicted solely on the basis of the two variables of political culture and role structure. According to the theory of crosscutting cleavages, one would expect the Low Countries, Switzerland, and Austria, with subcultures divided from each other by mutually reinforcing cleavages, to exhibit great immobilism and instability. But they

[13] "A Functional Approach," 42.

do not. These deviant cases of fragmented but stable democracies will be called "consociational democracies."[14] In general, deviant case analysis can lead to the discovery of additional relevant variables, and in this particular instance, a third variable can account for the stability of the consociational democracies: the behavior of the political elites. The leaders of the rival subcultures may engage in competitive behavior and thus further aggravate mutual tensions and political instability, but they may also make *deliberate efforts to counteract the immobilizing and unstabilizing effects of cultural fragmentation*. As a result of such overarching cooperation at the elite level, a country can, as Claude Ake states, "achieve a degree of political stability quite out of proportion to its social homogeneity."[15]

The clearest examples are the experiences of democratic Austria after the First World War and of pre-democratic Belgium in the early nineteenth century. The fragmented and unstable Austrian First Republic of the interwar years was transformed into the still fragmented but stable Second Republic after the Second World War by means of a consociational solution. As Frederick C. Engelmann states, "the central socio-political fact in the life of post-1918 Austria [was that] the Republic had developed under conditions of cleavage so deep as to leave it with a high potential for – and a sporadic actuality of – civil war." The instability caused by the deep cleavage and antagonism between the Catholic and Socialist *Lager* (subcultures) spelled the end of democracy and the establishment of a dictatorship. The leaders of the rival subcultures were anxious not to repeat the sorry experience of the First Republic, and decided to join in a grand coalition after the Second World War. According to Engelmann, "critics and objective observers agree with Austria's leading politicians in the assessment that the coalition was a response to the civil-war tension of the First Republic."[16] Otto Kirchheimer also attributes the consociational pattern of Austria's post-1945 poli-

[14] Cf. Johannes Althusius' concept of *consociatio* in his *Politica Methodice Digesta*, and the term "consociational" used by David E. Apter, *The Political Kingdom in Uganda: A Study in Bureaucratic Nationalism* (Princeton, 1961), 24-25.

[15] Claude Ake, *A Theory of Political Integration* (Homewood, 1967), 113. This possibility exists not only in the fragmented democracies, but also in fragmented predemocratic or nondemocratic systems, of course. See also Arend Lijphart, *The Politics of Accommodation: Pluralism and Democracy in the Netherlands* (Berkeley, 1968), 1-15, 197-211.

[16] Frederick C. Engelmann, "Haggling for the Equilibrium: The Renegotiation of the Austrian Coalition, 1959," *American Political Science Review*, Vol. 56 (September 1962), 651-52.

tics (until early 1966) to "the republic's historical record of political frustration and abiding suspicion."[17] Val R. Lorwin describes how the potential instability caused by subcultural cleavage was deliberately avoided at the time of the birth of independent Belgium: the Catholic and Liberal leaders had learned "the great lesson of mutual tolerance from the catastrophic experience of the Brabant Revolution of 1789, when the civil strife of their predecessors had so soon laid the country open to easy Habsburg reconquest. It was a remarkable and *self-conscious 'union of the oppositions'* that made the revolution of 1830, wrote the Constitution of 1831, and headed the government in its critical years."[18]

The grand coalition cabinet is the most typical and obvious, but not the only possible, consociational solution for a fragmented system. The essential characteristic of consociational democracy is not so much any particular institutional arrangement as the deliberate joint effort by the elites to stabilize the system. Instead of the term "grand coalition" with its rather narrow connotation, one could speak of universal participation, or as Ralf Dahrendorf does, of a "cartel of elites."[19] A grand coalition cabinet as in Austria represents the most comprehensive form of the cartel of elites, but one finds a variety of other devices in the other Western consociational democracies and, outside Western Europe, in the consociational politics of Lebanon, Uruguay (until early 1967), and Colombia. Even in Austria, not the cabinet itself but the small extra-constitutional "coalition committee," on which the top Socialist and Catholic leaders were equally represented, made the crucial decisions. In the Swiss system of government, which is a hybrid of the presidential and the parliamentary patterns, all four major parties are represented on the multi-member executive. In Uruguay's (now defunct) governmental system, fashioned after the Swiss model, there was *coparticipación* of the two parties on the executive.

In the Colombian and Lebanese presidential systems, such a sharing of the top executive post is not possible because the presidency is held by one person. The alternative solution pro-

[17] Kirchheimer, "The Waning of Opposition in Parliamentary Regimes," *Social Research*, Vol. 24 (Summer 1957), 137.

[18] Lorwin, "Constitutionalism and Controlled Violence in the Modern State: The Case of Belgium" (paper presented at the annual meeting of the American Historical Association, San Francisco, 1965), 4 (italics added). For a description of the establishment of consociational democracy in the Netherlands, see Lijphart, *The Politics of Accommodation*, 103-12.

[19] Dahrendorf, *Society and Democracy in Germany* (Garden City, 1967), 276.

vided by the Lebanese National Pact of 1943 is that the President of the Republic must be a Maronite and the President of the Council a Sunni, thus guaranteeing representation to the country's two major religious groups. In Colombia, the Liberal and Conservative parties agreed in 1958 to join in a consociational arrangement in order to deliver the country from its recurrent civil wars and dictatorships. The agreement stipulated that the presidency would be alternated for four-year terms between the two parties and that there would be equal representation (*paridad*) on all lower levels of government. In the Low Countries, the cabinets are usually broadly based coalitions, but not all major subcultures are permanently represented. The typical consociational devices in these democracies are the advisory councils and committees, which, in spite of their very limited formal powers, often have decisive influence. These councils and committees may be permanent organs, such as the powerful Social and Economic Council of the Netherlands – a perfect example of a cartel of economic elites – or *ad hoc* bodies, such as the cartels of top party leaders that negotiated the "school pacts" in Holland in 1917 and in Belgium in 1958.

The desire to avoid political competition may be so strong that the cartel of elites may decide to extend the consociational principle to the electoral level in order to prevent the passions aroused by elections from upsetting the carefully constructed, and possibly fragile, system of cooperation. This may apply to a single election or to a number of successive elections. The *paridad* and *alternación* principles in Colombia entail a controlled democracy for a period of sixteen years, during which the efficacy of the right to vote is severely restricted. Another example is the Dutch parliamentary election of 1917, in which all of the parties agreed not to contest the seats held by incumbents in order to safeguard the passage of a set of crucial constitutional amendments; these amendments, negotiated by cartels of top party leaders, contained the terms of the settlement of the sensitive issues of universal suffrage and state aid to church schools. A parallel agreement on the suffrage was adopted in Belgium in 1919 without holding the constitutionally prescribed election at all.

Consociational democracy violates the principle of majority rule, but it does not deviate very much from normative democratic theory. Most democratic constitutions prescribe majority rule for the normal transaction of business when the stakes are not too high, but extraordinary majorities or several successive majorities for the most important decisions, such as changes in the constitution. In fragmented systems, many other decisions in addition to constituent ones are perceived as involving high stakes, and therefore require more than simple majority rule. Similarly, majority rule does not suffice in times of grave crisis in even the most homogeneous and consensual of democracies. Great Britain and Sweden, both highly homogeneous countries, resorted to grand coalition cabinets during the Second World War. Julius Nyerere draws the correct lesson from the experience of the Western democracies, in which, he observes, "it is an accepted practice in times of emergency for opposition parties to sink their differences and join together in forming a national government."[20] And just as the formation of a national unity government is the appropriate response to an external emergency, so the formation of a grand coalition cabinet or an alternative form of elite cartel is the appropriate response to the internal crisis of fragmentation into hostile subcultures.

Furthermore, the concept of consociational democracy is also in agreement with the empirical "size principle," formulated by William H. Riker. This principle, based on game-theoretic assumptions, states: "In social situations similar to n-person, zero-sum games with side-payments [private agreements about the division of the payoff], participants create coalitions just as large as they believe will ensure winning and no larger." The tendency will be toward a "minimum winning coalition," which in a democracy will be a coalition with bare majority support – but only under the conditions specified in the size principle. The most important condition is the zero-sum assumption: "only the direct conflicts among participants are included and common advantages are ignored."[21] Common advantages will be completely ignored only in two diametrically opposite kinds of situations: (1) when the participants in the "game" do not perceive any common advantages, and when, consequently, they are likely to engage in unlimited warfare; and (2) when they are in such firm agreement on their common advantages that they can take them for granted. In the latter case, politics literally becomes a game. In other words, the zero-sum condition and the size principle apply only to societies with completely homogeneous political cultures and to societies with completely fragmented cultures. To the extent that political cultures deviate from these two extreme conditions, pressures will exist to fashion coalitions and other forms of cooperation that are more inclusive than the bare "minimum winning coalition" and that may be all-inclusive grand coalitions.

[20] Nyerere, "One-Party Rule," in Paul E. Sigmund, Jr., ed., *The Ideologies of the Developing Nations* (New York, 1963), 199.
[21] William H. Riker, *The Theory of Political Coalitions* (New Haven, 1962), 29, 32-33.

Almond aptly uses the metaphor of the game in characterizing the Anglo-American systems: "Because the political culture tends to be homogeneous and pragmatic, [the political process] takes on some of the atmosphere of a game. A game is a good game when the outcome is in doubt and when the stakes are not too high. When the stakes are too high, the tone changes from excitement to anxiety."[22] Political contests in severely fragmented societies are indeed not likely to be "good games." But the anxieties and hostilities attending the political process may be countered by removing its competitive features as much as possible. In consociational democracies, politics is treated not as a game but as a serious business.

FACTORS CONDUCIVE TO CONSOCIATIONAL DEMOCRACY

Consociational democracy means government by elite cartel designed to turn a democracy with a fragmented political culture into a stable democracy. Efforts at consociationalism are not necessarily successful, of course: consociational designs failed in Cyprus and Nigeria, and Uruguay abandoned its Swiss-style consociational system. Successful consociational democracy requires: (1) That the elites have the ability to accommodate the divergent interests and demands of the subcultures. (2) This requires that they have the ability to transcend cleavages and to join in a common effort with the elites of rival subcultures. (3) This in turn depends on their commitment to the maintenance of the system and to the improvement of its cohesion and stability. (4) Finally, all of the above requirements are based on the assumption that the elites understand the perils of political fragmentation. These four requirements are logically implied by the concept of consociational democracy as defined in this paper. Under what conditions are they likely to be fulfilled? An examination of the successful consociational democracies in the Low Countries, Switzerland, Austria, and Lebanon suggests a number of conditions favorable to the establishment and the persistence of this type of democracy. These have to do with inter-subcultural relations at the elite level, inter-subcultural relations at the mass level, and elite-mass relations within each of the subcultures.

RELATIONS AMONG THE ELITES OF THE SUBCULTURES

It is easier to assess the probability of continued success of an already established consociational democracy than to predict the chance of success that a fragmented system would have if it were to attempt consociationalism. In an existing consociational

[22] Almond, "Comparative Political Systems," 398-99.

democracy, an investigation of the institutional arrangements and the operational code of inter-elite accommodation can throw light on the question of how thorough a commitment to cooperation they represent and how effective they have been in solving the problems caused by fragmentation. *The length of time a consociational democracy has been in operation* is also a factor of importance. As inter-elite cooperation becomes habitual and does not represent a deliberate departure from competitive responses to political challenges, consociational norms become more firmly established. And, as Gerhard Lehmbruch states, these norms may become an important part of "the political socialization of elites and thus acquire a strong degree of persistence through time."[23]

There are three factors that appear to be strongly conducive to the establishment or maintenance of cooperation among elites in a fragmented system. The most striking of these is the existence of *external threats* to the country. In all of the consociational democracies, the cartel of elites was either initiated or greatly strengthened during periods of international crisis, especially the First and Second World Wars. During the First World War, the comprehensive settlement of the conflict among Holland's political subcultures firmly established the pattern of consociational democracy. "Unionism" – i.e., Catholic-Liberal grand coalitions – began during Belgium's struggle for independence in the early nineteenth century, but lapsed when the country appeared to be out of danger. As a result of the First World War, unionism was resumed and the Socialist leaders were soon admitted to the governing cartel. The Second World War marked the beginning of consociational democracy in Lebanon: the National Pact – the Islamo-Christian accord that provided the basis for consociational government for the country – was concluded in 1943. In Switzerland, consociational democracy developed more gradually, but reached its culmination with the admission of the Socialists to the grand coalition of the Federal Council, also in 1943. The Austrian grand coalition was formed soon after the Second World War, when the country was occupied by the allied forces. In all cases, the external threats impressed on the elites the need for internal unity and cooperation. External threats can also strengthen the ties among the subcultures at the mass level and the ties between leaders and followers within the subcultures.

---

[23] Lehmbruch, "A Non-Competitive Pattern of Conflict Management in Liberal Democracies: The Case of Switzerland, Austria and Lebanon" (paper presented at the Seventh World Congress of the International Political Science Association, Brussels, 1967), 6. See also Lehmbruch, *Proporzdemokratie: Politisches System und politische Kultur in der Schweiz und in Österreich* (Tübingen, 1967).

A second factor favorable to consociational democracy, in the sense that it helps the elites to recognize the necessity of cooperation, is a *multiple balance of power among the subcultures* instead of either a dual balance of power or a clear hegemony by one subculture. When one group is in the majority, its leaders may attempt to dominate rather than cooperate with the rival minority. Similarly, in a society with two evenly matched subcultures, the leaders of both may hope to achieve their aims by domination rather than cooperation, if they expect to win a majority at the polls. Robert Dahl argues that for this reason it is doubtful that the consociational arrangement in Colombia will last, because "the temptation to shift from coalition to competition is bound to be very great."[24] When political parties in a fragmented society are the organized manifestations of political subcultures, a multiparty system is more conducive to consociational democracy and therefore to stability than a two-party system. This proposition is at odds with the generally high esteem accorded to two-party systems. In an already homogeneous system, two-party systems may be more effective, but a moderate multiparty system, in which no party is close to a majority, appears preferable in a consociational democracy. The Netherlands, Switzerland, and Lebanon have the advantage that their subcultures are all minority groups. In the Austrian two-party system, consociational politics did work, but with considerable strain. Lehmbruch states: "Austrian political parties are strongly integrated social communities ... and the bipolar structure of the coalition reinforced their antagonisms."[25] The internal balance of power in Belgium has complicated the country's consociational politics in two ways. The Catholic, Socialist, and Liberal subcultures are minorities, but the Catholics are close to majority status. The Catholic party actually won a legislative majority in 1950, and attempted to settle the sensitive royal question by majority rule. This led to a short civil war, followed by a return to consociational government. Moreover, the Belgian situation is complicated as a result of the linguistic cleavage, which cuts across the three spiritual families. The linguistic balance of power is a dual balance in which the Walloons fear the numerical majority of the Flemings, while the Flemings resent the economic and social superiority of the Walloons.

Consociational democracy presupposes not only a willingness on the part of elites to cooperate but also a capability to solve the

---

[24] Dahl, *Political Oppositions in Western Democracies* (New Haven, 1966), 337.

[25] Lehmbruch, 8.

political problems of their countries. Fragmented societies have a tendency to immobilism, which consociational politics is designed to avoid. Nevertheless, decision-making that entails accommodation among all subcultures is a difficult process, and consociational democracies are always threatened by a degree of immobilism. Consequently, a third favorable factor to inter-elite cooperation is a *relatively low total load on the decision-making apparatus.* The stability of Lebanon is partly due to its productive economy and the social equilibrium it has maintained so far, but it may not be able to continue its successful consociational politics when the burdens on the system increase. Michael C. Hudson argues that the Lebanese political system is "attuned to incessant adjustment among primordial groups rather than policy planning and execution." As a result, its "apparent stability . . . is deceptively precarious: social mobilization appears to be overloading the circuits of the Lebanese political system."[26] In general, the size factor is important in this respect: the political burdens that large states have to shoulder tend to be disproportionately heavier than those of small countries. Ernest S. Griffith argues that "democracy is more likely to survive, other things being equal, in small states. Such states are more manageable. . . . "[27] In particular, small states are more likely to escape the onerous burdens entailed by an active foreign policy. Lehmbruch states that the Swiss, Austrian, and Lebanese cases "show that the preservation of the inner equilibrium presupposes a reduction of external demands to the political system." And he even goes so far as to conclude that the type of politics found in these three countries "seems to work in small states only."[28]

INTER-SUBCULTURAL RELATIONS AT THE MASS LEVEL

The political cultures of the countries belonging to Almond's Continental European type and to the consociational type are all fragmented, but the consociational countries have even clearer boundaries among their subcultures. Such *distinct lines of cleavage* appear to be conducive to consociational democracy and political stability. The explanation is that subcultures with widely divergent outlooks and interests may coexist without necessarily being in conflict; conflict arises only when they are in contact with each other. As Quincy Wright states: "Ideologies accepted

[26] Hudson, "A Case of Political Underdevelopment," *Journal of Politics,* Vol. 29 (November 1967), 836.

[27] Griffith, "Cultural Prerequisites to a Successfully Functioning Democracy," *American Political Science Review,* Vol. 50 (March 1956), 102.

[28] Lehmbruch, 9.

by different groups within a society may be inconsistent without creating tension; but if . . . the groups with inconsistent ideologies are in close contact . . . the tension will be great."[29] David Easton also endorses the thesis that good social fences may make good political neighbors, when he suggests a kind of voluntary *apartheid* policy as the best solution for a divided society: "Greater success may be attained through steps that conduce to the development of a deeper sense of mutual awareness and responsiveness among *encapsulated cultural units.*" This is "the major hope of avoiding stress."[30] And Sidney Verba follows the same line of reasoning when he argues that political and economic modernization in Africa is bringing "differing subcultures into contact with each other and *hence* into conflict."[31]

This argument appears to be a direct refutation of the overlapping-memberships proposition, but by adding two amendments to this proposition the discrepancy can be resolved. In the first place, the basic explanatory element in the concept of consociational democracy is that political elites may take joint actions to counter the effects of cultural fragmentation. This means that the overlapping-memberships propositions may become a self-denying hypothesis under certain conditions. Secondly, the view that any severe discontinuity in overlapping patterns of membership and allegiance is a danger to political stability needs to be restated in more refined form. A distinction has to be made between essentially homogeneous political cultures, where increased contacts are likely to lead to an increase in mutual understanding and further homogenization, and essentially heterogeneous cultures, where close contacts are likely to lead to strain and hostility. This is the distinction that Walker Connor makes when he argues that "increased contacts help to dissolve regional cultural distinctions within a state such as the United States. Yet, if one is dealing not with minor variations of the same culture, but with two quite distinct and self-differentiating cultures, are not increased contacts between the two apt to increase antagonisms?"[32] This proposition can be refined further by stating both the degree of homogeneity

---

[29] Wright, "The Nature of Conflict," *Western Political Quarterly*, Vol. 4 (June 1951), 196.

[30] Easton, *A Systems Analysis of Political Life* (New York, 1965), 250-51 (italics added). See also G. H. Scholten, "Het vergelijken van federaties met behulp van systeem-analyse," *Acta Politica*, Vol. 2 (1966-67), 51-68.

[31] Verba, "Some Dilemmas in Comparative Research," *World Politics*, Vol. 20 (October 1967), 126 (italics added).

[32] Connor, "Self-Determination: The New Phase," *World Politics*, Vol. 20 (October 1967), 49-50.

and the extent of mutual contacts in terms of continua rather than dichotomies. In order to safeguard political stability, the volume and intensity of contacts must not exceed the commensurate degree of homogeneity. Karl W. Deutsch states that stability depends on a "balance between transaction and integration" because "the number of opportunities for possible violent conflict will increase with the volume and range of mutual transactions."[33] Hence, it may be desirable to keep transactions among antagonistic subcultures in a divided society – or, similarly, among different nationalities in a multinational state – to a minimum.

ELITE-MASS RELATIONS WITHIN THE SUBCULTURES

Distinct lines of cleavage among the subcultures are also conducive to consociational democracy because they are likely to be concomitant with a high degree of *internal political cohesion of the subcultures*. This is vital to the success of consociational democracy. The elites have to cooperate and compromise with each other without losing the allegiance and support of their own rank and file. When the subcultures are cohesive political blocs, such support is more likely to be forthcoming. As Hans Daalder states, what is important is not only "the extent to which party leaders are more tolerant than their followers" but also the extent to which they "are yet able to carry them along."[34]

A second way in which distinct cleavages have a favorable effect on elite-mass relations in a consociational democracy is that they make it more likely that the parties and interest groups will be the organized representatives of the political subcultures. If this is the case, the political parties may not be the best aggregators, but there is at least an *adequate articulation of the interests of the subcultures*. Aggregation of the clearly articulated interests can then be performed by the cartel of elites. In Belgium, the three principal parties represent the Catholic, Socialist, and Liberal spiritual families, but the linguistic cleavage does not coincide with the cleavages dividing the spiritual families, and all three parties have both Flemings and Walloons among their followers. Lorwin describes the situation as follows: "The sentimental and practical interests of the two linguistic communities are not effectively organized, and the geographical regions have no administrative or formal political existence. There are no recognized representatives qualified to formulate demands, to negotiate, and to fulfill commitments."[35] The religious and class issues have been

[33] Deutsch, *Political Community at the International Level* (Garden City, 1954), 39.

[34] Daalder, 69.

[35] Lorwin, "Belgium: Religion, Class, and Language in National Poli-

effectively articulated by the political parties and have by and large been resolved, but the linguistic issue has not been clearly articulated and remains intractable. In Switzerland, the parties also represent the religious-ideological groups rather than the linguistic communities, but much of the country's decentralized political life takes place at the cantonal level, and most of the cantons are linguistically homogeneous.

A final factor which favors consociational democracy is *widespread approval of the principle of government by elite cartel.* This is a very obvious factor, but it is of considerable importance and deserves to be mentioned briefly. For example, Switzerland has a long and strong tradition of grand coalition executives, and this has immeasurably strengthened Swiss consociational democracy. On the other hand, the grand coalition in Austria was under constant attack by critics who alleged that the absence of a British-style opposition made Austrian politics "undemocratic." This attests to the strength of the British system as a normative model even in fragmented political systems, where the model is inappropriate and undermines the attempt to achieve political stability by consociational means.

CENTRIPETAL AND CENTRIFUGAL DEMOCRACIES

An examination of the other two types of the threefold typology of democracies in the light of the distinguishing characteristics of consociational democracy can contribute to the clarification and refinement of all three types and their prerequisites. In order to avoid any unintended geographical connotation, we shall refer to the homogeneous and stable democracies as the *centripetal* (instead of the Anglo-American democracies), and to the fragmented and unstable ones as the *centrifugal* (instead of the Continental European) democracies. The centrifugal democracies include the French Third and Fourth Republics, Italy, Weimar Germany, the Austrian First Republic, and the short-lived Spanish Republic of the early 1930's. The major examples of centripetal democracy are Great Britain, the Old Commonwealth countries, the United States, Ireland, the Scandinavian states, and the postwar Bonn Republic in Germany.

The French Fourth Republic is often regarded as the outstanding example of unstable, ineffective, and immobilist democracy, but the explanation of its political instability in terms of cultural fragmentation has been criticized on two grounds. In the first place, Eric A. Nordlinger rejects the argument that the "ideologi-

---

tics," in Dahl, ed., *Political Oppositions in Western Democracies*, 174.

cal inundation of French politics" and its "fragmented party system" were responsible for its chronic instability; he states that this explanation conveniently overlooks "the way in which the game of politics is actually played in France. Although ideologism pervades the parties' electoral and propaganda efforts, this public ideological posturing of French politicians does not prevent them from playing out their game of compromise in the Assembl., ...nd its *couloirs*. In fact, the political class thinks of compromise as a positive principle of action, with parliamentary activity largely revolving around nonideological squabbles. . . . "[36] The elites of the center parties that supported the Republic fulfilled to some extent all of the logical prerequisites for consociational democracy except the most important one: they lacked the ability to forge effective and lasting solutions to pressing political problems. They indeed played a nonideological game, but, as Nathan Leites observes, with a "well-developed capacity for avoiding their responsibility."[37] In other words, they were nonideological, but not constructively pragmatic. To turn a centrifugal into a consociational democracy, true statesmanship is required. Moreover, it is incorrect to assume that, because the elites were not divided by irreconcilable ideological differences, mass politics was not ideologically fragmented either.[38]

The second criticism of the cultural fragmentation thesis alleges, on the basis of independent evidence, that not only at the elite level but also at the mass level, ideology played a negligible role in France. Philip E. Converse and Georges Dupeux demonstrate that the French electorate was not highly politicized and felt little allegiance to the political parties.[39] But the lack of stable partisan attachments does not necessarily indicate that the political culture was not fragmented. Duncan MacRae argues persua-

---

[36] Nordlinger, "Democratic Stability and Instability: The French Case," *World Politics*, Vol. 18 (October 1965), 143.

[37] Leites, *On the Game of Politics in France* (Stanford, 1959), 2.

[38] Nor does the reverse assumption hold true. Giovanni Sartori relates the instability of Italian democracy to "poor leadership, both in the sense that the political elites lack the ability for problem-solving and that they do not provide a generalized leadership." This weakness of leadership, he continues, "is easily explained by the fragmentation of the party system and its ideological rigidity." ("European Political Parties: The Case of Polarized Pluralism," in LaPalombara and Weiner, eds., *Political Parties and Political Development*, 163.) The example of the consociational democracies shows that this is not a sufficient explanation.

[39] Converse and Dupeux, "Politicization of the Electorate in France and the United States," *Public Opinion Quarterly*, Vol. 26 (Spring 1962), 1-23.

sively that political divisions did extend to the electorate as a whole in spite of the apparent "lack of involvement of the average voter." Even though political allegiances were diffuse, there were "relatively fixed and non-overlapping *social* groupings" to which "separate leaders and separate media of communication had access."[40] The combination of fragmentation into subcultures and low politicization can in turn be explained by the negative French attitude toward authority. Stanley Hoffmann speaks of "potential insurrection against authority," and Michel Crozier observes that this attitude makes it "impossible for an individual of the group to become its leader."[41] Strong cohesion within the subcultures was mentioned earlier as a factor conducive to consociational democracy; the lack of it in France can explain both that the French people were fragmented but at the same time not politically involved, and that the political elites did not have the advantage of strong support from the rank and file for constructive cooperation.

On the other hand, the example of France also serves to make clear that the lack of problem-solving ability as a cause of political instability must not be overstated. After all, as Maurice Duverger points out, in spite of all of the Fourth Republic's flaws and weaknesses, it "would have continued to exist if it had not been for the Algerian war."[42] The critical factor was the too-heavy burden of an essentially external problem on the political system. Similarly, the fragmented Weimar Republic might have survived, too, if it had not been for the unusually difficult problems it was faced with.

Germany's experience with democracy also appears to throw some doubt on our threefold typology and the theory on which it is based. Weimar Germany was a centrifugal democracy but the Bonn Republic can be grouped with the centripetal democracies. In explaining this extraordinary shift, we have to keep in mind that cultural fragmentation must be measured on a continuum rather than as a dichotomy, as we have done so far. The degree of homogeneity of a political culture can change, although great changes at a rapid pace can normally not be expected. Three reasons can plausibly account for the change from the fragmented

---

[40] MacRae, *Parliament, Parties, and Society in France: 1946-1958* (New York, 1967), 333.

[41] Hoffmann and others, *In Search of France* (Cambridge, 1963), 8 (italics omitted); Crozier, *The Bureaucratic Phenomenon* (Chicago, 1964), 220.

[42] Duverger, "The Development of Democracy in France," in Henry W. Ehrmann, ed., *Democracy in a Changing Society* (New York, 1964), 77.

political culture of the unstable Weimar Republic to the much more homogeneous culture of the Bonn Republic: (1) the traumatic experiences of totalitarianism, war, defeat, and occupation; (2) "conscious manipulative change of fundamental political attitudes," which, as Verba states, added up to a "remaking of political culture";[43] (3) the loss of the eastern territories, which meant that, as Lipset argues, "the greater homogeneity of western Germany now became a national homogeneity."[44]

The degree of competitive or cooperative behavior by elites must also be seen as a continuum. Among the consociational democracies, some are more consociational than others; and many centripetal democracies have some consociational features. The phenomenon of wartime grand coalition cabinets has already been mentioned. The temporary Christian Democratic-Socialist grand coalition under Chancellor Kiesinger falls in the same category. In fact, the stability of the centripetal democracies depends not only on their essentially homogeneous political cultures but also on consociational devices, to the extent that a certain degree of heterogeneity exists. The alternation of English-speaking and French-speaking leaders of the Liberal party in Canada may be compared with the Colombian device of *alternación*. In the United States, where, as Dahl states, "the South has for nearly two centuries formed a distinctive regional subculture,"[45] cultural fragmentation led to secession and civil war. After the Civil War, a consociational arrangement developed that gave to the South a high degree of autonomy and to the Southern leaders – by such means as chairmanships of key Congressional committees and the filibuster – a crucial position in federal decision-making. This example also shows that, while consociational solutions may increase political cohesion, they also have a definite tendency to lead to a certain degree of immobilism.

Even in Denmark, which is among the most homogeneous of the centripetal democracies, one finds considerable consociationalism. This does not appear in grand coalition cabinets – in fact, Denmark is known for its long periods of government by minority cabinets – but in the far-reaching search for compromise in the legislature. The rule of the game prescribes that the top leaders of all four major parties do their utmost to reach a consensus. This

[43] Verba, "Germany: The Remaking of Political Culture," in Lucian W. Pye and Verba, eds., *Political Culture and Political Development* (Princeton, 1965), 133.
[44] Lipset, *The First New Nation: The United States in Historical and Comparative Perspective* (New York, 1963), 292.
[45] Dahl, 358.

is *glidningspolitik*, which Gerald R. McDaniel translates as the "politics of smoothness"[46] – an apt characterization of consociational politics.

---

[46] McDaniel, *The Danish Unicameral Parliament* (unpubl. Ph.D. diss., University of California, Berkeley, 1963), iv.

A NON-COMPETITIVE PATTERN OF CONFLICT MANAGEMENT IN LIBERAL DEMOCRACIES: THE CASE OF SWITZERLAND, AUSTRIA AND LEBANON[1]

Gerhard Lehmbruch

Source: Gerhard Lehmbruch, "A Non-competitive Pattern of Conflict Management in Liberal Democracies: the Case of Switzerland, Austria and Lebanon" (Paper presented at the Seventh World Congress of the International Political Science Association, Brussels, September 1967). Printed for the first time by permission of the author.

In current political typologies the existence of a fundamental and "normal" pattern of conflict settlement in liberal democracies is often taken for granted, namely, deciding controversial political issues by alternating parliamentary majorities which result from the competition of political parties in periodic elections (compare, for example, Schumpeter's still influential "theory of competitive leadership" in democracy). Such typologies often take the form of simple dichotomies, such as democracy versus dictatorship, or they are variants consisting of three members (e.g., totalitarian versus authoritarian versus democratic government). Recently, "developmental" typologies have gained increasing favour in the field of comparative politics. In these the competitive leadership model (often identified with Anglo-Saxon or, more precisely, the British two-party system) appears to be the final point of an ascending continuum of political development, whereas the multi-party coalition systems of continental Europe are viewed as an intermediate stage on this continuum and hence as a somehow imperfect type of liberal democracy. In this line of thinking we may include the well-known proposals for a transformation of those "imperfect" democracies into really competitive systems by constitutional or legal devices, for example by a change of the electoral system, or of the rules for selecting the head of government (as has been suggested in France by the advocates of a genuine presidential system).

The validity of such arguments has repeatedly been questioned. It has been argued recently that "it might be reasonable to consider multiparty systems as the natural way for government and oppositions to manage their conflicts in democracies, while the two-party systems ... are the deviant cases."[2] Though we

---

[1] This paper summarizes and develops further some hypotheses contained in the author's *Proporzdemokratie: politisches System und politische Kultur in der Schweiz und in Österreich* (Tübingen: J. C. B. Mohr, 1967).

[2] R. A. Dahl, *Political Oppositions in Western Democracies* (New Haven and London, 1966), 335.

doubt that it makes sense to consider any particular type of political system as a "natural" one, or inversely as a "deviant case," we think that the rather unique character of competitive two-party systems is well emphasized here. Comparative political science thus seems to be on the point of arriving at more appropriate schemes of classification which are free of hidden teleological implications.

This paper intends to contribute to such efforts by analyzing a type of political systems that has hitherto been rather neglected in comparative research: we speak of systems in which political groups like to settle their conflicts by negotiated agreements among all the relevant actors, the majority principle being applicable in fairly limited domains only. The most important cases are Switzerland (the Confederation as well as the cantons), Austria (the central government from 1945 to 1966, the *Laender* since 1918) and Lebanon. The most salient feature of these political systems is the distribution of public office among all important linguistic groups and regions (Switzerland), political parties (Austria, Switzerland), or, as in Lebanon (and in the Swiss Confederation until 1798), religious denominations. Another example is the Holy German Empire from 1648 to 1806, in which conflicts among the religious groups had to be settled by *amicabilis compositio*, and the majority principle was explicitly suspended for such matters; this principle was further guaranteed by the constitutional rule of "parity" of Protestants and Catholics in the distribution of offices.

It is tempting to explain this pattern on the basis of the peculiar social structure of the countries we are investigating. The political cleavages run along linguistic and/or denominational lines. The strong ideological tensions between the conservative and the socialist "camps" in Austria retain the imprint of quasi-religious antagonisms dating back to the Counter-reformation. The numerical relations of rival groups are therefore rather inflexible. This means that in a society thus divided along religious or ethnic boundaries a political strategy of maximization of votes – an essential feature of competitive political systems – cannot work. Hence if neither group has a clear numerical preponderance, negotiated agreement appears to be the only possible means by which civil peace can be preserved.

Such agreements are to be distinguished from those reached by bargaining in a "homogeneous" political culture. If actors agree on political ends and means their preferences tend to be generally compatible and transitive. Thus, if they differ on transitive preferences, they may agree on a compromise which constitutes an intermediate point on a common preference scale. This is usually done by incremental concessions of the bargaining actors, and often it is assumed that the intermediate solution is a "just," "natural" or "rational" one.

Instead, in a society divided by religious or strong ideological differences, or among linguistic groups, some (or the more important) preferences of the actors are incompatible and intransitive. Hence, there exists no common preference scale on which an intermediate solution may be found. In this case the following expedients may be used: either (1) the political system is divided into more or less autonomous spheres of influence in which the actors may be free to realize the preferences held by the respective groups; such spheres of influence may be on a regional basis (this is the Swiss solution of linguistic conflicts) or on a functional basis (this has resulted in Austria from the allocation of ministries among the political parties). Or (2) the actors may agree on large-scale barter similar to package deals as they occur not infrequently in international negotiations; this procedure means that one of the actors offers a concession he detests in exchange for a concession by his opponent that the latter detests equally strongly. This formula, known in Austria under the name of *Junktim*, amounts to a partial realization of the actors' incompatible and intransitive preferences in different domains; its significant mark is that often there exists no objective relation among the "junctimized" (*junktimiert*) matters, and that the solution can be labeled neither "intermediate" nor "just" nor "natural". Of course in all these countries there are issues which are characterized by compatibility and transitivity of preferences, for example in economic and social matters, but even these are often included in such exchange procedures.

That the social structure of the countries concerned is an essential condition of this pattern of conflict management, is quite obvious. But it offers no sufficient explanation. For it is equally obvious that there exist important countries with equally "fragmented" political cultures where conflicts are managed in a rather different fashion. The case of France, beginning with Jean Bodin's advocacy of authoritarian arbitration of religious conflicts by the sovereign power, may be an example in point.

From this we conclude that one must look for intervening variables which explain why a system of *amicabilis compositio* and *Proporz* correlates in some countries with a social structure in which the preferences of rival groups appear to be largely incompatible. One of these variables is the interaction of the conflicts within the political system and the conflicts in the surrounding international system, particularly if the same cleavages divide the one as well as the other. This is true of Lebanon and was true of Switzerland too, as long as religious or ethnic antagonisms played a major role in European politics. The groups within the state then have to be balanced in order to maintain the integrity of the political system against pressures from outside, while on the other hand internal equilibrium might be a condition of the equilibrium of the surrounding international system.

But the intervening variable most relevant to our topic seems to belong to the domain of "political culture": this is the fact that peculiar norms of conflict management develop under specific historical circumstances. Thus the most important historical roots of the Swiss system of proportional representation of all large groups in government seem to be (1) the principle of "parity" of Catholics and Protestants within the Confederation which, in analogy to the Holy German Empire, developed during the 16th to 18th centuries, and (2) the tradition of municipal government in which all patrician or otherwise privileged families used to be represented in the councils of towns and cantons. Later the same formulae were applied to the settlement of ethnic, and finally of inter-party, conflicts. The Lebanese system goes back to the Ottoman tradition of autonomy of the religious communities (millets) and to the cooperation of Christian and Druse millets in the Turkish province of Lebanon since the treaties of 1861 and 1864 which established Lebanese autonomy and provided for a multi-denominational council of notables to assist the governor.

As for Austria, political parties continue to manage their conflicts according to those rules of the parliamentary game which (as for example the *Junktim*) were used in the Habsburg Empire to establish the fragile modus vivendi of the different nations of the monarchy, and the political usages of the Republic still bear the impact of the politics of *Ausgleich*, that is, the settlement of ethnic antagonisms by institutional devices such as patronage, committees representing the different groups, demarcation of autonomous spheres of influence, and so on. Another factor of importance is the strong influence that corporate representation of interests exerts upon policy-making; this reinforces the strong inclination of Austrian political leaders and legislators to manage their conflicts by negotiated agreements (in the manner of union-employer bargains) rather than by political competition and the majority principle, which in the eyes of the minority often appears to be "undemocratic".

The common essence of these developments is this: under certain (and quite different) historical circumstances "fragmented" political cultures generate methods of conflict management which permit the survival and continued existence of the political system and the retention at the same time of a considerable measure of group autonomy. These methods consist in transactions which differ markedly from bargains in a "homogeneous" political culture and have much in common with agreements as they take place among nations. Then they become norms which are retransmitted by the learning processes in the political socialization of elites and thus acquire a strong degree of persistence through time. The case of Switzerland demonstrates that this pattern of conflict management may become so firmly established that it will remain essentially the same even if the issues change. Recent developments in that country as well as in Austria seem to indicate an increasing tendency to settle social and economic affairs by agreements – often rather highly formalized – among the large interest groups; this can be interpreted as an extension of the pattern to these domains too.

If our hypothesis is correct, this would mean that continued existence of fundamental cleavages is not an absolute condition for the persistence of this pattern. The point may come where polarization of the electorate is decreasing, as seems to be the case in present-day Austria. But if the elites are strongly integrated in parties of rigid discipline, as in Austria, their perception of political conflicts may differ markedly from the manner in which these are perceived by a majority of voters. Policy disagreements which voters regard as being of rather limited importance may then be interpreted by elites in terms of fundamental cleavages, and in critical situations the polarization of voters may even be reactivated by the elites. On the other hand, if elites cease to perceive the society as divided by fundamentals, they may nonetheless continue to uphold the supposed virtues of the "typical Austrian compromise" or "typical Swiss compromise" (a characteristic phrase quite current in both countries) and to prefer this pattern of cartelized decision-making to political competition of the "Anglo-Saxon" type. This hypothesis is supported by empirical evidence indicating that voters in different countries differ much less in their perception of political conflicts than do the political elites. An important example is the demonstration by Converse and Dupeux that the polarization of French public opinion, as compared with the less strong polarization in the United States, seems to be largely an elite phenomenon. This aspect is often somewhat neglected in the discussion on political culture and in voting research.

The discussion on *Proporz* government has concentrated on the efficiency of the system. Unfortunately, the problem of efficiency has been disregarded in comparative research on political systems. One reason may be the difficulty in finding an operational definition of such efficiency. We might define it as the capacity of a political system to resolve, within a reasonable time, the problems considered as vital or important by substantial segments of public opinion, including those problems that can be expected to gain such importance in the foreseeable future. But then we would be led to the conclusion that no political system at all is efficient, for it seems to be a structural fact of modern industrial society that the political system always lags behind the expectations placed upon it by some important groups. It seems highly improbable that any material definition of goals would enable us to measure and to compare the efficiency of political systems.

Instead we may inquire into the degree to which certain essential functions are performed in a given system, considering them at first from the standpoint of the mechanisms of conflict management, and thereafter from the standpoint of performance of vital tasks by the political system. As to the first aspect, comparison of the Swiss and the Austrian system is particularly instructive, for the mechanisms of conflict management obviously work much more smoothly in the Swiss system than they did in the Austrian coalition. Austrian political parties are strongly integrated social communities ("pillarized," in the sense of the Dutch *verzuiling*), and the bipolar structure of the coalition reinforced their antagonisms; moreover the coalition worked within the framework of a rather centralized political and administrative system. Although horizontal communication channels (for example, on the union-employer level) facilitated the solution of many problems and thus relieved the load on the system, important agreements often had to be worked out at the top by the leaders of the coalition parties. Such a system may of course quickly be deadlocked, whereas in Switzerland several factors contribute to render the mechanisms much more flexible: there are more than two cooperating parties (Radicals, Catholics, Socialists, conservative "Peasants and Bourgeois") which are rather loosely integrated and little disciplined; their mutual relationships are characterized by multiple intersections of cleavages (regional, linguistic, confessional, economic and social); and they work within the framework of a strongly decentralized federal system. This means that in Switzerland, unlike Austria, it remains possible to avoid deadlock by majority decisions. For majorities in the Swiss system are of a rather temporary and inconsistent character and do not infringe – as would the consistent majorities of the Austrian two-party antagonism – upon the fundamental principle of transactional conflict management and cooperation of all relevant groups. *Proporz* systems, like federal states, can thus be said to work better if there exist several independent centers of political power, because these can use the majority principle not as the fundamental device of conflict management and the ultimate source of legitimacy, but as an auxiliary expedient to avoid deadlock, whereas in a system consisting of only two parties the majority principle is quite inapplicable.

It is rather frequently assumed that *Proporz* systems perform less well the vital tasks of the commonwealth than do competitive or bureaucratic systems, especially because important constitutional functions are neutralized and paralyzed by the cartelization of groups and political parties. This criticism often overlooks the fact that, by a process of functional substitution, these tasks may be performed by other elements of the system than those to which the constitutional texts assign the respective tasks. Control has been exercised, as the late Otto Kirchheimer has underlined, by means of mutual *Bereichsopposition*, or of opposition restricted to certain domains, of the coalition partners. The same may be said of innovation, although the Austrian or the Swiss systems certainly include specific factors that may block innovative change as effectively as does, for example, the structure of British trade unionism. Admittedly, Lebanon offers numerous examples of impediments to social change and innovation which arise if an elaborate equilibrium of groups has to be preserved, but there is no reason to believe that the political systems of the Arab neighbour states are more efficient. Perhaps central coordination may be particularly difficult in a *Proporz* system, but competitive and bureaucratic systems have their own specific problems in this regard. The present rather unsatisfactory state of comparative research does not permit us to make a definitive judgment, but it appears difficult to credit competitive systems with a generally higher level of efficiency than *Proporz* systems. We can only specify which are the characteristic deficiencies and strong points of either system.

In one domain, it is true, *Proporz* systems seem to be less capable of effective performance of tasks, namely that of foreign policy. Switzerland, Austria and Lebanon show that the preservation of internal equilibrium presupposes a reduction of external demands on the political system. This may explain why, in a general fashion, *Proporz* seems to work in small states only.

This is not to say that the topic of this paper is of only marginal and limited relevance to comparative research. For it is evident that the pattern of conflict management described as *Proporz* has much in common with the phenomenon of "organized pluralism".[3] The most salient fact is that *Proporz* as well as "organized pluralism" are non-competitive systems in which issues are settled by *amicabilis compositio*, that is, by negotiated agreement rather than by majority. No doubt it is not by accident that the "organized pluralism" of interest groups is more highly devel-

[3] Dahl, *op. cit.* 395.

oped in Austria and Switzerland than in most other industrialized countries. Thus our topic may lead us to reconsider critically current political typologies which disregard non-competitive conflict management in favour of the competitive pattern on the one hand and the centralized bureaucratic and authoritarian patterns on the other. This disregard, incidentally, may be due to the fact that only the latter patterns have been accepted by constitutional theory; it thus reflects legalistic traditions of our discipline untouched by methodological progress.

We propose an alternative classification of political systems of the liberal-democratic type according to the predominance of one of the following patterns:

a) The competitive pattern of conflict management (the fundamental device of which is the majority principle);

b) the non-competitive, "cartelized" pluralist pattern (which works by *amicabilis compositio*, "amicable agreement");

c) conflict management by an interaction of bureaucratic arbitration (which works by hierarchy) and democratic control.

This third pattern seems to be characteristic of some larger countries of continental Europe which we propose to label "demo-bureaucratic systems." In these countries – especially in France, Italy and Germany – liberal democracy originated in parliamentary control of the monarchic-bureaucratic executive, and this distribution of roles is still largely characteristic of the structure of parliamentary government. Political parties are not really competitive leadership parties, and control of the executive power, instead of taking over executive leadership, is a predominant element in the role perceptions of legislators. This is particularly evident in the political culture of France and in French theories of parliamentary government, but West Germany's political culture too is still largely marked by the demo-bureaucratic pattern and is not as fully competitive as it might seem to the foreign observer.

These patterns, which are transmitted in the socialization processes of political elites, may of course intermingle and supplant each other in the course of historical developments.

Developmental typologies that tend to explain patterns of conflict management by socio-economic factors alone and that neglect intervening variables may lead to rather faulty projections of development trends. Particularly if we want to predict the future evolution of the "developing countries" or of the "socialist camp", we should consider that even an evolution towards a more "pluralistic" system might not render this a really competitive one. Historical circumstances may instead favour the coming into existence of norms of conflict management which are of the demo-bureaucratic or of the non-competitive *Proporz* type.

THE PRINCIPLES OF MAJORITY AND PROPORTIONALITY

Jürg Steiner

Source: J. Steiner, "The Principles of Majority and Proportionality," *British Journal of Political Science*, Vol. 1 (1970), 63-70, a translation by Geoffrey Hosking of the original German version published under the title "Majorz und Proporz," *Politische Vierteljahresschrift*, Vol. 11 (1970), 139-146. Reprinted by permission of the author.

It is only in connection with electoral law that the terms 'majority principle' and 'proportionality' are widely used. It seems to us meaningful to apply the two concepts also to the political decision-making process as a whole. In this broadened sense 'majority principle' and 'proportionality' denote certain models of conflict regulation. The majority model then denotes the regulation of conflict through majority decisions. The proportional model is much more difficult to describe: its basic characteristic is that all groups influence a decision in proportion to their numerical strength. Proportional conflict regulation is easiest to apply when a decision is concerned with several units, all of which are perceived as equivalent to one another. The classical case of this is the parliamentary election, for the parliamentary seats are perceived as equivalent to one another, so that by means of an appropriate electoral law they can relatively easily be distributed on a proportional basis among the different political groups. In Switzerland the election of the government by the parliament gives rise to an analogous situation, in that the seven seats in the Bundesrat (Federal Council) are perceived as equivalent to one another, so that they can likewise be relatively easily distributed on a proportional basis. In most other political systems the application of the rules of proportionality at the level of the government would entail greater difficulties, since the individual governmental posts are perceived as being of different value. The greatest difficulty presents itself when only a single office is to be filled, for example that of President. Here the application of proportional rules is only possible if rotation of office (i.e. proportionality in the temporal dimension) is brought into the reckoning, or if the disadvantage imposed on one group can be compensated by preference given to it in another decision.

In policy decisions it is as a rule even more difficult to proceed by proportionality than in decisions regarding persons. Policy problems are usually not structured in such a way that they can be reduced to a number of units perceived as equivalent to one another. A roughly proportional distribution of influence in policy problems can usually only be assured if the decision is bargained over with the participation of all groups. We may add that this bargaining process is also the most frequent indication of conflict regulation on the proportional principle. Gerhard Lehmbruch has revived for this bargaining process a concept originating from the Peace of Westphalia, that of the '*amicabilis compositio*'.[1] In the Swiss discussion the concept of 'concordance democracy' has often been used in this context, and has recently also been taken up by Lehmbruch.[2]

The models of conflict regulation on majority or proportional principles, which we here describe, are scarcely ever met with in their pure form. They constitute the extremes on a continuum which requires closer investigation. Unfortunately there do not as yet exist any studies which have undertaken to classify political systems according to the degree to which they settle political conflicts by majority or proportional rules. This would of course not simply be a matter of enumerating the electoral systems: rather, what requires investigation is the extent to which, in governments, in parliaments, in political parties, etc., majority or proportional rules are applied. It should be the aim of such investigations to compile for each political system a set of indices permitting a rank-ordering on the majority-proportionality continuum. We are conscious that the establishment of such indices will involve great difficulties. The major problem will be to determine what weight within the overall index should be attached to conflict resolution in the individual sub-systems. A provisional solution might be first of all to establish separate indices for the individual sub-systems – i.e. the parties, parliaments, governments, etc. – and to seek an international comparison on this level.

A classification of political systems on a majority-proportionality continuum would enable one to test hypotheses in which the method of conflict regulation could feature either as the dependent or as the independent variable. In what follows we will attempt to formulate some hypotheses of this kind. These rest on a narrow empirical basis: on the one hand, a description of the political system of Switzerland,[3] on the other, the secondary liter-

---

[1] Gerhard Lehmbruch, *Proporzdemokratie: Politisches System und politische Kultur in der Schweiz und in Oesterreich* (Tübingen, 1967).

[2] Gerhard Lehmbruch, 'Konkordanzdemokratie im politischen System der Schweiz: Ein Literaturbericht', *Politische Vierteljahresschrift*, 9 (1968), 443-459.

[3] See my book: *Gewaltlose Politik und kulturelle Vielfalt: Hypothesen entwickelt am Beispiel der Schweiz* (Bern-Stuttgart: Paul Haupt, 1970). For a summary of this book see my article: 'Nonviolent Conflict Resolution in Democratic Systems: Switzerland', *The Journal of Conflict Resolution*, Vol. 13, (1969) pp. 295-304.

ature on other political systems.[4] Since it is our conception of science that any theory must result from a constant interplay of the formulation and testing of hypotheses, it is quite natural that in the opening phase of an investigation the hypotheses are still predominantly speculative in nature. The present article has thus primarily an innovatory function, in that hypotheses are to be formulated which can later be tested systematically.

First of all we consider the degree of conflict-regulation on majority or proportional principles as a dependent variable. The first hypothesis takes the following form:

Hypothesis I: The smaller political systems are, the greater their tendency to regulate conflicts on proportional principles.

A first substantiation of this hypothesis may be seen in the fact that in smaller states the political elite is, compared to bigger states, relatively small. Hence the probability is greater that the members of the political elite will interact relatively frequently. But, as Homans postulates, frequent interaction tends to increase mutual goodwill.[5] As a result of this relatively high level of mutual goodwill, such groups generally prefer not to perceive politics as a zero-sum game, in which a strategy of 'all-or-nothing' is applied. For the winners in such a game would forfeit the loser's goodwill, and this would entail high costs relative to the rewards to be gained. The costs of a majority strategy in the sense of 'all-or-nothing' are only low if the participants do not feel much goodwill towards one another, and hence risk no great loss in this respect. If on the other hand the level of goodwill is relatively high, then the gains resulting from the balance between rewards and costs can be maximized by applying some kind of proportional rules in the resolution of conflicts. Of course the rewards to be gained are reduced, for it is no longer possible to achieve 'all' at the expense of the opponent. But on the other hand the costs in terms of goodwill are likely to be low, so that in the overall balance higher gains are much more likely to result than if majority rules had been followed.[6]

[4] A particularly rich source in this respect was Robert A. Dahl, ed., *Political Oppositions in Western Democracies* (New Haven and London: Yale University Press, 1966).

[5] George Caspar Homans, *Social Behavior: Its Elementary Forms* (New York: Harcourt Brace and World, 1961).

[6] The hypothesis put forward here, that small groups tend to avoid majority strategies, can also be found in W. H. Riker, *The Theory of Political Coalitions* (New Haven: Yale University Press, 1962), p. 51: 'Especially in small groups ... considerations of maintaining the solidarity of the group and the loyalty of members to it dominate considerations of maximum victory on particular decisions.'

A second reason why proportional rules are applied relatively frequently in small states is that in such states the resources available as rewards are by the nature of things smaller than in large states. Now if in small states high costs are incurred in distributing the modest rewards, it can easily happen that the balance between rewards and costs turns out to be negative. But the costs are generally high if political conflicts are settled according to majority rules, because in this mode of conflict regulation the winners risk forfeiting the losers' goodwill. Such costs are only irrelevant where in any case no mutual goodwill exists. If, however, goodwill does reach a certain level, then it will presumably be preferable to distribute the available resources according to proportional rules. In this way costs can be kept to a minimum, while the overall balance can show a gain, in spite of the modest rewards. We can formulate the same idea in a slightly different way by saying that, in a game where the rewards to be gained are meagre, one does not risk a large stake.

It is evident that both the elucidations hitherto offered for hypothesis I have a cumulative effect. Because in small states the mutual goodwill within the political elite tends to be relatively great, the probability will increase that, with a majority strategy, in view of the meagre resources available, the costs in terms of goodwill will exceed the rewards.

A third explanation of hypothesis I can be seen in the fact that small states are more exposed to the pressure of the international system than large ones. As small group research has demonstrated, the solidarity within a group increases under external pressure.[7] If we apply this result to large groups such as states – which is not unproblematic, but surely not wholly misleading – then we reach the conclusion that the pressure of the international system has a positive effect on the solidarity within small states. To be able to resist the pressure from outside it is perceived as essential to maintain internally as high a degree of solidarity as possible. But this solidarity could be reduced if in the regulation of internal conflicts a majority strategy in the sense of 'all-or-nothing' were mainly applied. In this connection it should be pointed out that in the Second World War Great Britain, the majority democracy *par excellence*, when it was under strong external pressure, deviated considerably from the majority model, in particular by setting up an all-party government.

Which point on the majority-proportionality continuum a political system occupies will probably depend not only on its size but also on its segmentation. On this second aspect we formulate the following hypothesis:

[7] Cf. for example Homans, *Social Behavior*.

Hypothesis 2: The more political systems are segmented, the greater their tendency to regulate conflicts on proportional principles.

We consider a political system segmented when most members of the individual sub-systems have in common two or more social characteristics with political relevance. Such segmentation is present, for example, when most members of a given sub-culture belong both to the same political party and to the same religious denomination; for both party and confessional allegiance are, as a rule, politically relevant. The segmentation can be dominated by a single characteristic, as for example in Austria between the two world wars, where two 'camps' (*Lager*) had been formed on a class-ideological dimension.[8] In such cases, we speak of a one-dimensional segmentation. We find a two-dimensional segmentation in Belgium, where besides the religious/anti-religious dimension language is also a dominant characteristic. From the combination of both these dimensions there results, for example, inside the Christian Socialist party a Flemish and a Walloon sub-culture.[9] Finally, in Switzerland we have multi-dimensional segmentation, for here the segmentation is determined roughly equally by language, religion, membership of social stratum and region. These dimensions cut across one another, so that a relatively large number of sub-cultures exists.[10]

In segmented political systems – whatever the nature of the segmentation – interests of the different segments are in many political questions perceived as incompatible. Hence the probability is small that the application of a majority strategy would lead to alternating majorities, for a segment which finds itself in a minority has scarcely any chance of winning over voters from the majority segment and thereby of becoming itself a majority. But if a group of the population remains constantly in a minority, it will presumably in time become so frustrated that it will make efforts to opt out of the system. The best way to prevent this kind of dissolution of the system will, in case of strong segmentation, probably be to apply some kind of proportional rules in the resolution of political conflicts.

The application of proportional rules appears as especially necessary when the segmentation within a political system corresponds to a segmentation of the international system. In the event of this kind of congruence it is particularly probable that a frustrated segment within a national system will make efforts to

[8] Lehmbruch, *Proporzdemokratie*, pp. 34 ff.

[9] Val R. Lorwin, "Belgium: Religion, Class, and Language in National Politics," in Dahl, ed., *Political Oppositions*.

[10] For the concept of segmentation, compare Steiner, *Gewaltlose Politik*.

opt out of that system. Switzerland was long in a situation where internal religious and linguistic segmentation was also dominated by the international system. We may suppose that Switzerland would have fallen apart had she not partially satisfied all her segments by the application of proportional rules.[11]

The third hypothesis we postulate is that the position of a political system on the majority-proportionality continuum depends not only on its size and its segmentation, but also on its social norms.

Hypothesis 3: The more weight the prevalent norm-system lays on amicable agreement, the more a political system tends to regulate conflicts on proportional principles.

In Switzerland, it is common to speak of a "true Swiss compromise". By that is meant that a solution has been reached as a kind of amicable agreement with the participation of all interested circles. The frequent use of the concept of the "true Swiss compromise" shows that the norm of amicable agreement possesses a high priority. That such a norm can emerge at all depends partly on its past application having been rewarded. This prerequisite is present in Switzerland, for in Switzerland's understanding of itself the view is widely accepted that the economic prosperity of the country, its peaceful internal community life, indeed its very existence, are largely derived from the fact that amicable agreement was always aimed at as a means of regulating conflict. It is also important for the generation of a norm that symbolic figures should exist which represent that norm. This too applies to Switzerland, if we think for example of Brother Klaus, who in the Ordinance of the Diet of Stans (1481) indicated the path of negotiation in the spirit of amicable agreement. Furthermore, the name of the Swiss Confederation (*Eidgenossenschaft*) points symbolically to amicable understanding between comrades (*Genossen*). Whether the prevalent norm inclines more to competition or to amicable agreement depends also on the nature of the socialization process in families, schools, play groups, workplaces, etc.

The position of a political system on the majority-proportionality continuum can also be treated as an independent variable, and as such be used to explain other variables. The next hypothesis attempts to show how the application of proportional models affects the channels of communication for the articulation of dissent:

[11] The first two hypotheses presented here can also be found, partly with similar explanations, but limited to electoral law, in Stein Rokkan, 'The Structuring of Mass Politics in the Smaller European Democracies: A Developmental Typology', *Comparative Studies in Society and History*, 10 (1968), 189 ff.

Hypothesis 4: The more conflicts in political systems are regulated by proportionality, the greater the tendency for ordinary citizens to have no functional channels for the articulation of dissent at their disposal.

The explanation of this hypothesis is that, with a proportional strategy, the political elites form a relatively closed group, as results from the necessity of reaching settlements by mutual bargaining. In the face of this relatively closed political elite the ordinary citizen is hardly in a position to discern who is responsible if his demands are not met. Nor has he access to the information necessary to articulate his dissent in a well-directed and hence functional manner. A diffuse protest against the dominant political group as a whole, however, is usually dysfunctional, since in this way nothing is likely to be achieved.

Hypothesis 5: The more conflicts in a political system are regulated by proportionality, the lower the learning capacity of the system tends to be.

By high learning capacity we understand with Karl W. Deutsch a combination of 'a high degree of richness and originality – that is, improbability – of new patterns, with a high degree of speed in their selection, and with a high probability of their relevance to the challenges offered to the organization by its environment'.[12] Because of the already mentioned relatively closed nature of the political elite, it is probable that the citizens' political interest will wane as they see only limited opportunities for making their influence felt.[13] But if the citizens behave politically relatively passively, then they communicate to the political elites correspondingly little information. Then the feed-back process within the system does not work optimally, since the political elites are inadequately informed about the reactions their decisions arouse from the ordinary citizens. This must affect the learning capacity negatively, by reducing the probability that solutions will be found which are relevant to the demands imposed on the system.

The learning capacity of the system is also adversely affected by the fact that a compromise solution in the spirit of amicable agreement can usually be reached only if the scope for innovation is very limited from the start. For if there is wide scope for innovation, then so many alternatives will present themselves that a decision can hardly be reached unless a good many alternatives are eliminated by the application of majority rules. If the scope for innovation is small, on the other hand, it is more likely to be

---

[12] Karl W. Deutsch, *The Nerves of Government. Models of Political Communication and Control* (New York and London: Free Press, 1966).

[13] For this point see my *Bürger und Politik* (Meisenheim: Anton Hain, 1969).

possible through amicable agreement to reduce the viewpoints to a common denominator. Small scope for innovation, however, also lessens the probability that very original solutions will be found, such as might be evolved in a system possessing high learning capacity.

Even when the scope for innovation is kept small, the bargaining for an agreed solution still takes a lot of time. Hence the system has difficulty in reacting fast, which is likewise not conducive to a high learning capacity.

What connection exists between the position of a political system on the majority-proportionality continuum and the *consensus* within the system? On the basis of Swiss experience one might assume that the frequent application of proportional rules increases the consensus within the system, for various indicators, such as the low incidence of the use of violence,[14] suggest that the Swiss system enjoys strong consensus. As confirmation one could point out that through the frequent application of proportional rules the demands of the various groups of the population are satisfied more or less equitably, so that nowhere can pronounced frustration arise.

But then, what about the connection between hypotheses 4 and 5 and the degree of consensus? Do dysfunctional communication channels for the articulation of dissent and a low learning capacity not operate to reduce the degree of consensus? We assume it hypothetically, but must point out that in Switzerland special conditions pertain which restrict the effects of these factors. For one thing, the political system of Switzerland has a relatively small input of demands, and consequently the deficient learning capacity of the system does not make itself strongly felt. The relatively small input of demands is connected with various factors: neutrality eases the burden of foreign affairs; by virtue of the federal structure demands are split up among different political levels; because of the small size of the state political problems remain within certain limits of complexity; and, finally, in Switzerland many problems elsewhere consigned to the state are traditionally settled privately.

A second consideration is that the Swiss elector has in the referendum an instrument at his disposal which constitutes considerable compensation for the way in which the frequent application of proportional rules renders other communication channels for the articulation of dissent dysfunctional.

However, even in Switzerland the input of demands has increased considerably recently.[15] Because of this development,

[14] Steiner, *Gewaltlose Politik*.
[15] For this point cf. for example: *Schätzungen der Einnahmen und Ausgaben des Bundes 1966-74*. Bericht der Eidgenössischen Exper-

the deficient learning capacity of the system is gradually beginning to have more noticeable effects. Furthermore – as we have expounded in another place[16] – it appears that with a growing input of demands the institution of the referendum degrades the learning capacity of the system. As a result, the ever more apparent deficiency in the learning capacity of the system has already led to a certain uneasiness, vividly captured by Max Imboden in the concept of the *malaise helvétique*.[17] Even in the case of Switzerland it must thus in the long run be regarded as uncertain whether a proportional strategy furthers consensus within a system.[18] So it would be at the very least hasty to want to transfer the Swiss proportional rules to other strongly segmented political systems. On the other hand it must not be forgotten – as we have already pointed out—that it is no less problematical for political systems with strong segmentation to apply majority rules. This problem indicates the dilemma in which many developing countries find themselves, and also modern industrial states like Belgium and Canada. With the progress of attempts at integration, this dilemma will also become ever more acute for supranational organizations. Considerable research endeavours will be needed so that it may gradually become clearer what connection exists under different systemic conditions between the application of majority and proportional strategies and the stability of democratic systems.[19]

tenkommission zur Bearbeitung der Grundlagen und Methoden einer langfristigen Finanzplanung im Bunde (Bern, 1966).

[16] Steiner, 'Aspekte des Referendums', *Schweizer Monatshefte,* Vol. 48, No. 12 (March, 1969).

[17] Max Imboden, *Helvetisches Malaise* (Zurich, 1964).

[18] Cf. Steiner, *Gewaltlose Politik.*

[19] Cf. my "Conflict Resolution and Democratic Stability in Subculturally Segmented Political Systems," *Res Publica.* Revue de l'Institut Belge de Science Politique, 11 (1969), 775-798, and also my *Amicable Agreement and Majority Rule: Conflict Resolution in Switzerland* (Chapel Hill: University of North Carolina Press, forthcoming).

ON BUILDING CONSOCIATIONAL NATIONS: THE CASES OF THE NETHERLANDS AND SWITZERLAND

Hans Daalder

Source: Hans Daalder, "On Building Consociational Nations: the Cases of the Netherlands and Switzerland", *International Social Science Journal*, Vol. 23, No. 3, 1971, pp. 355-370. Reprinted by permission of UNESCO and the author.

Introduction. Of late, the term "consociational" has been increasingly used to characterize a certain pattern of political life in which the political élites of distinct social groups succeed in establishing a viable, pluralistic State by a process of mutual forbearance and accommodation. In modern social science, the word was first used by David Apter.[1] The term was further elaborated into a general classificatory concept by Arend Lijphart.[2] Independently of him and sometimes under different terms like *Proporzdemokratie* or *Konkordanzdemokratie*, Gerhard Lehmbruch,[3] Jürg Steiner,[4] and Rodney Stiefbold[5] have sought to analyse comparable types of political experience.

The word *consociatio* originated with Johannes Althusius.[6] It is significant that a term first adopted to analyse the development of a new polity in the Low Countries in the early seventeenth century, is now being revived in the study of comparative political development in the twentieth century. A process of building up a new political society from below, to some degree by the consent of participating communities, in which deliberate compromises by élites carefully circumscribe and limit the extent to which political

[1] David Apter, *The Political Kingdom in Uganda: a Study in Bureaucratic Nationalism*, (Princeton, 1961), pp. 24-5.

[2] See his "Typologies of Democratic Systems," *Comparative Political Studies*, Vol. 1 (1968), p. 3-44; and "Consociational Democracy," *World Politics*, Vol. 21 (1968-69), p. 207-25.

[3] See his *Proporzdemokratie* (Tübingen, 1967); and "A Non-Competitive Pattern of Conflict Management in Liberal Democracies: the Cases of Switzerland, Austria and Lebanon," paper presented to the Brussels Congress of the International Political Science Association, 1967.

[4] Jürg Steiner, *Gewaltlose Politik und Kulturelle Vielfalt: Hypothesen Entwickelt am Beispiel der Schweiz* (Bern and Stuttgart, 1970).

[5] Rodney Stiefbold, "Elite-Mass Opinion Structure and Communication Flow in a Consociational Democracy (Austria)," paper presented to the annual meeting of the American Political Science Association, Washington, 1968.

[6] For a useful short summary see Otto Gierke, *Natural Law and the Theory of Society 1500 to 1800*, ed. and trans. by Ernest Barker (Boston, 1957), pp. 70-9.

power can be wielded by one political centre, may be a relatively
rare political phenomenon. Yet it provides at least a significant
footnote to the prevailing mood in the study of nation-building
which so often proceeds from the assumption that nationhood
should be forged from above, by the deliberate imposition of a
"modern" State on traditional society.

The term "consociational democracy" has been used by Lijphart
to characterize the political life of European countries (the Low
Countries, Austria, Switzerland) as well as countries on other
continents (e.g. Israel, Lebanon, Uruguay, Colombia). This article will deal only in its conclusion with the general model of
"consociational democracy." Its major emphasis will be on a
two-country comparison prompted by the suggestion of Stein
Rokkan that a treatment of the Dutch and Swiss cases of
nation-building might open "fascinating possibilities of comparative historical analysis."[7] Inevitably, in the context of a short
article, the argument will proceed mainly in the form of propositions which stand in need of more detailed historical substantiation.

Comparison presupposes common as well as contrasting characteristics. In the first section of this article, common elements in
the political development of the Netherlands and Switzerland will
be traced. In the second part, the focus will shift to differences
between the two countries. The paper will conclude with some
remarks on more theoretical questions which are prompted by a
comparison of Dutch and Swiss experiences in nation-building
with those of other countries.

COMMON CHARACTERISTICS OF SWISS AND DUTCH
NATION-BUILDING PROCESSES

Both the Netherlands and Switzerland provide examples of States
which attained international sovereignty with only minimal internal consolidation. Some violence did occur both in the processes
of external demarcation and internal integration; but nationhood
typically grew through extensive processes of accommodation and
compromise. In the typology of European States,[8] the two countries resemble the United Kingdom and Sweden in their centu-
ries-old status as independent polities which show strong tradi-

---

[7] Stein Rokkan, *Citizens, Elections, Parties – Approaches to the
Comparative Study of the Processes of Development* (Oslo, 1970),
p. 118

[8] Rokkan, *op. cit.*, Part 1, especially Chapter 3; see also Hans
Daalder, "Parties, Élites and Political Developments in Western
Europe," in: Joseph LaPalombara and Myron Weiner (eds.), *Politi-
cal Parties and Political Development* (Princeton, 1966), pp. 44-52

tions of continuous representative organs and which grew slowly – but without reversals – into modern democratic societies. But unlike these two countries, nationhood was achieved without dynastic guidance or early central government. Like Italy and Germany, the modern State developed through unification of once highly dispersed political communities. But whereas conquest and forceful unification stood at the cradle of Italian and German statehood, Swiss and Dutch statehood as well as nationhood were formed on the whole by compact and accommodation.

If one seeks to account for the Dutch and Swiss developments, the following factors would seem to stand out.

Geopolitical Factors. Otto Hintze long ago drew attention to the importance for later developments of the specific location of certain countries at the periphery of the Holy Roman Empire.[9] Due to the weakness of central authority in the Empire independent dukedoms, bishoprics, counties, cities, cantons and provinces maintained themselves with a high degree of political self-sufficiency and independence when in other countries like France, Spain, the United Kingdom and the Scandinavian countries dynastic rule resulted in centralized statehood. The development notably of the United Kingdom and France as strong power centres on the international scene, assisted the further development of political independence of Switzerland and the Netherlands: Swiss independence after the fifteenth century was strengthened by a special relationship with France, and Dutch nationhood was achieved not least because Habsburgs, Bourbons, and Stuarts were unwilling to see political control over the European Delta go to any one of them.

A second common geopolitical factor between the Netherlands and Switzerland is their location at some of the most important trade routes of Europe. This led to the early development of mercantile cities. Both in the Netherlands and in some of the more important Swiss cantons, cities thus gained a dominant position which they also extended over the surrounding countryside. But these cities remained at the same time highly particularist political communities. Both in the Netherlands and Switzerland a polycephalous city network developed in which no single city could become the "capital city" for the whole country. Switzerland as well as the Netherlands remained for long, much to the dislike of nineteenth-century unifiers like Friedrich List, a *Konglomerat von Munizipalitäten.*[10] Moreover, in both countries

---

[9] Otto Hintze, "Typologie der Ständischen Verfassung des Abendlandes," *Historisches Zeitschrift,* Vol. 141 (1930), p. 224-48.

[10] Quoted by Hans Kohn, *Nationalism and Liberty: the Swiss example,* (London, 1956), p. 57.

strong rural cantons and provinces retained an independent political title beside the more prosperous city-dominated polities.

Thirdly, for geographic reasons, neither country saw the development of large land-ownership. Communal grazing practices in Switzerland, common needs for the protection of land against the ever-present threat of the sea and rivers in the Lowlands, made for an early development of self-reliant peasant communities. If not always in practice, this provided at least in political theory for the idea of self-governing communes administered by commoners. Later political developments could therefore be inspired by ancient traditions.

The Peculiar Development of 'Sovereignty'. Both in the Netherlands and in Switzerland, independent national existence was originally decided by the force of arms. Territorial consolidation was achieved only by extensive military battles against foreign claimants and, to some extent, at least in Switzerland, by a show of strength against internal dissidents. Local military conflicts decided the course of later frontiers, and military alliances began the process of later development of national identity. To state that nationhood emerged from the completely voluntary association of free communities, would therefore be an unwarranted simplification. In the Netherlands, the seven United Provinces conquered Brabant and Limburg in the 1620s and 1630s and ruled them as dependent territories for 150 years. Switzerland for long was a patchwork of *Urkantone*, associated cantons and a host of dependencies of which Tessin and Vaud were the most important. The essence of Dutch and Swiss political life remained for very long a motley arrangement of particularist communities, not national co-operation among equals.

Yet this very particularism had important consequences for later developments. Interestingly, even the more important, potentially more powerful provinces and cantons did not aspire to become central administrative capitals. And even in dependent territories, local traditions and local governments were permitted to persist. A measure of traditionalist self-sufficiency could eventually substantiate later claims for a separate identity on a par with former overlords. The very dispersed power structure gave ample scope, moreover, for local élites to maintain themselves, and for the confederation as a whole to continue irrespective of political changes within any of the constituent political communities. If there was hardly any national political life, there were also no strong national cleavages or conflicts.

Both the Netherlands and Switzerland emerged therefore as independent political societies without either a strong central government apparatus or an articulate national identity. Common affairs were decided *ad hoc* by political procedures that resembled international conferences rather than legitimate national government. Neither the United Provinces, nor the Swiss Confederation knew a central army or a central bureaucracy. There were no organs of State which could act directly on the individual and there was no concept of common citizenship.

Does this mean that one cannot speak of a Dutch or a Swiss nationality in this period? The answer is somewhat in the nature of a *petitio principii*. If one defines "the central factor of nation-building" as "the orderly exercise of a nation-wide public authority,"[11] the answer must be negative as no such nation-wide public authority existed. If one speaks of nations only when there has been a "process whereby people *transfer* [my italics] their commitment and loyalty from smaller tribes, villages, or petty principalities to the larger central political system,"[12] the conclusion must be equally negative. But one could also argue that at least one condition of nationality – sovereign political existence – had been fulfilled. And if one defines nationality more in terms of at least some consciousness of togetherness rather than as an exclusivist transfer of loyalties to a new State, signs of an incipient nationhood could be found at least among the leading political strata of Swiss and Dutch society.

The Persistence of Pluralism in Modernization. The French revolution, undoubtedly, had a major effect on the development of Dutch and to a lesser extent on that of Swiss nationhood. In the Netherlands, French occupation brought a lasting unitary State, common citizenship, common laws and equal rights for the various religions. In Switzerland, the institutions of the Helvetic Republic proved abortive, but old inequalities between the cantons disappeared and virtually equal rights were secured for the main languages. Eventually, Switzerland too moved to more definite forms of (federal) statehood in 1848.

But the drive of radical forces for unification (as represented by the Dutch *Patriottenbeweging* or the Swiss Helvetic Society towards the end of the eighteenth century, or again by innovative radicals around 1848) never succeeded in achieving a sharp break with older pluralist traditions. If thinkers of the French Enlightenment put the twin concepts of absolutism and individualism against what they conceived as the dead weight of privileged corporate interests, Dutch and Swiss traditions consistently

[11] Reinhard Bendix, *Nation-building and Citizenship: Studies of our Changing Social Order* (New York, 1964), p. 18.

[12] Gabriel A. Almond and G. Bingham Powell, Jr., *Comparative Politics: a Developmental Approach* (Boston, 1966), p. 36.

regarded an entrenched pluralism as the safeguard of liberties. Admittedly, these old liberties (in the plural) might frustrate individual equality and individual liberty (in the singular). Yet, corporate rights were regarded as important in themselves, as well as a protection against threatening claims on the part of an omnipotent new State.

The formation of the Dutch and Swiss nations could therefore become the result of a slow process of genuine national integration, rather than of deliberate nation-building. It would be difficult to point to one social group, or one political centre, or one legal institution which might be regarded as the chief nation-building force.

Data on élite-recruitment (whether on Dutch Cabinet personnel[13] or on Swiss members of Parliament[14]) show that elite positions in the nineteenth century were shared widely by all the major regions of the country. National integration first evolved slowly on the level of accommodating élites, to filter down later to the more parochial orders of society. The slow development of a stronger national sentiment in the population at large was therefore in the main complementary to, rather than destructive of, older local allegiances.

In Dutch and Swiss nineteenth-century history one also looks in vain for a salient role of the usual agencies of nation-building: the army, the bureaucracy, national schools.

National armies appeared only relatively late on the Dutch and Swiss scene. Although they may have played some role in the political socialization of recruits into a developing national political culture – a role so often attributed to armies[15] – a definite sense of national identity preceded the introduction of compulsory military service.

Especially in Switzerland, the national bureaucracy has remained of relatively modest dimensions, not least because the cantonal governments retained very major political and administrative functions in the federal structure. But also in the Netherlands which was a unitary State from 1795 onwards, the central

---

[13] A machine-readable bibliographical file on all Dutch cabinet ministers since 1848 is available in the Leiden Department of Political Science, based on material originally collected by Mattei Dogan and Maria Scheffer-van der Veen. In the context of a larger study of the Dutch Parliament, a similar file is being prepared on all members of the Dutch Parliament from 1848 to the present.

[14] E. Gruner and K. Frei, *Schweizerische Bundesversammlung, 1848-1920* (Bern, 1966), 2 vols.

[15] See in particular Lucian W. Pye, *Aspects of Political Development,* (Boston, 1965), chapter 11.

bureaucracy remained of modest size until the early twentieth century. Recruitment to higher civil service roles has retained many of the features of earlier particularist élite practices. To this day, the Swiss and the Dutch bureaucracies remain in many respects not only nationalizing agencies, but also points of brokerage between highly differentiated subgroups of society.

Schools have undoubtedly played an important role in fostering the development of national sentiment. But in Switzerland control over education has, in practice, remained a highly regionalized and localized affair. In the Netherlands, an attempt on the part of secular liberal élite groups in the second part of the nineteenth century to build up a centralized school system soon ran into strong opposition from Calvinists and Catholics who successfully fought for autonomy of religious schools under their own control.[16] An inspection of the course content of Dutch and Swiss schools would probably reveal an insistence on both national and sub-national allegiances, typically regarded as fully compatible.

Thus, older traditions of élite accommodation which had grown from the necessities of the highly dispersed power structure of the pre-1789 confederations could be carried over into the modernization process. Older pluralist élite attitudes facilitated the gradual settlement of participation demands from new social groupings in society. Both in Switzerland and in the Netherlands verbal adherence to ancient ideals of accountable government had gone together in practice with effective rule by relatively narrow – albeit also pluralist – élite groups. But typically, these had enjoyed a high degree of legitimacy. The franchise was extended only slowly, and older practices by which policies were preferably determined in negotiations and compromises outside the public market place, have retained a strong hold in the political culture. Both the Netherlands and Switzerland substantiate two of Stein Rokkan's hypotheses: (a) "The stronger the inherited traditions of representative rule, whether within estates, territorial assemblies or city councils, the greater the chances of early legitimation of opposition"; and (b) "the stronger the inherited traditions of representative rule, the slower, and the less likely to be reversed, the processes of enfranchisement and equalization".[17]

Finally, in the two countries a strong emphasis on the need to make sure that political power could not become concentrated in one political centre, has continued to form part of the political culture. More so in Switzerland than in the Netherlands, this has

---

[16] See Hans Daalder, "The Netherlands: Opposition in a Segmented Society," in Robert A. Dahl (ed.), *Political Oppositions in Western Democracies* (New Haven, 1966), pp. 199ff.

[17] Rokkan, *op. cit.*, pp. 82-3.

been done by keeping local governments strong and relatively independent political sites.[18] In both countries, central government institutions have been so arranged as to ensure a definite duality between the executive and the legislature. Within each, older pluralist traditions and modern electoral devices have seen to it that political power has been divided over a variety of political parties: the distance which separates even the largest party from the majority point has been greater in Switzerland and the Netherlands than in practically any European country.[19] Coalition government is ingrained both within the official government structures and in the decision-making processes of the large number of interest groups.

In sum, ancient pluralism has facilitated the development of a stable, legitimate and consistently pluralist modern society.[20] Both the Netherlands and Switzerland are countries with strong subcultural divisions. Yet, of the six possible ways in which subcultural conflicts might be dealt with according to Robert A. Dahl,[21] violence and repression as well as secession or separation have been remarkably absent. Instead a respect for autonomy, a habitual reference to proportional representation, and sometimes a willingness to abide by mutual veto rather than undiluted majority decisions[22] have been characteristic features of Dutch and Swiss

---

[18] On the concept of political "site", see Dahl, *op. cit.*, pp. 338ff.

[19] See the classificatory table of the Smaller European Democracies by the Likelihood of Single-party Majorities and the Distribution of Minority Party Strength, in Rokkan, *op. cit.*, p. 94.

[20] This article concentrates above all on the distinct properties in the national development of Switzerland and the Netherlands. These countries have, of course, many other features in common with European States. Most of the general indicators specified by Rokkan, *op. cit.*, in his "Methods and Models in the Comparative Study of Nation-building," p. 65ff. would be highly relevant for a study of Dutch and Swiss experience. Swiss and Dutch national development might also be contrasted with that of the United States. In fact, both countries often resemble Huntington's "American" pattern of development more than his "European" type (whether "British" or "Continental"). See Samuel P. Huntington, "Political Modernization: America *vs.* Europe", *World Politics*, Vol. 18 (1965-66), pp. 378-414.

[21] These six possible ways of solving subcultural conflicts are: (a) violence and repression; (b) secession or separation; (c) mutual veto; (d) autonomy; (e) proportional representation; and (f) assimilation – see Dahl, *op. cit.*, pp. 358-9.

[22] Typically, the Swiss referendum has in practice become much more a weapon wielded by minorities who seek to resist majority decisions taken by the federal Parliament than an expression of will by "the" sovereign Swiss people as a whole.

political culture. And this instinctive respect for diversity has, paradoxically, eased modern processes of assimilation.

CONTRASTS BETWEEN DUTCH AND SWISS NATION-BUILDING PROCESSES

If "the inevitability of gradualness" in a consistently pluralist evolution is the most obvious common characteristic of the two countries, certain differences between them should also be noted.

Geopolitical Factors. Geographic factors have differentiated Dutch and Swiss political development on the following points.

First, Dutch geography provided less durable barriers to processes of social mobility than the Swiss terrain. Particularism was therefore broken up more easily once the homogenizing process of political modernization set in. The most conspicuous illustration of this process is the relatively unhindered development of one national language. To this day Frisian remains a separate language spoken by a few hundred thousand persons; in addition there are numerous slowly disappearing Dutch dialects. But there was never any real issue about the acceptance of the original tongue of the burghers of the cities of the Netherlands as the national language. This in turn, facilitated easy communication throughout the country, and paved the way for stronger assimilatory processes than could be found in Switzerland.

Secondly, Switzerland is a land-locked country, the Netherlands very much a sea-faring nation. The latter country acquired a colonial empire, and developed also other strong overseas links. At the same time, the Netherlands psychologically stood for a long time – to use a habitual Dutch metaphor – with its back against the European Continent (strong trading-links with the hinterland notwithstanding). The Dutch self-image was therefore relatively little influenced by the country's precarious position as a small European State at the borders of larger European powers. Switzerland, on the other hand, was acutely conscious of its larger neighbours. The very fact that Swiss citizens spoke the languages of three larger neighbouring States – and that each of these tended to define nationality in linguistic terms – made it imperative to separate the concept of nationhood from any possible link with seemingly objective "national" criteria of language, culture, or ethnic descent.[23] Of the two countries, the Netherlands became

---

[23] It has been argued that Switzerland owes its continued political independence to the very circumstance that it was not a German-speaking State only, but a multilingual political community. According to the historian William Martin, the conquest of French-speaking parts by the original Swiss Confederation in 1536 determined the very existence of a Swiss State: "On ne saurait exagérer

the more homogeneous, unconsciously nationalized society; Switzerland the more heterogeneous, diversified State which embraced a self-conscious "political" definition of nationhood.[24]

Differences in Political Centralization. Since 1795, the Netherlands has been the more centralized political community. But even before, some vestiges of centralization could be found in the Low Countries. The Dutch Republic, after all, developed when medieval traditions inspired particularist societies in the sixteenth century to revolt against the Burgundians who seemed destined to become the most successful centralizing dynasty of Europe.[25] If the Dutch Revolt arrested this drive towards centralization, some remnants of it could yet be found in some of the curious political organs of the Dutch Republic. Notably the office of the *stadtholder* (literally, the Sovereign's *remplaçant*) retained vestiges of earlier centralizing practices, and provided a political base for the Orange dynasty which had no counterpart in Swiss history. Technically, the *stadtholders* were servants of each of the provinces, and for long periods the city aristocracies successfully kept the Orange Princes from power. But the office carried the command of fleet and army, and eventually developed even before the arrival of the unitary State into a unifying force, complete with court and court circle.

Much more than the Swiss Confederation, the Dutch Republic

---

l'importance de cette conquête. Elle est comparable à celle du Tessin et la dépasse de beaucoup. Ce fut pour la Confédération une nouvelle naissance. Sans qu'il soit permis de refaire l'histoire, on peut affirmer que si la Suisse était restée purement allemande, elle n'aurait pas pu défendre son indépendance contre le mouvement des nationalités modernes qui a tendu à la création de grands États sur une base linguistique. Au moment où les Bernois ont conquis le Pays de Vaud, ils n'ont peut-être pas saisi toute la portée nationale de leur acte, car la diversité des langues n'étonnait alors aucun esprit. Mais la conquête n'en a pas moins régénéré, et peut-être sauvé, la Confédération." William Martin, *Histoire de la Suisse: Essai sur la Formation d'une Confédération d'États*, p. 112, Lausanne, 1943, as quoted by Hans Kohn, *op. cit.*, pp. 19-20, footnote 1.

[24] For a discussion on the definition of "nation" – and the political overtones in the debate about defining "nationhood" – older studies like those of C. A. Macartney, *National States and National Minorities* (London, 1934); Royal Institute of International Affairs, *Nationalism* (London, 1939); E. H. Carr, *Nationalism and After* (London, 1945); and Alfred Cobban, *National Self-determination* (Oxford, 1945), remain highly relevant.

[25] For a very good analysis, see B. H. M. Vlekke, *The Evolution of the Dutch Nation* (New York, 1945).

was for a time an active participant on the international scene. Some of the Orange Princes – as well as the Grand-Pensionary of Holland – were actively involved in high diplomatic manoeuvres. The Dutch fleet, and the Dutch colonies, also made for a stronger international presence. This more active international stance hardly contributed towards internal consolidation. In the seventeenth and eighteenth centuries, activist foreign policies were settled in the most narrow circles, in which the otherwise highly particularist representatives of the Province of Holland had a decisive voice. Typically, activism in foreign policy was more characteristic of the loosely structured Dutch Republic than of the nineteenth-century centralized kingdom. But the role played by the Republic in international affairs created at least a self-conscious image of the international importance of the Netherlands which later nationalist historians could exploit on behalf of nationalist mythology.

Both during the days of French supremacy, and after the defeat of Napoleon, there was a definite revulsion against centralized structures in both countries. But whereas Switzerland reverted almost completely to the old order in 1813, the Netherlands knew its period of strongest autocratic rule after 1815. Fears of the older diversity caused the new kings to obtain strong powers. Control over local governments remained strongly centralized, and to this day the appointment of provincial governors and local mayors rests with the central government.[26] Decisive powers were explicitly vested in the national government. Ever since 1813, Dutch political life has tended to be national in scope: constitutional conflicts centered on the national institutions, and political oppositions tended to develop as contestants in one national political arena.

In contrast, nineteenth- and twentieth-century developments in Switzerland have been far less centralistic in nature. Not only after 1813, but also after the formation of a genuine political federation in 1848, Swiss politics has remained a very specific compromise between local, regional, and national forms of government. The Swiss *Gemeinde* has retained many characteristics of autonomous polities, including lifelong administrative and sentimental ties with persons born within its boundaries. The Swiss cantons have remained powerful bodies, with great diversities in structure and politics. And even in the national institutions, regional interests hold an important place. The Swiss Upper

---

[26] It is again illustrative, however, of the forces of pluralism in the Netherlands that these central appointees nevertheless developed into highly independent magistrates rather than "prefects" on behalf of the centre.

House (like the American Senate) continues to give absolute parity to cantons, large or small; the Dutch *Eerste Kamer* is also elected by the provincial councils but only after a complex weighting arrangement makes the vote of each councillor proportional to population. The Swiss Executive (*Bundesrat*), composed of only seven members, preserves a careful balance between linguistic and regional interests, unlike the much larger Dutch Cabinets which are formed almost exclusively with an eye to the relative strength of political parties. Also in the election of the Lower House – as well as the day-to-day functioning of political parties – regional forces play a much greater role in Switzerland than in the Netherlands. Being more important than Dutch local government posts, cantonal government positions provide much greater sources of leverage for local politicians within their national parties than can be found in the Netherlands.

Differences in the Cleavage Structure. The much greater, continuing influence of regional factors in Swiss political life has a strong influence on the degree of politicization of various cleavages. This factor may perhaps best be illustrated in the very different manner in which religious factors have affected the growth of national integration.

Both the Netherlands and Switzerland belong to the mixed religious belt in Europe in which Protestants and Catholics live side by side. In the United Provinces, Calvinism became the established church, even though Catholics never numbered less than a third of the Dutch population. Catholics not only lived in the conquered provinces of Brabant and Limburg, but also formed large minorities – and locally even majorities – in the western parts of the country. Switzerland did not know a national established church; the effective independence of each of the cantons made for the development of specific Catholic and specific Protestant cantons (true to the old Augsburg formula of *cuius regio eius religio*). Much more so than in the Netherlands, religion was therefore tied to specific regional positions.

This had great effect on later developments. The localization of religion in Switzerland in particular cantons exacerbated regional strife. It polarized conflict to such an extent that religious conflict led to the regional *Sonderbund* war in 1847.[27]

In the Netherlands, on the other hand, national unification

---

[27] It testifies to the lasting strength of accommodationist practices in Switzerland that immediately after the civil war victors and vanquished sat together in elaborating the Swiss Constitution of 1848 which retained much of the older regional particularism and to a large degree depoliticized religious cleavages.

after 1795 had ensured equal rights for all religious groups throughout the State. But both the secular claims of the new State – and the widespread processes of secularization in society at large – provoked Calvinists and Catholics to demand autonomy for their churches and denominational control over education. This issue made religion the dominant dividing line in the formation of modern political parties in the latter part of the nineteenth century. Paradoxically, religion therefore became both an integrative and a divisive force. It split mixed religious local communities, and built strong organizational links among like-minded believers across the nation. The strong institutional build-up of Calvinist and Catholic organizations led to a strong segmentation of the Dutch nation in separate subcultural communities of Calvinists, Catholics and more secular groups. But this new division, while splitting the country along a new dimension, integrated and nationalized political life.

The subordination of regional to religious cleavages can be best illustrated by the example of the Dutch Catholics. About half the number of Dutch Catholics live in the two southern provinces of Brabant and Limburg. These provinces shared a common history, similar patterns of speech, and religious outlook with neighbouring Belgium. Belgian Catholicism exercised a strong influence on these southern provinces, not least because a Catholic hierarchy had disappeared in the north when Calvinists captured the leadership of the Dutch Revolt at the end of the sixteenth century. Until very late, only weak administrative links and at most tenuous integrationist contacts on the level of a narrow political élite linked Brabant and Limburg between 1650 and 1850 with the remainder of the Netherlands. These circumstances would seem to make Brabant and Limburg natural candidates for secessionist stirrings. Why then did these not materialize?

The explanation probably lies in differences in the timing of political mobilization. Brabant and Limburg remained for long the least developed, most traditional part of the Netherlands. Northern Catholics, on the other hand – living as distinct minority groups in a part of the country which modernized earliest – developed a more definite political consciousness than their southern brethren. Sensitive to the massive Protestantism which surrounded them, these Catholic minorities demanded a return of the Roman Catholic hierarchy, so as to secure their identity with a definite organizational base. The resurrection of the Catholic hierarchy in 1853 – and later joint political action for other Catholic interests – strengthened organizational links between Catholics of all parts of the country. The fight on behalf of separate Catholic interests simultaneously promoted the integration of Brabant and Limburg in the Dutch nation.

In both the Netherlands and in Switzerland, then, religion was an important cleavage line. But the much greater political centralization of the Dutch State made religion less a regional than a national source of political conflict. Much more so than in Switzerland, regional factors were subordinated to national partisan alignments. If in Switzerland religion was one factor in a highly diversified society, in the Netherlands the contest between Calvinists, Catholics and more secular elements of the society became of overriding importance; in this process a strongly integrated, but religiously segmented political community developed.

One can make this statement more general. Partly due to the much greater role of regional factors, Swiss political culture is more highly fragmented[28] than Dutch political culture. Factors of class, religion, language and regionalism intersect one another at numerous points. None of these factors has assumed dominant importance, and in many cases the potential for politicization of any one cleavage line has been minimized by rival claims of other possible divisions. Swiss politics, too, might be dubbed "the politics of accommodation."[29] But accommodationist practices are diffused among many more sites and arenas than in the Netherlands, where religion (and to a lesser extent class) came to subordinate other potential cleavages as the basis on which political organizations were formed and political decisions taken.

CONSOCIATIONAL DEMOCRACY AND DUTCH AND SWISS
EXPERIENCE
In this final section, we shall raise, on the basis of Swiss and Dutch experience, some more general theoretical questions. These are important if one seeks to generalize from the experiences of these two countries to wider issues of possible models of nation-building. Two issues deserve special attention: (a) to what extent is "consociationalism" a matter of free choice for political élite groups?; and (b) is the model of "consociationalism" restricted to nations of smaller size?

Consociationalism as Free Choice? In the argument of Arend Lijphart[30] consociational democracy should be seen above all as a

---

[28] See especially the theoretical study on Switzerland by Jürg Steiner, *op. cit.*

[29] This is the well-chosen title of Arend Lijphart's important study, *The Politics of Accommodation: Pluralism and Democracy in the Netherlands* (Berkeley, 1968).

[30] The following quotes are all from Arend Lijphart, "Consociational Democracy," *World Politics,* Vol. 21 (1960), p. 212ff. [see above, pp. 75-79].

result of "*deliberate efforts to counteract the immobilizing and unstabilizing effects of cultural fragmentation*," undertaken by leaders of rival subcultures; Lijphart defines "consociational democracy" as "government by élite cartel designed to turn a democracy with a fragmented political culture into a stable democracy." Implicit in this reasoning is the statement that certain political societies develop such sharp cleavages, that only the "deliberate joint effort by the élites [can] stabilize the system."

Lijphart's argument is directed against the writings of a generation of scholars who have ascribed the stability of political systems to a combination of a homogeneous political culture and a group structure in which "cross-cutting cleavages" make for overlapping memberships and hence for political moderation. He attributes a vital importance to the stance of political élites who may turn the expected dangers of a fragmented political culture into a "self-denying prophecy," by counteracting the divisive effects through conscious policies of accommodation. He mentions certain conditions which should be fulfilled for a successful consociational democracy: "(1) . . . that the élites have the ability to accommodate the divergent interests and demands of the subcultures; (2) . . . that they have the ability to transcend cleavages and to join in a common effort with the élites of rival subcultures; (3) [that they have] a commitment to the maintenance of the system and to the improvement of its cohesion and stability; (4) finally . . . that the élites understand the perils of political fragmentation."

These are demanding conditions; but they remain largely on the level of free choice on the part of strategic elite groups. The major theme of the earlier part of this article has been that, in the Netherlands and Switzerland, traditions of pluralism and political accommodation long preceded the processes of political modernization. Against Lijphart's views of consociational democracy as the outcome of a desire on the part of élites to counteract the potential threat of political divisions, one might put the reverse thesis: earlier consociational practices facilitated the peaceful transition towards newer forms of pluralist political organization in these two countries. Consociationalism, in this view, is not a response to the perils of subcultural splits, but the prior reason why subcultural divisions never did become perilous.

Whereas our analysis starts from a developmental perspective of centuries, Lijphart gives a critical analysis of certain general sociological models that have a somewhat static character. In doing so, Lijphart remains, to some extent, hostage to some of the mechanistic fallacies which underlie the literature on political cleavages. This body of literature often assumes, without adequate political analysis, that social divisions automatically translate themselves into political conflicts. Hence the search for cross-cutting cleavages, to dampen the explosive potential of polarized cleavage lines. Hence also Lijphart's quest for counteracting forces on the élite level when he finds societies in which cross-cutting cleavages seem replaced by mutually reinforcing dividing lines. Both views tend to neglect the important question of what forces make for the politicization, or non-politicization of dividing lines. Under general terms like "subcultural splits," "segmentation," "fragmentation," "cleavages," all manner of social divisions are regarded as loaded with potential political content. Rarely are different cleavage lines distinguished according to their potential for politicization. Too little attention is paid to the issue of whether earlier politicization of one cleavage line may prevent the exploitation of other possible cleavages. Élite cultures are regarded too much as a dependent variable only: Lijphart's élites act to counteract the perils of "objective" cleavages. In our view, on the other hand, the élite culture is in itself a most important independent variable which may go far to determine how cleavages are handled in a political society, to what extent they become loaded with political tension, and to what degree subcultural divisions are solved in a spirit of tolerance and accommodation, or by violence and repression.

The importance of these theoretical matters for the comparative study of nation-building processes should be obvious. The view of élite culture as an important independent variable forces one to take a long developmental perspective. Differences between existing nation-States are seen to be to a considerable extent the product of earlier forms of State formation.[31] Similarly, the future of nation-building efforts in the new States becomes highly dependent on prior élite experiences. Prevailing ideological outlooks in the new States are not favourable for consociationalist choices. Older pluralist traditions in the new States are strong. But they are regarded generally by present-day political élites as obstacles which should be cleared away, rather than as building-stones from which a new, pluralist nation might be constructed. Later developments will depend to a very large extent on choices now taken. The importance of stressing the various alternative roads to modern Statehood, including the consociational one, lies in the need to destroy the widespread assumption that *Blut und Eisen* is the "normal" path to nation-building.[32]

Consociationalism – A Luxury of Small Nations? Both the Netherlands and Switzerland are smaller nations. It has often been argued

[31] See the article mentioned in note 8 above.
[32] See Hans Daalder, "Government and Opposition in the New States," *Government and Opposition*, Vol. 1, (1966), pp. 205-26.

that their specific political experiences are related to that fact. A standard argument holds that smaller nations can practise a certain pattern of political life that larger States could not endure, exactly because these latter States cannot escape the international responsibilities which their size forces on them.[33] According to this theory, larger States carry a greater political load. They must have certain institutions which allow them to act with sufficient decisiveness. Considerations of defence necessitate a larger army which in turn requires a strong bureaucracy. The need to act rules out the cumbersome accommodationist styles of Swiss or Dutch politics; for that reason electoral systems like proportional representation or accommodationist coalition systems on the level of the Cabinet or chief executive are impracticable. In the particular case of Switzerland (or the Netherlands before 1940), their stance was moreover facilitated by the fact that the surrounding powers liked to see neutral States in charge of strategic locations. Even if this implied neutrality by imposition, it gave these countries a licence for internal tolerance and cumbersome pluralism that larger nations could not afford.[34]

It is not easy to assess the justification of this body of reasoning. Undoubtedly, countries like Switzerland and the Netherlands fared better in international politics than many of the larger States, and to the extent to which small size assisted this development, it helped them to maintain the accommodationist practices of older times. But should one grant the argument that larger States must carry the burden of international politics as distinct from actually carrying, let alone preferring to carry it? Did not the once-subject inhabitants of Tessin consciously prefer in 1798 to join the archaic Swiss Republic rather than an incipient national State in Italy, because they preferred internal freedoms to foreign grandeur? Did not in the early nineteenth century many *Kleinstaatler* in Germany foresee the dangers which the development of a large new German State might spell both for internal freedoms and external aggressiveness?

The statement that smaller States carry in fact a smaller load in international politics remains debatable. Handling a foreign environment – and the impact of foreign influences within their boundaries – pose large problems for small States. Not the least of these is survival itself. If both the Netherlands and Switzerland

---

[33] These views are particularly evident in the writings of Ferdinand Hermens, Carl J. Friedrich and Barrington Moore. See on this same point Lijphart, "Consociational Democracy," p. 217; Lehmbruch, *Proporzdemokratie, passim,* and Rokkan, *op. cit.,* pp. 88ff.

[34] In a similar vein, the greater freedom characteristic of the United Kingdom and the United States is often explained by their ability to avoid entanglements in large-scale land wars.

belonged to the surviving States of Europe, this may possibly be due in some measure to their ability not only to handle internal diversity, but also foreign-imposed loads.

PART III
APPLICATIONS AND ILLUSTRATIONS:
EUROPE

The material in this section has been chosen to illustrate the working of the social and political systems of the four "classic" examples of consociational democracy in Western Europe, namely the Netherlands, Austria, Belgium, and Switzerland. Most of these selections were written prior to the theoretical articles in Part II, and this is an advantage in the sense that they are substantially independent of the explicit consociational model. Yet the selection has been made so as to illustrate more comprehensively the broad themes already developed above, that is, the implications of segmented social structure, political accommodation at elite level, and the cultural context in which such patterns occur.

For the Netherlands, J. P. Kruijt's article "The Influence of Denominationalism on Social Life and Organizational Patterns" (1959) is one of the earliest statements in English to call attention to cumulative religious-ideological segmentation as a phenomenon deserving sociological study. While Kruijt poses the question in general terms the bulk of his brief paper gives an overview of the structure and dynamics of verzuiling in the Netherlands. The passage by Arend Lijphart, on the other hand, is concerned with the context of conflict resolution at elite level. In this chapter drawn from The Politics of Accommodation *(1968) he describes certain informal but well understood norms of parliamentary behavior that have enabled members of coalition ministries in the Netherlands to reach agreement on issues that find their respective parties sharply opposed to one another.*

For Austria, Alfred Diamant's pages on the three Lager *are drawn from his* Austrian Catholics and the First Republic *(1960), a full-length study of Catholic political thought and action between the two World Wars. Even though his topic is the First Austrian Republic, he is describing a pattern of classically segmented social structure that re-emerged with little change in the Second Republic despite the upheavals of Austrian annexation to Germany and the Second World War. Peter Pulzer's article, "The Legitimizing Role of Political Parties" (1969), is concerned with the party system and its long-term evolution from the Habsburg Empire to the present. In particular, his theme is the successful legitimization in the Second Republic of a previously strife-ridden party structure and faltering democratic process in spite of formidable obstacles and a relatively unchanging social and electoral base. While elements of consociationalism are not specifically emphasized in this broad study, the central role of coalition politics in the changed political climate of the Second Republic emerges clearly.*

Val Lorwin's paper "Conflict and Compromise in Belgian Pol-

itics" was presented to the Annual Meeting of the American Political Science Association in 1965. Although some aspects of it have been developed in his later work, it has not been published previously in its original form. In this paper Lorwin touches on three major themes of Belgian politics and society. First, he describes the organization and development of segmented social structures in terms of the three traditional familles spirituelles and the system of political parties that resulted from this segmentation around the twin issues of confessionality and social class. Secondly, he shows how the three major political parties developed a practice of coalition ministries based on a politics of continuous accommodation and adjustment among the coalition partners. Finally he examines in some detail the impact on this system of a major and persistent issue that crosscuts the traditional alignments of religious-ideological verzuiling, the increasingly sensitive linguistic-cultural cleavage between Dutch-speaking and French-speaking Belgians.

Roger Girod's "Geography of the Swiss Party System" (1964) deals with the structure of parties in the Swiss political system and particularly with interparty cooperation at executive level. While Girod is particularly concerned to identify variations in the system by region and level of government, the non-Swiss observer may be more impressed by the similarities of executive composition and behavior among regions of widely different social structure and political representation. This is especially noticeable concerning the norms of interparty representation and cooperation on executive councils at all three levels of government. The politics of interparty "compromise on a permanent basis" has spread even to cantons and communes where a single party dominates the legislature. Girod makes it clear that the multi-party executive is a relatively recent development in Switzerland, but it is now sufficiently widespread to be considered an integral part of the political culture.

THE NETHERLANDS: THE INFLUENCE OF DENOMINATIONALISM ON SOCIAL LIFE AND ORGANIZATIONAL PATTERNS

J. P. Kruijt

Source: J. P. Kruijt, "The Influence of Denominationalism on Social Life and Organizational Patterns," *Archives de Sociologie des Religions* (Paris: Editions du C.N.R.S.), Vol. 4, no. 8 (1959), 105-111. Reprinted by permission of the Centre National de la Recherche Scientifique and the author.

In the Western world there are many nations with two or more Christian denominations, for example the Catholic Church and some Protestant denominations (Germany, Switzerland, England, Scotland, U.S.A., the Netherlands, etc.). A variation, as in the case of France, Italy, or Belgium, is that of a majority of Roman Catholics, only a small percentage of Protestants, but with a great number of persons who are only nominal Catholics and in fact religiously indifferent or even antagonistic to the Roman Catholic Church. In both categories we find varying degrees of religious tension: between Roman Catholics and Protestants, between more orthodox and more modernistic Protestants, between High Church and non-conformists, between churches and sects, between Christians and non-Christians.

Now the *general* problem I address, and which I shall illuminate for my own country, the Netherlands, is this: what are the influences of those *religious* tensions on all the other areas of social life, especially on the cooperation or non-cooperation of individuals and groups of different denominations in economic, social, political, educational, cultural, scientific, and artistic organizations or activities, in family life, cliques, neighbourhood or clubs, in schools, factories, offices and the army, etc.?

Theoretically there are two extreme possibilities:

1) *no* correlation between church membership (or non-membership) and the selection, in terms of religion, of persons and groups with which one is participating or cooperating in all the other above-mentioned activities and organizations. This would mean that each organization, if large enough, is a representative sample of the whole population, or of that part of the population which may be expected to perform the particular activities of that organization or to be interested in it.

2) a *complete* correlation, which would mean that all activities are performed by (or all organizations have a membership consisting of) persons with the same denomination or belonging to the same group of congenial denominations, having the same or related religious (or non-religious) philosophies or ideologies.

These two *extreme* possibilities have never been realized in our modern Western world, and will probably never be realized, at least not on a national level. We might call them two extreme ideal types. However, between those two extremes lies the possibility of – and in fact exists – a whole scale of descending or ascending degrees of correlations as stated above. Some countries in the Western world have a situation not far from the first ideal type, others are not far from the second, and the remaining countries lie more or less midway between.

It is not my intention to give a detailed international comparison, however important this may be. Let me only give some examples. In my opinion, the Anglo-Saxon and Scandinavian countries are not far from the first ideal type, that is, with some but not many correlations, though in recent times some authors have seen several symptoms that in the United States the distance from that point of comparison is increasing.[1] On the other hand my own country, the Netherlands, lies rather close to the second ideal type, or at least at the shortest distance from this point as compared with other Western countries, with perhaps Belgium coming next after the Netherlands.

I think this is a very important theological, ecclesiastical and political problem. Here we are especially interested in the sociological aspects. Now, in giving my survey of the Dutch situation, I hope to stimulate similar sketches of the situation in other countries in this respect and perhaps, to animate other sociologists (and theologians!) to do the same. Only then will it be possible to give a more exact comparison and – what is still more important – to try to find a socio-historical explanation of why the Western countries differ so much in this respect.

First, some remarks about our terminology. What is the best name for this phenomenon in its different degrees? The situation not far from the second ideal type might be typified as *religious-ideological segregation*: there is a preference for participating in all activities with persons of the same ideology, there is isolation from and discrimination of other persons and groups. The consequence is the development within the same nation of two or more complex sets of organizations and activities, two or more competing blocs, each based on and bound together by a particular philosophy.

It is no accident that the only language which has a name for

[1] David O. Moberg (Bethel College, St. Paul, Minnesota), "Religion and society in the Netherlands and in America," unpublished paper, 1959 [later published in *American Quarterly*, 13 (1961), 172–178, and reprinted in *Social Compass*, 9 (1962), 11–19 – ed.]; Will Herberg, *Protestant, Catholic, Jew* (New York, 1955).

such a bloc is the Dutch language. In our country we call such a bloc a *zuil*. German friends will understand the word: *eine Säule*, that is, a pillar, a column (in French: *un pilier*, *une colonne*).The word pillar is a rather apt metaphor. A pillar or column is a thing apart, resting on its own base (in our case a particular religious or non-religious faith) separated from other pillars, which are units similar to the first; they are standing upright, perpendicular sets of persons and groups separated from other sets. Perpendicular means that each pillar is cutting vertically the horizontal socio-economic strata which we call social classes. For a pillar is not a social class; it contains persons out of every social class or stratification. We might say that the "horizontal functional integration" is crossed by the "vertical ideological integration." Further, a pillar is solid; the ideological pillars of the Dutch nation are indeed strong super-organizations, and the Roman Catholic pillar is the strongest, the most solid of all.

Finally, all the pillars together generally serve as a support to something resting on the top; in our case, that something is the whole Dutch nation. At least, that is what is signified by this word pillar. However, whether the whole Dutch nation is stronger through this "pillarization"[2] than if it were sustained by one mighty pillar remains a problem which has to be resolved not by an architect, but by sociologists, psychologists, historians, political scientists and theologians. For those religious-ideological pillars are also pressure groups, and while pressure groups may be a necessity in a modern pluralistic democratic society, as such they may be more dysfunctional than eufunctional for the whole nation. We can now understand why Fogarty[3] uses the term "vertical pluralism" for this Dutch phenomenon. But we know that the presence of several ethnic groups besides the Yankees in the American population is also a form of vertical pluralism and therefore I make the term more specific by speaking of "vertical ideological pluralism."

And now we must give a more detailed and concrete sketch of the Dutch situation. Several authors say that the roots go back to the Reformation. Indeed, since that time we have had (somewhat simplified) two religious blocs: the Calvinist "Reformed Church," a State Church, at least sustained and privileged by the State, and a rather numerous minority of barely tolerated Roman Catholics. From the beginning the Protestant world had two wings, one more liberal-minded and undogmatic, the other the more aggres-

---

[2] This word is from David Moberg (see note 1). A French word might be *colonnisation* (with two *n*'s!).

[3] Michael P. Fogarty, *Christian Democracy in Western Europe, 1820-1953* (London, 1957).

sive dogmatic Calvinists and among them many diehards. At the beginning of the 17th century came a schism; the less dogmatic ministers were driven out of the State Church and formed a new nonconformist church, still existing, the "Remonstrants." The 19th century brought a new separation; the most orthodox members of the Dutch Reformed Church – no longer a State Church but still the "national church" – resigned their membership and formed new groups which later on were for the greater part united by the famous Dr. Abraham Kuyper in a new and very active Neo-Calvinist Free Church, "the Reformed Churches." So the former State Church lost many active members on its right wing, modernistic-minded members on its left wing, and moreover, since the last decades of the 19th century, hundreds of thousands of people who gradually went over to the unorganized army of people without any church. In the meantime the Roman Catholic Church restored its hierarchy and began to grow in influence, and in our century also in membership through a higher birthrate. The result was that, according to the census of 1947,[4] the Roman Catholic Church was, with more than 38 per cent of the population, the largest church, the Dutch Reformed Church was still the largest Protestant Church but had only 31 per cent of the population, the Neo-Calvinist Free Church had, together with some smaller related groups, about 10 per cent, a great number of smaller churches and sects about 4 per cent, while 17 per cent of the population had no religious membership at all.

We know that the religious situation in the United States is about the same, although with different percentages: a strong and growing minority of Roman Catholics, many Protestant Churches and sects with a whole scale of theologies from fundamentalism to modernism, and a numerous group of unchurched. Hence it will be clear that this kind of frequency distribution cannot by itself explain the high degree of pillarization of the Dutch people. Without attempting a total explanation I shall mention here some significant points:

1)   The adherents of the Neo-Calvinist movement were in general "little people" with a low social status. Among the Roman Catholics were some well-do-do families, but the majority also had a low status. Both groups were second-class citizens and their religious struggle was also a struggle for emancipation, which gave a strong stimulus for very close cooperation with people of the same creed.

---

[4] [By the 1971 census the religious distribution was as follows: Roman Catholics, 39.5 per cent; Dutch Reformed, 23 per cent; Neo-Calvinists and related groups, 10 per cent; other smaller churches and sects, 5 per cent; no religious membership, 22.5 per cent.]

2) In the first half of the 19th century our country had a public school system. The Roman Catholics as well as a part of the orthodox Protestants wanted to have their own religious schools, Catholic schools or "schools with the Bible" respectively. On the side of the Neo-Calvinists this was promoted by Abraham Kuyper's theological doctrine of the so-called "sphere sovereignty": family, state, church, school, and society each ought to have a certain autonomy, however all dominated by God's sovereignty. The Roman Catholic principle of subsidiarity goes, *mutatis mutandis*, in a similar direction. Therefore the controversy between the adherents of the public school and those of the religious school became, in the second half of the 19th century, one of the principal and very emotional topics of Dutch political life.

3) To get more possibilities for their religious schools, the Neo-Calvinists and the Roman Catholics each founded a political party, the Anti-Revolutionary party and the Roman Catholic party. From 1888 till 1938 Protestant and Roman Catholic political parties cooperated in a so-called "Christian" coalition and in most elections won a majority varying between 51 and 55 per cent of the votes. For most of these 50 years this "Christian coalition" had the political power in the national government; the "Christian" or "right" parties were in government, the "left" or "non-Christian" parties in the opposition.

4) Especially in the view of the Neo-Calvinists, this was *the* principal line of separation: the antithesis between the "Christians" (i.e., adherents of these "Christian" political parties) at the right, and the "paganists," pagans, non-Christians, at the left. As a matter of fact there were and are, among voters and representatives of the left, many Christians, most modernists, and increasingly after the Second World War many orthodox Protestants and even some Roman Catholics. This means that the antithetical separation between right and left never coincided with the religious dividing line between Christians and non-Christians, and in recent times even less than before 1940.

5) The emotional school struggle came to an end with a kind of armistice, the Pacification of 1917. This provided a way out which is really unique in the Western world: a total financial equality between public education and free (that is, mostly religious) education, since 1920 for the primary schools, and gradually in later years also for the secondary and higher schools, even for all kinds of technical schools! About 62 per cent of the parents are now sending their children to the religious primary school and only 38 per cent to the public primary school. In the elections of 1959, 52 per cent voted for the Roman Catholic

Party and the four Protestant parties. That means that the degree of "pillarization" for the primary school is higher than that for the political parties.

6) I called this pacification an "armistice." In fact it was not a real peace. The great purpose for the parties of the right was equalization for their religious schools. They had attained this result in 1917 and we might expect a reduction of the tension between right and left after 1917. However, even during the emotional school struggle before 1917, and with the background of belief in a total antithesis between right and left, the adherents of the right had already turned to other controversial topics and they continued this work after 1917. The result is that nowadays the number of "confessional" (either Roman Catholic or orthodox Protestant) organizations, clubs, foundations, societies, unions, institutes, etc. is multitudinous.

I shall now try to give you an idea of the extent of the Dutch pillarization. The two groups have not only their own schools, their own political parties, their own press, but also in general:

- their own trade unions, farmers' unions, employers' unions, shopkeepers' unions, co-operatives, agricultural loan banks;
- their own institutes for social research and societies for physicians, for lawyers, for teachers, for social workers, for scientists, for employees, for artists, for musicians, for authors;
- their own music bands, choral societies, sport clubs, theatre clubs, travellers' clubs, dance clubs, clubs for adult education, "public" libraries, broadcasting;
- their own youth organizations, women's clubs, student clubs, fraternities, and sororities;
- their own hospitals, sanatoriums, organizations for all kinds of social work and charitable work, etc.

I stop without even trying to be complete. In addition I have to mention that the frequency of religiously mixed marriages is rather low: 10 per cent for the Roman Catholics, 25 per cent for the Neo-Calvinists. And finally, in selecting employees (especially for smaller enterprises) or in choosing a dealer, many people have a preference for persons of their own pillar.

So, from all those thousands of organizations, clubs, etc. there are, for each activity, at least *three* associations: one Roman Catholic organization; one Protestant organization (sometimes more than one: an orthodox and a modernist Protestant organization, or a Neo-Calvinist organization and one for members of the Dutch Reformed Church); and then, of course, one "general" organization, that is, an organization which admits members irrespective of their creed, but which in fact has only members who oppose the principle of total antithesis. Usually they are called neutral organizations, and in that sense they form together a third pillar, the neutral pillar. But these organizations themselves say that they do not want to form a pillar, they are general, they are open to all people. We may distinguish three kinds of such "general" organizations:

a) those which have a majority of unchurched people and are in fact not neutral, e.g., they arrange meetings on Sunday morning;

b) those which strive for a passive, negative neutrality, that is, they try to avoid all things which may offend religious feelings;

c) those which strive for a positive attitude towards the religious pluralism, that is, they not only recognize the diversity of creeds of their members, but also stimulate them to work in the organization and for the common purpose of that organization on the foundation of their own creed, and try therefore to formulate the principles of the organization in accordance with that religious pluralism.

Whereas before the Second World War the first two types were dominant, after that war the third has been winning ground. This opens the possibility for a future de-pillarization.

Meanwhile the whole structure is still strongly pillarized. This is promoted by government subsidies, just the same as in the case of the school system. Every time that an activity (social work, adult education, sport, libraries, youth work, etc.) is subsidized, the money is "honestly," that is, proportionally, divided: so much for the Roman Catholics, so much for the orthodox Protestants, and so much for the third pillar, the general or "neutral" organizations.

If this system were complete, and wholly closed, there would be three totally closed sub-cultures, sub-nations in the Netherlands. Therefore I must stress the fact that the system is not complete, not wholly closed, that it is very complex and in continuous movement. The system has developed in a highly urbanized and industrialized society. Therefore some villages, only recently taken up in modern traffic, still have some traits of what a Dutch sociologist called the "folk oecumene," that is, the territorial ties with neighbours are stronger than the religious differences. But even there the pillar integration grows to the same degree that the territorial ties become looser. This explains why, during the last century, the whole pillar system became stronger and stronger. It was a kind of counter-offensive of some churches to protect their members against the secularizing effects of modern society; it increased the social control of church members by promoting group exclusiveness, exclusiveness of the religious ingroup.

On the other hand it seems that the whole system, although structurally very strong, has already reached or passed its culminating point. It still performs favourable functions for the Roman Catholic and Neo-Calvinist churches in terms of enculturation, but for the whole nation it works rather dysfunctionally. In general people belonging to different pillars do not really meet, and that means they do not really know each other. This is a situation in which very peculiar stereotypes about the persons in the other pillars may develop and spread. And even for the churches themselves the system may be dysfunctional. The material interests of a pillar may be identified with the spiritual interests of the church. The Roman Catholic Church in particular, and the Neo-Calvinist Church too, are accustomed, more than in other democratic countries, not only to give advice on some worldly affairs (elections, membership of trade-unions), but even to impose sanctions in this respect. The most recent example is a Letter from the Roman Catholic Bishops in 1954, in which they declared: "We maintain the rule that the Holy Sacraments must be refused – and, in case of death without conversion, the ecclesiastical funeral also – to any Catholic who is known to be a member of a Socialist association, or who, without being a member, still regularly attends Socialist meetings, or is a regular reader of Socialist periodicals or papers." And this has been written in a country in which the Socialist Party shows perhaps the greatest distance of any in Europe from former Marxian attitudes towards religion and church. Membership in the Socialist Party itself was strongly discouraged by the Roman Catholic Church, which however did not formally ban it. A few hundred Roman Catholics, mostly intellectuals, were members of this Party and remained in it after the publication of the Letter. The public reaction was exceptionally strong. It was a declaration of war from the Roman Catholic Church against the idea of breaking through the antithetical lines of demarcation set up by the Neo-Calvinists and their Catholic allies. The principal vehicles of this "break-through" idea are, on the theological and ecclesiastical side, the "Dutch Reformed Church," the former State Church, whose members are partly influenced by the doctrine of Karl Barth, and, on the political side, the already mentioned socialist Labour Party. It is symptomatic that the Dutch Reformed Church published a Protestant Pastoral Letter in which this pressure on the consciences of the Episcopal Letter is rejected, but that the Anti-Revolutionary

Party, the most militant Protestant political party, heartily agreed with it. However, there are also other opinions among the Neo-Calvinists; Dr. Schippers, Professor at the Neo-Calvinist "Free University" in Amsterdam, declared that "the way in which the Bishops direct the consciences of their church members is not acceptable to Christians of the Reformation".

It is clear that the Dutch nation is now in a period of heavy crisis in this respect. This period may last several years. The struggle goes on. In my opinion it is not probable that it will end in a complete pillarization. More probable is a gradual depillarization, especially in those fields which are most remote from the essence of religion (sport, recreation, economic life). But we know that Roman Catholic ideas about the separation between Church and State, and between Church and public life, are different from those of Churches of the Reformation. And we have seen that in several aspects the Neo-Calvinists in the Netherlands came very near to Roman Catholic ideas. It is also symptomatic that these Neo-Calvinistic Churches are not members of the World Council of Churches. The result of the struggle will be very important for the Dutch nation – but also very interesting for other Western countries which have hitherto had a smaller degree of pillarization and which may learn from the Dutch example.

THE NETHERLANDS: THE RULES OF THE GAME

Arend Lijphart

Source: A. Lijphart, *The Politics of Accommodation: Pluralism and Democracy in the Netherlands* (Berkeley and Los Angeles, 1968), Chapter 7, "The Rules of the Game," 122-138. Originally published by the University of California Press; reprinted by permission of The Regents of the University of California and the author.

The politics of accommodation places heavy burdens on the political leaders. Successful policymaking and settlement of divisive issues under the adverse conditions of a minimally consensual milieu requires a clear recognition of the perennial disintegrative tendencies in the system and the capability to take either preventive or remedial action. In the Netherlands, the process of accommodation is greatly facilitated by the existence of a number of rules that govern the "game" of accommodation. These rules are not part of a comprehensive national consensus; they apply mainly to the political elite. Or, to follow the terminology of political culture analysis, the rules of the game are a part of the "role culture" developed by and instilled in the elite, and not of the mass culture.[1] Furthermore, they consist of a mixture of procedural rules and general orientations toward politics, and do not have much substantive content. It must be emphasized that the seven rules specified below are unwritten, informal, and implicit. No convenient book of rules exists; they have to be inferred from the actions of the leaders especially under conditions of political tension.[2]

RULE I: THE BUSINESS OF POLITICS

The first and foremost rule of the Dutch political game is that politics should not be regarded as a game at all. It is, to borrow von Clausewitz's phrase, "a serious means to a serious end." Or, to put it even more succinctly, it is a business. This attitude is in accord with Holland's long tradition as a merchant nation and with the crucial political role the merchant middle classes have played in Dutch history. This attitude toward politics has a

---

[1] See Gabriel A. Almond and Sidney Verba, *The Civic Culture: Political Attitudes and Democracy in Five Nations* (Princeton: Princeton University Press, 1963), pp. 29-31. These rules of the game differ in the same way from what Truman calls the "rules of the game" (i.e. the "general ideological consensus"); see Arend Lijphart, *The Politics of Accommodation*, pp. 13-14.

[2] Hans Daalder has done the most significant pioneering work in calling attention to these rules. See especially his *Leiding en lijdelijkheid in de Nederlandse politiek* (Assen: Van Gorcum, 1964).

pervasive and highly beneficial influence on democratic stability. Hans Daalder calls it the "businesslike determination that the job should not be allowed to suffer"; and Alan D. Robinson refers to the "attitude that doctrinal disputes should not stand in the way of getting the work done."[3] The political elite is oriented toward results. In this respect, Dutch politics is sharply different from what Nathan Leites has called the "game of politics in France" with its tactics of delay, equivocation, and avoidance of responsibility, regardless of the consequences for the nation.[4]

Without this result-oriented attitude, Dutch politics would look quite different. Neither the great political settlement of 1917 nor the continuing pattern of accommodation since then would have been possible without it. It is the axiom underlying all other "rules of the political business."

RULE II: THE AGREEMENT TO DISAGREE

Probably the second most important rule that governs the Dutch political business is the pragmatic acceptance of the ideological differences as basic realities which cannot and should not be changed. The fundamental convictions of other blocs must be tolerated if not respected. Disagreements must not be allowed to turn into either mutual contempt or proselytizing zeal.

In the policy-making process, a pure and consistent application of this rule would lead to paralysis. Decisions on controversial matters have to be made, and continuous inaction would have disastrous consequences. In its pure form, therefore, the rule is only applied to questions not requiring immediate answers. An excellent illustration is the cabinet crisis of 1951. The four-party coalition cabinet, based on all major parties except the Anti-Revolutionaries, fell apart on the highly emotional issue of colonial policy. In the negotiations to end the crisis, it was clear that the realities of both the international situation and the domestic constellation of opinion would not permit any major change of policy. The four parties were thus able to mend their differences by simply agreeing to disagree on the colonial question because it had no direct policy consequences. The new cabinet was a virtual carbon copy of its predecessor, and could be formed only because of the conviction that the widely divergent and deeply felt dis-

---

[3] H. Daalder, "Parties and Politics in the Netherlands," *Political Studies,* Vol. 3, No. 1 (February 1955), p. 16; Alan D. Robinson, *Dutch Organised Agriculture in International Politics* (The Hague, Nijhoff, 1961), p. 37. See also Daalder, "Politiek in Nederlands kader," in *Mensen en machten* (Utrecht: Spectrum, 1965), pp. 117-118.

[4] Nathan Leites, *On the Game of Politics in France* (Stanford: Stanford University Press, 1959), passim.

agreements over colonial policy should not stand in the way of fruitful cooperation on more pressing questions. This policy, or rather nonpolicy, was appropriately referred to as the "icebox policy."[5] Here the agreement to disagree allowed a vexatious issue to be temporarily frozen.

Such perfect conditions for the pure and simple application of the agreement-to-disagree rule are rare, of course. Most issues do require some kind of substantive decision. An attempt is then made to involve all blocs in finding a fair compromise. Or, if a compromise acceptable to all blocs cannot be reached because of ideological opposition by one or more blocs, the other groups will go to great lengths in trying to avoid antagonizing their opponents. Decisions are not made by a majority simply outvoting a minority. For instance, when a cabinet proposal to institute a football pool was debated in parliament in 1960 and again in 1964, the Calvinists, and especially the orthodox Anti-Revolutionary party, were fundamentally opposed on religious grounds – not allowing any pragmatic compromise. On the other hand, a large majority were in favor and had the votes to pass the bill over Calvinist opposition. But this was not done. The majority parties made a number of concessions – like limiting the amount an individual could wager and instituting a relatively low maximum for the highest prize to be won – not so much in order to fashion a majority to pass the bill, but mainly to placate the minority. This also made it possible for the Anti-Revolutionaries to remain in the cabinet.

In this form, the agreement-to-disagree rule comes close to Calhoun's doctrine of concurrent majority. On issues considered vital by any bloc, no decision can be made without either their concurrence or at least substantial concessions to them. The veto power is not absolute. No single group can block action completely, but its wishes will be considered seriously and accommodated as much as possible by the others. In short, the rule is majoritarianism tempered by the spirit of concurrent majority.

RULE III: SUMMIT DIPLOMACY

The politics of accommodation entails government by the elite. The leaders of the religious-ideological blocs have the duty to make the political decisions and to work out compromises. This pattern has become increasingly more institutionalized, as was discussed in the previous chapter.[6]

[5] See Arend Lijphart, *The Trauma of Decolonization: The Dutch and West New Guinea* (New Haven: Yale University Press, 1966), pp. 164-177.

[6] *The Politics of Accommodation*, pp. 112-115.

The more serious the political question that is at stake, the higher will be the elite level at which it will be resolved. This means that the crucial issues have to be handled at the summit. The problems of state aid to religious schools and of extending the suffrage were solved by summit conferences of the top leaders of all major parties. This culminated in the peaceful settlement of 1917.[7] Summit diplomacy was resorted to again in later crises. When the Germans occupied Holland in May 1940, the cabinet went into exile and parliament disbanded. But the political leaders remaining in the Netherlands decided immediately on the necessity of close cooperation. An informal summit conference was established which consisted of twelve persons: the two highest leaders of each of the six major parties (Catholics, Social Democrats, Anti-Revolutionaries, Christian Historical Union, and the two Liberal parties in existence at that time). This important group, which eventually received the unpretentious name of "Political Council" *(Politiek Convent)*, met for the first time on July 1, 1940, and continued to be active in one form or another during the entire war period in spite of growing Nazi persecution.[8]

Another example was the group referred to in popular parlance as the "Irene Quartet." Its task was to resolve the crisis over Princess Irene's conversion and marriage in 1964. It consisted of four cabinet ministers: Prime Minister V. G. M. Marijnen, his second-in-command B. W. Biesheuvel, Minister of Internal Affairs E. H. Toxopeus, and Minister of Justice Y. Scholten. These four were chosen ostensibly on the grounds that the issue involved their special jurisdictions as ministers. But it was no accident that they also belonged to the four different parties represented in the cabinet. The only gap in this summit arrangement was the absence of a Labor party leader from the temporary supercabinet. A Laborite was not included because the party was in the opposition from 1958 to 1965, but the Irene Quartet was informally in close touch with the Labor party leadership, too.

A somewhat similar arrangement is the so-called "Seniors' Assembly" *(Seniorenconvent)* in the Second Chamber of the States-General. It is a five-man committee made up of the parliamentary chairmen of the five major parties. It has no formal

[7] *Ibid.*, pp. 109-112.

[8] W. Drees, "1940-1945: Het Politiek Convent," in P. J. Bouman, et al., eds., *150 Jaar Koninkrijk der Nederlanden* (Amsterdam: De Bussy, 1963), pp. 232-239. See also Werner Warmbrunn, *The Dutch under German Occupation: 1940-1945* (Stanford: Stanford University Press, 1963), pp. 216-218.

status, and it operates only intermittently.[9] But it assumes great political significance at times of actual or threatening crises and deadlocks in the chamber.

RULE IV: PROPORTIONALITY

The rule of proportionality is a simple procedural device capable of solving a host of troublesome problems. The most important of these is the allocation of the necessarily scarce financial resources at the government's disposal. The peaceful settlement of the schools issue in 1917 set the pattern: all schools, private as well as public, would receive government funds in proportion to the number of students enrolled. The same rule is applied in the allocation of governmental assistance to hospitals and other welfare functions. It does not solve the problem of deciding the *kinds* of projects the government should finance; for example, should more money be spent on secondary education or on hospital expansion or on land reclamation? But once this decision is made, it does solve the problem of allocation among the blocs, which is politically the most sensitive one. Hans Daalder puts it this way: "the essence of political action has shifted from strife to distribution" with the government's task limited to "the allocation of subsidies according to objective criteria."[10]

Proportionality applies to other areas as well. Network time on the state-owned radio and television stations is allocated to the bloc organizations that arrange virtually all programs, roughly in proportion to their memberships. Appointments to public office are on the basis of a rough proportionality. The almost one thousand burgomasters and the eleven provincial governors are appointed with the idea of approximate proportionality in mind. The composition of the national civil service in The Hague is patterned after the relative strengths of the blocs in the population as a whole, although the Catholics are still slightly underrepresented.[11] It is significant, however, that the Catholics invariably base their protests against this bias on the grounds of injustice defined as lack of proportionality. Such an argument is most persuasive and is bound to win eventually. In the local civil services, proportionality is also the rule. Gadourek reports the

---

[9] E. van Raalte, *Het Nederlandse Parlement* (The Hague: Staatsdruk-kerij- en Uitgeverijbedrijf, 1958), p. 155.

[10] Daalder, *Leiding en lijdelijkheid in de Nederlandse politiek*, p. 24 See also S. W. Couwenberg, "Nederland meer een corporatieve dan parlementaire democratie," *Oost-West*, Vol. 3., No. 7 (October 1964), p.228.

[11] *The Politics of Accommodation*, pp. 90-92.

formula, based on both the number of civil servants belonging to each bloc and their salaries, used by the town council in the small town of Sassenheim:

> The total amount of money for the salaries of the personnel is divided among them roughly in the same way as the electorate is divided into various political (virtually *religious*) factions. Thus, for instance, if about one half of the population is Roman Catholic, the money which is paid to the Roman Catholic clerks at the village-hall will amount to about one half of the total sum. Hirings are governed by the same rule. As there are no sudden changes in the political composition of the electorate, elections do not disturb this system.[12]

The rule of proportionality is of fundamental importance to the success of the politics of accommodation in Holland. The establishment of the accommodation pattern of politics by the peaceful settlement of 1917 was intimately related to this rule: both the suffrage and the schools questions were settled on the basis of proportionality. The rule has been faithfully adhered to ever since.

RULE V: DEPOLITICIZATION

Proportionality is one method for the neutralization of potentially divisive political disputes. But it can be applied only when there are valued items like appointments, subsidies, or broadcast hours to be distributed. A different method of neutralizing sensitive issues and justifying compromises to the rank and file, especially in postwar politics, has been the use of complicated economic arguments and the juggling of economic facts and figures incomprehensible to most people.

Another frequent tool of depoliticization is the resort to legal and constitutional principles. The handling of the crisis over Princess Irene's conversion and marriage can again serve as an example. The issue was most embarrassing: should a Catholic be allowed to ascend the Dutch throne? A positive answer would deeply offend especially the more orthodox Calvinists, and a negative answer would be an insult to the Catholics. If the issue had been limited to Irene's conversion to Catholicism, the agreement-to-disagree rule could have been followed: the government could have argued that the constitution did not bar Catholics from succession to the throne, but that Irene was not first in the

[12] I. Gadourek, *A Dutch Community: Social and Cultural Structure and Process in a Bulb-Growing Region in the Netherlands* (2nd ed., Groningen: Wolters, 1961), p. 62.

line of succession and that hence the issue was purely hypothetical. Thus the dilemma could perhaps have been avoided altogether, and at least postponed. But the question was more difficult: a definite decision on Irene's right of succession was absolutely necessary, because of the constitutional provision that royal marriages require parliamentary approval. Irene was engaged to a Spanish nobleman. Without parliamentary approval, she and her descendants would be excluded from the right of succession.

Coincidentally, Irene's fiancé was involved in Spanish politics. The possibility of a future prince consort being embroiled in politics, and even more seriously, in the politics of a foreign country, definitely conflicted with an important unwritten rule in the Dutch constitution: the monarch and the royal family must stay out of politics. This was the main argument on which the cabinet based its decision not to propose parliamentary consent to the marriage. Thus the most troublesome issue – which concerned the monarch's religion and which was therefore a potential strain on interbloc peaceful coexistence – could be avoided. If a decision on a Catholic princess' right to become the Dutch queen would have been inescapable, the government and parliament would undoubtedly have supported this right – the Catholic, Socialist, and Liberal leaders whole-heartedly, and the leaders of the two main Protestant parties perhaps more reluctantly. But such a decision was not necessary, because the issue could be formulated in less embarrassing and, therefore, politically more acceptable terms. It was deliberately neutralized by the skillful resort to a generally approved constitutional principle.

RULE VI: SECRECY

Successful accommodation by the bloc leaders requires a high degree of flexibility. They have to be able to make concessions and to arrive at pragmatic compromises even when religious or ideological values are at stake. The process of accommodation must, therefore, be shielded from publicity. The leaders' moves in negotiations among the blocs must be carefully insulated from the knowledge of the rank and file. Because an "information gap" is desirable, secrecy is a most important rule. In this respect, the politics of accommodation again resembles international politics. Woodrow Wilson's prescriptions of "open covenants of peace, openly arrived at" and a "diplomacy [which] shall proceed always frankly and in the public view"[13] are obstacles to compromises between ideologically opposed rivals in the international as well as in domestic systems. In Holland, covenants are usually, though

[13] Albert Bushnell Hart, ed., *Selected Addresses and Public Papers of Woodrow Wilson* (New York: Boni and Liveright, 1918), p. 248.

not always, open, but covenants openly arrived at are rare indeed.

Democracy would suffocate under complete secrecy, of course. The principal public forum for the discussion and disclosure of political facts and issues is the States-General, and particularly the Second Chamber. Here the parties confront each other and the cabinet in the presence of the parliamentary reporters of the major newspapers and those citizens who are lucky enough to gain access to the two short rows of seats – a symbolically significant limitation! – of the public gallery.[14] Parliamentary approval represents no more than the final stage of the accommodation process. Until recently, all meetings of parliamentary committees were closed to the public. What is held up for public view on the floor of the chambers is the result of the interbloc negotiations which now merely requires ratification. Covenants that were worked out in secret, now become open. Daalder characterizes parliamentary debates as "more elaborate than informative ... because policy has already been determined in another place and because a compromise itself looks much better in half-lights than in the glare of a real parliamentary search-light."[15] Clashes between the chamber and the cabinet do occur, of course; amendments are introduced and often passed; and adverse votes can topple cabinets. But the leaders usually do their utmost to avoid it, and to safeguard at least the essence of the *fait accompli*. And when the parliamentary battle gets out of control, they often resort to the device of suspending the public debate and retiring to the proverbial "smoke-filled rooms."

Parliament does have considerable constitutional powers to force the cabinet into a public disclosure of facts: investigation, interpellation, and questions. The most potent of these – parliamentary investigation – has been used only nine times since 1850, and mainly before 1887. From 1887 to 1947, no commissions of investigation were set up. The best-known instance of investigation since the Second World War is the nine-member commission which labored for almost ten years on a thorough inquiry into the activities of the wartime government-in-exile in London – more a matter of historical interest than of current political excitement. Interpellations are held more frequently: in the 1930's about ten per year, but no more than four or five per year in the postwar period. This is, therefore, not a strong weapon against elite secrecy either. Besides, secrecy is safeguarded by the custom that the interpellator submits his questions in advance to the minister

---

[14] However, in recent years a number of important parliamentary debates have been televised.

[15] H. Daalder, "The Relation Between Cabinet and Parliament in the Netherlands" (unpublished paper presented at the Rome Congress of the International Political Science Association, 1958), p. 17.

involved. The most innocuous parliamentary weapon is the question. Hundreds of questions are asked during each annual session, but the overwhelming majority deal with very minor matters and are written. And ministers usually take their time to write the answers. Few questions entail a lively confrontation on the floor of the chambers.[16] In short, parliament has the power to bridge the information gap but does not take advantage of it. Its members, or at least those belonging to the Big Five of the parties, conscientiously participate in the conspiracy of silence.

The academic world also tends to protect this secrecy. Goudsblom, pointing out that the question of social stratification in Holland has not been subjected to a thorough scholarly investigation and that "least of all is known about the elites," speculates that one reason for this lack of information is the elite's "discretion [which] has always been part and parcel of its self-assured dignity and authority; the modern university graduates, ascended from lower levels of society, have generally tended without questioning to adopt this paternalistic attitude."[17]

There are other conspirators, too, notably the press. Indeed the communications elite play the most vital role in preserving the secrecy of the accommodation process. Most of the national newspapers are closely linked to a particular bloc by organizational, ideological, or personal ties. Editors and journalists belong to the "establishment" of the politics of accommodation. An independent paper like *De Telegraaf* is more adventurous and does not feel bound to guard all political secrets. But its access to such classified information is severely limited, and it tends to be more noisy than knowledgeable.

In a speech to the National Newspaper Association in 1964, Prime Minister Marijnen cautioned the press to exercise self-control in deciding what is and what is not fit to print[18] – a totally unnecessary reminder to the highly self-disciplined Dutch newspaperman. In commenting on the editorial speculation of another paper, the *Nieuwe Rotterdamse Courant* wrote: "They give the impression of knowing more than they can tell at the moment (which is not abnormal for newspapers; they are often like icebergs)."[19] This would also be an apt description of the entire political process, of which only a small part is visible and the rest is kept hidden under the dark and sometimes muddy water.

[16] Van Raalte, pp. 207-217, 232-238.
[17] Johan Goudsblom, *Dutch Society* (New York: Random House, 1967), p. 70.
[18] *Nieuwe Rotterdamse Courant* (May 26, 1964).
[19] *Ibid.* (February 1, 1964), quoted in Dick Schaap and Bert Pasterkamp, *De zaak Irene* (Amsterdam: ABC-Boeken, 1964), p. 68.

RULE VII: THE GOVERNMENT'S RIGHT TO GOVERN

All rules discussed so far are closely related to the first rule or axiom that politics is a serious business. The seventh rule is a direct deduction from this axiom. What is important in both politics and business is to get the job done, and this applies first and foremost to the highest rulers: the cabinet. When the Dutch refer to the "government" (*regering*) they refer primarily to the cabinet rather than all branches of government or the entire administration. The government or cabinet must do the job of governing. The corollary to this is that others, specifically the parties in parliament, must allow them to govern. To be sure, the cabinet or individual ministers may be challenged and criticized but only with decent and polite restraint. The cabinet must not be harassed.

Parliament, that is, the two chambers of the States-General, is theoretically sovereign. The principle that the cabinet is entirely dependent on the confidence of parliament was firmly established in the protracted battle between the Second Chamber and the cabinet from 1866 to 1868. The Second Chamber repeatedly passed motions of censure against the cabinet and voted down the cabinet's budget proposals. The cabinet tried to maintain itself in office by twice dissolving the chamber, but the newly-elected chambers still had strong majorities opposed to the cabinet. In the end, the cabinet resigned and was replaced by a new cabinet that had the chamber's confidence. Parliamentarism had triumphed. Furthermore, the constitutional provision that "the laws are inviolable" means that the judiciary is not allowed to test the constitutionality of laws passed by the States-General. Judicial review is unknown.[20] In this respect, too, parliament is fully sovereign.

It is impossible, therefore, to apply the concept of separation of powers to the relationship between cabinet and parliament. Yet, in practice, the cabinet enjoys a large measure of independence, based on the attitude that it is the government's task to govern. This "semi-separation of powers" is based not on constitutional provisions but on informal, but nonetheless deeply ingrained political practice. The semi-independent position of the cabinet is reinforced by the prevalent concept that cabinets are King's or Queen's cabinets, although they are all, at least after 1868, parliamentary cabinets, and by the strong tradition that membership in the cabinet is not compatible with membership in the States-

---

[20] R. Kranenburg, *Het Nederlands staatsrecht* (8th ed., Haarlem: Tjeenk Willink, 1958), pp. 118-120, 288-293. See also J. V. Rijpperda Wiersma, *Dualisme in ons staatsbestel* (Assen: Van Gorcum, 1961).

General. Ministers have special reserved seats in the chambers and they may speak there, but they are not members and may not vote. Also, cabinet members have traditionally been recruited primarily from outside the States-General. Of the 334 ministers between 1848 and 1958, almost half never served in parliament and almost a fifth entered parliamentary service only after first having been on the cabinet; only slightly more than a third of the ministers had prior experience in parliament.[21] The semi-independence of the cabinets is further enhanced by the labels they frequently attach to themselves. Virtually all cabinets are based on a majority coalition in parliament, but many have described themselves as "extraparliamentary cabinets," "business cabinets," "crisis cabinets," and the like, thus emphasizing their autonomous status.

The practice of semi-separation of powers is eminently suited to the politics of accommodation. Dutch cabinets are egalitarian bodies. The prime minister stands out only slightly above his colleagues; the title prime minister (*Minister President*) did not even exist officially until 1945. The person charged with the formation of a new cabinet does not necessarily become its prime minister. In 1948, J. R. H. van Schaik formed the cabinet, but W. Drees became its prime minister and Van Schaik himself took the vice-premiership and the less exalted official title of minister without portfolio. Again, in 1951, Drees became the head of a new cabinet formed by someone else, C. P. M. Romme, who did not enter the cabinet himself.[22] The prime minister is undoubtedly *primus inter pares* but without undue emphasis on *primus*. The parties joining in a cabinet coalition do not have to be afraid, therefore, of being dominated by the strongman of a different party.

Furthermore, cabinets have usually been based on broad majorities in the Second Chamber, especially after 1946. The major parties have ample opportunities to participate in cabinets, and if they do participate, to occupy a number of posts roughly proportional to their parliamentary strength. Not all major parties are permanently in the cabinet, of course. But being in opposition does not entail being excluded from the policy-making process. There is no sharp line between government and opposition parties. Major pieces of legislation are often passed with the help of

[21] Mattei Dogan and Maria Scheffer-Van der Veen, "Le personnel ministériel hollandais (1848-1958)," *L'Année Sociologique,* 3rd series, 1957-58, p. 100.

[22] E. van Raalte, *De ontwikkeling van het minister-presidentschap in Nederland, België, Frankrijk, Engeland en enige andere landen* (Leyden: Universitaire Pers, 1954), pp. 24-26, 44-45.

some "opposition" parties and with a "government" party voting against. The departmental budgets are usually approved by all major parties with only one or more of the splinter groups in the opposition.

The cabinet's semi-independent status and its flexible partnership with all major parties – representing the four blocs – in the Second Chamber, give it a dual function in the politics of accommodation. Because of its broad composition, it is another confederal organ *within* which accommodation takes place. At the same time, because of its autonomous position above parliament and the parties and its presumed impartiality, it acts collectively as a mediator or balancer *between* the rival groups in the process of accommodation. In its first role, it resembles the Social and Economic Council, although its tasks are more comprehensive. Its second role is epitomized by the fifteen cabinet-appointed neutral members in the Social and Economic Council who hold the balance of power that is divided proportionally among the blocs and equally between workers and employers. The rule of the government's right to govern on which its special position in the politics of accommodation is based, is therefore of great importance.

These informal, unwritten rules govern the political business in Holland. They may not always be scrupulously followed, and because they are stated in general terms, they may be subject to different interpretations, but they are sufficiently salient to be regarded as *the* rules of the game. They contribute much to the success of the elite's efforts to govern the divided nation.

Another effect of the rules is to make politics dull and to keep popular interest at low ebb. Especially the rules of secrecy, proportionality, and depoliticization keep much of the fire and excitement out of politics. It would be wrong to assume, however, that the dullness of Dutch politics must be attributed to a lack of issues and tensions. The opposite is true: potentially divisive issues and disintegrative tendencies are ever present, but they are carefully controlled. The lack of excitement does not reflect a nearly perfect consensus, but rather the elite's conscious and deliberate attempts to cope with the system's fragility. Hence popular apathy and disinterest in politics and its apparent dullness have a positive value.

POSTSCRIPT BY THE AUTHOR, AUGUST 1973

When I was writing the final version of the manuscript of my *The Politics of Accommodation* in 1967, there were already clear signs that Dutch politics was changing in a number of fundamental respects. I therefore included a chapter on "Dutch Politics in

Transition" in which I paid special attention to the fact that the religious and ideological cleavages had become less deep and less relevant to the political process during the late 1950's and the 1960's. Therefore, I stated, "the highly oligarchical and elitist patterns of authority are not as necessary and consequently not as justifiable as before, and . . . a greater degree of openness and popular participation can be allowed without grave risks to the system's stability" (p. 193). In the years since 1967, strong pressures have in fact been building up to change the rules of the game in the direction that I indicated. One clear manifestation of these pressures is the growing support for the proposal to introduce a popularly elected prime minister (or, in a less far-reaching version of the proposal, a directly elected cabinet *formateur*) who would be much more than a *primus inter pares*. A second important innovation is the "shadow cabinet" formed by the left-wing parties to challenge the incumbent cabinet in the parliamentary election campaigns of the spring of 1971 and the fall of 1972. These developments entail a tendency to draw a sharper line between government parties and opposition parties, to accentuate political differences rather than to depoliticize them and resolve them in secret negotiations, and to downgrade the principles of concurrent majority and proportional participation in decision-making.

AUSTRIA: THE THREE *LAGER* AND THE FIRST REPUBLIC

Alfred Diamant

Source: "Austrian Society and the Three *Lager*," in Alfred Diamant, *Austrian Catholics and the First Republic: Democracy, Capitalism, and the Social Order 1918-1934* (copyright © 1960 by Princeton University Press), pp. 73-80. Reprinted by permission of Princeton University Press and the author.

The political and social development of the Austrian Republic was dominated by the existence of three major groups which the Austrian historian, Adam Wandruszka, had called *Lager*.[1] Each *Lager* drew its support from specific social groups and each had a political organization which acted as the political representative of its interests. Each *Lager* also attempted to develop a *Weltanschauung*, and to foster social and ideological homogeneity among its followers. Thus it hoped to establish "totalitarian" control over its members and shape their entire lives. These three *Lager* were the Socialist, the Nationalist, and the Christian-social conservative (*christlichsozial-konservativ*).[2] Their origin can be traced to the national, social, and religious struggles of the Empire during the nineteenth century. The development of Austrian politics since 1945 gives proof of the persistence of the three-*Lager* pattern. The growth of National Socialism and the question of *Anschluss* upset the "normal" pattern in the early 1930's, but when Austrian politics returned to normal in 1945 the three *Lager* re-emerged. The Socialist and Christian-social conservative camps again dominate the scene while a small Nationalist movement attempts to play the role of a balancer. However, the determination of the two large camps to avoid the mistakes of the First Republic has so far prevented the Nationalists from exercising a decisive influence over the distribution of political power as they had done between 1918 and 1934.

(A) THE SOCIALIST LAGER

Of the three, the Socialist *Lager*, the camp of the industrial workers, most nearly attained homogeneity. Its political representative was the Social Democratic party. In addition, the so-called Free Trade Unions were so closely allied with the Social Demo-

---

[1] Adam Wandruszka, "Österreichs politische Struktur. Die Entwicklung der Parteien und der politischen Bewegungen," *Geschichte der Republik Österreich*, Heinrich Benedikt, editor (Vienna: Verlag für Geschichte und Politik, 1954), pp. 289-485.

[2] *Ibid.*, pp. 291-292.

cratic party organization that they were considered an integral part of the Socialist *Lager*. Through the Social Democratic party, the trade unions, and a host of other organizations the Socialist *Lager* had created a separate sphere of life for its members,[3] a separate universe in which the workers lived among fellow Socialists in municipal public housing units, read Socialist newspapers, and joined Socialist stamp collecting or pigeon fancying clubs. They enrolled their children in the Socialist youth organization, hiked through the Vienna woods with comrades from the Socialist *Naturfreunde*, and stayed overnight in mountain lodges maintained by Socialist Alpine Clubs. At work they belonged to a trade union whose principal leaders sat in parliament as Social Democrats. After their death they were cremated in a municipal crematorium operated by a Socialist city administration. This last act of their earthly career was also their ultimate gesture of defiance against a clerical bourgeois world. The Christian Social Government, urged by the church, had tried to stop the construction and operation of the crematorium ostensibly on technical, legal grounds. Actually, the Christian-social conservative camp opposed cremation on religious grounds and attempted in this way to enforce its *Weltanschauung* on a resisting proletariat.

The Austrian worker considered active membership in the Socialist *Lager* his way of protesting against the privileged position of the old nobility, the clergy, and the industrialists. This protest also found expression in an extremely militant ideology, *Austro-Marxismus*,[4] a term which became synonymous in Europe

[3] "After 1918 the party had not only grown to be a mass organization of unique size and vigor but a spiritual power whose effects were lasting and profound. . . . Far beyond the realm of politics it shaped the lives and thoughts of its active members. . . . Its broad organizational structure had room for all trades and professions. It enabled all ages to organize their entertainment requirements, their educational plans, their purposes in life, their cultural desires, their hobbies, even their follies, and to fuse them 'ideologically' with the aims of the party in serious and ridiculous fashion. In this mass of hundreds of thousands, anyone capable of rising above the merely personal, found in the party a new meaning to his life. This fulfillment was as strong and as enduring as a religious tie." Joseph Buttinger, *In the Twilight of Socialism. A History of the Revolutionary Socialists of Austria* (New York: Frederick A. Praeger, 1953), pp. 20-22. Buttinger was one of the principal figures in the illegal Socialist movement between 1934 and 1938.

[4] In spite of his pro-Socialist bias, Gulick's chapter on Austro-Marxism is an excellent summary and critique. Charles A. Gulick, *Austria from Habsburg to Hitler*, vol. II: *Fascism's Subversion of Democracy* (Berkeley: University of California Press, 1948), ch. XXVII, "Theory and Practice of Austro-Marxism," pp. 1363-1400.

with extreme left-wing Marxism. This ideology was given an especially radical formulation in the Social Democratic party's *Linz* program of 1926. The emphasis on a violent class struggle and the determination to seize power by force contained in the *Linz* program greatly exaggerated the doctrinaire Marxist tendencies of the Socialist *Lager*. Austrian Socialists never applied this doctrinaire Marxism,[5] but pursued instead a gradualist policy and were committed to change by peaceful means. Nevertheless, Austrian Catholics came to identify the Republic of 1918 with the Socialist *Lager* and considered Social Democracy its principal enemy.

The Socialist *Lager* drew its principal strength from the industrial workers in Vienna and the industrial centers in the provinces.[6] It also had a large following of intellectuals, especially Jewish intellectuals who found in it career opportunities as organizers, educators, and party theorists not open to Jewish intellectuals elsewhere.[7]

Gulick showed that in spite of an appearance of violent Marxism the theories of Austrian Socialism were "dictated by their steadfast adherence to the principles of democracy and of intellectual and spiritual freedom ... and by their deep sympathy with those who suffer and need help" (p. 1400).

[5] Anton Rintelen for many years *Land* governor of Styria and one of the more sinister figures in republican Austria admitted: "It was a miracle that Marxism did not sweep away all conservative obstacles in its march to total power.... Communism radicalized Social Democracy but was unable to carry it along all the way. In fact, on crucial issues Social Democracy resisted, and even opposed Communism actively." Rintelen, *Erinnerungen an Österreichs Weg. Versailles-Berchtesgaden-Grossdeutschland* (Munich: Verlag F. Bruckmann, 1941), p. 98. Rintelen was slated to be chancellor in the government to be installed after the assassination of Dollfuss in July 1934. The book is largely anti-Christian Social and anti-clerical and, therefore, more favorably disposed to anyone else who also might have been anti-clerical. Rintelen recalled that in 1919 at the height of what he called Communist riots in Graz only the support given to the regular police forces by the Socialist *Arbeiterhilfskorps* saved the day and broke the fury of the riots. *Ibid.*, p. 104.

[6] Rudolf Schlesinger, *Central European Democracy and its Background; Economic and Political Group Organization* (London: Routledge & Kegan Paul, Limited, 1953), pp. 178-179.

[7] Buttinger estimated that eighty percent of the intellectuals who joined the Socialist movement were Jewish and that there were secret arrangements by the party executive to insure an "Aryan" majority in the party's top echelons: "The Austrian worker's awe of mental achievement gave to many intellectual Jews the first and deepest happiness of their lives. This was their real escape from the loathsome Ghetto ..." *op. cit.*, pp. 80-81. Even though Jewish

(B) THE NATIONALIST LAGER.

During the first decade of the Republic the Nationalist *Lager* was the weakest of the three. It was composed of anti-clerical middle-class groups in urban as well as rural areas. Under the influence of the social question and of the nationality struggles the German middle class of the Empire had split in two. Those who emphasized social and economic problems followed Lueger into the Christian-social conservative *Lager*. Those who were more concerned with threats to the national position of the Germans within the Empire followed Georg von Schönerer and his anti-clerical, Pan-German program. These anti-clerical nationalist groups formed the nucleus of the Nationalist *Lager* in 1918.

Two political parties represented the Nationalist *Lager* between 1918 and 1934. The *Grossdeutsche Volkspartei* drew its strength from urban middle-class groups, especially civil servants. In fact, defense of the civil servants and lobbying for civil service legislation consumed most of the energies of that party.[8] The *Landbund* represented a group of well-to-do anti-clerical peasants in Carinthia and Styria. In Carinthia the *Landbund* gained the support of East Prussian Protestant peasants who had fled from the East Prussian territories ceded to Poland after the war, and had taken over land vacated by Carinthian Slovenes who had been forced to return to Yugoslavia in 1918.[9] Both parties collaborated with the Christian Socials until 1934. In fact, their votes in Parliament were indispensable for an anti-socialist majority. The rise of the Nazi movement deprived these two parties of all their followers. Ultimately the Nazis drew a large number of middle and lower middle-class supporters into the Nationalist *Lager*.

---

intellectuals joined the Social Democratic party in large numbers, the Jewish members of high finance, big business, and industry did not share this radicalism and supported the *Heimwehr*, in spite of its open anti-Semitism, because it "protected" business and industry. Franz Borkenau, *Austria and After* (London: Faber and Faber, 1938), pp. 106-107.

[8] George Maria von Alexich, *A Study of the Political Parties in Austria, 1918-1938* (Georgetown University Ph.D. dissertation, 1948), pp. 218-226. Alexich was a member of the Austrian diplomatic service until 1938. The dissertation has an outspoken pro-Christian Social bias.

[9] *Ibid.*, pp. 227-229. In Styria the Landbund was fairly strong and Rintelen, who led the Christian Socials in that *Land*, complained that his party could fight the *Landbund* only with difficulty. The Christian Socials could not entirely neglect either rural-agricultural or urban-industrial interests while the *Landbund*, a purely agricultural interest group, could appeal to the peasants strictly on their own terms. Rintelen, *op. cit.*, p. 57.

(C) THE CHRISTIAN-SOCIAL CONSERVATIVE LAGER.

The Christian-social conservative *Lager* centered around the church and those groups which accepted Catholic social theory: peasants and the urban petty bourgeoisie. It also received the support of financial and industrial leaders who sought to fashion a political instrument with which to destroy the powerful position of the workers. In this manner the Christian-social conservative *Lager* became the focal point of an anti-socialist alliance.

The lower middle class in the cities and on the farm comprised the principal support of the Christian-social conservative *Lager*. Artisans, shopkeepers, some white-collar workers, and above all the peasants constituted the social base of that *Lager*. The Christian Social party and a multitude of Catholic organizations, most of them closely supervised by the clergy, were the principal organizational weapons of the Christian-social conservative *Lager*.[10] Catholics considered this network of organizations indispensable in their struggle against bourgeois-liberal as well as socialist influences in Austrian life. They feared that the Socialists would be able to win over a majority of Austrians and establish a dictatorship of the proletariat on the Russian model – a fear which seemed well-founded in view of the extreme doctrinaire Marxian program proclaimed repeatedly by the Socialists. The Christian-social camp realized that it was engaged in a grim struggle: "The fight must be conducted along two fronts: in parliament among deputies, and outside parliament among the Austrian people. Therefore Catholicism must be prepared to do combat on both fronts. . . . Because Socialists have focused their energies on the task of obtaining a majority in the legislature, Catholic Action must do everything to create the sort of electorate which will choose a parliament where the Socialists' strength will be reduced and the enemies of religion will not have a majority."[11] Aemilian Schöpfer, a prelate of the Catholic Church and a leader of the Christian Social party in the Tyrol, reflected in that statement the commonly accepted assumption during the interwar period that a political movement which would gain a clear majority in the legislature would immediately proceed with a complete reshaping of the country's social, economic, and political institutions, in line with that party's *Weltanschauung*.

To counter the Socialist network of trade unions, youth organi-

[10] Aemilian Schöpfer, "Katholizismus und Politik," *Katholizismus in Österreich*, pp. 448-449. However, Alexich was of the opinion that the youth groups, for example, which had a highly complex organizational structure in parishes and dioceses, did not amount to very much, *op. cit.*, pp. 86-87.

[11] Schöpfer, *op. cit.*, pp. 442-443.

zations, hiking clubs, weight lifting and pigeon fancying societies, Catholics attempted to create a similar network of organizations in which the faithful would follow a Catholic pattern of life
and a Catholic *Weltanschauung*, just as the Socialist *Lager* tried
to create a Socialist world for its own people.

The Catholic camp could not match the homogeneity of its
Socialist rival. Under the influence of industrialists and large land
holders who traditionally play a prominent role in Austrian life,
Christian Social governments pursued policies which did not
always favor the small holders and the artisans, the Christian
Social rank-and-file. Some of the provincial politicians, like
Anton Rintelen, and Catholic trade union leaders like Leopold
Kunschak, castigated their own party chieftains for their pro-big
business bias.[12]

(D) THE THREE LAGER AND THE FAILURE OF CONSENSUS.
The failure of the major Austrian social groups to establish a
consensus on fundamentals of political and social organization
perpetuated the division of the country into three *Lager*. The
major opponents in this struggle were the Socialist and the Catholic camps, with the Nationalists joining the Catholics in a bourgeois anti-Socialist alliance. In spite of this parliamentary alliance
between two of the *Lager*, the three were divided on fundamental
issues involving the social question, church-state relationships, and
German nationalism. Austria, therefore, lacked what P. T. Lux, a
Swiss, long-time resident of Austria, has called a "vital, unified,
national idea."[13] Consequently, each *Lager* tried to become the
centre of all loyalties of its followers, and the struggle for the
votes of the people turned into a struggle for their souls. Aemilian
Schöpfer was correct when he insisted that "...the Socialist

[12] Rintelen seems to be very bitter about the policies which favored
industry at the expense of the peasants. One must remember,
though, that Rintelen, in writing his memoirs, would tend to over-
emphasize the differences between him and the less nationalist and
more strongly clerical views of those in Christian Social party head-
quarters in Vienna, *op. cit.*, pp. 48-51. Rintelen pointed out that
before the First World War there had been no contact at all between
the peasants, safely rooted in the Catholic conservative fold, and the
nationalist bourgeoisie of the small and medium-sized towns of
Austria. Men like Rintelen were largely responsible for assuming the
leadership of part of the peasantry and also for alienating the peasants from the clerical leadership. They thereby prepared the way for
the sweeping victories of National Socialism especially in Styria and
Carinthia.

[13] P. T. Lux, *Österreich 1918-1938. Eine Demokratie?* (Graz: Leykam
Verlag, G.m.b.H., 1946), p. 76.

youth organizations and the freethinker societies were non-political means to a political end and had, therefore, tremendous political significance."[14] They were part of the network of organizations with which the Socialists tried to spread their theology to win new followers and maintain the loyalty of the faithful. Otto Bauer, the Socialist, on the other hand, considered the Catholic Church not simply a religious institution but the propaganda arm of the Socialists' principal opponent: "The clergy fanned the flame of peasant resentment against the workers. . . . They organized and strengthened the peasant movement as the most effective counterforce to the proletarian revolution. Newspapers and sermons reminded the peasants . . . that the revolution would socialize their property and destroy the Church."[15] C. A. Macartney, whose *The Social Revolution in Austria* is critical of the Social Democrats, wrote: "The Catholic Church of Austria is the real enemy of Socialism. She is the living representative of the old order. . . . She is the upholder of conservatism, loyalty, piety, respect and obedience. . . . Until her hold over the spirits of the people has been weakened, Socialism, the very reverse of all this, cannot move. The Catholic Church, too, was and is an active political force. . . . Therefore we find that even to this day the real battle of Austrian Socialism is directed against the Church. . . . For under these circumstances the Socialist maxim that 'religion is every man's private affair' is already a direct challenge, since Catholicism admits no neutrality."[16]

Ever since the days of the Josephinist reforms and of Schöner-er's *Los von Rom* campaign, political struggles in Austria have been religious rivalries, and religious rivalries have been turned into political controversies. Under such conditions political parties become armed camps of religious crusaders, determined to drive the infidels from the field: "Parties which serve as a shield for powerful private interests have a tendency to become totalitarian and to suppress all those who disagree with them. This was especially true in Austria whose parties were extremely doctrinaire and committed to definite ideologies. This gave them the character of secular religions – and distinguished them sharply from most Western parties which were held together not by an ideology but by common traditions or interests. As a result, all parties in Austria tended to identify their own interest with that of the entire country."[17]

[14] Schöpfer, *op. cit.*, p. 441.

[15] Otto Bauer, *Die österreichische Revolution* (Vienna: Wiener Volks-buchhandlung, 1934), p. 124.

[16] C. A. Macartney, *The Social Revolution in Austria* (Cambridge: University Press, 1926), p. 54.

[17] Lux, *op. cit.*, p. 3.

AUSTRIA: THE LEGITIMIZING ROLE OF POLITICAL PARTIES

Peter Pulzer

Source: P. G. J. Pulzer, "The Legitimizing Role of Political Parties: the Second Austrian Republic," *Government and Opposition*, Vol. 4, No. 3 (1969), 324-344. Reprinted by permission of the publisher, and with a 1973 postscript by the author.

Can parliamentary institutions thrive in countries with little or no tradition in the habits of self-government?[1] Is multi-party competition viable in states where compromise is not accepted as a political virtue? The questions are familiar and are asked whenever the advisability of exporting the Westminister model (or the Capitol Hill or Palais Bourbon model) is raised.

The proposition to be examined is that a parliamentary and party system was transplanted into an initially unfavourable environment and eventually acclimatized itself. The ecological difficulties are familiar; indeed, they form the substance of the debate about the export of systems. In the Third World, at the point of decolonization it involves the former colonial power bequeathing liberal-democratic institutions as a device for legitimizing the new native regime.[2] In Central and Eastern Europe it was native elites – generally the intelligentsia, but sometimes enlightened nobles and bureaucrats – who sought to bring their societies into line with the archetypal nation-states of the West. One distinguished historian of Eastern Europe has outlined the process as follows:

> The ideas of Voltaire, the rhetoric of Gladstone, derived – even if by tortuous routes – from the reality of France or Britain. The Russian intellectual and the Russian peasant belonged to different cultures. The ideas of the Russian intellectual did not derive from Russian conditions, but were imported prefabricated from abroad . . . Eastern Europe (including Russia) was the first part of the world in which Western ideas, imported ready made, were used to remould societies neither economically nor culturally prepared for them.[3]

It is, of course, the case, that the intelligentsia of the Third World have also imbibed ideas which derive more from the experience

---

[1] A version of this paper was presented to the Comparative Politics Panel of the Political Science Association in York, April 1969.

[2] D. E. Apter, *The Politics of Modernisation*, p. 271, n. 4.

[3] H. Seton-Watson, "Intellectuals and Revolution: Social Forces in Eastern Europe since 1848" in: R. Pares & A. J. P. Taylor (eds.), *Essays Presented to Sir Lewis Namier*, pp. 399, 428.

of advanced countries than of their own, but these ideas have been largely concerned with national self-determination and industrialization, not with constitutional forms. In continental Europe it was the ideas of the Enlightenment and the institutions of liberalism which travelled southwards and eastwards during the 19th and early 20th centuries. We may therefore say that while parliamentary government was *exported* by de-colonizing powers to largely unappreciative or uncomprehending elites outside Europe, it was *imported* by enthusiastic though unreflecting elites in Europe outside the liberalized North-West. The learned works on parliamentary procedure by 19th century Germans and Austrians, such as Robert von Mohl, Rudolf von Gneist and Josef Redlich, show the extent to which the Westminister model was explicitly regarded as a norm.[4]

Given that Austria presents virtually the only example of a European state in which an initially unsuccessful parliamentary system turned into a successful one, and in which constitutional and party-structural factors can be held constant over half a century (1919-1969), I propose to examine Austrian political experience. I propose to treat it as a problem in *political culture*; more specifically as a problem in isolating the main determinants of such a culture and in distinguishing between the static and evolving elements in it.

PARTY FORMATION IN THE EMPIRE

The principal components of the Austrian political culture emerged in the final, constitutional era of the Habsburg empire (1861-1918) and particularly between the two franchise reforms of 1882 and 1906. The Habsburg empire differed from the post-1918 republics not merely in area and social structure but in its multi-nationality. I intend to discuss the historical continuity only of the German-speaking parties, though bearing in mind that the empire's multi-nationality had a decisive impact on the nature of these parties.

Austrian parliamentary institutions, as established by the 'February Patent' of 1861, gave little scope for popular participation and provided little need for elaborate party organization. Until 1872 the members of the *Reichsrat* were elected indirectly, by the diets of the individual crown-lands. Within these crown-lands the franchise varied widely. When in 1872 direct elections were introduced, the variations in the franchise remained. A further feature

[4] This point is discussed by G. Loewenberg, *Parliament in the German Political System*, pp. 8-9, 14-15; and by R. J. Lamer, *Der englische Parlamentarismus in der deutschen politischen Theorie im Zeitalter Bismarcks (1857 bis 1890). Historische Schriften*, 387.

of the electoral system, carried over from that prevailing in the crown-lands, was representation by classes or *curiae*. In 1882 the franchise in the third and fourth *curiae* was standardized at an annual tax burden of five florins bringing in one adult male in three. A fifth *curia*, to be elected by universal suffrage, was added in 1896.[5] In 1906 universal male suffrage for all seats was introduced.

Party formation in the 1860s reflected the inherited cleavages of Austrian public life: on the one hand, a Catholic Church, accustomed since the Counter-Reformation to a dominant share in directing the state, allied with agriculture and the power of the territorial aristocracy; on the other, a secularizing, centralizing, mainly German-speaking urban middle class, the local representative of the challenge expressed by the Enlightenment and the French Revolution. It also took the form characteristic of early parliamentary systems with a restricted suffrage. It was intra-parliamentary, and the parties so formed divided dichotomously into groups supporting or opposing the government of the day.

There quickly emerged a Left (collectively known as *Verfassungspartei* or Constitutional Party) and a Right, though neither was rigorously disciplined and both tended to fragment into subordinate groupings known as *Klubs*. There was virtually no constituency organization and, until direct elections were introduced, no need for any. Partisanship was defined by intellectual affinity, not organization. The Right/Left duality did not arise in response to any demands which the new constitution made on parliamentarians. Neither the February Patent nor the 1867 Constitutional Laws which amended it provided for ministerial responsibility, and the government retained considerable reserve powers of legislation by decree. It arose rather, as observers have noted for many states,[6] because the merits of the representative institutions were themselves still in dispute; it arose, in other words, out of a *crisis of legitimacy*. The Left supported, in principle if not necessarily in detail, the 1861-7 constitution: hence their name. The Right favoured the historic rights of the individual crown-lands. Left and Right were therefore not rivals for ministerial office, otherwise prepared to observe the same rules. They were the heirs of an ancient ideological dispute; their antagonism survived them, and was inherited by the newer parties which emerged in the 1880's and 1890's.

[5] 12 fl. = £1,

[6] For Sweden, see D. A. Rustow, *The Politics of Compromise. A Study of Parties and Cabinet Government in Sweden*, pp. 11-12, 26-34; for the U.S.A., S. M. Lipset, *The First New Nation*, pp. 15-23. The evolution of parties in Britain between 1679 and 1760, though not uniformly interpreted, is no doubt the best-known example of all.

The intra-parliamentary parties of the 1860's and 1870's were unable to resolve the crisis of legitimacy. In general such a crisis can be overcome by parliamentary means only if the participants are able to concentrate on solving to the exclusion of other critical strains on the system (Britain, Sweden, Netherlands). It is not too difficult for a system to carry one critical 'load' at a time. But it is a characteristic of late-developing countries that various loads are placed on the system at very short intervals or even simultaneously. Three other types of historical crisis, in addition to that of legitimacy are most salient in the formation of parties: territorial incorporation, economic distribution and political participation.[7]

The *crisis of incorporation*, involving the ability of different ethnic communities to co-exist within the same state, may be said to date from 1848 in Austrian politics, and was never solved. Indeed, their ability to co-exist declined between 1848 and 1918. The reason for this is to be found in the forms that the crises of distribution and participation took.

The *crisis of distribution* was sparked off by the accelerating modernization of the Austrian economy in the 1860's and even more by the bank and stock exchange crash of 1873. It affected first the lower middle class and peasantry and was able to influence party formation thanks to the electoral reform of 1882 which benefited principally these classes. Because this reform enfranchised proportionately more non-Germans than Germans, the division into Catholic, liberal-national, radical and agrarian parties took place among most nationalities – Czechs, Poles, Ruthenes and Slovenes. By bringing about party divisions on ethnic lines it helped to perpetuate and exacerbate the crisis of incorporation, and the electoral system, with its socially homogeneous *curiae* and constituencies, further encouraged the division on class lines. These dual divisions caused the extreme fragmentation of parties in the last years of the empire.

The enfranchisement of the five-florin voters also led to the formation of the first extra-parliamentary parties. This move was symptomatic of the *crisis of participation*. Such a crisis may be overcome – as in Britain – if the politically dominant groups accommodate the claimants to a share in power. The effect on the dominant political parties of such accommodation is a slow evolu-

[7] My definition of these "developmental crises" resembles those of Verba in Pye & Verba's *Political Culture and Political Development.*, pp. 557-9 and La Palombara and Weiner in their *Political Parties and Political Development,* pp. 14-19. I prefer "incorporation" to their "integration," since integration already has an accepted meaning in political sociology, not related to territorial problems.

tion from cadre to mass-membership parties, as envisaged by John Gorst and Joseph Chamberlain in the years after the 1867 Reform Act.

In Austria there was little accommodation. Peasants and tradesmen in the German-speaking areas rebelled against the political leadership of aristocrats and *grand bourgeois*, and against the economic encroachments of industrial and financial capitalists. Civil servants and professional men feared the growing competition of non-Germans, especially Czechs. All groups demanded increasingly protectionist, German-nationalist and anti-Semitic policies.[8] The response from the established parties was in the main inhospitable, forcing the new formations to seek an extra-parliamentary base. Georg von Schönerer's Pan-German League (1882) was the first of several to seek the support of the provincial, anti-clerical middle class. Catholic social reformers formed the *Christlich-Sozialer Verein* (1887) which soon emerged as a fully fledged party. In the election of 1901, the last to be fought under the *curia* system, the extraparliamentary parties gained 76 out of the 118 seats with predominantly German electorates in the third and fourth *curiae*, and an anti-Semitic electoral coalition under Karl Lueger gained control of the municipality of Vienna in 1895.

The refusal of the dominant classes to accommodate the claims of the lower middle-class electorate helped to emphasize the difference between the older, intra-parliamentary parties and the newer extra-parliamentary ones,[9] and encouraged the newer parties to see in the *Reichsrat* little more than a platform for sectional claims. Such parties naturally identify less closely with the conventions of parliamentary institutions, they radicalize the process of electoral competition and they tend – as I shall amplify below – to rely on 'totalistic' programmes.

The final claim for participation came from the growing industrial working class. In the 1870's and 1880's the spread of anarchist ideas on the one hand, and government repression on the other, had both inhibited the emergence of a working-class party. This, the Social Democratic Party, with a Marxist programme, was born in 1889. It got its first electoral chance in 1897 after the creation of the fifth *curia* in which it won 14 of the 72 seats.

After 1907 some rationalization of the party structure was necessary in response to the requirements of the new political culture. The Conservatives, already driven into a corner under the

[8] P. G. J. Pulzer, *The Origins of Political Anti-Semitism in Germany and Austria*, pp. 144-70.
[9] For the importance of the distinction in organizational origin see, e.g. M. Duverger, *Political Parties*, pp. xxiv-xxxvii.

old franchise, were absorbed into the Christian-Social Party and the Liberals, similarly constricted, joined forces with the other German nationalist parties to form a rather loosely integrated *Deutscher Nationalverband*. The primary ideological cleavage of Austrian public life was thus perpetuated. The Social Democratic Party, which had initially prided itself on being a "little International," succumbed to nationalist pressures in 1910, thus leaving the official party overwhelmingly German-speaking.

The new geography of political fragmentation was further emphasized by the relationship between parties, classes and interest groups. The patriarchal and paternalistic character of state and society had inhibited the growth of self-help associations. Interest groups grew up in the shadow of, and in subservience to, political parties. Workers' and peasants' organizations, which were the most important, illustrate this. Trade unions and working men's associations were, from their beginnings, dominated by socialists. In the 1860s this meant Lassalleans;[10] when trade unions revived in the 1880s they were dominated by Marxists. In country-wide organization they lagged behind the Social Democratic Party: the *provisorische Kommission der Gewerkschaften Österreichs* was not set up until 1892, three years after foundation of the party; its first Congress declared that "in order to be able to carry on the struggle effectively on all fronts [trade unions] will not be able to neglect political means to this end and therefore take their stand unreservedly on the foundations and principles of Social Democracy."[11] The only rivals to the socialist trade unions were also ideologically based, as membership for 1908 shows:[12]

Socialist (all nationalities)	513,769
Christian-Social	94,011
German Nationalist	37,446
Czech Nationalist	16,141

Peasant associations were equally strongly tied to the Christian Social party. The most important of these, that of Lower Austria, was at first politically neutral, but declared itself for the Christian-Socials in 1901, partly under the influence of the village clergy who had been prominent in building it up. When it was reconstituted in 1904 thirteen of its eighteen executive members were political office holders. The same domination by politicians characterized the Tyrolean *Bauernbund*, founded in 1904, though

[10] J. Deutsch, *Geschichte der österreichischen Gewerkschaftsbewegung*, pp. 34-6.

[11] *Ibid.*, p. 196.

[12] Calculated by A. G. Whiteside, *Austrian National Socialism Before 1918*, p. 33.

the local clergy, who were mainly sympathetic, were barred from supporting it.[13]

Thus, by 1914, the principal sub-cultures had become institutionalized. Among the German-speaking population these were (a) a predominantly *Catholic-conservative* one, representing largely pre-industrial strata ideologically continuous with the Old Right, (b) a *secular, liberal-national* one, ideologically continuous with the Old Left, and (c) a *working-class, industrial* one, ideologically dominated by Marxism. In the last *Reichsrat* election of the old empire the Christian-Social party gained 36 per cent of the German vote, the parties of the *Nationalverband* 32 per cent, the Social Democrats 31 per cent; in those crown-lands that constituted the post-1918 Austrian republic the percentages were 53, 18 and 29 respectively. Given that the other nationalities had also by this time been drawn into participation and that their party structures showed similar divisions along class and ideological lines, the picture that the *Reichsrat* presented was a highly fragmented one. There was not a single one among its 28 parties that could claim to represent more than one nationality, class or *Weltanschauung*.

All fragmentation makes parliamentary institutions difficult to operate, but it is not the fragmentation as such which is the chief obstacle. Divergent influences in a society may be compensated by countervailing, convergent factors, such as patriotism; or the practice of pluralistic reconciliation may derive from the traditionally democratic structure of subordinate social units, such as the family, the Church or the school.

Merely to describe these centripetal forces is to emphasize their absence from Austria. One reason for this was constitutional. In the absence of ministerial responsibility parties had no incentive to consider the consequences of pressing their demands, and indeed no function beyond articulating the sectional interests of their followers. The executive or the judiciary were not penetrated by new parties: this was not because the new parties were satisfied by the controls which parliamentary government gave them, but because these institutions remained the monopoly of the older elites. Indeed, the constitutional structure of the empire illustrated the difficulty of resolving the crises of legitimacy and participation. The rulers of the empire were convinced that the sole, reliable centripetal force in it was the dynasty, and the dynasty's appeal to the loyalty of its subjects could rest on only one of

---

[13] T. Kraus, *Die Entstehung des niederösterreichischen Bauernbundes,* Unpublished dissertation, pp. 162, 189-90; N. Miko, *Die Vereinigung der Konservativen in der Christlich-sozialen Partei,* Unpublished dissertation, p. 52.

Weber's three authority types, the traditional.[14] Once the traditional authority of the dynasty was challenged, as it increasingly
was from 1848 onwards, entrusting its future to the mechanism of
popular consent was too risky. This constitutional deadlock had
profound effects on the political culture and gave it the following
characteristics:

1) Government was thought of in administrative, not parliamentary, terms.
2) All parties were opposition parties, judging the government in the light of its response to their sectional
   demands.
3) All parties were identified with well-defined interest-
   groups; they reflected the fragmentation of political life,
   but also encouraged it, since interest groups were seen as
   useful sources of political mobilization.

All parties aimed, through a network of affiliated economic and
cultural groups, at spiritual and organizational self-containment,
as a defence against both the executive and other rivals.

The most effective agent of such external isolation and internal
coherence is ideology. The Social Democrats were not only the
most highly organized of the three main party groups, they were
also the most highly ideologized, but the difference between them
and their rivals was one of degree only. The liberal-national
groups became increasingly affected by Pan-German and racialist
notions, the Christian-conservative groups by various schools of
Catholic social theory.[15] Such was the internal coherence of each of
these institutionalized sub-cultures, such the hostility with which it
regarded its rivals, so strong the consciousness of belonging to a
movement, that historians have tended to refer to these embattled
sub-cultures as *Lager* (encampments).[16]

The emergence of the *Lager* had a crucial effect on the way the
crisis of legitimacy unfolded under the impact of the First World
War. The traditional authority which had commanded the loyalty
of the empire's citizens in the early part of the war disintegrated
in the face of military defeat.

[14] M. Weber, *The Theory of Social and Economic Organization* (ed.
    T. Parsons), pp. 328-9, 341-58.
[15] P. Molisch, *Geschichte der deutschnationalen Bewegung in Öster-
    reich*, pp. 140-51, 182-5, 215; A. Diamant, *Austrian Catholics and
    the First Republic. Democracy, Capitalism and the Social Order*,
    pp. 3-69.
[16] A. Wandruszka, "Österreichs politische Struktur," in: H. Benedikt
    (ed.) *Geschichte der Republik Österreich*; A. Diamant, "The Group
    Basis of Austrian Politics," *Journal of Central European Affairs*,
    Vol. 18 (July 1958).

THE FIRST REPUBLIC AND THE *Lager*

In October 1918 the *Reichsrat* members of the three German
parties formed themselves into a "provisional national assembly,"
drew up a provisional constitution and called for the election of a
Constituent Assembly. This, consisting of the three parties which
had called it into being, merely ratified the draft. That the draft
had emanated from the parties which were, at the parliamentary
and electoral level, the secular arms of hermetic, millenarian
sub-cultures, was sufficient legitimation for the new parliamentary
republic. As Otto Bauer, the chief theoretician of the Social
Democratic Party, put it, "The German-Austrian state had
emerged from a *contrat social*, a state-founding treaty between
the political parties representing the classes of the German-
Austrian people."[17]

A corollary of this contract was that legitimacy could last only
as long as the parties continued to collaborate. But the obstacles
to such collaboration were too great. Just as under the empire the
crisis of legitimacy was perpetuated because the crisis of participation remained unresolved, so now under the republic it was
perpetuated by the unresolved crisis of distribution. The peculiar
difficulties surrounding the Austrian distribution crisis can be
traced to the political culture – and its chief component, the *Lager*
– which the republic inherited from the empire. The relative
strengths of the *Lager* did not shift dramatically compared with
pre-war. In the 1919 elections the Social Democrats gained 41
per cent of the votes, the Christian-Social Party 36 per cent, the
liberal-national groups, which re-formed themselves into two parties, the Pan-German People's Party (*Grossdeutsche Volkspartei*)
and the Rural League (*Landbund*), 18 per cent. This party constellation looked, on the surface, promising for a viable parliamentary system: at no subsequent election did the two leading
parties gain fewer than 75 per cent of the total votes. In fact,
after the collapse of the Christian-Social/Social-Democrat coalition in 1920, the future of the republic itself was in doubt. For
though political life was dominated by two major parties their
relationship was not, in Sartori's vocabulary "bi-polar" – "tending
to converge to the centre and therefore centripetal" – but polarized "where the spectrum of political opinion is extremized."[18]

Though Sartori's terminology is helpful in an analysis of the
Austrian party system, his categories are not. He rightly urges us
to abandon analysis of party systems by reference to the number
of competing parties: instead we should adopt "a model-oriented

[17] O. Bauer, *Die österreichische Revolution*, p. 96.
[18] G. Sartori, "European Political Parties. The Case of Polarised Pluralism" in La Palombara & Weiner, *op. cit.*, pp. 138-9.

distinction between bi-polar and multi-polar systems which, first, accounts for the positioning and pattern of interaction of the parties (regardless of their number) and, second, breaks down the undifferentiated category of the multi-party systems." In addition what matters is "not only the number of poles but the distance between them. . . . Finally we must take into account the drives of the polity [i.e., centripetal or centrifugal]." Consideration (a) of the number of the poles (b) of the predominating drive, enables him to arrive at three main types of party system:

1) "simple pluralism": two poles, no polarity, hence an over- whelmingly centripetal drive (e.g. Great Britain);
2) "moderate pluralism": two poles, some polarity, hence predominantly centripetal drives (e.g. Scandinavia);
3) "extreme pluralism": many poles, overwhelming polarity, hence centrifugal drives (e.g. Italy).

These types may be illustrated as follows: –

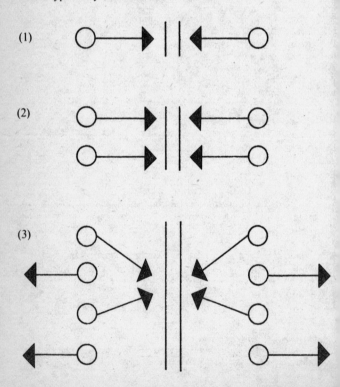

Sartori's typology, though in many ways original, shares the old-fashioned assumption that polarization occurs only in company with multi-polarity. What is missing is type (4):

two poles, extreme polarity, hence centrifugal drive. It is, of course, arguable that such a system cannot survive: that where the only two important political forces are pulling in opposite directions, disintegration is the only possible outcome. And it is true that in Austria it survived for only fourteen years (1919-33), though this is no shorter a life than that of the Weimar Republic and the Fourth French Republic. What Austria lacked was the characteristic which Sartori has located in the other two examples I have cited, as well as in post-war Italy: "a large area which is unequivocally central despite its centre-left and centre-right shades and subtleties."[19] Thus, though a multi-polar, polarized system may contain anti-system parties whose opposition is irresponsible, it can keep going provided that the *ministrable* parties command a majority. It is this centre that was lacking in Austria: the Austrian system could survive only on condition that the two poles had convergent drives. Between 1919 and 1933 these drives were divergent.

The reasons for this are to be found in the political culture that the republic inherited, one which in the extended territory of the empire had been genuinely multi-polar. The republic inherited a geographical fragment of the imperial party system. Moreover the *Lager* mentality luxuriated as never before. Each of the parties was able to engage not merely in intense political mobilization but, since it now held executive power (national or local), to provide patronage as well. Membership of the Social Democratic Party rose from 92,000 in 1913 to 332,000 in 1919 and 718,000 in 1929.[20] In 1930 three out of five male socialist voters were party members; in Vienna it was four out of five.[21]

The coalition government which had, in 1918-19, legitimated the republican constitution broke up in 1920 in the face of increasingly bitter class conflicts; thereafter the Christian-Social Party ruled with the support of the liberal-national groups. What compelled the *Lager* to co-exist was what Otto Bauer termed the

[19] *Ibid.*, p. 155.
[20] Bauer, *op. cit.*, p. 137.
[21] *Statistische Nachrichten* (Vienna: Bundesamt für Statistik) Sonderheft: *Die Nationalratswahlen vom. 9 November 1930*, Tabelle 34.

"equilibrium of class forces" *(das Gleichgewicht der Klassen-
kräfte)*,[22] which prevented either of the partners from dealing a
knock-out blow. The percentage of votes polled by the Marxist
Lager (Social Democrats plus the very small Communist Party)
was as follows:

1919	41%
1923	40%
1927	43%
1930	42%

Changes in list combinations make it difficult to compare the
shares of the two "bourgeois" *Lager*, but the Christian-Social
Party, fighting alone, never dropped below 35 per cent and the
national-liberal groups never below 13 per cent. These figures are
not very different from those of 1907 and 1911[23] and illustrate the
rigid delineations between the encampments. Moreover, the term
Lager was ceasing to be metaphorical as each of the major parties
formed its own private army.

It would be tedious to go through all the parties' programmes
to count how frequently words like *Kampf* and *Macht* are reiterated. Of course all political parties, even the most liberal-minded,
are apt to use military metaphors (campaign, strategy, rank-
and-file) and Michels had pointed out long ago that "Socialist
terminology . . . is largely borrowed from military science."[24] Nevertheless there was an exceptional relish in the *Lager's* anticipa-
tion of ideological Armageddon, and a calm certitude in the way
in which the Social Democrats' 1926 programme equated interest
and ideology: "The class struggle is not only a struggle between
opposed class interests, it is at the same time a struggle between
opposed class ideals. . . . "[25] Thus the distribution crisis was deadlocked; as long as it was deadlocked a state with low legitimacy
survived, *faute de mieux*. The deadlock was broken in 1933-4 by
Chancellor Dollfuss's suspension of parliament, the banning of
the Social Democratic Party, the defeat of its armed formation,
the *Republikanischer Schutzbund*, and the proclamation of an
authoritarian-corporatist constitution in force until the *Anschluss*
of 1938.

But the late-imperial political culture survived, intact, the dictatorship of the 1930's, incorporation into the Third Reich and the

[22] Bauer, *op. cit.*, pp. 126, 196-213.
[23] See below, p. 169.
[24] R. Michels, *Political Parties. A Sociological Study of the Oligarchical Tendencies of Modern Democracy* (introd. S. M. Lipset), p. 80.
I am grateful to Professor David Rapoport, of U.C.L.A., for his
illuminating comments on this topic.
[25] L. Berchtold, *Österreichische Parteiprogramme, 1868-1966*, p. 250.

Second World War, and imprinted itself on the second as on the first Austrian Republic. The very manner in which the republican constitution was reinstated in 1945 illustrates this continuity. As in 1918, it was the party leaders who took the initiative – this time not in parliament (for there was none), but in their private residences and hiding places. On 27 April the members of the provisional government acting as "executives of the political parties of Austria" proclaimed the "restoration of the democratic republic of Austria".[26] Once more a constitution was apparently accepted by the population because it was acceptable to the parties. The first parliamentary election showed that little had changed in the relative strengths of the *Lager*: the People's Party (ÖVP), broadly the successor of the Christian-Socials, polled 50 per cent, the Socialists (SPÖ) 45 per cent and the Communists 5 per cent. The Allied military authorities refused to license a party to represent the national-liberal *Lager*, and many of its potential voters were among the 480,000 temporarily disfranchised for their Nazi activities. When, in 1949, such a party was licensed and former Nazis were again allowed to vote, it polled 12 per cent. Not very much had shifted since 1911:

Percentage Support for Lager
1911-49 (post-1918 frontiers)

	1911	1930	1949
Marxist	29	42	44
Liberal-National	18	16	12
Christian-Conservative	53	42	44

One critical load of which the Austrian political system was relieved in 1945 was that of incorporation. The experience of the *Anschluss* convinced most Austrians that they wished to live in a sovereign state, bounded by the frontiers fixed at the Paris Peace Conference. For the first time since 1848 patriotism and the sense of nationality could work towards the same goal.

In every other respect the viability of the system was still in question. As in 1918-19 its legitimacy depended on the combined support of the major parties; if that support disappeared, so would the legitimacy. If the political parties concentrated their efforts on reconstructing and maintaining their internal cohesion and ideological purity, then *Lagermentalität* would once more triumph over common interest. All the initial evidence showed how tenacious were the habits of life of the sub-cultures. Party

[26] A. Schärf, *Österreichs Wiederaufrichtung im Jahre 1945*, p. 74.

enrolment quickly rose to pre-war levels. The SPÖ had over 600,000 members by 1948; in the past twenty years between 36 and 38 per cent of the party's electors have been paid-up members, compared with under 10 per cent in West Germany. The effective membership of the ÖVP is about 515,000,[27] representing some 25-30 per cent of its regular electorate – an extraordinarily high level for a European Christian-Democratic party. Electoral participation exceeds 90 per cent in every one of the nine provinces, including those where voting is not compulsory.

The ancillary organizations of the political parties continued to flourish. There are, according to the latest figures, 4,000 socialist philatelists, 11,000 socialist fishing enthusiasts and 85,000 socialist motorists.[28] The parties' rival athletic organizations vie in proclaiming their contributions to the country's Olympic medals. An elaborate multiple regression survey in 1965-6, using seven variables, came to the conclusion that three out of five Austrians are firmly integrated into either the working-class-socialist or Catholic-conservative sub-culture, and that the proportion of persons susceptible to cross-pressures is exceptionally low.[29]

COALITION IN THE SECOND REPUBLIC
Although the extent of commitment to the life of the sub-cultures has not changed since the first republic, its intensity evidently has. The coalition government which saw the second republic in lasted twenty-one years, not a mere two.

The most pressing reason for continuing the coalition beyond the initial phase of political reconstruction was external. It was necessary to maintain national unity in the face of Allied military occupation which lasted until 1955. Even after the signature of the State Treaty there were diplomatic reasons for preserving the coalition, since a condition of the treaty was "perpetual neutrality" on the part of Austria – a condition which the Austrian public initially accepted only grudgingly, as the price to be paid for Soviet withdrawal, and which only later came to be seen as an ornament of Austrian sovereignty, rather than as a diminution of it. The importance of the treaty for internal politics was that it enabled the coalition leaders to claim a patriotic achievement, unlike the political leaders of the first republic, who had to bear

[27] The difficulties of assessing ÖVP membership are discussed in P. G. J. Pulzer, "Austria" in S. Henig & J. Pinder (eds.), European Political Parties, p. 295.
[28] Sozialistische Partei Österreichs. Bericht an den Parteitag 1968, pp. 137, 130, 127.
[29] K. Liepelt, "Esquisse d'une typologie des électeurs allemands et autrichiens," Revue française de Sociologie, 11 (janvier-mars 1968), pp. 16, 23.

the odium of having stabbed the empire in the back. (The parallel with the fate of the political parties of West Germany is strikingly suggestive.) These patriotic achievements, and their diplomatic consequences, quite apart from their legitimating effect, also ensured that there would be no revival of the incorporation crisis.

But there were also purely domestic reasons which explain the slow solution of the legitimacy crisis. I shall argue that the longevity of the coalition; the modes of political collaboration devised within it; and the special relationship between the coalition partners and the principal pressure groups have had a de-polarizing effect on the system. Ideology is not an end in Austria. As the Liepelt survey has shown, *Lager*-based traditionalism is widespread, but what was once a millenarian vision has become a set of routinized dogmatic attitudes. The *Lager* have not disintegrated. They have merely colluded in letting their ammunition rust. The character of the parties has not changed beyond recognition. What *has* happened is that those wings of the parties which favour peaceful co-existence have gained strength compared with the inter-war period.

Both before 1934 and since 1945 it was the party organizations of the provinces which were more favourable to coalition than those of Vienna,[30] partly because the constitutions of the eight non-metropolitan provinces provide for coalition government on the Swiss, collegial model. The post-war shift of economic and demographic preponderance from metropolitan to provincial Austria has had predictable political effects.

The political dominance of moderate men and the exigencies of foreign policy helped to make the coalition viable; but they would not have sufficed if the coalition had been unable to satisfy the aspirations of the country's major organized interests.

Polarity as it exists in Austria can be explained in three ways. In the first place Austria is unique among European polarized systems in having two overwhelmingly strong major parties. In post-war elections they have totalled an average of 87.4 per cent of the vote compared with 88.7 per cent in "two-party" Britain. The reason for this, as I have suggested above, is that the post-1918 party alignment, like the post-1918 territory of Austria, was a fragment of the multi-national, multi-party empire.

Then, the weakness of autonomous pressure groups, and their dependence on political parties as patrons, makes the articulation of interests easier. When interest groups depend on the leadership of ideological parties in multi-party systems, the result is fragmentation of interest representation – witness the rival trade unions and farmers' organizations in Italy, France or Belgium. In Aus-

[30] A. Wandruszka, *op. cit.*, pp. 324, 344-5; 452, 455-6.

tria there is no reason for this fragmentation. The Liepelt survey demonstrates what Austrian political managers have for decades assumed, that each major interest group is almost exclusively integrated into one of the *Lager*. Of the peasants 80 per cent are integrated into the Catholic sub-culture. Forty-nine per cent of socialist support comes from industrial or white-collar workers who are classified as integrated and a further 24 per cent from industrial workers who are not fully integrated; the ÖVP draws only 5 per cent and 9 per cent respectively of its support from these two groups.[31]

Finally, not only does each party effectively articulate one of the major interests in the country, it also aggregates them, as indeed it must in a two-party situation.

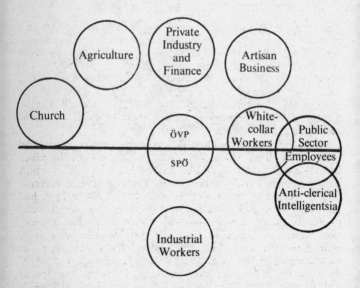

The only group apparently cross-pressurized is that of public sector employees (which includes a considerable proportion of the country's white-collar labour force). However, the conventions of party patronage elaborated under the coalition turned the "red"

[31] Adapted from Liepelt, *op. cit.*, pp. 18-19, p. 27, n. 8.

and "black" wings of the public sector into virtually separate, non-competing interests.

The exceptionally clear-cut relationship between interest groups and parties contributed to the smooth functioning of the coalition. Each party knew in which direction it had to look over its shoulder. The process was further facilitated by the corporatist traditions and semi-corporatist institutions of Austrian economic life. Each major economic interest is enrolled in a statutory representative organ known as a chamber; the three most important and politically significant of these are the Chamber of Commerce (*Handelskammer*), the Chamber of Agriculture (*Landwirtschaftskammer*), and the Chamber of Labour (*Arbeitskammer*), embracing both industrial workers and clerical employees.[32] Since elections to the executives of these chambers are by party list, the ÖVP permanently dominates the first two, the SPÖ the third. The same corporatist features are displayed by the internal constitution of the People's Party: membership is recruited through one of three occupational "leagues" – economic (*Wirtschaftsbund*), agricultural (*Bauernbund*) and wage-earners' (*Arbeiter- und Angestelltenbund*). Leadership of the chambers, the leagues, and therefore also of those ministries in the coalition which came under ÖVP patronage, overlapped heavily. The Socialist Party in contrast has a unitary structure, but there is a noticeable interlocking of offices between its leaders, those of the trade unions and those of the Chamber of Labour.

While the authority with which the party leaders acted owed much to the direct way in which they could speak for the major interest organizations, it derived equally from the way in which the governmental coalition functioned. The modalities of coalition politics recognized that it was the parties which, as in 1918, had "created" the organs of state. The character of this *contrat social* (to repeat Bauer's formulation) was ratified by a series of coalition pacts, first signed in 1947 and then repeated after every general election until 1962, which bound the signatories to an exclusive partnership, to be ended only by a dissolution of parliament. At first these pacts were secret, but following a newspaper leak those of 1956, 1959 and 1962 were published immediately on being signed. The pacts provided for a coalition commission (*Koalitionsausschuss*) with power to decide any matters of interpretation. Except for the two party leaders (who would be the Chancellor and Vice-Chancellor of the government) the delegates to the commission were whips and party functionaries, not cabi-

[32] H. P. Secher, "Representative Democracy or 'Chamber State': The Ambiguous Role of Interest Groups in Austrian Politics." *Western Political Quarterly*, Vol. 13 (December 1960) pp. 892-6.

net members. It is evident that in terms of policy-making power the cabinet was subordinate to the commission, as parliament was subordinate to both, since it was the duty of the parliamentary whips to ensure compliance with the decisions of the commission. But even the commission was not completely master in its own house. The parties' dominance over the interest groups was strong, but not complete: "business," "agriculture" and "labour" do not, after all, constitute single, homogeneous lobbies, but are subject to intra-group rivalries. Especially in the period of greatest economic stringency, from 1947 to 1952, the annual wage-price agreements, a national collective bargain in which the country's leading politicians certainly participated but in which the chambers and trade unions came uniquely into their own, constituted "the core of political decision-making."[33] To that extent they presented *faits accomplis* to the bodies constitutionally designated for ratifying these agreements.

The coalition's style of decision-making had its faults: it encouraged a corporatist immobilism, protection for the least productive sectors, and inflation; it gave Austria a *per capita* income which is one-half that of Switzerland. But it also created full employment and the beginnings of consumer affluence, and both these material satisfactions are a great improvement on the Austrians' previous experience. What the coalition did achieve, equally by its methods of work and by the material improvements which took place under its aegis, was to defuse the crisis of distribution. Economic conflicts were no longer seen as driving inexorably towards civil war.

The coalition equally helped to resolve the crisis of participation. The introduction of universal suffrage in 1907, and of full parliamentary government in 1918, had, of course, gone a long way towards achieving this. Neither of these reforms, however, had given the non-official classes, represented by the extra-parliamentary parties, full access to the administration and the judiciary. Before 1918 both these branches had, at any rate in the higher ranks, been near-monopolies of the liberal bourgeoisie. The academic requirements were stringent and membership of the correct student corporation helped. After 1918, with governments dominated by the Christian-Social Party, the older elites had to share their privileges with nominees of the *Cartell-Verband*, the Catholic academic corporation. But only in a limited number of municipalities, chiefly Vienna, was public service advancement open to persons of working-class or Jewish origin.

This changed with the coming of the post-1945 coalition. Under the terms of the coalition pacts, each party gained partisan

[33] *Ibid.*, p. 899.

patronage in the ministries and public corporations that it controlled. The right to nominate rested on the *Proporz* – the relative strengths of the parties as revealed by the most recent election. The *Proporz* also applied to any new institutions that might be set up: the broadcasting services and the armed forces, as these were released from allied military control after 1955, or new universities and research institutes.[34] Through the *Proporz* the socialists at last gained parity within the state, and it was one of their main reasons for supporting the coalition.

The *Proporz* no doubt encouraged bureaucratization and careerism in the SPÖ, thereby offending some rank-and-file members. However, the number of jobs at stake was large, partly as a result of the nationalizations of 1945-6. The Ministry of Nationalized Industries, headed from 1949 to 1956 by the chief SPÖ technocrat, Karl Waldbrunner, was the most important part of the socialist patronage machine, and one whose partition the ÖVP achieved when they gained 8 seats in the 1956 election.

With two of the heaviest critical loads shed, the chances that the crisis of legitimacy might also be solved were improved. There were still obstacles to this. Most importantly, the machinery of economic consultation necessarily devalued the purely political institutions of the country – parliament and the cabinet – and the purely political mechanisms, such as elections. Everybody knew that the real decisions were made by the chambers, the caucuses and the coalition commission. In addition, a powerful factor in cementing the coalition was precisely the mutual distrust which the two *Lager* had inherited as part of the common political culture. Only if shackled to each other by the coalition pact could they avert foul play. This explains why elections were only semi-competitive. Both the SPÖ and the ÖVP pledged themselves in advance to continue the coalition after the election – this was true even in 1966 when the coalition was, in fact, not continued. Neither of the true opposition parties – the communists on the Left and the revived liberal-national parties on the Right[35] – had any prospect of sharing power. All that the election could decide was the exact proportions in which office was to be distributed within the next government. Given the rigidity of voter loyalties the movements were necessarily minute.

Some aspects of coalition government suggested that the coalition was intended to be a permanent feature of the country's

---

[34] H. P. Secher, "Coalition Government: The Case of the Austrian Second Republic," *American Political Science Review*, Vol. 51 (September 1958), pp. 799-801, 805-7.

[35] League of Independents (VdU) until 1956, Freedom Party (FPÖ) thereafter.

political life. The *Proporz* was one symptom of this institutionalization. Another was the convention of "departmental opposition" *(Bereichsopposition)*; since the genuine parliamentary opposition had no opportunity to act as a control on the actions of the government, each coalition partner acted as a critic of the departments dominated by the other. Some political observers even went so far as to regard coalition *à l'autrichienne* as a unique contribution to political institutions,[36] and one expert on constitutional law forecast in 1959 that to end the coalition would be the equivalent of a political revolution.[37]

What the enforced collaboration of the coalition did ensure, since its leading members were at the same time representatives of the main economic interests, was a trend towards pragmatic discussion and piece-meal reformism. The parties' dependence on ideology was also diminished: in the SPÖ by the formal renunciation of an exclusively Marxist inspiration in 1958[38] and on the Right by the withdrawal of the Church from party politics, begun in 1945.[39] These developments, common in the post-war world, helped to neutralize the otherwise powerful survivals of *Lager* culture in Austria.

THE END OF THE COALITION

Whether the regime had been truly legitimated, however, would emerge only when it was no longer supported jointly by the parties which had called it into existence. This happened as a result of the 1966 election when the ÖVP emerged with 48.3 per cent of the vote (a gain of 2.9 per cent) and an absolute parliamentary majority. Although the SPÖ was temporarily weakened at that election by a dissident list, formed by the former trade union leader Franz Olah, what was really significant on this occasion was the evidence of new, and large-scale, electoral volatility. At the beginning of the election campaign 22 per cent of the electorate were still undecided, compared with under 10 per cent at previous elections.[40] This volatility cannot be treated as an inde-

---

[36] E.g. A. Schärf, *Österreichs Erneuerung 1945-1955* (revised edn., 1960), p. 412. Schärf was Vice-Chancellor, 1945-57 and President, 1957-65.

[37] G. E. Kafka, "Die verfassungsrechtliche Stellung der politischen Parteien im modernen Staat," *Veröffentlichungen der Vereinigung der deutschen Staatsrechtslehrer,* 17 (1959), p. 90.

[38] K. L. Shell, *The Transformation of Austrian Socialism*, pp. 126-58.

[39] H. Magenschab, *Die zweite Republik zwischen Kirche und Parteien*, passim.

[40] For 1966: K. Blecha & H. Kienzl, "Österreichs Wähler sind in Bewegung," *Die Zukunft*, May 1966, p. 26; for 1962: K. Blecha, H. Kienzl & R. Gmoser, *Der durchleuchtete Wähler. Beiträge zur politischen Soziologie in Österreich*, p. 37.

pendent factor: the pragmatism which the political leaders had been practising for two decades was beginning to influence the rank-and-file elector.

Many Austrians viewed the return of single-party government with apprehension. One observer warned that "the work of building up a consensus was broken off too soon and competition introduced prematurely."[41] But economic bargaining has continued much as before and the trade unions have shown no inclination to use industrial action for political ends. The ÖVP government has not seriously abused its powers of patronage. Moreover, a series of provincial and municipal elections during 1967 and 1968 has demonstrated continuing electoral volatility, this time in terms of an anti-government swing which, if maintained at the parliamentary election of 1970, make it conceivable that the ÖVP will have to resign its monopoly of power to the ŠPO. It is not too early to say that the mechanism of self-government has "taken off" and is now self-sustained.

Since the emergence of extra-parliamentary parties in the 1880's, it has been these parties, with their combination of ideology and interest articulation, that have succeeded in attracting the political loyalties of a population whom successive regimes offered insufficient participation and unsatisfactory distribution. The way in which these parties exercised an authority that the institutions of the state could not aspire to was demonstrated in 1918 and 1945. The failure of the state-founding coalition to legitimate the First Republic, because the parties reverted, after two years, to their disintegrative roles, contrasts with the largely integrative role of the state-founding parties in the much longer coalition of the second republic. By successfully operating, in concert, the institutions which they had called into being, they legitimated them. Those very qualities which turned the parties into *Lager* enabled them to turn towards co-operation – or at least peaceful competition – with the same disciplined unanimity with which they had previously fought each other in the streets.

POSTSCRIPT BY THE AUTHOR, JULY 1973

Consociationalism is a specific remedy for a specific ill. It is a conspiratorial device arising out of the assumption by the leaders of the main opinion groups that their followers cannot be trusted to compete freely for power in the state. Its defects are a diffusion of responsibility and a lack of external controls on decision-making.

As with other educative constraints, we can judge its success only when it is no longer needed. Since 1966, the Austrian

---

[41] E. F. Winter, "Bilanz der Nachkriegszeit Österreichs," *Politische Studien,* 19, (March-April 1968), p. 184.

federal government has been formed by single parties, not coalitions. The majority ÖVP government was replaced in 1970 by a minority SPÖ government and a new election in 1971 gave the SPÖ an absolute majority. Alternating majorities have therefore not placed an intolerable load on the system.

Some of the devices of the coalition, such as departmental opposition, are now redundant. *Proporz* in appointments remains, though more fluidly, especially since most provincial and municipal government is still by coalition. In any case, large-scale purges would undo the work of integration. The coalition of producer groups, institutionalised in the Parity Commission for Wages and Prices, has remained intact and the ending of the coalition has not exacerbated social conflict.

Lagermentalität survives in attenuated forms. Party membership is as high as ever and will continue to be so as long as parties exercise the patronage they do. But voter volatility has come to stay, as municipal elections since 1971 have shown. If it increases, it could introduce into the system an element of instability, the avoidance of which is something to which the parties and interest groups have hitherto subordinated almost all other objectives.

BELGIUM: CONFLICT AND COMPROMISE

Val R. Lorwin

Source: V. R. Lorwin, "Conflict and Compromise in Belgian Politics" (Paper presented at the Annual Meeting of the American Political Science Association, Washington, D.C., September, 1965). It is printed here for the first time by permission of the author, who has reviewed and revised the text for this volume. He notes: "I have made stylistic changes in the text to improve on imprecise or unclear phrasing, and to put most present and present perfect tenses into the more neutral past tense. I have resisted the obvious temptation to alter language to show wisdom after the event." A French translation appeared in the *Courrier hebdomadaire* of the Centre de Recherche et d'Information Socio-Politiques (Brussels), No. 323, June 10, 1966.

Three issues dominated the first century and a third of the national political life of Belgium. The first in time was the religious issue, the problem of relations of Church and State, especially with regard to the schools. Out of this conflict arose the first two of the nation's three "traditional parties," the Liberal Party and the Catholic Party.

A second set of issues, arising from the claims of the working class for equality of citizenship, and for social justice, gave rise to the Socialist Party. It coupled its defense of workers' interests with an opposition to the Church and to religion which allied it with the Liberal Party against the Catholic Party in the school fight. The Socialist Party's and socialist unions' attitudes toward religion and the Church, and the Church's intense hostility toward socialism, caused Catholic workers to organize largely within specifically Catholic labor organizations and to act politically as a wing of the Catholic party.

The third set of issues opposed Flemish and French-speaking (francophone) Belgians, sometimes in a confrontation of the two linguistic communities, sometimes in a confrontation of the two regions of Flanders and Wallonia, and sometimes – especially in more recent times – in conflict among the three regions of Flanders, Wallonia, and Brussels. These issues did not become party-forming until after World War One.

Kulturkampf, class conflict, linguistic and regional tensions are classic issues of modern European politics. But if no single element in the Belgian political system was unique, its structures of conflict and compromise, and the historical circumstances under which these developed, represented a unique pattern interesting for itself and for comparative analysis.

The most inclusive system of conflict and compromise was that of the "spiritual families" – Catholic, Liberal, and Socialist. This I have called the system of "*verzuiling*," to use a word which the

Dutch first used after World War Two.[1] The term was not current in Belgium, but it identified a system of relationships as basic for several generations to that country's politics as to those of its northern neighbor.

A "*zuil*" is a pillar. If we insisted on translating the Dutch with an English neologism, *verzuiling* would be "pillarization." (A better English translation would be "segmented pluralism," but it too requires explanation.) *Verzuiling* was first used in the affirmative sense of the basic unity of Dutch society resting on the separateness of the several pillars which are the spiritual families.

The *zuilen*, however, not only supported; they also separated. They were – to change the metaphor – compartments as well as pillars. Each ideology had its own party, press, cultural, and socio-economic organizations, and – in the case of Catholicism (and in Holland, Protestantism) – religious and educational institutions. Historically the three parties of Belgian *verzuiling* dominated the political scene, in their hostilities and, later, their coalitions. Their bases of support in the spiritual families and their networks of organizations gave each of them a certain security in the cooperation entailed by the coalition government necessary in the era of universal equal manhood suffrage.

Verzuiling expressed, but it might also absorb, or deflect, conflicts. It fully reflected the religious conflict which dominated the first half century of the new nation's political life, a conflict extending from the two ideological parties of the taxpayers' suffrage era to the voteless crowds which each of the parties summoned from time to time in demonstration against its opponents. The entry of the Socialist Party on the scene did not change the essentially bipartite nature of this conflict, for the Socialists were at one with the Liberals in opposition to Catholic claims. The forms of settlement changed, but problems were managed, more or less effectively, by the *verzuiling* system, in its three political parties and the Church, until they arrived at the apparently lasting compromise of the 1958 school pact.[2]

[1] See the witty and informative brief volume of J. P. Kruijt and others, *Verzuiling* (2nd ed., Zaandijk, Heijnis, 1959); J. P. Kruijt and W. Goddijn, "Verzuiling en ontzuiling als sociologisch proces," in A. N. J. Den Hollander et al., eds., *Drift en Koers: Een halve eeuw sociale verandering in Nederland* (2nd ed., Assen, 1962), pp. 227-63 and bibliography, and the chapter on The Netherlands by Hans Daalder in the volume in press as this was written, Robert A. Dahl, ed., *Political Oppositions in Western Democracies*, (New Haven: Yale University Press, 1966).

[2] For some discussion of the history and present state of the other conflicts, see two volumes in press as this was written: Jean Mey-

Class issues were partly represented, partly absorbed, in the *verzuiling* system. Socialist organization quickly disciplined the industrial and political protest of one section of the working class to manageable levels. Catholic workers pressed their case within their own spiritual family, which finally legitimized the Catholic labor movement as one of its "estates." The system was strong enough to keep workers' patience within bounds until their most elementary demands were granted after the First World War. But only what remained of State authority above and beyond its immersion in the *verzuiling* system could force the employer organizations to accept the various forms of collective bargaining which after World War Two achieved a more or less continuous adjustment of class interests. *Verzuiling* helped maintain the discipline of the unions and health insurance societies which represented labor in those bargaining processes inside and outside of government agencies. Belgium was one of the very few countries where divided labor movements were strong.

Linguistic claims were long kept within bounds by the political parties, but they were too long denied legitimacy. After World War One, these claims repeatedly erupted outside the party system or beyond its capacity to handle them effectively.[3]

It was the opposition of linguistic regions, joined to that of the spiritual families, which between 1944 and 1950 made the "royal affair" – the struggle over the return of Leopold III to his throne – the sharpest conflict of Belgium's internal history. The system was further shaken because the issue concerned the person who symbolized and enacted the role of constitutional guarantor of the *verzuiling* system itself. Here, in 1950, the popular violence of a Socialist general strike reversed the original decision to bring the King back. But the constitutionally and electorally stronger party (the Christian Social Party) could afford to bow to this violence because it did not threaten the continuation of the *verzuiling* system or its continuing guarantee.

Verzuiling and its political party system took care of much of the regular business of government, allocating jobs and responsi-

naud, Jean Ladrière, and François Perin, eds., *La Décision politique en Belgique: le pouvoir et les groupes* (Paris: Cahiers de la Fondation Nationale des Sciences Politiques, no. 138, 1965), and my chapter on Belgium in the volume edited by Dahl (see note 1).

[3] H. J. Elias, *Geschiedenis van de Vlaamse gedachte, 1780-1914* (4 vols., Antwerp, 1963-65); S. B. Clough, *A History of the Flemish Movement in Belgium* (New York, 1930); A. W. Willemsen, *Het Vlaamse nationalisme, 1914-40* (Groningen, 1958); J. A. Van Houtte *et al.*, *Algemene Geschiedenis der Nederlanden* (Zeist, 1956-58), vols. IX-XII, and Theo Luykx, *Politieke geschiedenis van België* (Brussels, 1964).

bilities to system participants. But some major issues, notably regional demands and the mutual fears and resentments of the two linguistic communities, occasionally broke onto the scene from without, upsetting previous system compromises or electoral decisions. So far, common interests and habits – and other factors which I consider later – have been strong enough to maintain the functioning of the national state and national social organizations.

THE PARTY SYSTEM

The party system had great continuity. The new state was launched with an interesting period of "unionism," in which Catholics and Liberals cooperated in successive cabinets, while the state was establishing its right and ability to survive. Then Liberals and Catholics alternated in national power for four decades. In 1884, the Catholics, taking full advantage of Liberal dissensions and the resentments aroused by anticlerical school legislation, installed themselves in exclusive national power until the First World War.

The Socialist Party entered upon the political scene in the 1880's tying in the claims of the working class with the attack on revealed religion so common on the Continent and so different from the British or Scandinavian socialist positions. Anticlericalism remained the dogmatism of the Socialist Party as, becoming a force in Parliament in 1894, it quickly abandoned the revolutionary dreams of its youth to become a party of the "loyal opposition."

The national suffrage was not broadened from 1848 to 1893 in this country whose early factories, mines, and railroads set the pace of the Industrial Revolution on the Continent. Universal manhood suffrage was introduced in 1893, but weighted for property, education, and family status. Universal, compulsory primary education did not come until 1913. Only in 1919 was universal equal suffrage for men granted (and only in 1949 for women). By 1919, it was a politically rather mature working class whose male members had arrived at full political rights.

The long struggle for the right to vote and for equality of the vote, as well as for the public schools, for compulsory primary education, and for equality in military service, disciplined the Socialist Party in the acceptance of limited political aims and in the tactics of coalition (with the progressive wing of the Liberal Party). The Socialists sat in the national government for the first time, as in many countries, during the First World War. But, contrary to the experience of other Socialist Parties, they continued in the cabinet after the war, and with pragmatic gains to show. In style and function, they became a "party of government," one of the three "traditional parties."

Belgian social groups, and first among them the industrial workers, showed a considerable capacity for self-organization. "The future belongs to the class which builds its own institutions," said the Socialist Emile Vandervelde. But classes do not build; men and women build. Men and women have other loyalties, and other interests, than those of class. Expressing their loyalties within the framework of *verzuiling*, Belgian workers built as Socialists and Catholics and (to a much smaller degree) as Liberals.

The Socialists led the way with their network of friendly societies, consumer cooperatives, and labor unions, all closely tied in with – and for a long time rather dominated by – the political party. The Catholics established similar workers' organizations and powerful farmers' and middle-class organizations, mainly in Flanders, which gained recognition as corporate elements or "estates" within the Catholic Party. The Liberals, although predominantly of the middle and professional classes, also established friendly societies and trade unions. Thus the Belgian parties at the turn of the century took on their close association with the cultural and socio-economic organizations grouped by religious-ideological affinities and antipathies, although the great burst of organizing activity of the workers came after World War One.

The party system was remarkably stable for many decades. It withstood two world wars and two enemy occupations, changes in social structure, the rise of regional-linguistic movements, the introduction of universal suffrage and of proportional representation, the great depression, the tides of international communism and fascism, the shifts from Belgian neutrality to international commitment and back and forth again, the acceptance of the welfare state, the forced abdication of a monarch, and the loss of a vast colony. It withstood changes of name and structure by each of the parties. (For simplicity, I shall sometimes speak of the "Catholic Party" in a context which includes the years since 1945, when it was reborn as the Christian Social Party, of the "Socialist Party" to signify what was until 1940 the Belgian Workers' Party, and of the "Liberal Party" and the "Liberals" to denote those who in 1961 reorganized as the Party of Liberty and Progress. The continuity is least clear for the Liberals, but I shall follow Belgian usage and speak of the members or voters of the Party of Liberty and Progress, PLP, for whom there is as yet no other noun, as the "Liberals." I shall use the initials of the French names, although obviously each party also had its Flemish name.)

The period of single-party cabinets ended with the equalization of male suffrage. Since 1919, except for a single legislature (1950-54), no one party has ever had a majority in both Houses.

Table 1 Seats in House of Representatives, by Party, Period of Equal Universal Suffrage, 1919-1965*(in number of seats immediately after each national election).

	Soc.	Comm.	Lib.	Flem. Nat.	Rex	Cath.	Diss. Cath.	Misc.	Total
1919	70	–	34	5		73		4	186
1921	68	–	33	4		76	4	1	186
1925	78	2	23	6		75	3		187
1929	70	1	28	11		71	6		187
1932	73	3	24	8		79			187
1936	70	9	23	16	21	61	2		202
1939	64	9	33	17	4	73		2	202
					UDB				
1946	69	23	17	–	1	92			202
1949	66	12	29	–		105			212
1950	77	7	20	–		108			212
1954	86	4	25	1		95	1		212
1958	84	2	21	1		104			212
1961	84	5	20	5		96		2	212
			PLP						
1965	64	6	48	12		77		5	212

Abbreviations: Soc. – Socialist Party (Workers' Party until 1940; since 1945, Socialist Party)
Comm. – Communist Party
Lib. – Liberal Party; PLP – Party of Liberty and Progress – after 1961
Flem. Nat. – Various Flemish nationalist groups; since 1954, Flemish People's Union
Cath. – Until 1940, Catholic Party; since 1945, Christian Social Party
Diss. Cath. – Dissident Catholic tickets
UDB – Belgian Democratic Union (Catholic laborite)

* Male suffrage only before 1949.

Sources: R. E. Smet, R. Evalenko, and W. Fraeys, *Atlas des élections belges, 1919-1954*, *Annexe*, pp. 14-15, for 1919-1954, and Ministry of Interior figures for 1958, 1961, and 1965.

Table I gives the distribution of seats in the House of Representatives after each national election since 1919.

The Catholic Party was the strongest at almost every national election, with the Socialists not far behind and occasionally ahead, and the Liberals a distant but significant third. The Catholics were strongest in Flanders and the Socialists in Wallonia; the Liberals had their greatest strength in Brussels, where the balance fluctuated most.

The only flash-party success of this whole period was that of the anti-democratic Rexists in the crisis year of 1936. The Communists were the one persistent splinter party. Various Flemish nationalist parties become a permanent feature of the parliamentary landscape, and in the 1960's a Walloon and a Brussels francophone party each appeared in significant numbers.

Since there was no willingness to support minority governments and no backing for cabinets of non-parliamentary figures, coalition cabinets became the rule. Between the wars, the most frequent combinations were Catholic-Liberal and tripartite cabinets. One cabinet broke out of the *verzuiling* mold: that formed in 1925 by the Catholic Party's Flemish-laborite wing and the Socialists. Its eleven months in office gave the Socialists the tantalizing hope, unrealized but never quite abandoned in 40 years, of a breakup of the Catholic Party on socio-economic lines, with its labor elements going over to the Socialist Party.

After World War Two there was a brief period in which the Communists were admitted to the sanctum of power. Then followed the first one-party cabinets under universal equal suffrage, the all-Catholic governments of the 1950-54 legislature. After, national government took the form of each possible combination – Socialist-Liberal, Catholic-Liberal, and Catholic-Socialist.[4] The latter, the "grand alliance" in the size of its parliamentary majority and the importance of the social forces behind it, was the formula from 1961 to the time this was written. Despite *verzuiling*, the political distance between parties was sufficiently reduced to permit any combination of two or three in a cabinet.

Between the wars the Catholic Party became a loose federation of its component social forces – the organizations of farmers, labor, and middle-class, and the clubs of local notables – and, in the late 1930's, a loose federation of two separate regional wings, Flemish and French-speaking. After the war, it reemerged as the Christian Social Party (the Parti Social Chrétien, PSC). It was now based on individual, not group, affiliations, and adopted a tighter national structure. It proclaimed its intention to "deconfes-

---

[4] In addition, a minority all-PSC cabinet held office for 4½ months after the 1958 election.

sionalize" itself (to use a rather barbarous word for which it found no happier synonym), and to pursue more progressive social policies than its pre-war predecessor.

The years submerged some of these intentions, but confirmed others. Individual membership continued to be the rule, but the social organizations, especially those of labor, became stronger, and asserted their group interests in the party's mechanisms of decision-making and selection of candidates. Farmers' leagues, middle-class groups, and the Catholic Workers' Movement (which grouped trade unions, friendly societies, and the Young Catholic Workers) were given recognition, along with traditional bourgeois elements, in the naming of candidates. This recognition came through negotiation and agreement, or by the primary elections which – in most large cities and many smaller ones – might confirm candidates or resolve disputes about slates of candidates, in the PSC as in the two other major parties. The electoral system of multi-member constituencies facilitated the recognition of the various social organizations of the Catholic community in any single slate.

The party did indeed become much more "social," while experiencing a continual tension between a progressive tendency, whose mass support was labor, with intellectual sympathizers of labor, and a conservative and traditionalist tendency. The Flemish wing was on the whole more progressive, reflecting the weight of the Flemish Catholic labor movement. The much smaller Walloon wing of the party was more conservative, dominated as it was by middle-class and aristocratic elements, albeit in frequent conflict with a left-wing Walloon minority.

In its national structure, the PSC recognized the two language groups in its midst. By the early 1960's, old strains between the Flemish majority and the francophone minority were again greatly in evidence. The difference in the party's social base in the two regions deepened the linguistic-regional tensions which threatened its national unity.

One aim the party soon forgot about: "deconfessionalization." In leadership, in electoral constituency, and in ties with the increasingly strong Catholic social groups, the party did not depart from the basis of *verzuiling*. The school war of the 1950's strengthened the ties of organized Catholic social groups, especially labor, with the PSC.

Immediately after World War Two one attempt was made to free political action from the old mold of religious affinities and antipathies. A group of Socialists and chiefly – as it turned out – Catholics attempted to launch a Labour-Party form of political action. Influenced by wartime reflection on the British experience, they hoped for a realignment of parties, more "modern" and less affective, primarily on social and economic issues. But the old party structures and the spirit of *verzuiling* reaffirmed themselves too soon for the new Belgian Democratic Union (Union Démocratique Belge) to take hold. The UDB entered the election campaign of 1946 as a mildly left-laborite, chiefly Walloon Catholic group. To many, therefore, it looked like only a dissident Catholic formation, with a high percentage of intellectuals, and without the mass base its orientation demanded, as most Catholic and Socialist trade union leaders returned to habitual party affinities. Electoral disaster in its first and last election brought the experiment to an abrupt end. The UDB's failure confirmed the confessional character which Catholic political action had once again assumed.

The old Worker's Party was reborn too in 1945, as the Socialist Party (Parti Socialiste Belge, PSB). It abandoned the group affiliation of members (through the trade unions, cooperatives, and friendly societies) in favor of individual affiliation, like the PSC. But its hopes of attracting support from other classes were largely disappointed as its chief recruitment came from its traditional sources: manual workers, white collar, and professional people.

A formal structure called the Common Action was created (in 1949) to coordinate the political action of unions, friendly societies, and cooperatives with that of the PSB. Its role remained limited. More important was the network of informal personal contacts, overlapping directorates, common social base, generally common aims, and financial aid by the social organizations to the party. Some of the party's leaders showed a certain nostalgia, without practical consequences, for the old days of fuller *verzuiling*, when the party had the more assured base and financing of formal collective affiliation by the social organizations.

The Liberal Party had been the leading party of government, of centralization of the unitary state, and of *laïcité* in the first half century of independence. Like many other lay bourgeois parties, in the age of mass suffrage it was far outdistanced by Catholic and Socialist appeals. It continued, however, to play a significant minority role, in national government and in local politics, with some strong local organizations, most notably in Brussels.

In 1961 the party merged with several right-wing splinter parties, took the name of the Party of Liberty and Progress (PLP), and launched an ambitious "catch-all" appeal. The Liberals shed the old party's historic anti-clericalism in an effort at modernization and appeal to the Catholic petty and upper bourgeoisie, especially those dissatisfied with the Christian Social Party's cohabitation in government with the Socialists. The PLP achieved a double breach in the wall of *verzuiling* by its appeal to Catholic voters and its linguistic emphases, appropriately varied in each region.

The Communist Party represented a significant opposition only – paradoxically – when its tactics were those of identification with the national interest, in resistance and reconstruction. Soon after Liberation, for the first time, it had members in the government, a sizable labor union following, much public sympathy, and even more friendly curiosity. In 1946, it obtained one-eighth of the total vote. For the first and last time since universal equal manhood suffrage, a fourth party surpassed the Liberals in votes and House seats. Then the CP declined to its present low state.

The Socialists fused their unions with those which emerged under Communist leadership at the liberation. Trade union fusion was possible without suffocation by the Communists, thanks to the *verzuiling* of close Socialist union ties with other Socialist organizations and to Socialist freedom from the paralyzing French myth of "no enemies to the left." The Communist Party retained some following in Walloon industrial centers and among Brussels white-collar and public service employees. But it was weak in numbers, leadership, press, and intellectual support. Almost pathetically mild and colorless, it shuffled along in the wake of the Socialist Party, half-heartedly claiming to be in advance of it, until in the 1960's it was riven by the Moscow-Peking schism.

One significant, but small, regional party appeared on the national scene after World War Two, the Volksunie or Flemish People's Union. But the chief representatives of Flemish interests were still to be found in the Flemish wings of the PSC and, to a smaller extent, of the two other national parties. An out-and-out linguistic party, the Francophone Front, made a strong first appearance in Brussels, whose overwhelmingly French-speaking population resented national legislative efforts to protect the language of the Flemish minority. A Walloon party also appeared on the national scene, in defense of regional economic and French-language interests.

THE FLEMISH QUESTION

The nation born in 1830 was bisected by an internal linguistic frontier, which had hardly shifted since the fifth century A.D., running from west to east just south of Brussels. The southern provinces spoke French and Romance dialects, chiefly Walloon; the northern provinces, chiefly Flemish dialects. But within Flanders itself there was a more complex and provocative frontier, a linguistic-social barrier between the Flemish-speaking masses – peasants, workers and lower middle classes – and their French-speaking native elites, some of whom hardly even knew Flemish.

"French in the parlor; Flemish in the kitchen" ran the telling, scornful phrase.

The linguistic patriotism of the romantic revival coincided with the surge of national or regional consciousness, in Flanders as in so many parts of nineteenth-century Europe. The advocates of the Flemish cause first saw it only in linguistic and sentimental terms: "the language is the whole people." The Flemish masses must be free to learn and to use their own language; their language must have equal standing with French. But the protagonists of Flemish had first to define, and then to diffuse, the language of a cultured Flemish speech, for the rich tongue of medieval literature had fallen into a divided and degraded state. Most Flemings spoke one of a number of often mutually incomprehensible local dialects. Only a tiny minority spoke a correct Flemish or Dutch ("Nederlands" as it came officially to be called). Illiteracy was high, and the defenders of Flemish had first, literally, to "teach their people to read."

The cultural backwardness of the Flemish masses reflected their region's economic backwardness. After the heyday of its medieval communes, after the glory of sixteenth-century Antwerp, Flanders had fallen far behind Wallonia. Wallonia paced the continent's industrial revolution while Flanders had only its agriculture, its textiles, the port of Antwerp, and its great numbers.[5] In its overpopulated villages, a wretched peasantry long tried to keep cottage industries alive, while many of its sons went off to work in Walloon coal mines and steel mills, in Brussels, in France and the United States.

Differences in the pace of industrialization accentuated regional contrasts. In Wallonia, as in many other industrializing areas of Europe, most of the new working classes turned away from, or grew up outside, the church of their fathers. Not until well on in the twentieth century did a modernized Catholicism stay the loss of workers' support brought on by industrialization, emigration, and urbanization.

In the Belgian self-image, Wallonia became dechristianized while Flanders remained Catholic. The reality was more nuanced, although the self-image was a significant reality in itself. Actually the contrast was chiefly between industrial-and-urban and rural-and-small-town populations. Rural areas in Wallonia too retained their Catholic practice. In Flanders also, in the two large cities, Antwerp and Ghent, most industrial workers were lost to the Church.

The dominance of the French language reflected the political

[5] The first linguistic census, in 1846, showed 2,471,000 Flemish-speaking and 1,827,000 French-speaking Belgians.

and social dominance of the French-speaking property holders and professional elites of nineteenth-century Belgium. Naturally they carried on the national government and most local government in their own tongue. Some, moreover, saw the French language as a vehicle of national unification and centralization. Parliament and all but three city councils debated in French; the courts judged in French. For several generations, education in Flemish stopped with the primary schools; secondary schools and universities taught exclusively in French. Only in French could one make a professional or civil-service career. "To be Belgian," complained Flemish intellectuals, "we have to cease being Flemish."

The first leaders of the Flemish movement came chiefly from modest strata of the intelligentsia—lower civil servants, school teachers, priests. To many of these, especially the lower clergy, the tide of godlessness that threatened pious Flanders was peculiarly associated with the French language and literature, with the nation of Voltaire and the anticlerical Third Republic, with French-speaking industrial Wallonia, where Flemish immigrants lost their faith, and with the francophone Liberal bourgeoisie of Flanders itself.

The emphasis on language diverted the attention of the Flemish movement from the social and economic bases of Flemish inferiority in Belgian life. The myth that "the language is the whole people" for a long time dominated the thinking of leaders of the Flemish movement.[6] That movement took form first in literary and cultural associations. There were occasional political forays at the municipal level, but no regional political parties yet. Individual Flemish leaders in all three national parties began some concerted action, notably in favor of a Flemish-language university. As all aspects of civic life became politicized, the Flemish cultural movements split along Liberal and Catholic and Socialist lines.

Only at the very end of the century had the government come around to requiring an official text of its laws in Flemish as well as French, but there was, oddly, still no official text of the Constitution in Flemish. By the First World War, it had made some place for Flemish, alongside of French, in secondary education, administration, and criminal justice in Flanders.

The war gave new dimensions to the Flemish problem. If it deepened national feeling among many Belgians, it also deepened the opposition between the Flemish and "the others." Military sacrifice was glaringly unequal, by the direction of invasion and

---

[6] "Telemachus," "De Spanning tussen de Taalgroepen: een sociologische benadering," *De Maand*, Vol. 6 (1963), p. 332.

the nature of Belgian social structure. The Germans overran the country too fast for the Walloon contingents to be mobilized as fully as the more distant Flemish. The skilled workers taken out of the lines for jobs in French industries were mostly Walloons. Remaining in the trenches were mostly Flemings, with a majority of their officers French-speaking. Grave incidents in some units in the lines and in punishment camps behind the lines pitted Flemish soldiers against often uncomprehending commanders.

The Germans encouraged Flemish separatism, leaving a train of political booby traps for the Belgian nation after the war. But the Flemish "Activists," as they were called, who accepted measures of regional autonomy from the occupation authorities, were mostly literary and cultural figures, rather than political leaders.

After the years of people's sufferings in the trenches, in occupied Belgium, and in deportation, the old Flemish demands had a new urgency. Equal manhood suffrage, moreover, gave a new political weight to the large numbers of Flemish peasants and workingmen. But the war had also called forth a surge of Belgian nationalism, which brought a stiffening against Flemish claims. The prosecutions of the Activists after 1918 caused some French-speaking Belgians, consciously or unconsciously, to identify not only the men on trial, but all the Flemish movement, with treason. By a comparable reflex many loyal Flemings felt, resentfully, that not just Activists but the whole Flemish people were being put in the dock.

THE LINGUISTIC LAWS OF THE 1930's

It was a long time before Parliament enacted the equality for the Flemish language which King Albert had promised from the throne on the liberation of the country in 1918. The Flemish showed increasing bitterness at the delays in giving effect to solemn promises, while the Francophones showed irritation at the aggressiveness of the Flemish leaders.

Specific Flemish parties made their appearance in 1919, rising to a modest peak in 1939, when they won 15 percent of the total vote in Flemish areas, and elected 17 out of 202 members of the House. Their threat to the established parties, especially to the Catholic Party, and especially after 1930, was much greater than their percentage of the electorate. For they functioned, in effect, much like groups of pressure upon the national parties and the government.[7]

[7] Jan Dhondt, "De evolutie van de partijen tussen de twee wereldoorlogen," *Res Publica*, Vol. 4 (1962), pp. 370-380; A. W. Willemsen, (see note 3) and also his "Sociologie als Therapie?" in *De Maand*, Vol 6 (1963), p. 493.

The Flemish movement earlier had been essentially democratic in style. In the 1930's, its extremists – the Vlaams National Verbond (The Flemish National League) and the Verdinaso (Verbond van Dietsche Nationaalsolidaristen, the Dutch-Speaking National Solidarity League, with its racial, Greater Netherlands slant) – took on an authoritarian style. But the main agitation went on outside the extremist groups.

Preoccupation with linguistic issues in the 1930's kept Parliament in a state of recurring turmoil. It made the formation of cabinets laborious, and their existence precarious. It took the attention of parties, governments, and electorate from the challenges of the depression and European fascism.[8]

A series of laws in the 1930's finally enacted a long-delayed equality for the Flemish language in education, administration, justice, and the army. The polity would be bilingual, but the people would not. Flanders and Wallonia would each be unilingual, and only in Brussels would there be an attempt at institutional and personal bilingualism. There would be some instruction in the second national language in the schools, but that language would be a foreign tongue to almost all. A number of Flemings, and a few rare Francophones, would be more or less bilingual, but only as the result of personal effort or family circumstances. The hopes for bilingualism as a national unifying factor – as earlier for the French language – had failed. But French continued in national and economic life, in the higher ranks of public administration, and in Brussels municipal government and social and cultural life to hold a predominance which roused the opposition of many Flemings. So did the failure fully to implement the language laws, except in the courts.

THE "FLEMISH PROBLEM" AFTER WORLD WAR TWO

The occupation authorities did not favor Flemish autonomism in World War Two as much as they had a generation earlier, although Flemish prisoners were released soon after the Belgian surrender while Walloons were held until the bitter end. Contrary to the belief of many Walloons and Bruxellois, the Francophones had no monopoly of resistance to the Nazis, nor the Flemings of collaboration. Contrary to the belief of many Flemings, the wide-

[8] In 1939, for example, a tripartite government fell and Parliament had to be dissolved in a dispute over the government's naming to the Flemish Academy of Medicine of a convicted and amnestied Activist: this within half a year of the outbreak of war. On the inter-war period, see the excellent work by the late Swedish scholar, Carl-Henrik Höjer, *Le Regime Parlementaire belge de 1918 à 1940* (Uppsala, Almkvist and Wiksell, 1946).

spread and perhaps excessive purge after the war struck French-speaking Belgians as well as Flemings.[9] But, as after the First World War, the bitterest recollections of the purge and the demands for an amnesty were those of the Flemings.

After the decimation of its leadership by the purge, Flemish nationalist action resumed slowly, at first under the cautious forms of cultural and youth movements. In the 1950's, the Volksunie could demonstrate that a Flemish federalist party had a permanent, if minor, place in regional and national politics. Between 1961 and 1965, it sharply increased its national representation, from five to 12 (out of 212) House members, receiving in the 1965 election almost 12 percent of the votes in the Flemish constituencies, and its potential appeal represented pressures upon the traditional political parties considerably greater than its own electoral showing.

Outside of Parliament, Flemish organizations were not above troubling the public order now and then. The Flemish Action Committee for Brussels and the Language Frontier organized "marches on Brussels" – the classic form of Belgian protest – and other demonstrations whose force impressed public opinion. For a time the Volksunie maintained a paramilitary youth organization. But, whatever the latent threat to democratic processes from some "hard" elements, up to 1965 they had done no more than interrupt services in several Antwerp and Ghent churches that had French-language sermons, deface French-language highway markers and business signs on Flemish soil, and rough up bystanders in occasional "border incidents" around Brussels.

Economic development, meanwhile, eliminated many Flemish disadvantages. An overwhelming percentage of post-war investment, especially by foreign interests (notably American), and most of that in the new types of industry, was in Flanders. While sub-marginal old Walloon coal mines were being shut down, more productive new seams were opened in Flanders.

These changes would take time to produce their social and psychological and political consequences, even their clear economic consequences. For the time being, the Walloon provinces as a whole still had more of the higher-wage industries and higher personal incomes than the Flemish provinces (with Brussels higher than either), but their lead was narrowing. If the structural unemployment which had so long plagued Flanders was finally on the way to being absorbed, in the 1950's the Flemish provinces as a whole still showed almost 2½ times as much unemployment as

[9] John Gilissen, "Etude statistique sur la repression de l'incivisme," *Revue de Droit Pénal et de Criminologie*, Vol. 31 (1950-51), pp. 513-628, especially the summary, pp. 624-626.

the Walloon provinces.[10] As one moved from secondary to university-level education, the ratio of Flemish to French-language students was reversed, to the disadvantage of the Flemish. While the Dutch language was advancing, French still dominated in the highest echelons of the economy and administration.[11]

THE "WALLOON PROBLEM"

As long as Wallonia had prospered and Francophones had run the nation, there had been no "Walloon problem." Nor was there a Walloon consciousness comparable to Flemish consciousness; people of the southern provinces had long thought of themselves more in local terms, as Liégois or men of the Borinage, for example, than as Walloons. But increased regional consciousness was a byproduct of economic distress – and of Flemish demands.

By the 1950's, the shift in the relative economic position of Wallonia began to alarm a region once so confident of its destinies. To the continued experience of demographic stagnation and decline in some areas was joined the newer, more harrowing experience of economic stagnation due to superannuated coal mines, old factories and equipment, and an industrial structure still reflecting the first Industrial Revolution.

Frustrations and fears came to a head in a general strike of 34 days' duration in December 1960 and January 1961. The strike began, over the opposition of the national leaders of the Socialist unions and party, as a protest against the PSC-Liberal government's omnibus economic retrenchment bill (the "loi unique") after the loss of the Congo. Soon it turned in Wallonia into a violent protest against government and (incidentally) Socialist leaders' alleged neglect of Walloon interests. In the heat of the strike, as their immediate economic demands were getting nowhere, left-Socialist trade union leaders of the region switched to federalist demands. When they founded the Walloon People's Movement (Mouvement Populaire Wallon, the MPW), Walloon federalism for the first time had a mass organization.

Flemish federalists proposed regional autonomy for its own sake or chiefly for cultural reasons. Walloon federalists proposed regional autonomy to improve their region's economic prospects and to carry out the socialist economic reforms they could not

---

[10] L. Coetsier and A. Bonte, *Doorstroming naar de universiteit* (2 Vols., Antwerp, Kulturraad voor Vlaanderen, 1963), Vol. II, p. 20.

[11] On student ratios, see *Ibid.* Vols. I and II. On ratios of higher civil servants, see E. Van Leuven, *De Evolutie van de Personeelseffectieven in Overheidsdienst* (Brussels (?), 1963?), pp. 25-27, offprint of two articles originally in the *Tijdschrift voor Bestuurswetenschappen en publiek Recht* (1962), nos. 4 and 5, pp. 230-237 and 304-319.

win on a national basis. The MPW called itself a pressure group – not afraid of a term which alarmed many citizens – but it led to a series of independent political thrusts, mostly at the expense of the Belgian Socialist Party, eventuating in the Rassemblement Wallon.

Walloon Socialists very optimistically foresaw an absolute majority for themselves in their own region. But Flemish Socialists opposed a federalism which would leave them so clearly a minority in their region. The general strike and the formation of the MPW exacerbated divisions between Walloons and Flemings. Even more it exacerbated divisions between the right-wing majority and the small but significant left minority which has been a permanent feature of the Socialist trade unions and party.

THE PROBLEM OF BRUSSELS

Brussels and its environs showed a special form of the center-periphery opposition to be seen in many nations. A pole for Flemish immigration and the center of the nation's French-speaking elites, Brussels became for Flemish leaders both a domination to overcome and a *terra irredenta* to recover.

Near the capital the old language frontier had shifted in the course of a century of national life, and the once quiet little Flemish city had become a French-speaking metropolis. Here not even Dutch, let alone the Flemish dialects, could compete with French – and most Flemish spoke dialects rather than standard Dutch. For the culturally stronger language was also the language of upward social and economic mobility. Until recently most Flemish immigrants, or at least their children, were lost to Flemish culture. The 1932 laws to make Brussels bilingual in administration and education were honored in the breach by the authorities of a number of predominantly French-speaking communes of metropolitan Brussels. Flemish citizens complained that they did not feel at home in a national capital which looked down upon, and discriminated against, their mother tongue.

Another dimension of the problem was that of the migration of Brussels families, mostly French-speaking, to the suburbs and rural communes of surrounding Flemish Brabant. Naturally they wanted to use their own language and have their children taught in it. Militant Flemings viewed this development, not merely as a local manifestation of a universal urban-suburban migration, but as a "robbery of Flemish soil." For the proximity of French speech would bring an increasing and intolerable competition for Flemish. In other ways too, they saw an "oil stain" spreading out from Brussels over the Flemish countryside. Some of the newcomers were indifferent Catholics, and some freethinkers, and they disturbed the political balance in hitherto overwhelmingly

Catholic Flemish communes. Even when the newcomers were indeed good Catholics, there were often conflicts with old settlers of other traditional habits and outlook.

THE LINGUISTIC LAWS OF THE 1960's
In 1962 and 1963, the Catholic-Socialist government managed, with the greatest difficulty, to put through a series of laws, some giving greater force to old prescriptions and some enacting new principles, in the hope of taking language conflicts out of national politics.

The new principle was that of fixity of the language frontier. One law[12] scrapped the 1932 principle of administrative conformity to language practices in communes along the language frontier, as determined by a periodic language census. The census had become more a referendum on preferences than a finding of facts about existing knowledge and use of languages.[13] The new law fixed the existing frontier[14] and administrative practices along it, in theory permanently. Here was a long step toward an undeclared federalism.[15]

In behalf of Flemish rights, another law sought to give more reality to official bilingualism in the municipal administrations of the Brussels metropolitan area, by creating sanctions and a mechanism for enforcement.[16] In behalf of the Francophones, it recognized some of the facts of migration out of the capital to its outskirts by concessions in the language of administration in certain Flemish communes with large French-speaking minorities.

A third in the triptych of language laws confirmed the principle, accepted in the 1930's, of unilingualism in the schools of Flanders and Wallonia. But it aimed to improve the quality and augment the amount of instruction in the second language in each area. In metropolitan Brussels it aimed to provide more Flemish

[12] Law of Nov. 8, 1962, *Moniteur Belge* (Nov. 22, 1962), pages 10315-10319.
[13] Paul M. G. Lévy, *La Querelle du recensement* (Brussels: Institut Belge de Science Politique, 1960); Vlaams Aktiekomitee voor Brussel en Taalgrens, *Geen talentelling* (Brussels, 1959).
[14] Some small shifts in administrative frontiers made eight of the nine provinces unilingual, four Flemish and four French in expression, with Brabant bilingual. The shift of some 4,500 inhabitants of a group of small towns (known in French as the Fourons) from Liège to Flemish-speaking Limburg province caused a wave of indignation in Wallonia.
[15] On undeclared federalism in other forms, see the excellent article by Lode Claes, "Het federaliseringsproces in België," *Streven*, April 1963 (English translation in *Delta*, Winter 1963-64, pp. 43-52).
[16] Law of August 2, 1963, *Moniteur Belge* (Aug. 22, 1963), pp. 8217-8233.

chools in francophone communes, while making it harder for
Flemish parents to have their children educated in French
chools.[17]

From Flemish movements and from Walloon and francophone
circles alike came loud protests against the 1962-1963 legislation.
In the painfully elaborated compromises between the two parties
of the majority and between their respective francophone and
Flemish wings, ardent Flemings and Francophones alike saw only
the concessions they had had to make, and not the concessions
made to them.

THE INTRACTABILITY OF LINGUISTIC-REGIONAL OPPOSITIONS

By the mid-1960's the linguistic-regional tensions appeared more
intractable than those of ideological difference or social class.
Why?

1. The sentimental and practical interests of the linguistic
communities were not effectively organized, and the geographical
regions had no administrative or formal political existence as yet.
There were no recognized representatives qualified to formulate
demands, to negotiate, and to fulfill commitments. The 1962-1963
language laws were negotiated within and between the PSC and
the PSB, the two governing parties. This aggregation of linguistic
and regional claims by the governing parties was challenged, not
only by the leading opposition party and by the regional and
linguistic parties, but also by self-designated linguistic and
regional spokesmen within the governing parties.

2. Inequality, the bane of relations between man and man,
poisoned the relations of the linguistic groups. Flemings resented
continuing francophone snobbishness toward the Flemish language, still touched with some of the old assumptions of social
superiority. French-speaking Belgians, always a numerical minority, now feared to become a sociological minority. In addition to
their numerical disadvantage, they lacked the feeling of community (some said the "national feeling") of their Flemish-speaking
compatriots. Francophones had no concept and – significantly –
no phrase comparable to the powerful Flemish "*ons volk.*" And
ons volk" embraced the Flemish-speaking people of Brussels as
well as Flanders; there was no such firm identification between
Walloons and French-speaking Bruxellois.

3. Flemings knew little of Walloon thinking, and Walloons
even less of Flemish thinking. On any specific issue Walloons and
even Flemings were far from monolithic, yet each group tended
to see the other as a solid bloc opposing its vital interests.[18]

---

[17] Law of July 30, 1963, *Ibid.*, pp. 8210-8214.
[18] Even the distinguished Catholic philosopher, Msgr. Jacques

4. Many of the Flemish elite passed their days in a Brussels environment which kept linguistic sensitivities raw. If they worked in, or dealt with, national institutions in Brussels, they generally found French still the dominant language. They might assert the rights of the Dutch language to equality, at the cost of frictions with Francophones who did not speak the second national language. Or they might, as "good fellows," carry on in a language which many spoke fairly well, but few as they did their mother tongue, and at the cost of frictions with more punctilious Flemings.

5. In the arguments over the Brussels area, the thorniest complex of linguistic opposition, Flemish and Francophones appealed past each other to different sets of values. The contrast was classic. In behalf of the socially disadvantaged, the Flemish asserted the rights of the collectivity; in behalf of the socially dominant, the Francophones asserted the rights of the individual. The Flemish demanded that the State protect the continuity of their language community, even against those of their own people who wished their children to be assimilated into the more prestigious language community. The Francophones defending Flemish individuals' rights to choose the French language for their children's education, ignored the social and economic pressure, the "silent intolerance,"[19] weighing upon humbler Flemish in the Brussels milieu.

6. There was an incongruity between many of the basic problems and the remedies sought. Legal equality for Dutch could not alone make up for a lack of precision, uniformity, and style in most Flemings' use of their own language. No official policy could preserve for the Walloons an equal share of responsible government posts when their numbers were so much less than those of the Flemish and when so few of them made the effort to learn the other national language.

7. The Flemish still saw themselves as oppressed, despite the political weight of their numbers, the progress in use of the Dutch language everywhere except in the Brussels area, and the recent economic growth in Flanders. What Michael Balfour once called

---

Leclercq, wrote that "the Flemish form a homogeneous community."' *Les Catholiques et la question wallonne* (Liège: Comité d'étude pour une nouvelle action wallonne, 1963), p. 5.

[19] The phrase is that of "Telemachus" (cited above, note 6), p. 334. On the social bases of the "Flemish problem," see also "Onze Taalpolitieke Spanningen en Hun Toekomst," *De Maand*. Vol. (1965), pp. 207-39, consisting of a number of critical comments by various authors on my article, "Factoren van conflict en factoren van samenhorigheid," in the same review, 7 (1964), pp. 596-604.

"the reflexes of underdogs"[20] continued far beyond the conditions which had created them. The reflexes of "overdogs" or former overdogs were equally far from reality. The Walloons looked backward too, recalling past security in the light of their fears for the future. Brussels still determined and administered much, too much, of the nation's life, yet many Bruxellois felt threatened by Flemish aggressiveness and resentful of Walloon indifference toward their special interests. In this unique national triangle of one oppressed majority and two oppressed minorities, rational and tolerant discourse was not easy.

8.   Local and regional leaders and interest groups competed for public and private investment and for other advantages in public policy. Such normal clashes of local and regional economic interest were intensified because they were seen in the sentimental light of ethnic-linguistic conflict.

9.   Money had met many of the historic demands of the working classes. Greatly enhanced public expenditures made the school pact acceptable to Catholic and to public institutions. Money could meet regional economic demands. But money could do little to meet critical linguistic demands and counter-demands; it would not resolve to the satisfaction of both parties the issue of whether a child should be taught in Dutch or in French.

10.   National sentiment was milder in Belgium than in any other European nation except Austria. Political socialization, especially in Flanders, emphasized the regional rather than the national. Belgians knew a Flemish culture and a French culture (and in folklore a Walloon culture) – but hardly a Belgian culture.

Except for the King, few national symbols had power to move or to hold. Even the monarchy, although generally accepted, was far from universally popular. The army had little value as a symbol, because of a realistic assessment of its weakness in the nuclear age, and because of the anti-militarism traditional among the Flemish in general and among the Socialists in Wallonia. The historic memories of Flanders were regional rather than national; the anniversary of the Battle of the Golden Spurs in 1302 evoked more enthusiasm than the national holiday commemorating 1831, and the Flemish lion more enthusiasm than the national flag. In what other national capital of a democratic polity would federalists have given the unfurling of the national colors as excuse for assault and battery?[21]

---

[20] Michael J. L. G. Balfour, *States and Mind* (London: Cresset Press, 1953), p. 97.

[21] In Wemmel, a Flemish suburb of Brussels, in June 1962, Flemish nationalist demonstrators assaulted some citizens from whose windows flew the national colors. A Volksunie leader did not hesitate to

In what other Western nation (except Canada) did informed citizens feel no taboo against public inquiry, not only as to whether the national state would survive, but even as to whether it deserved to survive? "We are faced with this choice," said the leading Flemish daily newspaper in its issue for the national holiday in 1964, "either we reach an understanding as to how to continue to live together, or each of us [each region or linguistic community] goes its own way. Belgium is not condemned, but it must prove its right to live."[22]

Discussion of the survival of Belgium added to the hazards of its continuance. That it continued despite the discussion was a tribute to the *sang-froid* of the Belgians. It was also a reflection of many factors of sentiment, of institutions, and of social and economic advantage which – along with inertia – contributed to the national reality.

FACTORS OF UNITY

1. The Constitution was, to be sure, no longer venerated as it had been. But, except for the federalist proposals, its institutions were accepted with little question. In the "royal question," both sides had appealed to the Constitution, while taking opposing views of the constitutionality of the King's wartime acts. In the long school conflict, neither side questioned the constitutional provision for the freedom of education while each asserted that only its own approach could realize that freedom in practice.[23]

2. The monarchy, born with the nation, was a symbol of its existence and unity. Except for the decade of the 1940's, the kings had been not only symbols, but mediators. The royal function had "some of all three of Max Weber's ideal types of power: the traditional, the charismatic, and the rational."[24]

3. Communal (municipal) politics, on the whole, served as a factor of unity. The commune was the normal ladder to national political office, and a high percentage of M.P.'s continued to hold communal office. With communal councils elected by proportional representation, only a coalition could secure the needed majority in most of the larger communes. Municipal coalitions formed and fell apart with scant reference to ideology, and gener-

---

say, publicly and privately, that the flags had been "a provocation" to the demonstrators.
[22] M. Ruys, "Bouwen aan België," *De Standaard* (July 20-21), 1964, p. 1.
[23] On the constitution, see the excellent discussion in André Mast, "Une Constitution du temps de Louis-Philippe," *Revue de Droit Public et de la Science Politique* (Nov.-Dec. 1957), pp. 987-1030.
[24] "La Couronne et le Pays," *Revue Nouvelle*, 30 (July 15, 1959), p. 57.

ally with little reference to national coalition patterns. Politicians thus were likely to have considerable experience of alliance at one level of government with people they opposed at another level. On balance,[25] this experience tended to diminish hostilities among politicians by making the reasons for hostility seem relative rather than absolute.

4. Brussels had a "national vocation." Its very existence as a metropolis depended upon the performance of national political, administrative, commercial, financial, and cultural services. Out of interest and out of sentiment, Brussels needed the national framework; its new international "vocation" did not obviate that necessity. Conversely, advocates of regional separation or federalism à deux found Brussels the greatest stumbling-block.

5. Economic life reflected the national experience, and helped to shape it. Most large industrial and financial enterprises were national. Exports and the transit trade, upon which Belgium was so heavily dependent, called for national action. The highly structured system of labor relations was largely on a national basis, and in no case on a regional basis.

6. Most social and economic interests, except those of a specifically local or regional character, were organized nationally. National organizations preserved their unity by recognizing diversity. Some differentiation between Flemish and French-speaking members was imposed by language differences. The formal or informal recognition of two language communities or of two-or-three regional interests permitted national organizations to accommodate differences in outlook and in style of action among their Walloon, Flemish, and Brussels memberships.

7. If all the lines of cleavage in Belgium had run in the same direction, the tensions might well have become unbearable. But each of the other great factors of division – religion, social class, and party – was also a factor of national cohesion across regional and language lines. The Church and the national labor and employer organizations were, at the the top, conscious of national responsibilities. In the political parties, although secondary leaders defended chiefly Flemish or Walloon or francophone interests, the top leaders assumed an explicit role in the aggregation of linguistic and regional claims.

THE IDEOLOGIES RECEDE; THE PILLARS STAND
By the school pact of 1958, the PSC had consciously divested itself

---

[25] "On balance" only, since local frictions sometimes impede national agreements and national frictions sometimes impede or disarrange local accords.

of the historic basis and the chief argument for Catholic political cohesion, as well as for the political intervention of the hierarchy. The school pact also took much of what ideological starch there had been out of the anti-clerical Socialist Party as well. The Liberals' "deconfessionalization" in 1961 was an appropriately timed bid to keep up with more pragmatic times – more pragmatic in reference to religious and political ideology, but not language.

Floating voters had hitherto come chiefly from the middle classes, less disciplined and less effectively organized by the *verzuiling* system than workers and Flemish peasants. "Do you know the Friendly Society, the Union, the Movement, the Party of the Bourgeois?" ironically asked a Catholic employers' journal.[26] The 1965 elections showed that more working-class voters were moving into the floating-voter category. To be sure, Belgian society was still rather highly stratified; there were sharp class differences in style of life and in access to higher education, and workers felt the possibilities of upward mobility to be very limited. But few workers concerned themselves with the structural reforms which would alter the locus of economic power,[27] while most felt that welfare-state benefits were assured under any conceivable government. Thus some workers were moving into a more modern age to vote, not along the lines of economic group interest, but along those of language. Or they might be protesting against the leadership of parties and unions of the system of *verzuiling* by voting along the linguistic or regional lines which escaped that system.

There were other signs of diminished *verzuiling*. There were increasing contacts among the elites of the Catholic, Socialist, and Liberal worlds. The partial integration of Socialist, Catholic, and Liberal friendly societies into the social insurance system de-emphasized somewhat the ideological-political bases of their foundation. Yet if the ideologies of *verzuiling* receded, the pillars still stood.

The thoughtful journal of a Catholic ginger group made light of some persons' stress on the old philosophical and religious barriers " . . . as if Belgium were peopled with philosophers and theologians."[28] But a year later the same journal was complaining

[26] Jean Nolet de Brauwère, "Un Coup d'oeil sur les bourgeoisies," *Bulletin Social des Industriels* (April 1965), page 227.

[27] See Marcel Bolle de Bal, "Les sociologues, la conscience de classe, et la grande grève belge de l'hiver 1960-61," in *Revue de l'Institut de Sociologie*, (1961, no. 3), and Maurice Chaumont, "Grèves, syndicalisme et attitudes ouvrières: les grèves belges de décembre 1960-janvier 1961," *Revue de sociologie du travail*, Vol. 4 (1962), pp. 142-158.

[28] *La Relève*, March 7, 1964, p. 2, untitled article on Guy Cudell, unsigned (by F. Coupé).

about the excess weight of "ideological a-priori's" in party programs.[29]

It was not the programs or even the ideologies which constituted the chief barriers between people and people. But while the ideologies became *Privatsachen*, the organizations originally based on them had become well established in most of organized social life and in the innumerable agencies of a highly developed administrative pluralism.[30]

In the United States, multiple memberships in voluntary associations were thought to dilute loyalties and lessen the rigidity of individuals' attitudes. In Belgium they reflected and confirmed primary loyalties, since the individual's memberships were ordinarily all within one spiritual family and one language group.

The Socialists lacked the schools and parish organizations, the farmers' and middle-class groups, of their Catholic rivals. But they had organizations of most of the other conceivable socio-economic and cultural interests, from pigeon fanciers to old-age pensioners. The Liberals had almost as many, although generally less numerous in membership. There were even Liberal trade unions, divided though they were, and anomalous as the idea was to some PLP leaders.

The largest complex of voluntary organizations was that which asserted the values and interests of Catholicism. It was possible to live one's life in a Catholic sub-culture: parish, school, youth movement, trade union or farmers' league or other occupational group, family association, consumer cooperative, credit union, insurance, friendly society, clinic and hospital, cultural organizations, women's movement or men's study group, and pensioners' organization. This was a sociological or "protective" Christianity, which to an older Catholic mentality had the value of minimizing the "dangerous outside contacts" of the faithful. To many earnest and thoughtful Catholics after the war, however, it kept fellow-Catholics in a "ghetto" which was no less confining – and discouraging to Christian witness – for being that of the most numerous group in the nation.[31]

The comprehensiveness of Catholic socio-political organization offered its own challenge however. The tensions among the socially diverse organizations of the Catholic sub-culture were

[29] "Programmes," *Ibid.*, July 17, 1965, p. 1.

[30] See especially various numbers of the *Courrier Hebdomadaire* of the Centre de Recherches et d'Information Socio-Politiques (CRISP), 1959 – .

[31] See the remarkable summary (unsigned) by Jules Gérard-Libois, "Débats actuels des Catholiques belges," *Informations Catholiques Internationales* (June 1, 1958), pp. 15-22, and a number of *Courriers Hebdomadaires* of the CRISP.

perhaps one of the reasons for the greater recent vitality of Catholic labor organizations, as compared to their Socialist rivals, who operated in a socially less heterogeneous sub-culture.

Proportional representation for all recognized interests was enshrined in almost every aspect of life affected with a public interest. It ran from elected local and national political assemblies, the Central Economic Council and the joint collective bargaining commissions, to the three brass bands – Catholic, Socialist, and Liberal – which sounded forth, with the aid of subsidies, in any large city.

The institutionalization of the nation's particularisms in turn helped to maintain the attitudes to which they had once given more militant expression. The attitudes remained after the ideologies had lost their thrust, as in Austria under the continuing coalition and the "proporz."[32] In Belgium, in normal times, these attitudes were pervasive rather than virulent, brooding rather than bellicose. If meaningful personal contacts with people of other spiritual families were few, so were the occasions for personal hostility.

For many, organizational membership was a dull gray rather than a militant Red or a faithful Black. Normal man would not be political man much of the time. Even party membership – not to speak of voting – might be, not an act of commitment or even a *prise de position*, but only conformism to a social milieu, a key to a housing project, or an insurance policy for a career in a highly politicized civil service.[33]

Even the anti-heroes of such behavior usually responded to demands for support on the set occasions of political balloting or shop-or-office elections, or on the unpredictable occasions when a royal affair or a regional strike raised gusts of old passions. As Otto Kirchheimer demonstrated in a now-classic essay, some nineteenth-century forms of opposition had indeed waned.[34] But that waning left the structure of other old oppositions intact. Even

---

[32] See the chapter on Austria by Frederick C. Engelmann in Dahl, (see above, note 1).

[33] See the admirable essay by André Molitor, "L'Administration dans la société belge," in Institut Belge de Science Politique, *Aspects de la société belge* (Brussels, 1958), pp. 113-134; J. Vandendries, "L'Influence de la politique dans la vie de l'administration en Belgique," *International Review of Administrative Sciences*, Vol. 24 (1958), pp. 512-522; Victor Crabbe, "Les Commissions de réforme administrative en Belgique," *Ibid.*, Vol. 20 (1954), pp. 869-903, and the reports of the commissions of inquiry cited in that article; E. Van Leuven, cited in note 11, above; also Val R. Lorwin, "The Politicization of the Bureaucracy in Belgium," Stanford, Center for Advanced Study in the Behavioral Sciences, 1962 (mimeographed).

[34] Otto Kirchheimer, "The Waning of Opposition in Parliamentary

if their ideological bases sank into the ground, the structures of *verzuiling* still conditioned the affinities and antipathies of many people along old lines.

How can one explain the contrast between the continuing pervasiveness of *verzuiling*, on the one hand, and – on the other hand – the recurrent eruptions of disorder and the recent increase of political action outside the system?

At a fairly modest level of expectations, the system produced the services and the political representation satisfactory to an increasingly consumer-oriented society. But the decline of ideological commitment on the part of both organizations and masses opened the way to the unpredictable bursts of individual indignation and collective protest against the bureaucratization and compromise which were of the very nature of the successful operations of *verzuiling*. People accepted, even took for granted, the services which they got from the *verzuild* social organizations integrated into the administration of universalized welfare functions. But from time to unpredictable time, some of them acted to kick over the traces of affiliations which for their fathers and grandfathers had represented liberating movements.

In all this Belgium was perhaps contributing only its own version of apathy and alienation and the search for more meaningful forms of political participation in a society whose complexity was so much greater than its size.[35] Thus a pristine loyalty, tied to the intimacies of a once-scorned mother tongue or to the clouded destinies of a once-proud region, moved some people to action opposed to the compromises of *verzuiling*. To occasional outbursts and to continuing threats, the managers of the system of *verzuiling* responded by the time-honored policies of concession and attempted absorption. But the threats remained, and the pillars, still standing, weakened.

POSTSCRIPT BY THE AUTHOR, JULY 1973

Most of my 1965 paper was already written before the Belgian national elections of that year, which marked a considerable rupture with the patterns of *verzuiling* politics; my paper took

Regimes," *Social Research*, Vol. 24 (1957), reprinted in R. C. Macridis and B. E. Brown, eds., *Comparative Politics* (Homewood, Ill.: Dorsey, 1961), pp. 216-227, *Cf.* Gabriel A. Almond, "A Comparative Study of Interest Groups and the Political Process," *American Political Science Review*, Vol. 52 (1958), pp. 270-282, and Robert A. Dahl, cited above, note 1.

[35] On the basis of her researches in Belgium, Renée C. Fox suggests wryly that there may be an inverse relationship between the size of a country and the complexity of its social system. "Belgian Medical Research," in Phillip E. Hammond, ed., *Sociologists at Work* (New York: Basic Books, 1964), p. 349.

insufficient account of the changes which those elections indicated. Since then the chief tendencies have been as follows:

1. A steady series of gains for the linguistic and regional parties, in Wallonia and even more in Brussels; least in Flanders, but significantly there too. The most spectacular electoral achievement of these parties was the absolute majority of the Front Démocratique des Francophones in the elections for the assembly of the newly created Brussels Agglomeration in late 1971.

2. The obverse – both cause and consequence of the first phenomenon – the steadily declining share of total electoral or affective support for the two major national parties of the *verzuiling* system, the Christian Socials and the Socialists.

3. The general decline of the segmentation on religious-ideological lines of Belgian society and politics. This phenomenon of "*ontzuiling*" I have discussed in comparative perspective in "Segmented Pluralism: Ideological Cleavages and Political Cohesion in the Smaller European Democracies," in *Comparative Politics*, Vol. 3, No. 2 (January 1971), pp. 141-75 [*cf.* above, 33-69]

4. Continued moves toward federalism on language and regional lines in Belgian government, politics, and society. Constitutional revision has produced some Byzantine patterns of institutions, whose scope, functioning, and resource allocations are still (in mid-1973) very far from clear to most members of the political class, let alone even the most conscientious of average voters. I have discussed the background of these changes in "Linguistic Pluralism and Political Tension in Modern Belgium," in J. A. Fishman, ed., *Advances in the Sociology of Language*, (Paris and The Hague: Mouton, 1972), vol. II, pp. 386-412.

5. The maintenance, nevertheless, of most of the *structures* of segmented pluralism or consociational democracy in Belgium.

SWITZERLAND: GEOGRAPHY OF THE SWISS PARTY SYSTEM

Roger Girod

Source: R. Girod, "Geography of the Swiss Party System", in E. Allardt and Y. Littunen, eds., *Cleavages, Ideologies and Party Systems*, Transactions of the Westermarck Society, Vol 10 (Helsinki, 1964), 132-161. Reprinted by permission of the editors and the author.

The party system which operates in Switzerland today is without doubt of a particular kind. All the parties, with the exception of certain marginal groups, cooperate on a permanent basis within the executive councils. This overall alliance is not in any way disturbed by competition in elections, which serve only to record the very small fluctuations in party popularity. Such competition also enables rival forces within each party (right and left tendencies, urban and rural factions, contesting leaders, etc.) to test their influence.

This system applies more or less to the whole country. It presents itself according to regions as well as levels (federal, cantonal, communal) under varied aspects. This article will be devoted to examining in a very preliminary way some aspects of these variations. Chiefly, the article aims at classifying the different forms of the Swiss party system into several broad categories. A few remarks will however be made on the question of determining whether each one of these categories corresponds to a definite type of social organisation.

The relationship of the parties on the federal level is fairly widely known. Therefore this point will only be mentioned without development. A more detailed examination will be made of the system (number of parties, relative importance, style of their relationship) found on the cantonal level. A comparative analysis of these systems may prove to be interesting, since as far as we know no such analysis has been made to date, although on the whole Swiss political life is mainly on a cantonal basis.[1]

[1] William Rappard, *The Government of Switzerland* (New York, 1936), in particular pp. 31 and 104-105. This author emphasizes the fact that in Switzerland the activity of their cantonal grouping determines the existence of political parties. National committees have but limited influence over these groups.

"In fact it could not unreasonably be claimed that, with the possible exception of the socialist party, there were no autonomous national parties in Switzerland, but only alliances for federal purposes of otherwise completely independent cantonal organizations." It may also be added that the role of national party "great leader"

Information on this point has mainly been drawn from the answers given by all the cantonal chancelleries to several questionnaires which we had sent them. We would like to extend our thanks to the chancelleries for that help.[2]

An outline of the conditions to be found on the communal level will also be given, reference being made solely to the case of the Genevese elections.

A few of the limitations to this work must be pointed out. The question of the influence of the electoral system on the party formula will only be briefly touched on, not because the question is considered unimportant but rather because it was thought preferable not to enlarge upon an already broad subject.

Apart from a few historical reminders, the period under consideration in this article is that which stretches from 1945 till the 1960's. Before that period the Swiss party system was rather different.

We leave aside the parties and miscellaneous groups (for the most part ephemeral and unimportant) which have taken part in the elections under consideration, but without ever having a single candidate elected.

I. ON THE FEDERAL LEVEL

The Confederation is governed by an executive collegiate body consisting of seven members (the Federal Council) elected by the federal assembly which is made up of two chambers, the National Council and the Council of States. The members of the National Council are directly elected by the people, according to the system of proportional representation based on population. Each canton or half-canton[3] constitutes an electoral district and elects at least one representative. Today the council comprises 200 representatives. The Council of States consists of 44 members, two for each canton and one for each half-canton. The same method of

---

does not exist in Switzerland. On the contrary, parties have cantonal leading figures who are generally unknown to the average citizen in the rest of the country. Not even the Communist party has a national figure-head, a kind of Swiss Thorez or Togliatti, but has a leading team in every canton where it is represented.

[2] We also like to thank the Department of Home and Agricultural Affairs of Geneva, to whose remarkably kept archives we were given access. Mr. Firouz Tofigh and Mr. Jean-Claude Thoenig proved to be worthy collaborators during the preparation of this study.

[3] The cantons of Basle, Appenzell and Unterwalden are divided (Basle-City and Basle-Country, Appenzell Ausser Rhoden and Inner Rhoden, Obwalden and Nidwalden). Each of these half-cantons is a sovereign state with its own government, but elects only one state representative to the Council of States instead of two.

electing members of this Council does not prevail everywhere (17 cantons elect their members by secret popular vote, 4 by the cantonal legislature, and 4 by the *Landsgemeinde* which is an open-air gathering of all citizens.)

The present-day balance of power in these institutions is the result of a slow political evolution. For nearly fifty years the Radical party[4] dominated federal politics. It was not until 1891 that a representative of the Catholic-Conservative party[5] became a member of the Federal Council.

Since 1919 this last party has occupied two seats in the Federal Council. Since then, writes Rappard, "the Radicals and Conservatives have, as a rule, supported together the common governmental measures and have constantly voted for each other's candidates in all important elections."[6]

In 1929 the Bourgeois and Farmers party, a regional group (see Table I) formed ten years earlier, representing a type of radicalism broken away from its progressive tendencies, gained a seat in the Federal Council. The admission of a member of this party to the Federal government was then considered useful by the governing forces for strengthening the ranks of anti-Socialists. Since then the Bourgeois and Farmers party has retained this seat.

But the Socialists, who had become more and more moderate in a rapidly changing world, gaining some seats in the National Council, whilst the Radicals were experiencing a contrary move, managed to have a federal councillor elected in 1943 due to the closely knit political union of the time. Since 1959 they have held two seats. The composition of the Federal Council today is the following: two Radicals, two Socialists, two Catholic-Conservatives, and one Bourgeois and Farmers. It corresponds more or less to the composition of the National Council, whose figures are shown below for the years 1925, 1935, and 1963.

[4] The Radical party (which is named differently according to cantons) exists in nearly all parts of the country. Nearly all levels of society are influenced by it. It can be seen in various forms: opposition in Catholic cantons, the traditional party in rural Protestant regions, the party of the common man in towns, in close relations also with big business.

[5] The other party active throughout nearly the whole country. Open to all Christians, but in fact essentially Catholic. It is as varied in its components as the Radical party. The party has a Christian-social wing with progressive tendencies and amongst which certain members have clearly left tendencies. The party will be called the Catholic-Conservative party in this study although the name may not be the same throughout the country.

[6] *Op. cit.*, p. 97.

Party	Seats		
	1925	1935	1963[7]
Catholic-Conservative	42	42	48
Radical	60	48	51
Liberal	7	6	6
Bourgeois and Farmers	30	21	22
Socialist	49	50	53
Independent party	—	7	10
Democrats	5	4	4
Communist	3	2	4
Others	2	7	2[8]
Total	198	187	200

This table shows not only the basic stability of the political forces, but also clearly indicates that the lower house is dominated by three major political parties, the Catholic, Socialist and Radical. A few moderate regional groups may be added, amongst which the most important, the Bourgeois and Farmers, is represented in the government. The others (Liberal,[9] Democrat,[10] Independent[11]) have a governmental orientation in varying degrees.

The very small Communist party alone does not enter at all into the governmental circle.

Any Socialist penetration into the Council of States is difficult. An appreciable number of the members of this institution are elected by cantons in the mountains regions, where the Socialist party plays only a small role. In the other cantons the middle-class parties represent the majority, and thus the chances of Socialist candidates being elected are very small, except under certain circumstances.

In November 1963 the Council of States was made up in the following manner (in parentheses its composition in 1925): Catholic-Conservatives 18 (18); Radicals 13 (21); Socialists 3 (2); Bourgeois and Farmers 4 (1)); Liberals 3 (1); Democrats and Evangelicals 3 (1).

[7] After the elections of 25-27 October 1963.
[8] The Evangelical party of Zürich.
[9] The Liberal party today is a regional group (see Table I) with right tendencies, drawn from Protestant circles mainly. The "Journal de Genève" and the "Gazette de Lausanne" are its main French-language mouthpieces.
[10] Regional party (See Table I). Placed generally in the category of centre.
[11] Regional party (See Table I). Pro-dynamic economy, guaranteeing satisfactory living conditions for the people.

II. ON THE CANTONAL LEVEL

A unicameral system is found in the cantons. The members of the "Grand Conseil" (name given to the legislative body in French-speaking cantons) are elected on the basis of proportional representation, with the exception of some cantons that have retained the majority vote system (see table I). Each canton is governed by a collegiate Executive Council. This Executive Council is elected by popular vote, either by secret ballot as in 20 of the cantons, or by a show of hands in the *Landsgemeinde* (Obwalden, Nidwalden, Glaris, Appenzell Ausser Rhoden, Appenzell Inner Rhoden).

Table I (which shows the party structure of the Grand Conseil of the different cantons just following the Second World War, and today) and Table II (showing the party structure of the cantonal Executive Councils at approximately the same time) will enable us to distinguish the forms of the party system in the different cantons. In order to define these forms, certain expressions utilized by Maurice Duverger in his terminology, or terms suggested by that terminology, will be used.[12] There should however be no confusion in the reader's mind: Duverger proposed his classification in order to distinguish between a series of completely different systems, whereas in this case the classification is being used to distinguish the variations in one system. This system, as was explained at the beginning, is defined by a tendency towards an overall permanent alliance within the executive itself, of all the parties having a minimum of importance. For this reason, we shall speak here of different "formulas" (the "formula" of the predominant party, the "formula" of multipartism, etc.) and not of different systems. These "formulas" correspond to different ways of practising the system.

The cantons will be divided into two basic groups: those where the Grand Conseil and the Executive Council are dominated by one party, and those which have a multiparty formula. A subdivision will be made in each one of these categories.

A) FORMULA OF THE DOMINANT PARTY

In this group, a distinction is to be made between the formula of the solitary party and the formula of the predominant party.

1. Solitary Party. An extreme form of the dominant party formula exists in one canton, Appenzell Inner Rhoden. The somewhat cheerless name of solitary party may apply particularly well

---

[12] Maurice Duverger, *Les partis politiques* (4th ed., Paris, 1961), and the chapter on "Sociologie des partis" prepared by the same author for the *Traité de Sociologie*, published under the direction of Georges Gurvitch, Volume II, Paris, 1960, pp. 22-45.

in this case: in this canton, the Catholic-Conservative party finds itself without any partner to play the game of pluralism as this party does everywhere else in the country. All the members of the executive belong to this party, and there is no partisan opposition within the legislative assembly. Opposition, of course, is always possible. All the different trends of thought found throughout the country may be expressed freely without hindrance. This formula has therefore nothing in common with the authoritarian versions of the one-party system. If a political movement succeeded in grouping together a certain number of citizens outside the Catholic-Conservative party, it may safely be said that this new movement would soon be represented in the executive, as for example, the Socialist minority at Appenzell Ausser Rhoden, Zoug or Schwyz. For that reason, the solitary party formula belongs in essence to the above defined party system which tends towards an overall alliance of all political forces. This formula is but one incomplete (embryonic or degenerate) variety of that system.

In the case of Appenzell Inner Rhoden, party pluralism seems to have become impossible for purely sociological reasons. It would be interesting to specify these reasons in greater detail. For the present, it can be maintained that the solitary party formula of this very old, small and mountainous republic of Catholic faith (with a total population of 13,000, of whom nearly 5,000 inhabit the main town which is simply a large village) is the result of its marked religious unity, of the economic and social homogeneity of its people, and of the simplicity and cohesion of its traditional hierarchic structure. In the state doctrine nothing prevents a multiparty formula. The common practice of all cantons strongly favours plurality. However, in Appenzell Inner Rhoden, apparently because of an insufficient social differentiation, an opposition party capable of lasting has not taken root. In fact, the Radical party ceased all activities twenty years ago.

This situation would only be of folkloric interest, were it not a normal case in traditionally rural communities not only in Switzerland but in other countries as well. It shows that even when the system applied by the rest of the country is one of strong pluralism, as it is in the case of Switzerland, party plurality is not possible under a certain level of evolution.

The solitary party in Appenzell Inner Rhoden seems to correspond approximately to these movements which form at election time in rural communes of the traditional type with a political colour which is rather vague. The Catholic-Conservative party in this canton appears to limit its activities to an annual assembly at which 30 – 40 citizens participate.

It should be mentioned that the idea of a party is hardly more consistent in the other small and mountainous cantons.

In Appenzell Ausser Rhoden, as a footnote to Table II shows, a number of members of the Executive Council have only a very loose connection with the predominant party to which they are statistically assigned. In Nidwalden the parties disappeared for several years one generation ago, and were replaced by two pressure groups, one supporting the building of an electrical power plant, and the other opposing it. This situation has since changed and once again the party names are used to classify political leaders. The federal statisticians, for instance, consider that the members of the legislative councils of the two Appenzells and Obwalden cannot be classified by party (see Table I).

2. The Predominant Party. This term is used here to describe one strong form of the dominant party formula. The predominant party enjoys a double advantage: its ideological inspiration is in close harmony with the cultural and religious traditions of the bulk of the population; on the other hand, the party had in the past and continues to have the absolute majority of the legislative body at its disposal. Even in that case, in present-day Switzerland, the minority party (or parties) is represented in the executive, with the exception of extremely small groups.

The cantons where this formula is found are Appenzell Ausser Rhoden (Protestant) and all the cantons which during the Civil War of 1847 formed the Catholic league called the Sonderbund (Lucerne, Uri, Schwyz, Obwalden, Nidwalden, Zoug, Fribourg and Valais).

The fact that these cantons even today form a singular group must indeed draw one's attention to the astonishing permanence of certain fundamental political characteristics. It is impossible to explain these essential characteristics simply by comparisons of the present degree of economic development in the different cantons, in terms of production, standards of living, and so on. An adequate explanation cannot be found either in the language difference (Valais and Fribourg are mainly French-speaking) or in the contrasting electoral systems. Some of the cantons in question elect their legislative council on a majoritarian basis (for the most part the smallest of these cantons, and those where on the whole the Catholic-Conservative party is the more predominant), but in the remainder of this group of cantons this election is organized according to the proportional system.

The Catholic-Conservative movement dominates these Sonderbund cantons. In some of them the Social-Christian groups constitute a special organization with a certain degree of autonomy.

The Catholic forces have a special margin of safety in Uri, Nidwalden and Obwalden, as well as in the Valais. These cantons form the most mountainous regions of Catholic Switzerland. The

Catholic superiority is less overwhelming in Lucerne, Schwyz, Zoug and Fribourg.

In the cantons of the Sonderbund, the number of parties is between two and five. In Obwalden the two local parties form the Executive Council. In Schwyz, where three parties are represented in the Grand Conseil, these three parties form the Executive Council. However, in the latter canton, the Socialist party has only about 15 deputies out of the total of 105 in the cantonal legislature. In Nidwalden, the Radical party has representatives in the Executive Council but not the Socialists whose establishment is only recent and who have very few electors, and only one deputy in the legislative body. In Uri, Fribourg and the Valais, the Socialist minority is not represented in the executive. This minority amounts to between 5 and 9 per cent of the representatives in the legislative body. However, in Lucerne and Zoug, where the Socialist party has roughly the same degree of importance (7.7 per cent of the deputies in the former and 10.5 per cent in the latter) a place in the government has been accorded to it. In the two latter cantons the Independent party, which is active but very small, is the only party remaining outside the executive.

In Appenzell Ausser Rhoden, the Radical party traditionally holds six out of the seven seats within the Executive Council, the last seat being held by the Socialist party. The presence of this Protestant canton within the category of those which practise the predominant party formula, would indicate that religion as such is not at the basis of this solution. The reasons for the establishment of this combination of political forces may be sought rather in economic and social history.

The cantons with a solitary party or a predominant party formula number ten in all. They are mainly sparsely populated regions with a total population of approximately 690,000, which is 12.5 per cent of the total population of the country. In the Council of States their influence is quite large (16 deputies out of 44) but in the National Council they have only 33 deputies out of 200.

B) FORMULA OF MULTIPARTISM

In the majority of the States of the Confederation the political equilibrium is of the multiparty type. Not without a minimum of discretion, two cases may be characterized: the three-party formula and the pronounced multiparty formula.

1. The Three-Party Formula.   In this case, three parties dominate the political life of the canton, none of the three having a majority in the Grand Conseil, all three (and only they) being represented regularly in the Executive Council. This is to be found in the cantons of Berne, Soleure, Schaffhouse, St-Gall and Ticino.

The three dominating parties in the cantons of Berne and Schaffhouse are the Radicals, the Bourgeois and Farmers, and the Socialists. In Ticino, St-Gall and Soleure, the three dominating parties being Radical, Catholic-Conservative, and Socialist.

Berne and Schaffhouse are cantons with a large Protestant majority where the number of Catholic electors is relatively small. Industry has brought about a Social Democrat tendency, more to the left than the Radicals. On the other hand, the Bourgeois and Farmers party reacted by gaining importance on the right wing. The political power is therefore mainly shared by these three political parties. In Ticino, a Catholic canton, one finds a situation common to a Latin milieu. The present day Radicals are the mild inheritors of an anti-clerical tradition which had its period of virulence in the past. They have slightly more seats in the Grand Conseil than the Catholic-Conservatives. The Socialist party constitutes a third fairly important group. In Soleure and St-Gall, which are mixed from a religious point of view, the same three parties form the major political forces. But here the political climate is of a rather different kind.

In Soleure the three-party formula applies in its pure form, for only three parties have deputies in the Grand Conseil, and these three parties are represented in the executive. In Ticino there are four parties represented in the legislative assembly. The very weak Communist party is not included in the executive. In St-Gall the Independent party has a small number of deputies, but no state councillors, and a fifth party, the "Free Conservatives" has a single deputy in the Grand Conseil. In Berne there are seven parties and in Schaffhouse there are eight. The four parties in Berne, which take no part in governmental responsibilities, are small. The Catholic-Conservatives have eleven deputies out of 200, the Independent and Popular Evangelical parties have one each, and the "Youth of Berne" party has two. In Schaffhouse the situation is more or less similar.

2. Pronounced Multiple Party Formula. Four parties (possibly more) are represented in the Executive Council, and the number of those who play a certain role in the Grand Conseil may be higher. None of these parties has a majority in the Grand Conseil. The formula is the same on the federal level, as we have seen.

In 1962, in the cantons which are being considered here, the Executive Council had the following characteristics:

  a) It was composed of representatives of four parties.
  b) In none of these cantons did any one of these parties constitute the majority in the executive body. (The parties with the greatest number of representatives were the Rad-

icals in the canton of Vaud with 3 out of the 7 seats, and the Socialists in Basle-City who also had 3 out of the 7 seats.)

c) In each of these cantons the Radical and the Socialist parties belong to the governmental team along with two moderate parties. Consequently in every case the non-socialist forces are dominant.

The two moderate parties whose representatives cooperate on a governmental level with representatives of the Socialist and Radical parties differ from canton to canton. In seven cantons, (Glaris, Grisons, Basle-Country, Basle-City, Argovie, Thurgovie, Geneva) the Catholic-Conservative party is represented. The second moderate party is generally either the Democratic or the Bourgeois and Farmers in the German-speaking part of Switzerland. In Geneva and Basle-City it is the Liberal party. In Zurich,[13] Vaud and Neuchâtel the Catholic-Conservative party is not represented in the government. In the former of these three cantons, both the Independent party and the Bourgeois and Farmers are to be found in the executive. In Neuchâtel the National Progressive party (centre-right) works in conjunction with the Liberal, Socialist and Radical parties.

In 1946 the Radical party still had a majority in the canton of Vaud's Executive Council. At the same time, the executive councillors of Basle-City were taken from 5 parties (1 Communist in addition to the representatives of the 4 other parties). In Neuchâtel there were also representatives of 5 parties in the executive (including 2 local parties).

Glaris has only four parties in the Grand Conseil and all are represented in the executive. For the other cases, remarks concerning the cantons with a three-party formula may be repeated here. Those parties which have no executive councillor according to table II carry negligible electoral weight except in two possible cases: that of the Catholic-Conservative party in Zurich (this exception disappeared in 1963, see footnote 13) and the Communist party in Geneva.[14] The work of electoral coalitions prevented this party from belonging to the executive after its post-war success

[13] In April 1963 (Table II ends in 1962) a representative of the Catholic-Conservative party became a member of the Executive Council of Zurich. This council was subsequently made up of representatives of 5 parties, and no longer four: 2 Bourgeois and Farmers, 1 Socialist, 2 Radicals, 1 Independent party, 1 Catholic-Conservative.

[14] And also lately in the cantons of Vaud and Neuchâtel, where the Communist party has had a relatively important representation in the legislative body.

(except in Basle-City just after the war) and continues to have the same effect now that it is losing importance. The fact that this party has no representative in the cantonal executive does not prevent it from being active on the legislative level in cantons where it has some influence on public opinion. In the same regions this party has also an appreciable critical action through its press (not mentioning the role it plays at the municipal level). Fear of seeing the Communists increase their influence has made the other parties feel more sharply the need for reform. This may be one of the reasons for the disparity in matters of social legislation between the cantons of Geneva, Vaud, and Neuchâtel on one side, and the majority of other cantons during recent years.

Attention should also be drawn to the fact that those cantons in which there is a pronounced multipartism, do not have more parties than those with a three-party formula: 5 or 6 in Geneva, Neuchâtel, Vaud and Thurgovie; 8 in Basle-City, Basle Country, Zurich and Argovie. The balance of power between the parties is simply different. Because of the particular state of the social structures, a fourth group and sometimes a fifth has been able to gain sufficient support to have at least one executive councillor elected.

III. ON THE COMMUNAL LEVEL

It is obvious that the political party formula in a canton does not necessarily apply to the communes. A few remarks will be made to clarify this point, without going into too much detail.

Even in the very small region of Geneva, there are very marked political contrasts from the point of view of the relative influence of the different parties between two groups of communes. These contrasts have very ancient historical origins, as the major differences shown between the cantons had. The first of these two groups of communes is formed by those communes which were formerly possessions of the old Protestant Republic, and the second by those Catholic communes ceded by France and Sardinia just after the Napoleonic wars.

For example, in the elections of the Geneva Grand Conseil, the left parties obtain very few votes in the communes of the first group (apart from some which have become suburban constituencies). The Catholic-Conservative party does not obtain any great number. This indicates that the Radical and Liberal parties are predominant. These two parties alone get between 75 per cent and 85 per cent of the votes in the majority of these communes, and between 60 per cent and 75 per cent in the others. In the most typical cases, the Radical party alone has the majority, getting approximately 55 per cent to 70 per cent of the votes. However, in certain more residential communes the number of

Liberal electors is usually greater than that of the Radical electors.[15]

In the majority of the communes of the second type (excluding also those purely suburban) the situation tends to be reversed in favour of the Catholic-Conservative party. But the majority is not generally overwhelming.

This applies only to cantonal elections where the canton constitutes a single electoral district. Every party draws up a list of candidates, which are therefore the same in all the communes. Municipal elections (communal councils, mayors and their deputies) are obviously quite different.

In the small communes (up to 800 inhabitants) the election of the municipal council (7-11 members according to the number of inhabitants) is by the majority vote system. Quite often the local political committees (that is to say a few "notables") agree amongst each other on drawing up a single balanced list, to gain the satisfaction of the main groups of electors, naturally starting with the traditionally predominant categories. The number of candidates on the list is equal to the number of seats to be filled. Formerly, election was understood ("tacit") in such cases. Today the election takes place and for the candidates to be elected they must obtain at least one third of the votes cast. In other small communes two or more lists oppose each other, with non-political labels (list of communal interests, communal defence, and so on). However, these lists are drawn up according to more or less vague ideological affinities and to local interests. That may give them a certain political character. In communes of more than 800 inhabitants, the municipal councillors (from 13 to 25 according to commune, apart from the city of Geneva which elects a council of 80 members) are elected according to the system of proportional representation. In some of these communes, amongst the less urbanized, only non-political lists are presented. But in the others the parties draw up lists (only two or three parties in the communes of medium importance, four or five in the largest) which sometimes oppose candidates supported by more or less ephemeral local groupings. Similar remarks could also be made about the mayoral elections.

Throughout the country, the communes where there is a predominant political group, solitary or not, (either with Radical or Catholic or other tendencies) are probably numerous. Further research on the structure and climate of communal political life would be of interest. In some municipalities the Socialists domi-

---

[15] Geneva cantonal archives. Percentages concern the last election of the Grand Conseil (1961). In previous elections the situation was similar.

nate public life. In Bienne, for example, the municipal executive consists of 5 Socialists and 4 Radicals. In the two watch-making cities of Le Locle and La Chaux-de-Fonds the Communist party has one member in the executive (in La Chaux-de-Fonds the executive is made up of 1 Communist, 3 Socialists and 1 Liberal). Thus the formulas practised on the communal level are more varied than on the cantonal level, with political pluralism in its developed form tending apparently to limit itself to the more urbanized regions.

IV. THE SPIRIT OF THE SYSTEM

The general mode of relationship between the parties in Switzerland seems to be midway between a struggle in which everyone is trying to eliminate the other in order to rule alone, and federal co-operation in which each of the partners recognizes the other's right to retain his individuality, and any hostile action towards the other is mutually forbidden.

This situation did not come about immediately. The main parties today, on the contrary, were formed during a period of battles without concessions, amongst which the most important were the Liberal insurrection movements in the 1830's, the Sonderbund War between Radical and Catholic Switzerland, the *Kulturkampf*, and the clash between the army and the workers during the General Strike of 1918.

Nearly half a century lapsed after the Sonderbund War before a member of the Catholic-Conservative party became a member of the Federal Government, and 25 years passed between the Strike of 1918 and the election of the first Socialist federal councillor.

In Soleure, all executive councillors were Radicals up to the end of the 19th century. The first councillor of the Catholic-Conservative party was elected in 1887, the first Socialist in 1917. In Fribourg, at the end of the 19th century and at the beginning of the 20th century, the government was on the contrary entirely Catholic-Conservative. The first Socialist executive councillor of Vaud was elected in 1946. Many other examples could be quoted to show that the "all-parties government" is not at all inherent in the Swiss regime as such, but a construction of the latest period of history.

Once in the government, a party continues to oppose the other parties by propaganda, but generally in a moderate fashion. In addition, at election time the contest between the parties is relatively sharp. These elections enable the relative strength of the parties to be estimated, especially at the election of the cantonal legislative body and the National Council. But often enough agreements reduce stakes at election of deputies to this federal organ. The most remarkable case is perhaps that of Uri, where for many years the Catholic-Conservatives, who have a large majority, reserve two seats to themselves in the federal Council of States, and in exchange do not oppose the election of a Radical to the single seat of the canton in the National Council.

There is usually little or no struggle in the election of the executive councillors in the cantons. It is the people, as was said before, who elect these councillors. The voting is held on a majority basis except in two cantons where the system of proportional representation is used in these elections (Ticino, Zoug). In these two cantons, the right of minority parties to assume their role of governmental responsibility is thus constitutionally confirmed.[16] But although this is not a codified rule, in the other cantons it is nonetheless almost fully applied. The ordinary explanation given is that a party (or group of parties having similar interests) which numerically has the majority of the votes would act in contradiction with the rules protecting minorities by electing only magistrates of its own ranks.

Due to that present rule (apart from some exceptional restrictions such as those applied today to the Communists) every political group having even the minimum of importance in the legislature must be represented in the executive.

This means that the parties must be considered rather like natural political divisions of the population. The guarantees which federalism gives to local political entities, to languages, cultures and religions, must be largely extended to them especially where they are in a minority.

Under these conditions the electoral agreements between parties become all-important, and the popular vote less so, since often this vote serves to ratify the nominations agreed upon by party leaders. Even more often it serves to prolong automatically the mandate of the government in power.

In order to clarify this point, a questionnaire relating to the elections of executive councillors was sent to the cantonal chancelleries. It would be interesting to undertake comparative studies of this kind on the subject of other types of election (especially of

---

[16] It should be noted that although not going as far as Ticino and Zoug, several cantons explicitly recognise the right of certain minorities to be represented in the government. The constitution of the canton of Berne specifies that the minority in the Jura region, which is French-speaking, has two seats in the executive. The constitution of Argovie contains a similar principle which applies to the Catholic minority. Valais specifies that each of the major geographical regions of the canton (of which one is German-speaking) shall elect at least one executive councillor.

deputies to the Federal chambers). The questionnaire was along the following lines:

1) During the period from 1945 to August 1963, did it at any time occur in your canton, that the number of candidates equalled the number of seats available at the time of the election of one or more executive councillors?

2) If so, did the election actually take place or was there merely a tacit agreement?[17]

According to the replies received, the cantons were classified as follows:

A) Automatic Renewal of the Government's Term of Office. At the expiration of its term, the government is re-elected as a whole without opposition. Only supplementary elections, for example for the replacement of a deceased or retired councillor, are occasionally contested. The cantons of Group A are Berne, Lucerne, Uri, St-Gall, Thurgovie. Amongst these, two have a predominant party, two practise the three-party formula, and one the multiparty formula. These distinctions thus do not explain the habits acquired by these cantons as regards the nomination of the executive. This remark also applies to groups B and C which will be dealt with later on.

There is an extract from the Thurgovie reply which is fairly typical of the logic of the automatic renewal of the government: "At the time of the elections of cantonal government every three years ... the rule is that only the five magistrates in office shall be brought forward as candidates." The general idea motivating this practice is obviously that there is no valid reason for depriving men of their office when they have proved their worth, and whose distribution according to parties corresponds to a lasting balance between the political powers in the canton. If an appreciable change in this balance would be noticed, partial elections would enable the structure of the executive to be modified. But this is quite unusual. Since 1945 Berne, Uri, and Thurgovie have witnessed on two or three occasions contested supplementary elections. This has not taken place in Lucerne or St-Gall, where for the appointment of new magistrates the number has never exceeded the number of seats to be filled during the period under consideration here. It should also be added that none of the cantons of Group A allow a tacit agreement for the nomination of executive councillors. Even if not contested, these elections always take place.

[17] Tacit agreement: the authorities, noting that the number of candidates proposed in the prescribed time limit is not greater than the seats available, declares them elected without any vote.

B) Renewal Giving Rise to a Relatively Contested Electoral Campaign. The cantons classed here are those in which since 1945 the candidates have always been more numerous than the number of offices open at the time of the renewal of the term of office of the Executive Council. These cantons are Fribourg, Basle-Country, Ticino, Neuchâtel and Geneva.

The limitations to electoral campaigns which take place under these circumstances can clearly be seen from the following examples. In 1957 some people maintained that the elections of the Geneva executive councillors[18] were particularly contested, because not all the bourgeois parties had agreed on retaining the composition of the executive as it was at the time of the preceding legislature (4 Radicals, 1 Liberal, 1 Catholic-Conservative, 1 Socialist). The Catholic-Conservatives were claiming one supplementary seat for them. The electoral lists presented to the electorate were the following:

1) *Radical register:* four Radical candidates (R1, R2, R3, R4), 1 Liberal (L), 1 Socialist (S) and 1 Catholic-Conservative (C1)

2) *Catholic-Conservative register:* the same candidates except the Socialist replaced by a second Catholic-Conservative (C2)

3) *Liberal register:* the candidates R1, R2, R3, R4, C1 and L of the Radical register with the 7th line left empty.

4) *Socialist register:* R1, R2, R3, R4 and S.

Finally C2 was defeated and all the other candidates were elected. The Communist party, isolated, put no candidates forward. In the following election (1961) another contest, slightly different in detail, took place. Exceptionally, two councillors in office were defeated.

The contest is usually still less sharp. In Geneva, in 1948, 1951, and 1954 only candidates brought forward by non-political provisional groups without the slightest chance of being elected opposed the candidates of governmental parties. The number of candidates of these governmental parties was seven, corresponding to the number of seats in the Executive Council.

In the cantons of Group B, the supplementary elections for the replacement of state councillors are conducted more or less on the same lines as those for the periodic renewal of the government's term.

In Geneva, Basle-Country and Neuchâtel, the election of the executive councillors has never been tacit since 1945. In Fribourg a two-round election takes place, where the second may be tacit.

[18] Their term of office is 4 years.

In Ticino, too, this election may be tacit (as in 1943), but in general, this is not the case.

Even in the cantons of Group B the councillors, once elected, generally remain in office as long as they do not choose to retire. The limited electoral campaigns brought about by the renewal of their term of office simply means that this rule is subject to certain exceptions. Therefore the average governmental career of the members of the executive is long in these cantons, in spite of the fact that they may appear to be rather "unstable" to some in comparison with the other states of the Confederation. In Geneva, which is probably the most "unstable" of these republics, a governmental career lasting ten years is usually considered short and those lasting about twenty years are not exceptional.

C) Occasionally Contested Renewals. Cantons where the renewal of the executive councillors' mandate has given rise, since 1945, to elections which were sometimes contested and sometimes not: Zurich, Schwyz, Zoug, Soleure, Schaffhouse, Basle-City, Argovie, Grisons, Valais, and Vaud. Some of these cantons are very similar to those of Group A because contested elections are exceptional (for example Zoug which will be discussed later on) and others are for the opposite reason close to those of Group B (for instance Vaud).

In the canton of Vaud, the election of state councillors (periodic re-election or supplementary election) may be tacit. Basle-City uses the system of a two-round election for the same purpose, with the second round possibly being tacit.

Zoug would certainly be better placed in Group A, for the election of the Executive Council follows an almost unchanging pattern. Nevertheless this pattern was slightly disturbed in 1954. In this canton, where the councillors are elected proportionally, their distribution according to party has remained unchanged since 1918 (4 Catholic-Conservatives, 2 Radicals, and 1 Socialist). The parties represented in the government always put forward seven candidates in all, which generally meet with no opposition. Exceptionally, in 1954 ten candidates were put forward, but nonetheless the structure of the governing body did not change at all. In Zoug the periodic election for the government's mandate always takes place, but supplementary elections are tacit if the number of candidates corresponds to the number of officials to be elected. In practice this is what always happens. In the other cantons of group C, the election of executive councillors has always effectively taken place since 1945 up to the 1960's, whether contested or not.

D) Cantons Where the Executive Councillors Are Elected by the Landsgemeinde. These are Obwalden, Nidwalden, Glaris and the two Appenzells. In these cantons (the form of the election aside) the appointment of the members of the government is similar to those of group A: that is to say that there is an automatic renewal of the mandates of the magistrates in office, with the possibility of a contested election if a seat is empty. But in this last case the party mechanism apparently plays but a small part and the personal prestige of the candidates is the deciding factor. "When it concerns the renewal of the government's mandate and there is no seat vacant, then no names are put forward in fact, apart from those of the councillors already in office. On the other hand if one or more new councillors have to be proposed, then it is not unusual that several names are put forward for each position" (extract from the reply from Glaris). This is perhaps more unusual in some other of these cantons. In Nidwalden, for example, uncontested elections took place for the appointments of the new councillors in 1945, 1946, 1952 and 1959.

Because of the electoral system, the election always takes place effectively. "When only one candidate is proposed . . . the vote (by a show of hands) takes place. The *Landammann* then asks the assembly of the people if they do not wish to propose any other names. If this is not the case, he then declares that the election has taken place," (from Obwalden's reply). When several candidates are put forward they oppose each other face to face before their fellow-citizens. Every citizen has the right to propose names, and from time to time this right is implemented.

The election of the members of the Federal Council is made according to a scaled pattern of distribution, which only changes at rather long intervals, by virtue of the changes in the number of national councillors of each party, and other considerations (the international situation, public opinion climate, the attitude of the major trade union movements and the directing bodies of the economy, and so on). Neglecting the details of tactics, one may say that whenever such a change takes place, it is usually obtained without spectacular electoral dispute. The party which sees itself losing a seat does not put forward a candidate, at least not officially. In actual fact only representatives of the "moving up" party oppose each other, and the members of the Assembly choose between them.

The situation corresponding to these practices is very different from that in countries where the opposition systematically opposes a government party (or coalition) with the hopes of replacing it. The collegiate government as now seen in Switzerland forces the parties to reach a compromise on a permanent basis. Obviously each one of the parties tries to have its own ideas incorporated to the highest possible degree in this compromise. But the political conditions make it unrealistic for the members of a party to cherish the hope of seeing their party programme applied completely for a while. Therefore a permanent co-existence of the parties is left which does not differ very much in essence from that federalistic equilibrium which regulates relationships between cantonal sovereign states, between linguistic or religious groups, etc., except that the balance of power amongst the parties still fluctuates slightly instead of being completely stabilized.

FINAL REMARKS

The contrast between the predominant party cantons and the multiparty cantons would largely be explained by reference to their long-term historical evolution.

On the whole, the main reason for the development of the system practised by the multiparty cantons is the formation of urban economic centres since the end of the Middle Ages. The society which grew up within these centres soon gave birth to several different classes of people, all with claims to a part in the city's government, but with varied interests and concepts. To this may be added the opposition between the sovereign cities and subjected rural regions.

The economic changes of the 19th and 20th centuries added to this cleavage, especially by promoting the working class movement and parties corresponding to it. It also stimulated migrations which enabled Catholic-inspired parties to take root on Protestant soil and vice versa.

However, even in the cantons with the most pronounced multiparty formula, the influential political forces are certainly very few outside the towns. The small and relatively homogeneous population of their rural communes is not a ground where the multiparty formula may function. The persistence of the dominant party formula in a series of cantons is understandable along the same lines.

These last cantons are predominantly rural communities. The majority of them have no urban concentration of importance. Their greatest towns are Fribourg (32,500 inhabitants) and Lucerne (72,000). In addition, their population is comparatively homogeneous from the point of view of religious traditions. Under these circumstances, the number of organized political forces could hardly have been anything but restricted.

Both groups of cantons show now the same preference for the "all-party government," in spite of their structural differences.

Note by the author, June 1973: The system described here is very stable. Since the time of first publication of the paper, no significant change has occurred.

Table I

Composition of the «Grand Conseil» (legislative council) in Cantons, post-war and recent years in % with indications of the method of voting[1]

Method of Voting	Canton		Catholic-Conservatives[2]	Radicals	Liberals	Bourgeois and Farmers	Socialists	Democrats	Independent party	Communist party	Other parties, Without party	Total of seats (=100%)
	Zürich	1947	8.9	13.9	—	20.0	27.2	11.7	11.1	6.7	0.5	180
P		1959	13.3	18.3	—	19.4	27.2	5.6	10.6	1.1	4.5 [3]	180
P	**Berne**	1946	5.2	13.4	—	41.2	35.1	—	0.5	1.5	3.1	194
P		1962	5.5	19.5	—	39.0	34.0	—	0.5	—	1.5 [4]	200
P	**Lucerne**	1947	52.7	34.1	—	—	9.0	—	3.0	1.2	—	167
P		1959	53.6	36.9	—	—	7.7	—	1.8	—	—	168
P	**Uri**	1948	72.7	20.0	—	—	7.3	—	—	—	—	55
M		1960	75.9	18.5	—	—	5.6	—	—	—	—	54
M	**Schwyz**	1948	53.5	29.3	—	—	12.1	—	—	—	5.1	99
P		1960	54.3	27.6	—	—	14.3	—	—	—	3.8 [5]	105
P	**Obwalden**[6]	1963					—				—	38
M	**Nidwalden**	1949										
M												

Canton	Year											
Glaris	1947	P	13.2	36.8	—	—	19.1	30.9	—	—	—	68
	1962	M+P	16.0	34.6	—	—	16.0	33.4	—	—	—	81
Zoug	1946	P	48.7	32.1	—	—	19.2	—	—	—	—	78
	1962	P	55.0	33.0	—	—	10.5	—	1.5	—	—	78
Fribourg	1946	P	62.2	25.2	—	2.4	10.2	—	—	—	—	127
	1961	P	56.2	25.4	—	9.2	9.2	—	—	—	—	130
Soleure	1945	P	26.2	42.3	—	0.7	30.8	—	—	—	—	130
	1961	P	23.6	47.9	—	—	28.5	—	—	—	—	144
Basle-City	1947	P	10.0	15.4	14.6	4.6	25.4	—	4.6	23.9	1.5	130
	1960	P	15.4	19.2	16.2	—	30.0	—	6.9	6.2	6.2[8]	130
Basle-Country	1947	P	11.3	23.7	—	11.3	30.0	15.0	—	8.7	—	80
	1959	P	13.7	31.3	—	10.0	30.0	—	1.2	—	13.7[9]	80
Schaffhouse	1948	M	6.2	22.5	—	32.5	25.0	—	2.5	—	11.3	80
	1960	P	8.5	24.4	—	26.8	31.7	2.4	3.7	—	2.4[10]	82
App. Auss. Rhod.[6]	1963	M	—	—	—	—	—	—	—	—	—	61

Method of Voting	Canton	Catholic-Conservatives	Radicals	Liberals	Bourgeois and Farmers	Socialists	Democrats	Independent party	Communist party	Other parties. Without party	Total of seats (=100%)
M	App. Inn. Rhod.[6] 1963	—	—	—	—	—	—	—	—	—	60
	St-Gall										
P	1945	43.3	28.1	—	—	16.3	3.9	2.8	2.2	3.4	178
P	1960	47.6	30.6	—	—	16.1	—	5.2	—	0.5 [11]	193
	Grisons										
M	1945	32.7	13.2	—	—	7.1	43.9	—	—	3.1	98
M	1961	34.5	25.7	—	—	6.2	32.7	—	—	0.9 [7]	113
	Argovie										
P	1945	22.2	19.2	—	17.6	34.7	—	2.1	1.0	3.2	193
P	1961	23.5	20.5	—	14.0	32.0	—	4.0	—	6.0 [12]	200
	Thurgovie										
P	1947	23.0	48.4 [13]	—	—	24.6	—	—	0.7	3.3	122
P	1962	25.6	46.4 [12]	—	—	21.6	0.8	—	—	5.6 [3]	125
	Ticino										
P	1947	36.9	41.6	—	4.6	13.8	—	—	3.1	—	65
P	1959	35.4	44.6	—	3.1	15.4	—	—	1.5	—	65
	Vaud										
M	1945	—	46.5	16.1	3.7	12.0	—	—	19.4	2.3	217
P	1962	3.0	39.1	20.8	7.6	23.4	—	—	5.1	1.0 [7]	197

	Year										
Valais											
P	1945	70.2	24.4	—	—	5.4	—	—	—	—	131
P	1961	67.7	20.8	—	—	9.2	—	0.8	—	1.5 [14]	130
Neuchâtel											
P	1945	—	27.2	18.4	—	30.1	—	—	13.6	10.7	103
P	1961	—	29.6	20.8	—	32.2	—	—	5.2	12.2 [15]	115
Geneva											
P	1945	14.0	25.0	16.0	—	9.0	—	—	36.0	—	100
P	1961	21.0	27.0	20.0	—	18.0	—	—	14.0	—	100

[1] According to the Swiss statistical year-book, and correspondence with cantonal chancelleries.

P = proportional system.

M = majority vote system.

M + P = in circles electing one deputy, majority vote system; otherwise, proportional system.

[2] The Social-Christians form a separate movement, although joined with the Conservatives, in some cantons, in particular in Schwyz, Obwald and Lucern. In the latter canton, for example, the two groups form a single party in the Grand Conseil, and the Executive Council, but at election time, they present separate (and related) lists.

[3] Popular Evangelical party.

[4] Popular Evangelical party and «Youth of Berne».

[5] No indication, probably without party.

[6] Distinction according to party can not be made.

[7] Without party.

[8] Popular Evangelical party and Independent Socialists.

[9] Evangelical-Democratic party. List for the two Basles.

[10] Popular Evangelical party and Liberal-Socialist party.

[11] Free Conservatives.

[12] Popular Evangelical party, United movement for the compulsory vote, and list of dissident Catholic-Conservatives.

[13] Including the Bourgeois and Farmers party, the lists being identical in some districts.

[14] Farmers' social movement.

[15] National Progressive party (centre-right), Neuchâtel movement of the new Socialist left.

Table II

Composition of the Executive Council of each canton in 1946 and 1962[1]

Canton		Catholic-Conservatives	Radicals	Liberals	Bourgeois and Farmers	Socialists	Democrats	Independent party	Other party	Without party	Total of seats
Zürich	1946	—	2	—	2	2	1	—	—	—	7
	1962	—	2	—	2	2	—	1	—	—	7
Berne	1946	—	2	—	4	3	—	—	—	—	9
	1962	—	2	—	4	3	—	—	—	—	9
Lucerne	1946	5	2	—	—	—	—	—	—	—	7
	1962	4	2	—	—	1	—	—	—	—	7
Uri	1946	4	3	—	—	—	—	—	—	—	7
	1962	5	2	—	—	—	—	—	—	—	7
Schwyz	1946	4	2	—	—	1	—	—	—	—	7
	1962	4	1	—	—	1	—	—	—	1	7
Obwalden	1946	6	1	—	—	—	—	—	—	—	7
	1962	5	2	—	—	—	—	—	—	—	7

Canton	Year										Total
Nidwalden	1946	8	3	—	—	—	—	—	—	—	11
	1962	5	3	—	—	—	—	—	—	1	9
Glaris	1946	1	2	—	—	1	3	—	—	—	7
	1962	1	2	—	—	2	2	—	—	—	7
Zoug	1946	4	2	—	—	1	—	—	—	—	7
	1962	4	2	—	—	1	—	—	—	—	7
Fribourg	1946	6	1	—	—	—	—	—	—	—	7
	1962	5	1	1	—	—	—	—	—	—	7
Soleure	1946	1	3	—	—	1	—	—	—	—	5
	1962	1	2	—	—	2	—	—	—	—	5
Basle-City	1946	1	1	—	—	3	—	1	1[2]	—	7
	1962	1	2	1	—	3	—	—	—	—	7
Basle-Country	1946	1	1	—	1	2	1	—	—	—	5
	1962	1	1	—	—	2	—	—	—	—	5
Schaffhouse	1946	—	2	—	2	1	—	—	—	—	5
	1962	—	2	—	2	1	—	—	—	—	5

	Catholic-Conservatives	Radicals	Liberals	Bourgeois and Farmers	Socialists	Democrats	Independent party	Other party	Without party	Total of seats
App. Auss. Rhod.										
1946	—	6[2]	—	—	1	—	—	—	—	7
1962	—	6[3]	—	—	1	—	—	—	—	7
App. Inn. Rhod.										
1946	9	—	—	—	—	—	—	—	—	9
1962	9	—	—	—	—	—	—	—	—	9
St Gall										
1946	3	3	—	—	1	—	—	—	—	7
1962	3	3	—	—	1	—	—	—	—	7
Grisons										
1946	2	1	—	2	—	2	—	—	—	5
1962	2	1	—	1	1	1	—	—	—	5
Argovie										
1946	1	1	—	1	1	—	—	—	—	5
1962	1	2	—	1	1	—	—	—	—	5
Thurgovie										
1946	1	2	—	—	1	—	—	—	—	5
1962	1	2	—	—	1	—	—	—	—	5

		1	2	3	4	5	6	7	8	9	Total
Ticino	1946	2	2	—	—	1	—	—	—	—	5
	1962	2	2	—	—	1	—	—	—	—	5
Vaud	1946	—	4	2	—	1	—	—	—	—	7
	1962	—	3	1	1	2	—	—	—	—	7
Valais	1946	4	1	—	—	—	—	—	—	—	5
	1962	4	1	—	—	—	—	—	—	—	5
Neuchâtel	1946	—	1	1	—	1	—	—	2[4]	—	5
	1962	—	2	1	—	1	—	—	1[6]	—	5
Geneva	1946	1	3	2	—	1	—	—	—	—	7
	1962	2	1	2	—	2	—	—	—	—	7
Total	1946	64	51	6	11	23	7	—	3	—	165
	1962	60	49	5	13	29	3	1	1	2	163

[1] According to information kindly supplied by the Cantonal chancelleries in reply to a questionnaire.
[2] Communist party.
[3] The chancellery of this canton specifies that some of the councillors counted here as Radical, may not be party members at least formerly.
[4] One National Progressive party, and one member of another small local party.
[5] National Progressive party.

11

PART IV
APPLICATIONS AND ILLUSTRATIONS:
CANADA

The selections in Part IV are chosen to illustrate various aspects of consociationalism in Canada, although as in the case of Part III some of the material cannot be linked explicitly to the concept as it has been developed in recent political literature. My own paper on "Consociationalism and the Canadian Political System," like the introductory paper in Part I above, was prepared in its original form in conjunction with the International Round Table on Multilingual Political Systems sponsored by the International Political Science Association and the International Centre for Research on Bilingualism at Laval University in March 1972. In it I have attempted to assess the Canadian case from the standpoint of each of the three approaches to the consociational theme that were examined in Part I:

Probably the first scholar to apply the consociational model explicitly to Canada was S. J. R. Noel, who did so in a paper to the Canadian Political Science Association at Winnipeg in 1970 and again in October 1970 at a joint colloquium of the Canadian Political Science Association and the Société canadienne de science politique at Quebec. It is the second of these papers, revised, condensed, and confined to the consociational model alone, that is reprinted here. Noel is primarily influenced by Lijphart's approach to consociationalism and thus emphasizes the capacity and willingness of elites as a crucial factor in making the system work. But he also is impressed by the strength of regional identities and the working of federal-provincial mechanisms of accommodation to the point that he sees the provinces themselves as the basic subcultures within the Canadian system.

The next two selections are more historical. The pages from William Ormsby's The Emergence of the Federal Concept in Canada, 1839-1845 *are a reminder that for a quarter of a century following the Rebellions of 1837 Upper and Lower Canadians, English-speaking and French-speaking, Protestant and Roman Catholic, lived under a unified political system in the Province of Canada. A full-scale systematic study of the political accommodation of religious, linguistic and regional cleavages during the union period has yet to be attempted, but Ormsby indicates some of the themes to be explored in such a study. In particular he suggests how regional factors, fortified by the earlier separation of Upper and Lower Canada, pointed towards territorial federalism as the principal mechanism for the accommodation of pluralism.*

The view that Canadian Confederation rests upon a compact or contract has been affirmed and denied many times at both the political and the academic level. G. F. G. Stanley's "Act or Pact: Another Look at Confederation," delivered as the Presidential Address to the Canadian Historical Association in 1956, reconsi-

ders the evidence for regarding the terms of Confederation – from the standpoint of central Canada at least – as an interethnic entente that was later sanctioned by Imperial statute. The text reprinted here is considerably abridged, representing less than half of Stanley's original address. In particular two long sections, on French-English relations before the Confederation period and on judicial interpretation of the British North America Act, have been reluctantly omitted as less directly relevant to the general theme of this volume.

Janice Staples's paper, "The Erosion of Dualism in Manitoba," is a rewritten and condensed version of a considerably longer seminar paper on the same theme. While the institutions of dualism in Manitoba proved fragile and short-lived, this essay is a reminder that social segmentation and consociational politics can be found at the provincial level as well as federally, and that further provincial studies along the same lines might well be instructive. Consociationalism in Manitoba evolved gradually in the Red River colony over half a century and was destroyed in two decades after the province entered Confederation. The political processes and underlying public attitudes in the Manitoba case and in similar issues in other provinces deserve closer study than they have had hitherto, because whether religious and especially linguistic accommodation is possible – or impossible – at the provincial level has major implications for the future of the Canadian federation as a whole.

CONSOCIATIONALISM AND THE CANADIAN POLITICAL SYSTEM

K. D. McRae

When we look at Canadian society from the standpoint of consociational theory, we can use the three approaches to consociationalism described in Part I above as convenient categories for analysis and evaluation. Before doing so, however, we should recall that consociationalism is a classificatory device based on a number of complex political and social dimensions including the structure of political parties and voluntary associations, patterns of social action, attitudes and behavior of political elites, and even general historical traditions of accommodation of diversity. It is, therefore, primarily a matter of degree; one could expect to find at least some aspects of consociationalism in any democratic society having significant social cleavages. The consociational model may therefore be useful as an ideal type against which to measure societies that are consociational only to a limited extent. Furthermore, consociational patterns may increase or diminish dramatically over time, as the Austrian case illustrates. More generally, the literature on consociationalism reveals a pronounced tendency towards *ontzuiling*, or dismantling of the pillars, from the mid-1960's onwards in all of the European countries where segmented pluralism has been strong. In looking at the Canadian case, then, we may examine how closely the Canadian experience has approached the consociational model at any given point in time, and we may also consider whether the consociational model suggests possible reforms for the existing Canadian system.

SEGMENTATION IN CANADIAN SOCIAL STRUCTURE

In addition to the usual differences in socio-economic status it is fairly obvious that there are further social cleavages in Canada, but a closer look soon reveals difficulties in determining with any exactitude the segment boundaries or axes of cleavage. Unlike the European cases that we have examined, the political party system in Canada does not offer clear guideposts to these boundaries. Somewhat paradoxically, the most fully institutionalized cleavage in terms of segmented social structures need not be the cleavage of greatest salience or intensity, as we may recall from the example of Belgium in the 1960's when language differences became more intense than traditional formally institutionalized religious-ideological cleavages. In Canada the problem becomes more complex, in part because of the federal system. While differences between linguistic communities may appear at first glance to be the overriding cleavage of contemporary Canada in terms of intensity, the pattern of institutionalization of cleavages is not so simple, and we are faced with a number of alternative hypotheses.

In the most systematic attempt to date to apply the Lijphart model to Canada, S. J. R. Noel recognizes the need to make "certain adjustments" before applying it to Canada:

> The term "subculture" could be interpreted in a number of ways – it could be taken, for example, to refer to English Canada and French Canada, or to a number of distinct regions such as the Maritimes, Quebec, Ontario, and the West – but most usefully perhaps as "province."[1]

Lijphart himself appears to give this notion some sanction when he suggests that "if the subcultures are geographically concentrated, a federal pattern of government in which the internal political boundaries coincide with the subcultural cleavages can be an eminently suitable consociational device."[2] On the other hand another recent article, which refers only briefly to the consociational model, implies that the basic cleavage is primarily ethnic-linguistic:

> . . . we would suggest that Canadian Confederation, and in particular French-English relations, can be viewed as a consociational democracy, which has been faltering for some time, and which has since 1960 almost completely broken down.[3]

None of these articles, however, has examined systematically the structure of social or political segmentation in Canada.

There are obvious institutional arguments for interpreting Lijphart's model in terms of provinces. In the Canadian federal system the provinces provide a tangible institutional framework for articulating and aggregating local and regional interests which are then accommodated at the federal level and through various mechanisms of federal-provincial interaction. Much the same

---

[1] S. J. R. Noel, "Consociational Democracy and Canadian Federalism," *Canadian Journal of Political Science,* Vol. 4 (1971). 16 [below, 265].

[2] A Lijphart, "Cultural Diversity and Theories of Political Integration," *Canadian Journal of Political Science,* Vol. 4 (1971), 10. The paragraph in question does not appear in the original mimeographed version of the paper, which was presented at a joint colloquium of the Canadian Political Science Association and the Société canadienne de science politique at Quebec in October 1970.

[3] C. White, J. Millar, and W. Gagné, "Political Integration in Quebec during the 1960's", *Canadian Ethnic Studies,* Vol. 3 (1971), 57-58.

argument could be applied to any federal system, provided only that the component units of the federation coincide sufficiently with subcultural boundaries. The case of India suggests itself here, because there the state boundaries have been redrawn to coincide more closely with linguistic and cultural boundaries, and certain of the Swiss cantons – those that are small, intensely particularistic and homogeneous – afford a further example.

In Canada, however, one should not assume an automatic coincidence of provincial and subcultural boundaries, and even the nature of the cleavages themselves deserves closer analysis than it has had up to now. Basically, to recall the European examples, it is difficult to see the ten provinces – or even the four or five regions of Canada – as distinctive *familles spirituelles* or *Weltanschauungsgruppen* analogous to the European *zuilen* or *Lager*, that is, as blocs embodying distinctive, enduring, and possibly clashing value systems. If we compare Nova Scotia with Ontario or British Columbia in terms of value systems, life styles, and general cultural patterns, it seems likely – though we lack sufficient evidence to argue more strongly – that we would find greater differences *within* provinces than *between* them, and that interregional variations in Canada would be found to be significantly lower by most criteria than in many countries of Europe. It would therefore seem more appropriate, in the framework of consociational theory, to begin by regarding the Canadian provinces, like most Swiss cantons, not so much as independent subcultures in themselves but as additional *sites* for the accommodation of cleavages that do not necessarily coincide with provincial boundaries. Of course to the extent that subcultural boundaries do coincide with provincial boundaries, the federal system may itself become a device for accommodating subcultural differences, but this is a point to be investigated empirically rather than taken for granted from the start.

There is, however, one immediate exception. No very extensive investigation is needed to establish that Quebec is a province *pas comme les autres*. While all the other provinces are predominantly English-speaking, it is predominantly French-speaking. While all the others are either predominantly Protestant or almost evenly balanced between Protestants and Catholics, it is predominantly Roman Catholic. We encounter here a situation of overlapping and reinforcing cleavages by which province, language and religion are linked and interrelated, as indicated in Diagram 1. In this perspective Quebec is indeed a subculture that departs significantly from all other provinces and from the Canadian averages. And if the image of a *famille spirituelle* can no longer do justice to Quebec's diversity, the image of a *Lager*, a defensive complex in a hostile environment, is not inappropriate.

Nevertheless, as Diagram 1 indicates, the correlations between

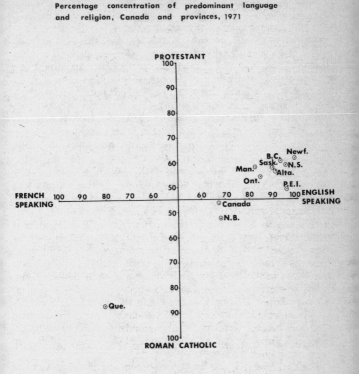

DIAGRAM 1
Percentage concentration of predominant language
and religion, Canada and provinces, 1971

Sources: Home language: *Statistics Canada Daily,* June 6, 1973.
          Religion: calculated from *Statistics Canada Daily,* July 3, 1973.

Note: In this table "Protestant" includes Anglican, Baptist, Jehovah's Witnesses, Lutheran, Mennonite, Pentecostal, Presbyterian, Salvation Army and United Church, but excludes smaller Protestant groups included in the residual category "Other". For Canada as a whole both Protestants and Roman Catholics are below 50 per cent (43 and 46 per cent respectively), and this occurs also in Prince Edward Island. Language data are based on the language most often spoken at home, which was recorded for the first time at the 1971 census.

religion, language and territory are far from perfect. Every province has both religious and linguistic minorities, though in every province except Quebec the religious minorities are larger than the linguistic ones. While virtually all French speakers are Roman Catholics, English speakers are far from being uniformly Protestant. This network of religious and linguistic cleavages, substantially reinforced but also partially cross-cut by the territorial dimension, gives rise to issues and tensions that cannot be resolved by mechanisms of decentralized federalism alone.

Because this pattern of cleavages is complex, it is important to observe carefully its institutionalization in historical context, for here, perhaps, lie clues to some present ambiguities. The most visible cleavage in Canadian history had its origin in France's double Cession to Britain of Acadia in 1713 and New France in 1763. With the Cession of New France Britain acquired for the first time a substantial colony whose population was alien in religion, legal system, language, and culture. For an imperial power whose own Roman Catholic population was still disfranchised and barred from any public office, the most important of these differences was religion, and with the influx of English-speaking settlement into Quebec differences between "new subjects" and "old subjects" tended to be institutionalized along religious lines. In 1774 the Quebec Act confirmed the position of the Catholic Church in the colony, and in 1791 the Constitutional Act made Roman Catholics in the Canadas eligible to vote and hold public office, rights not available to their co-religionists in Britain until 1829.

The line of religious cleavage and ethnic-linguistic cleavage coincided well enough until the 1840's, by which time extensive Irish immigration was giving rise to a substantial population of English-speaking Catholics. Religious issues were intensified by the importation into Canada of hereditary quarrels between Orangemen and Irish Catholics, and by the Catholic Church's counterattack on liberalism during the Papacy of Pius IX. Thus the second half of the nineteenth century witnessed a politics of significant religious confrontation, and after Confederation in 1867 this remained the most obvious line of cleavage at the federal level. As one pamphleteer remarked while analysing the distribution of appointments to the public service:

> I shall divide the whole population conformably with its two great religious sections – Catholic and Protestant – for all other distinctions seem minor perturbations, like the ripple on a wave, and merge in these. The former I shall divide into English and French-speaking.[4]

[4] J. L. P. O'Hanly, *The Political Standing of Irish Catholics in Canada* (Ottawa, 1872), 10.

The important thing to note is that a good deal of institutional segmentation took place during this period, and the Catholic population acquired not only publicly supported denominational schools in most provinces but a whole network of colleges, newspapers, hospitals and charitable and welfare institutions that made a substantial part of Catholic life a world apart. Linguistic issues might arise from time to time *within* the Catholic community, but the primary line of cleavage was religious during this important formative period.

Since about 1960 the pattern of institutional segmentation has appeared to be shifting slightly but perceptibly from religion to language. The evidence is found in many sectors. Schools are increasingly sharply segmented on a linguistic basis. In Ontario the private French-speaking Catholic high schools have entered the public system as French-language public schools. Denominational universities have been secularized under governmental and financial pressure but separate linguistic streaming is emphasized more strongly. Health care has become a public responsibility, and even Catholic hospitals are under pressure to establish abortion committees. The electronic media, which are segmented linguistically, have grown vastly in importance. Among the reasons for this changing pattern one could undoubtedly list a diminished interest in organized religion, the climate of ecumenism, and an increased salience of linguistic issues in the working world as urbanization and industrialism have advanced.

The shifting of patterns of segmentation from a religious to a linguistic base has certain political consequences. While all provinces except Quebec have quite substantial religious minorities (as defined by Diagram 1 above), the official-language linguistic minorities are proportionally small and politically weak in all provinces except Quebec and New Brunswick. As a consequence the French-speaking minorities outside Quebec are weaker and more vulnerable to majority pressures than were the politically significant Roman Catholic minorities of an earlier period, while within Quebec the English-speaking sector as a whole (including English-speaking Catholics) is larger and more significant than the relatively small Protestant sector alone. Thus the effect of a shifting pattern of segmentation towards a linguistic base is to throw the Canadian political system off balance at the provincial level; while the bargaining power of the minority in Quebec remains strong and even increases, that of the French-speaking linguistic minorities in the other provinces becomes significantly weaker and more precarious. Some of the present strains in the political system may doubtless be traced to the fact that it is badly structured for a situation in which linguistic and cultural issues are perceived to be more salient than religious ones.

Beyond the analysis of formal, institutionalized segmentation, however, certain troublesome analytical questions persist. Despite formal institutionalization along religious boundaries, there remains an alternative hypothesis that the most fundamental, the most basic, and the most enduring of social cleavages in Canada has been the dimension of ethnic-linguistic diversity, and that in this respect our history has perhaps been more homogeneous than the pattern of institutional segmentation suggests. Were not the initial phases of formal segmentation overly influenced by a British concern to integrate her Roman Catholic "new subjects" into the Imperial system, and was not the subsequent Protestant-Catholic rivalry in the nineteenth century in some sense a distortion of our own domestic tradition, an echo of foreign battles being fought at the time in Ireland and on the Continent? Was not Lord Durham essentially correct in his description of the Lower Canadian scene in 1838 as "a struggle, not of principles, but of races"?[5] And is not Arthur Lower correct, a century later, in characterizing the "deep division between French and English" as the "primary antithesis" of Canadian history?[6]

It is never easy to compare the salience or intensity of religious and ethnic-linguistic differences, and in the context of Canadian history it is particularly difficult. In the first place the two cleavages overlap substantially, but where they do not the patterns of interaction differ. The history of French-English relations has been characterized by relatively high geographical separation, and even where there was physical proximity substantial occupational differentiation tended to keep the groups apart. Further, as Louis Hartz has argued from the standpoint of comparative intellectual history, French Canada and English Canada arose from different phases of European ideological experience and constitute distinctive fragments of that experience, each with its own highly internalized value system and each insensitive to the values of the other.[7] Because of this ideological gulf, reinforced until recent decades by physical separation and occupational distance, the relationship of French and English Canadians in historical perspective has been less a confrontation of opposing forces than a coexistence of two solitudes. Given both physical and ideological separation, it is scarcely surprising that formal institutional segmentation on ethnic-linguistic lines was slower to develop than religious segmentation. With little inter-ethnic contact, it was simply less called for.

5 *The Report of the Earl of Durham* (new ed., London, 1902), 8.
6 A. R. M. Lower, "Two Ways of Life: The Primary Antithesis of Canadian History," *Canadian Historical Association Report*, 1943. Reprinted in C. Berger, ed., *Approaches to Canadian History* (Toronto, 1967), 15-28.
7 L. Hartz, et al., *The Founding of New Societies* (New York, 1964).

To some degree the very attempt to compare the salience of religious and ethnic cleavage may be an unreal quest, because a significant proportion of the population may not perceive the religious and the ethnic-linguistic dimensions as analytically distinct. It is possible that the distinction is felt primarily by the relatively small numbers who are cross-pressured, of whom perhaps the most obvious group are English-speaking Catholics in linguistically mixed areas. A thorough exploration of this question, which seems important to an understanding of Canadian society, would be too complex to pursue here. Our more modest objective in this paper has been to identify patterns of segmented pluralism primarily as they are manifested in the structure of formal institutions, but in a wider theoretical sense the study of segmentation could and should be extended across the entire spectrum of social action.

These special difficulties of the Canadian setting need not deter us from attempting some preliminary cross-national comparisons of areas and degrees of segmentation. We have identified three possible axes of segmentation for Canada – province, religion, and language. One method of comparison is to assess the degree of organized segmentation along each axis by sphere of activity, using Lorwin's categories, in order to compare the three Canadian axes with one another and also with Lorwin's results for Austria, Belgium, the Netherlands and Switzerland. The results of such a comparison are shown in Table 2, in which I have added certain political subcategories for Canada which are not included in Lorwin's original table.[8]

It must be emphasized at once that the ratings for Canada are both tentative and subjective. Our concern in Table 2 is with the degree to which groups are organizationally distinct and autonomous, or at least recognized and represented as distinct interest groups, with respect to the axis in question. A number of problems arise in establishing even approximate ratings. First, in Canada as in Europe different groups reveal different degrees of segmentation, Catholics more than Protestants, French Canadians more than English Canadians, and Quebec more than other provinces. Second, there are time differentials between the European and Canadian indicators. Lorwin refers to Europe at the peak of segmentation in the 1950's, while ours for Canada refer to about 1970; ratings for Canada in the 1950's might well have scored a few sectors higher on the religious axis and lower on the linguistic one. Third, since Canada's size and heterogeneity may give rise to different regional perspectives as to some of these ratings, I

[8] V. R. Lorwin, "Segmented Pluralism", *Comparative Politics*, Vol. 3 (1971), 155 [cf. above, 48].

Table 2. Degree of Segmented Pluralism, by Sphere of Activity.

	Austria	Belgium	Netherlands	Switzerland	Province¹	Canada Religion	Language
Education							
Primary		H	H	M	H	H or H	H
Secondary	M	H	H	M	H	M	H
Higher	M		M	L	H		H
Mass Media							
Press	H	M	M	M	L	L	H
Electronic	M		H		L	L	H
Socio-economic Organization							
Labor	H	H	H	H	M(H)	M	M
Farmers	H	H	H	M	M(H)	L	L
Small Business	M	L	M		L	L	L
Employers	M	M	M		L	L	L
Liberal Professions	M	H	H	L	M	L	L
Health Care	H	H		H	M	M	L
Consumers	H	H		L	L	L	L
Leisure Activities			M	M	L	L	L or M
Politics and Government							
Religion-Party ties	H	H	H	M			
Party Platforms²					L	L	L
Party Organization²					M	L	M
Variations in voter support²					M	M	M
Bureaucracy	H	H		H		L	L

Note: Degree of Segmented Pluralism: H = High; M = Medium; L = Low.

¹ Ratings in parentheses in this column refer to Quebec. ² Subcategories not included in Lorwin's table.

Source: For European countries, Lorwin (see above, p. 48).

should state that my own vantage point is that of central Canada. While I have tried to strike rough national averages, different provinces would probably yield somewhat different profiles on all three axes.

Finally, the ratings for the provincial column present a special problem. In a federal system some sectors may go to the provinces through the constitutional division of powers, but not necessarily because the provinces *themselves* represent divergent interests. In general a province may offer a base for mobilizing and expressing a particular regional interest in the wider political system, or else it may, as we have noted earlier, simply offer an alternative and possibly better *site* for the accommodation of divergent interests than the national level. Table 2 is not well adapted to bring out this distinction, especially as provinces may differ among themselves on this point. I have classified a sector as having medium or high segmentation on the provincial axis (1) where there is formal organizational autonomy (for example, in education), or (2) where associations in that sector are roughly as active at the provincial as at the federal level, or more so. In addition, since Quebec does represent a distinctive value system to a greater extent than other provinces, I have added extra ratings in parentheses for Quebec where these seem different from the Canadian norms.

In comparing the columns of Table 2 it is obvious from the crude nature of the data and the problems of establishing ratings that only very approximate comparisons should be attempted. From the three Canadian columns one notes first that none of the three axes reveals significantly stronger segmentation than the others. Once again the relative salience of province, religion and language as alternative lines of demarcation in organized social structure remains as unsettled as before. But the more interesting and significant comparisons in the table are between Canada and Europe. Unlike the European social movements that sought to embrace the "whole man" and to construct an organizational network encompassing all the social roles of the individual, social mobilization in Canada has left the various economic roles relatively unsegmented. The prime emphasis has been on education, with its large potential for structuring attitudes and values.

There is another crucial dissimilarity. In all four European cases the apex of the organizational network is a set of political parties which both mobilize and reflect the values of the subcultural blocs. In Canada this high correlation between political parties and *any* of the axes of cleavage has been conspicuously absent. Though parties may from time to time almost monopolize the representation of one province or region, they only rarely appeal to the electorate in specifically regional terms. Though parties may from time to time obtain disproportionate support from one religious or linguistic group, they almost invariably campaign to maximize support from the electorate as a whole rather than from any specific religious or ethnic segment as such.[9] Perhaps the chief obstacle to interpreting Canadian society in terms of European-style segmented pluralism is the low level of consistent, identifiable segmentation – whether regional, or religious, or linguistic – in the functioning of political parties. One might make an exception for separatist and nationalist parties in Quebec, but these have not been prominent at the federal level. The virtual absence of parties which might explicitly formulate and express segment interests has undoubtedly been a major obstacle to social mobilization along segment lines. The causes and consequences of this incomplete mobilization of segment interests will be seen in the next section.

ELITE COOPERATION IN THE CANADIAN POLITICAL SYSTEM.
In order to apply the consociational model to the Canadian political system, one must first consider certain basic differences between the Canadian case and all the European examples considered elsewhere in this book. These differences include (1) political parties with relatively low ideological profiles, (2) an electoral system that places a high premium on winning single-member constituencies, and (3) a strong tendency towards single-party control of the legislature and one-party ministries. These contrast with the European norms of more consciously ideological parties, proportional representation, and coalition ministries. The same contrasts exist at the provincial level; while the Swiss cantons tend strongly to proportional representation and coalition ministries like the Swiss federal pattern, Canadian provinces tend equally strongly to single-member constituencies and one-party ministries. It follows from these differences that patterns of elite cooperation may have to take very different forms in Canada from those found in Europe.

To take the question of party structures first, federal politics was characterized for half a century after Confederation by a two-party system in which both Liberals and Conservatives sought to obtain as wide a spectrum of support as possible. Although additional parties appeared in the 1920's and became an enduring feature of the political scene, the norm of a two-party system remained. As Denis Smith has pointed out:

[9] The 1971 Ontario provincial election, in which financial aid to Roman Catholic secondary schools became a major inter-party issue, was rather exceptional from this standpoint. More typical is the case of Manitoba, where the issue of aid to private sectarian schools has cross-cut political parties rather sharply during the 1960's.

> The leaders of the three western movements of political protest, the Progressives, the C.C.F., and Social Credit, insisted in their national campaigns from 1921 to 1958 that their purpose was not to complicate the Canadian party system by creating permanent minor groups, but to simplify it by forcing a realignment of political loyalty throughout the country. The professed national aim of each party was to create a national two-party system divided on lines of principle . . . [10]

In other words each of the minor parties sought to become a major party, an alternative to the government in power, and campaigned accordingly before the electorate. No federal party has sought to become identified as the representative primarily of a specific province, region, religious denomination, or linguistic-cultural group. Even the New Democratic Party and its predecessor the C.C.F., the most ideologically oriented of Canadian parties in terms of social class, have in most campaigns made a broad appeal for sympathetic middle-class support while seeking to maintain a special relationship with organized labour and farmers. At the formal level all federal political parties in Canada have stressed the aggregation of a maximum range of interests as their primary campaign goal, and hence in contrast to the European cases none of the possible axes of subcultural cleavage that we have examined has been consciously and deliberately embodied in the structure of parties. In practice there have been moderately significant variations in voter support along these same cleavage lines in recent elections,[11] and at more informal levels parties undoubtedly build upon whatever segment advantages they have.

There is an obvious link between the party system and the electoral system. The fact that a party must surpass all other parties to win a single-member constituency gives a bonus to the stronger subcultures in the constituency and discourages the full articulation of interests of minority groups. Under these circumstances the best electoral strategy is to emphasize common interests as fully as possible while minimizing the impact of divergent interests. In any given constituency minority interests will have no explicit parliamentary representation.

The same multiplier effect in the country as a whole enables the party with a simple plurality of votes to aspire to a clear majority of seats and to form a ministry dependent on no other parliamentary party. The system presupposes as a general rule the

---

[10] "Prairie Revolt, Federalism, and the Party System", in H. G. Thorburn, ed., *Party Politics in Canada* (Toronto, 1963), 126.

[11] J. Meisel, *Working Papers on Canadian Politics* (Montreal and London, 1972), ch. 1.

hegemony of one broadly based party in the legislature and the adequate representation within it of all major political interests, including regional, religious and linguistic-cultural interests. In practice, as Alan Cairns demonstrates in an important article, the electoral system has frequently produced a significant distortion between the parties' shares of the popular vote and the distribution of seats won, and – more important – each party's distribution of seats by region tends to be more distorted than one would expect from the distribution of the popular vote by region.[12] This is in sharp contrast not only with the European multi-party coalition model but even with those Scandinavian instances in which a single party having roughly comparable electoral support but only minority representation in the legislature will form a single-party minority ministry and remain in office for a considerable period through a politics of compromise. All the norms of the Canadian system favour one-party control of the legislature and a wide mandate to the majority party to rule as it sees fit. When an election does not produce this result, the members of a minority ministry, as Senator Forsey has pointed out,

> ... face three deeply rooted popular notions. ... The first is that minority governments are altogether exceptional, abnormal, almost unheard of, except, of course, among benighted continental Europeans ... .The second popular Canadian notion about minority government is that it is necessarily bad: incompetent, weak, indecisive, if not worse ... .The third popular notion about minority government is that it cannot last.[13]

If we look for consociational politics in Canada, then, we must normally seek it not in compromises *among* parliamentary parties but in accommodation *within* the party in power and in the mechanisms of the federal system.

---

[12] A. C. Cairns, "The Electoral System and the Party System in Canada, 1921-1965", *Canadian Journal of Political Science*, Vol. 1 (1968), especially pp. 58-63, and see also the further discussion by J. A. A. Lovink and Cairns in the same journal, Vol. 3 (1970), 497-521.

[13] E. A. Forsey, "The Problem of 'Minority' Government in Canada", *Canadian Journal of Economics and Political Science*, Vol. 30 (1964), 1-4. These "popular notions" may be most strongly held, however, by the party elites and activists who expect to gain from them. That the public at large may take a more pragmatic view is suggested by a March 1973 CIPO poll which showed 54 per cent of the public expressing favorable attitudes to minority government against 27 per cent who disapproved it (*Ottawa Citizen*, April 25 and 28, 1973).

The focal point for accommodation within the party in power is, of course, the federal cabinet. Longstanding and firm traditions require the Cabinet to be faithfully representative not only of provinces but also of religion and language, even to the extent of some sacrifice of efficiency. Alexander Mackenzie in 1873 took pride in his delicately balanced cabinet of "five Catholics, three members of the Church of England, three Presbyterians, two Methodists, one Congregationalist, and one Baptist."[14] More recent studies by Gibson and Van Loon[15] have focussed on the question of linguistic representation; both give data on a quantitive basis, but they also remind us that beyond the simple arithmetic of representation lie more complex questions of the importance of portfolios held, the varying stature of individual cabinet members, and the influence that these exert on cabinet decisions. As Noel observes, the secrecy of cabinet proceedings makes it difficult to relate representational factors to decision-making in any direct way.[16]

Our concern here is not to trace the detailed history of representational patterns in the Canadian cabinet system but to assess the cabinet as a possible consociational model. Such a context suggests certain possible dangers. In the first place adequate representation of subcultural interests is heavily dependent on the ability of the party in power to win significant support from all major segments. To illustrate in simple terms, this can be taken first and foremost to mean significant backing from both English and French Canada. Cabinet representation drawn from the elites of both sides must be sufficient in numbers and stature to press for and obtain decisions on national policy acceptable to the respective rank and file groups. If the inputs of one side are incompletely formulated or insufficiently heeded, the outcome will not be acceptable to the rank and file, which will then become less interested in, or even alienated from, federal politics. At this point the process tends to become circular, because alienation of the rank and file may produce less elite interest in federal politics and a correspondingly lower calibre of federal representation, which will then win less respect from the other side, and so on.

[14] R. M. Dawson, *The Government of Canada* (2nd ed., Toronto, 1954), 215-216.
[15] F. W. Gibson, *Cabinet Formation and Bicultural Relations* (Studies of the Royal Commission on Bilingualism and Biculturalism, 6, Ottawa, 1970), and R. Van Loon, *The Structure and Membership of the Canadian Cabinet* (mimeographed, Ottawa, 1966), a study prepared for the Royal Commission on Bilingualism and Biculturalism.
[16] Noel, *op. cit.*, 17 [below, 265].

Though the model is hypothetical, it is suggestive of the recurring difficulties of the Conservative Party in Quebec ever since the conscription crisis of 1917. From 1918 to 1920 the Unionist Government had only one French-Canadian minister in a cabinet of 22, and in 1957 the first Diefenbaker ministry began with one French Canadian in a cabinet of 17.[17] Though the number of representatives gradually increased to five, French-Canadian influence in the Cabinet remained relatively unimportant throughout the Diefenbaker period. These years of Conservative rule in Ottawa were parallelled by a remarkable resurgence of energy and talent in Quebec provincial politics, and it is worth noting that a number of senior French-Canadian politicians and public servants moved from the federal to the Quebec provincial stage during these years.

There is a second danger to the process of accommodation among subcultures in the Canadian political system. Governing parties in federal politics have always been loose coalitions of many divergent interests, highly volatile in terms of party loyalty. The power of party elites to control rank and file supporters is somewhat tenuous at best. Hence agreements arrived at by negotiation between the subcultural elites within a party may not be enforceable upon the mass of party supporters, particularly in English Canada where majoritarian values are prominent in the political culture. If elite-mass relationships are not cohesive, the whole process of negotiation between the subcultures begins to lose meaning, and if accommodation negotiated between the elites is rejected by the English-speaking electorate, the French-speaking electorate will lose confidence in its spokesmen at the federal level. This situation has perhaps been more typical of the Liberal Party in recent years, because while Liberal ministries have had strong parliamentary representation from both linguistic sectors, they have had difficulty in persuading their English-speaking followers of the need for a restructuring of French-English relations.[18]

However, the problem is not confined to the Liberal Party. All parties supported the Official Languages Act of 1969, but some Conservative backbenchers refused to follow the party leadership on this issue and it would appear that a substantial portion of the English-Canadian electorate of all political persuasions does not yet accept the changes agreed to by all parties in Parliament. These weaknesses of the Canadian political system may be sum-

[17] Gibson, *op. cit.*, 176-177.
[18] The above paragraphs were written prior to the federal election of October 1972; the results of this election appear to add emphasis to tendencies visible before.

marized by borrowing the terminology of Lijphart:[19] *adequate articulation of the interests of the subcultures* is not guaranteed at cabinet level because of uncertainty and distortion in the electoral system, and *internal political cohesion of the subcultures* is not strong enough to assure that agreements reached in cabinet will be accepted by the electorate.

While the cabinet is the main institution for elite accommodation in federal politics, one could pursue the question further by examining the working of other federal boards, departments, agencies and tribunals. In general we might expect to find patterns of accommodation similar to those pursued by the Cabinet, with the qualification however that most of these agencies are less sensitive than the Cabinet to pressures from the electorate and therefore less likely to have policies of intergroup compromise rendered unenforceable by reactions of the rank and file on one side or the other.

A more interesting question is the impact of the federal system itself upon patterns of elite accommodation. As in Switzerland, federalism in Canada can reduce levels of tension by offering more sites for the resolution of differences between subcultures. Its very flexibility means that in cases of malfunction at the federal level the provincial level offers a safety valve, a possible alternate staging point for the mobilization of subcultural interests. The concentration of French-Canadian interest on Quebec during the 1960's is an obvious example. There are, however, some limits to this alternative. First, if a subculture becomes thoroughly frustrated at Ottawa its interest will diminish to the point that Lijphart's second prerequisite condition, a minimal level of commitment to maintain the system, is no longer fulfilled.[20] Further, disagreements among the subcultures as to the appropriate degree of decentralization may be particularly difficult to resolve.

Finally, as we have noted earlier, provincial boundaries do not coincide fully with either religious or linguistic cleavages. While the religious minorities have been generally strong enough to fend for themselves at the provincial level, the French-speaking minorities in the English-speaking provinces are economically and politically weak. To move further towards the provincialization of linguistic and cultural differences is therefore to abandon the linguistic minorities and to force the subcultural boundaries to coincide with provincial boundaries. At the provincial level only

---

[19] Consociational Democracy", *World Politics*, Vol. 21 (1969), 221, [above, 84].

[20] A. Lijphart, "Typologies of Democratic Systems", *Comparative Political Studies*, Vol. 1 (1968), 23.

the English-speaking minority in Quebec, economically strong and reinforced by the cultural dominance of English in Canada and North America, has been able to obtain a fully effective politics of accommodation, and even this group has felt increasingly insecure in the face of escalating Quebec nationalism since 1960.

The Royal Commission on Bilingualism recognized this dilemma and proposed various federal initiatives to strengthen the position of the minorities: "We take as a guiding principle the recognition of both official languages, in law and in practice, wherever the minority is numerous enough to be viable as a group."[21] But while its linguistic recommendations were largely embodied in the federal Official Languages Act of 1969, the Commission terminated its work without producing a concluding volume in which it had planned to deal with "constitutional questions concerning the relations and the future of the two societies" of French and English Canada.[22] Thus the present federal system and its shortcomings from the standpoint of linguistic-cultural accommodation remain an unresolved constitutional problem. While the European multiparty systems run the obvious risk of immobilism due to stalemate among the parties, it is not so readily acknowledged that the Canadian system, through its inadequate representation of segment interests at the federal level, may also run a similar risk of immobilism and stalemate owing to subcultural disagreements over issues of decentralization and federal-provincial relations, and in this case the machinery for dialogue and accommodation is more cumbersome.

THE IMPACT OF OLDER POLITICAL TRADITIONS.
The political traditions of Canada originated from the two European powers that colonized the area, France and Britain. Both were archetypal nation-states whose political traditions differed sharply from those of the Holy Roman Empire and its successor states. Further, both colonial experiments represented a selective fragmentation from the parent society,[23] and it can be argued that the net effect of this filtering was to enhance centralizing tendencies. New France was a projection of the France of Louis XIV and Colbert, but it lacked the counterbalance of older feudalism. British North America after the loss of the American colonies was dominated by Imperial governors and British military garrisons, and until the 1840's it lacked an effective political counter-

---

[21] Royal Commission on Bilingualism and Biculturalism, *Report*, Book I (Ottawa, 1967), 86.

[22] *Ibid.*, I, xviii.

[23] Hartz, *op. cit.*

force to this strong executive influence. When responsible government came in the 1840's, it came in the form of parliamentary supremacy rather than of a balanced separation of powers. On both sides the tendencies of older tradition were heavily weighted in favour of the central authority; the accommodation of religious and cultural pluralism would clearly have to be learned in the New World. From one standpoint the political development of Canada since 1763 can be viewed as a series of attempts to find a satisfactory pattern of accommodation within the limits imposed by these older political traditions. Two centuries later, that quest remains conspicuously unfinished.

After American Loyalist immigration in the 1780's had introduced a substantial English-speaking population, the first response to diversity, implemented by the Constitutional Act of 1791, was to divide the province into the separate colonies of Upper and Lower Canada. In the latter French Canadians enjoyed a substantial majority in the Legislative Assembly but found themselves blocked by a colonial executive responsible only to London, an executive which increasingly came to reflect the outlook and aspirations of the commercially oriented English-speaking minority in the colony. When Lord Durham recommended colonial responsible government in his celebrated *Report* in 1839, this proposal was linked with a plan to reunite the two Canadas and to assimilate the French Canadians to the language and value structure of the British settlers.

Contrary to Durham's expectations, the French Canadians remained unassimilated, and the Union period produced perhaps the closest approach to an institutionalized politics of accommodation to be found in Canadian history. After the winning of responsible government in 1848 there developed a system of double prime ministerships and twinned ministerial portfolios in ministries which were carefully balanced to give equal weight to the eastern and western sections of the United Province. Despite the Union, parallel departmental establishments persisted and even the provincial capital rotated at intervals from one section to the other.[24] Both sections developed a two-party system and each of the four parliamentary groups worked primarily in loose coalition with its counterpart in the other section, Lower Canada *Bleus* with Upper Canada Conservatives, Lower Canada *Rouges* with Upper Canada Reformers. But in successive elections these coalitions became increasingly evenly balanced and politically deadlocked, and although some advocated a "double-majority"

[24] J. E. Hodgetts, *Pioneer Public Service: an Administrative History of the United Canadas, 1841-1867* (Toronto, 1955), 55-62.

principle whereby the dominant group in each section should collaborate regardless of party platform, the dominant *Bleus* of Canada East could not work with the increasingly anti-Catholic Reformers of Canada West. Nor could political stability be achieved through a grand coalition; the only example of this type during the Union period, the *Bleu*-Conservative-Reform coalition of 1864, was formed for the explicit purpose of breaking the deadlock through radical constitutional reform.[25] It is significant that the Union period, the one noteworthy example of French-English political collaboration on approximately equal terms, is remembered today primarily as a period of immobilism and dead-lock.

Confederation resolved the deadlock of the Province of Canada essentially by encapsulating the dominant religious and linguistic groups of each territorial section into their own respective provincial frameworks, subject only to certain minority guarantees. Although the new provinces of Nova Scotia and New Brunswick tilted the federal balance further in favour of Anglophones and Protestants, the eventual uniqueness of Quebec within Confederation was not a foregone conclusion at this point, for there still remained the question of Western Canada.

Long before its incorporation into Canada, the tiny Red River colony had evolved an accommodation among English and Scottish personnel of the Hudson's Bay Company, French-Canadian employees of the Montreal fur trade, Scottish agricultural settlers, and native Indians and half-breeds or *métis*. Following the Riel uprising in defence of these local interests against Canadian annexationists, the new Province of Manitoba entered Confederation endowed with similarly consociational institutions, including an ethnically balanced upper house, equality of the French and English languages in the legislature and courts, and a denominational school system. Further west, the Northwest Territories, eventually to become the provinces of Saskatchewan and Alberta, were also organized so as to extend the federal language guarantees for French and English to the territorial legislature and courts in 1877 and later to establish a dual Catholic and Protestant school system. Briefly, for two decades after Confederation there lingered the possibility of a second – and perhaps even a third – province of the Canadian federation which would incorporate in its institutions the principle of cultural duality according to the model of Quebec.

[25] P. G. Cornell, *The Alignment of Political Groups in Canada, 1841-1867* (Toronto, 1962), and see also his "The Alignment of Political Groups in the United Province of Canada, 1854-1864," *Canadian Historical Review*, Vol. 30 (1949), 22-46.

All of these hopes were abruptly terminated in the 1890's in the wake of massive English-speaking migration to the West. A Manitoba statute of 1890 ended the equal status of the French language and made English the sole official language; the Legislative Assembly of the Northwest Territories followed suit in 1892 as soon as it received from the federal government the power to determine its own language policy. But more important was the Manitoba Public Schools Act of 1890, which terminated public support for Roman Catholic schools and initiated a controversy that clouded federal politics for several years. The failure of federal intervention in 1896 served only to emphasize the inability of the federal government to protect religious or linguistic minorities and the political vulnerability of the minority constitutional guarantees of 1867. By 1905, the Western prairies, which had entered Canada with embryonic political institutions reflecting the cultural pluralism of their variegated populations, were refashioned by increasingly powerful local elites into the Anglo-Saxon, Protestant image of Ontario.[26]

Even at this date, however, another approach lay open at the federal level. During the early 1900's the influential French-Canadian nationalist Henri Bourassa was urging a pan-Canadian nationalism built on dualistic cultural foundations, in language that has strikingly contemporary consociational overtones:

> Our nationalism is Canadian nationalism founded on the duality of races and on the particular traditions which accompany this duality.... The fatherland, for us, is the whole of Canada, that is to say a federation of distinct races and autonomous provinces. The nation which we wish to see developed is the Canadian nation, composed of French Canadians and English Canadians, that is to say a nation of two elements separated by language and religion and by the legal arrangements necessary for the preservation of their respective traditions, but united by a sentiment of brotherhood in a common attachment to a common country.[27]

With respect to language, his advocacy as early as 1902 of bilingualism among the elites coupled with unilingualism of the French-speaking and English-speaking masses foreshadows almost exactly the federal language policy of the later 1960's and incidentally provides an apt blueprint for the consociational accommodation of linguistic diversity:

> On the question of language, I do not believe that it is

---

[26] For a closer study of the Manitoba case, see below, 288-299.

[27] J. Levitt, ed., *Henri Bourassa on Imperialism and Bi-culturalism, 1900-1918* (Toronto, 1970), 107.

possible or desirable for the mass of our people to learn and speak English. The common man can generally use only one language. The diffusion of the English language among the populace will take place at the expense of the national idiom and will soon harm the inner fibres of our ethnic temperament. This would be the surest road to the annihilation of our nationality. The case is not the same for our elite, those who by their wealth, intellectual culture and political and social position, ought to lead our people and maintain the union between ourselves and our neighbours. On them falls the duty of learning English, of drawing close to the elite of the English majority, of thoroughly studying the temperament, aspirations and the traits of English Canada. Moreover, the English elite have the same responsibility. If the most influential and most enlightened of the two races tried to have more to do with each other and got to know each other better, our national future would not be so precarious.[28]

Nevertheless in Bourassa's thought the linguistic issue is ultimately subordinate to the religious, a means to a more exalted end, for French Canadians must above all fulfil their providential mission as Catholics in the New World: "Let us not strive solely to protect our language, nor to protect *language and faith*; let us fight for the language *in order the better to protect the faith*".[29]

Like many other political figures, Bourassa based his arguments for French-Canadian rights on the contractarian nature of Confederation, but Ramsay Cook has pointed out that Bourassa was perhaps the first to argue in terms of a compact of cultures rather than of provinces, and this shift was clearly indicated after 1890 when questions arose of defending religious and linguistic minorities against provincial majorities. But to do so, Cook notes, he had to argue more in moral than in legal terms, for constitutional texts in support of such a position were lacking. More important, however, was the fact that the notion of cultural compact was taken up by no major interest group, while the alternative theory of Confederation as a compact of provinces had already found powerful backing from several provincial governments.[30] In the circumstances, Bourassa's views were not to pre-

---

[28] *Ibid.*, 105.

[29] H. Bourassa, *La langue, gardienne de la foi*, ([Montreal], [1918]), 51.

[30] R. Cook, *Provincial Autonomy, Minority Rights and the Compact Theory, 1867-1921* (Studies of the Royal Commission on Bilingualism and Biculturalism, 4, Ottawa, 1969), ch. 5. For a wider review of compact doctrines, see R. Arès, *Dossier sur le pacte fédératif de 1867* (rev. ed., Montreal, 1967).

vail in his generation, and very few English Canadians heard and understood his message. In place of bicultural accommodation, the move to abolish French-language schools in Ontario in 1913 and the wartime conscription policy of 1917 led to further and sharper polarization.

It is scarcely surprising that the period after the First World War saw a tendency for many French Canadians in Quebec to show little interest in federal issues and more concern for their own province, the only arena in which their political influence could find full expression. Gradually there emerged on both sides a tacit "Quebec reserve" theory, whereby French-Canadian leaders played only minor roles in broad federal issues while Quebec politics remained a world apart. Such an accommodation was possible as long as Quebec life remained traditional and politically passive, but under the impact of modernization it pointed directly to a gradual separation of the two political systems. When the federal government in 1963 appointed a Royal Commission on Bilingualism and Biculturalism to examine the whole question of equal partnership between the linguistic communities, it was late, very late indeed, to develop an alternative strategy.

The Commission published its *Final Report* between 1967 and 1970, and governmental implementation has been reflected in the Official Languages Act of 1969 and other measures. In its barest essentials the policy of the federal government since 1969 has called for full legal equality of French and English as official languages of Canada, provision of federal services to the public in both languages wherever there are significant concentrations of Francophones and Anglophones, and equal access to posts in the federal public service for speakers of either language. Once again we are close to the vision of pan-Canadian biculturalism envisioned by Henri Bourassa two generations ago, but the question of political accommodation that he raised still remains largely unexplored.

In retrospect, the quest to accommodate linguistic diversity in Canada may be viewed as a series of lost opportunities. While religious diversity has been accommodated with moderate success in Canadian history, linguistic and cultural cleavages have given rise to a variety of institutional arrangements and proposals none of which has been conspicuously successful on a long-term basis. Even by the most charitable interpretation, the political system's capacity to learn and to adapt to linguistic-cultural diversity has not been high, and it seems likely that this low capacity of the system to devise effective solutions has helped to increase the intensity of linguistic and cultural cleavage in recent decades.

SUMMARY AND CONCLUSION.

From several standpoints the Canadian political system defies simple classification, and in this respect it is of course not unique. The clarity of a model is seldom found in the real world. It is tempting to apply the consociational model to the Canadian political system, but closer analysis has revealed a number of major divergences from the model and even from the working consociational systems examined above. Despite these differences, however, the use of the consociational model helps to differentiate Canadian politics from its usual Anglo-American context and permits new insights at both the analytical and the normative levels.

In the above pages I have tried to assess the Canadian political system in the light of the three major approaches to consociationalism that are represented earlier in this book, but since the question is a complex one the argument may perhaps be clarified by a summary of its essentials:

1. The primary lines of segmentation in Canada are difficult to identify with precision on account of the reinforcing but not completely overlapping effects of province, language and religion. Because provinces are partially autonomous political units in the federal system, they offer a convenient but also a distorting forum for the expression of segment interests.

2. Historically, the formal institutionalization of cleavage has followed mainly religious rather than linguistic lines. However this does not demonstrate beyond dispute the greater salience of the religious issue because (a) formal institutionalization in the 18th and 19th centuries reflected norms of the Imperial authority as well as colonial values, (b) prior to 1840 the lines of religious and ethnic cleavage coincided closely, and (c) even after 1840 the line of linguistic-ethnic cleavage was characterized by high geographical and occupational separation, precluding any need for further institutional separation.

3. A rough attempt to compare the present extent of organized segmentation in various spheres of activity along the respective axes of province, religion, and language is inconclusive, but by any of these criteria Canada must be ranked significantly lower than any of the four "classic" consociational countries.

4. Because of the nature of the party system and the electoral system, modern political parties in Canada have not divided along any of the axes of subcultural cleavage. Because ministries are generally composed of a single party only, accommodations between subcultures must take place *within* the governing party on the basis of whatever pattern of subcultural representation that party may currently possess.

5. The principal mechanism for the accommodation of subcultural interests of all types is the federal cabinet, but accommodation may be unsatisfactory (a) if the cabinet reflects inadequate

representation of any subculture, or (b) if decisions arrived at in cabinet are not acceptable to any major subcultural segment of the government's followers. Either situation may lead to the alienation of a minority subculture from federal politics and in some circumstances to a transfer of allegiance to the provincial arena.

6. While the classic cases of consociationalism run a risk of stalemate through deadlock among parties, the Canadian case seems to run a comparable risk of immobilism in terms of subcultural disagreements over the federal-provincial division of power.

7. The older political traditions of both France and Great Britain have been typical of centralizing nation-states from an early date, and they offer little as foundations for pluralist accommodation in Canada.

8. In the Canadian setting a number of approaches to accommodating French-English linguistic-cultural cleavage have been attempted or proposed at different periods, but success has been rather limited and the learning capacity of the political system in this respect must be rated as low.

The pattern of religious and ethnic cleavages has not so far provoked a major catastrophe. Canadians have not been through the agonies of a Bangladesh, a Biafra, or a Cyprus. They are not trapped in the situation of a Northern Ireland, though there were occasions in the nineteenth century when such a turn of events seemed entirely possible. They have not fought a Boer War. But neither have they profited intellectually and politically from the less intense ethnic and religious tensions that have been a constant of their history. It may well be that the absence of more acute phases of tension has diminished the capacity of the political system to respond creatively to the problems of cultural diversity. In a sense Canadians have occupied the rather colourless middle ground between rational problem-solving and ultimate disaster. It would be unreasonable to assume that so precarious a balance can be maintained indefinitely.

CONSOCIATIONAL DEMOCRACY AND CANADIAN FEDERALISM

S. J. R. Noel

Source: S. J. R. Noel, "Consociational Democracy and Canadian Federalism," *Canadian Journal of Political Science*, Vol. 4 (1971), 15-18. Reprinted by permission of the Canadian Political Science Association and the author.

It is only natural that Canada should most frequently be compared with the United States, and that models, metaphors, and theories of the political system that are applicable to the one should be assumed to be applicable to the other. That there are certain close similarities is obvious: both are federations, both span the North American continent, both are affluent Western democracies, and both exist within the common economic framework of modern capitalism. These and other similarities, however, too often obscure the significance of those differences which do exist, or cause similarities which exist with other countries to be neglected. This is particularly true of European countries, even though it would appear to be the case that Canadians, with their strong linguistic and cultural differences, have a good deal in common with at least some Europeans. This is not to say that Canada is more European than American. It is merely to suggest that there may be some advantages to be gained from occasionally viewing Canadian politics from a European perspective.

First, however, it is necessary to discuss briefly the political culture of the Canadian federation. Canada, it is often said, is a country without a strong national identity; indeed, as John Meisel has put it, Canada "is almost totally lacking in a genuinely shared set of symbols, heroes, historical incidents, enemies, or even ambitions."[1] Implicit in such a view is a comparison with the United States: what is missing north of the border is an equivalent of the American national myth. Yet this comparison, while indisputable, can also be seriously misleading. For, among the countries of the world, Canada is by no means unique in its deviation from the American pattern and, moreover, excessive attention to the question of national identity obscures the fact that within Canada there are a number of strong regional and provincial identities, a recognition of which is vital to a proper understanding of the country's nature. As the historian J. M. S. Careless has pointed out, what Canadians have "sought, and to some degree achieved, is not really unification or consolidation,

[1] "Canadian Parties and Politics," in R. H. Leach, ed., *Contemporary Canada* (Durham, 1968), 135.

but the articulation of regional patterns in one transcontinental state."[2]

By what means, therefore, has the Canadian federal system been able to achieve the minimum level of harmony between its regional components which, despite the lack of a strong national identity, has allowed it to maintain itself and function with relative effectiveness for more than a century?

Perhaps the commonest response of political scientists to this question is to attribute to the national political parties in Canada the same role of "consensus-building" as that performed by national parties in the United States – even though in the case of Canada the content of the alleged consensus cannot be empirically identified.[3] A non-American but possibly more promising approach is to enquire instead into the basis of the political order in other economically advanced but culturally divided societies, particularly in Western Europe, where a number of countries resemble Canada in their lack of an overriding national identity, yet possess distinct "limited" identities of region and culture. A theory which attempts to explain their operation should therefore be of considerable interest to the student of Canadian politics. One such theory is that of "consociational democracy" advanced by Arend Lijphart.[4]

American pluralist theory, Lijphart points out, is unable to explain the politics of "fragmented but stable democracies" (such as The Netherlands, Austria, Belgium, and Switzerland) other than by treating them as "deviant" cases. In none of these societies is there a situation of "cross-cutting cleavages," or national consensus, such as pluralist theory holds to be necessary for the successful functioning of democratic government, yet each must be regarded as a functioning and relatively effective democ-

[2] "'Limited Identities' in Canada," *Canadian Historical Review*, Vol. 50, no. 1 (March 1969), 9. A parallel view may be found in the field of literary criticism: "When we speak of a recognizably Canadian poet we usually mean a regional poet who uses the distinctive objects and actions of his locality as poetic materials." Milton Wilson, "Other Canadians and After," *Tamarack Review*, Vol. 9 (1958-9), 89.

[3] For a more extended discussion of consensus and the role of parties, see my paper "Political Parties and Elite Accommodation: Interpretations of Canadian Federalism," Canadian Political Science Association, Winnipeg, June 1970, printed in J. P. Meekison, ed., *Canadian Federalism: Myth or Reality?* (2nd ed., Toronto, London etc., 1971), 121-140.

[4] For a more extensive presentation of the theory, see his "Consociational Democracy," *World Politics*, Vol. 21, no. 2 (Jan. 1969), 207-25 [above, 70-89].

racy. The explanation, he suggests, is to be found in the role played by political élites in each of these countries in deliberately overcoming the effects of cultural fragmentation. Given the existence of strong limited identities or subcultures, and the absence of a national consensus on symbols and goals, it becomes the task of the political leaders of these separate subcultures to practise accommodation at the élite level in order to maintain the national political system and make it work. In other words, bargains can be made and compromises reached among political leaders which would not be possible if they required popular ratification. This type of government Lijphart refers to as "consociational democracy."[5]

For it to function successfully, those who occupy positions of political leadership must understand the perils of political fragmentation and be committed to the maintenance of the national system; they must also be able, within their respective subcultures, to accommodate divergent interests and demands. For the masses, on the other hand, all that is required is that they be committed to their own subcultures and that they trust and support their respective élites. Since the more contact and interaction there is between the masses of the subcultures the greater the likelihood of friction between them, Lijphart suggests, "it may be desirable to keep transactions among antagonistic subcultures in a divided society . . . to a minimum."[6] In theory there is no reason why a consociational democracy could not function satisfactorily even if among the masses of the different subcultures there was absolutely no attachment to the national political system and no sense whatever of a national identity. In actual systems, however, some degree of popular national sentiment is invariably present. The distinguishing feature of a consociational political system is the relative weakness of popular national sentiment and the overcoming of this weakness through a process of élite accommodation.

Thus, not only does Lijphart's model suggest parallels between Canada's experience and the experience of a number of other countries, it also offers a possible explanation of the way the Canadian political process operates. First, in broadest terms, it suggests that the lack of a pan-Canadian identity combined with strong regional subcultures is not necessarily a dysfunctional feature in terms of the successful operation of a federal political system, as long as within each subculture demands are effectively articulated through its political élite. Secondly, it suggests that in the relative absence of a national mass consensus Canadian feder-

[5] This usage follows David E. Apter, *The Political Kingdom in Uganda: A Study in Bureaucratic Nationalism* (Princeton, 1961).
[6] "Consociational Democracy," 220-1.

alism has been maintained and made to work mainly through a process of accommodation at the élite level.

It is necessary, however, to make certain adjustments in Lijphart's consociational model before it can be applied to Canada. The term "subculture" could be interpreted in a number of ways – it could be taken, for example, to refer to English Canada and French Canada, or to a number of distinct regions such as the Maritimes, Quebec, Ontario, and the West – but most usefully perhaps as "province." Moreover, because of the federal constitution of Canada, a distinction should be made between federal and provincial political "élites" (defined simply as the holders of the most important offices in federal and provincial political institutions). Federal and provincial bureaucratic élites could be similarly identified. To employ Lijphart's term, élite accommodation in Canada could therefore be said to take place at several levels: in the numerous federal boards, commissions, and councils which, through convention, have provincial representation as their basis of membership; in the patterns of communication and consultation which have developed among senior provincial civil servants; in the meetings of such interprovincial bodies as the Council of Ministers of Education; in federal-provincial conferences; and, above all, in the federal cabinet. These are the institutions which are central to the day-to-day maintenance and operation of the Canadian federal system.

The representative character of the cabinet, and particularly the emphasis placed on provincial representation, is well known. What is uncertain is the practical significance of this fact in the functioning of the political system. Since constitutional convention ensures that the proceedings of cabinet are secret, it is possible only to surmise about provincial influences on decision-making. If, however, the cabinet is viewed in the broad framework of consociational theory, it can be seen as a mechanism of élite accommodation quite apart from the specific decisions it makes. Its importance, in other words, can be seen to lie more in its function of bringing together political leaders from the provinces and maintaining their continuous involvement in the decision-making process than in the actual outputs of that process. And one of the most important roles of the prime minister is to maintain among cabinet members drawn from the various provinces a degree of commitment to the national political system which does not exist to nearly the same extent at the popular or mass level within the provinces themselves; in other words, he must be able to maintain and operate successfully a system of élite accommodation.

Canadian political history contains ample confirmation of such a view. Two cases may be briefly mentioned. First, the inability of the Diefenbaker government to involve a Quebec political élite in a process of accommodation at the federal level was surely one of the major factors contributing to its downfall. Its policies and decisions were not anti-Quebec; its failure to appreciate the importance of élite accommodation was.[7] Secondly, as P. D. Stevens has shown in his study of the collapse of the Liberal party in Ontario in 1911, the failure of Laurier was not so much a failure of policy as a failure to maintain the involvement at the federal level of an Ontario political élite. After Sir Oliver Mowat's resignation in 1897 the Laurier cabinet increasingly lacked effective representation from Ontario, a deficiency which contributed largely to its electoral defeat.[8]

Interprovincial conferences and, since 1906, federal-provincial conferences have also provided an important institutional framework for the process of élite accommodation. Even more than in the case of the cabinet, their mere existence is more important than the agreements which they produce. Moreover, they dramatically illustrate a prime ministerial role of considerable consequence in the operation of the federal system: the presenting of a national viewpoint to provincial political leaders whose positions within the system are even more crucial than those of federal cabinet ministers. A federal-provincial conference, therefore, has a dual symbolic function: it symbolizes the vitality of the provincial fact in Canada and also the prime minister's unique position as the personification of inter-élite accommodation. It is politics as theatre, highlighting for a brief moment the prime minister's role in extracting the necessary national commitment from provincial élites (grudging and minimal though it may sometimes be) without which the federal system could not work.

Successful federal leadership in Canada requires an attention to provincial political élites which is matched only by the need for similar accommodation in the consociational democracies of Western Europe. Canadian political history reveals a pattern of élite accommodation which must be taken into account in any attempt to explain the longevity of the federation. From Joseph Howe, who moved from the leadership of the Nova Scotia secessionists to a seat in the federal cabinet, to Donald Jamieson, the present minister of transport, who in 1948-9 was one of the leading figures in the campaign to keep Newfoundland out of

---

[7] For a glimpse into the origin of this failure, see Dalton Camp, *Gentlemen, Players and Politicians* (Toronto, Montreal, 1970), 238-52.

[8] See Stevens, "Laurier, Aylesworth, and the Decline of the Liberal Party in Ontario," *Historical Papers*, Canadian Historical Association, 1968, pp. 94-113.

Confederation,[9] the pattern has been the same. Time after time, provincial politicians with no more attachment to the federal system than the mass of their constituents become transformed in Ottawa into cabinet ministers intent on making the system work. The two cases cited are but the extreme examples of how the process of élite accommodation in Canada has provided a workable substitute for mass national integration.

As Arend Lijphart rightly points out, his theory of consociational democracy also contains certain normative implications. Hence, if a consociational perspective is adopted towards some recent trends in Canadian politics, a number of conclusions would appear to follow. First, a decline of "élitism" in Canada and its replacement by a general acceptance of the Jacksonian myth of popular or "participatory" democracy may be detrimental to the maintenance of Canadian federalism if it leads to a situation in which the mass of the people are unwilling to accept the inter-élite accommodations made by their political leaders. If inter-élite accommodations must be popularly ratified they may be impossible to achieve. Secondly, "national" policies aimed at promoting bilingualism and biculturalism may be misguided in the sense that they may increase friction between separate communities which previously had little direct contact with one another. It may be that a system of consociational federalism works best when the "two solitudes" are preserved. Thirdly, if there were to emerge within any one of the provinces an élite who for nationalistic, economic, ideological, or any other reasons are unwilling to provide "overarching cooperation at the élite level with the deliberate aim of counteracting disintegrative tendencies in the system," the system would become inoperable. It may be, therefore, that the ultimate precept of consociationalism as a normative theory is that new élites must either be accommodated or suppressed. On the other hand, it must be noted that consociationalism combined with federalism creates at least the possibility of a conflict between competing federal and provincial élites within the same provincial subculture (as would presumably be the case if, for example, Quebec were to elect a Parti québécois government provincially yet continue to give a majority of its federal seats to the Liberal party). It would appear that the duality of political élites in a federal system makes the outcome of subcultural conflict more uncertain than it would be in a unitary state.

For the student of Canadian politics, however, the value of consociational theory lies less in its normative implications than in its capacity to provide a framework for historical explanation.

---

[9] See Richard Gwyn, *Smallwood: The Unlikely Revolutionary* (Toronto, 1968), 102-3.

What it offers is a way of viewing the Canadian political process which accounts for its successful maintenance yet requires no dubious assumptions about the role of political parties and posits no chimerical notion of an "underlying" national identity.

THE PROVINCE OF CANADA: THE EMERGENCE OF CONSOCIATIONAL POLITICS

William Ormsby

Source: William Ormsby, *The Emergence of the Federal Concept in Canada, 1839-1845* (Toronto, 1969), pp. 3, 122-5. Copyright © University of Toronto Press 1969. Reprinted by permission of the publisher and the author.

It has become traditional to regard the 1840's as the "responsible government" decade in Canadian history. While this emphasis on constitutional development is no doubt warranted, it has tended to obscure the fact that it was during these same years that the federal implications of the Canadian situation began to be recognized. The continued existence of two distinct cultures within the Province of Canada demanded the development of some guarantee for the peculiar interests and values of each group. In short, the survival of French Canada, despite the deliberate attempt to overwhelm it in a union of the two Canadas, demanded the emergence of a federal concept....

The advent of the United Empire Loyalists created the elements of a bi-cultural problem in the old province of Quebec, but it was almost seventy years before the full significance of this fact began to be recognized. In 1791, the division of the province was an attempt to find a solution for the problem of two distinct cultures endeavouring to exist within a single geographic unit. But it was a solution which side-stepped the basic question of whether French Canada was to be assimilated or the two cultures were to continue to exist side by side. During the debate on the Constitutional Act, Charles James Fox called for measures which would "form the two descriptions of people into one body, and endeavour to annihilate all national distinctions," but William Pitt replied that any attempt to implement such a policy would produce "a perpetual scene of factious altercation."[1] Nonetheless, Pitt sanguinely predicted that assimilation would take place indirectly through Lower Canada's emulation of Upper Canada.

Although the ensuing years revealed the fallacy of Pitt's prediction, they failed to produce any positive indication of the British Government's ultimate objective. Had the attempted union of 1822 been carried through, it would have amounted to a decision in favour of assimilation, but the rapidity with which it was dropped when opposition developed was indicative both of the

[1] *The Annual Register or a View of the History, Politics, and Literature for the year 1791* (London, 1795), pp. 110-11.

Government's reluctance to bring thorny colonial problems before Parliament and of the force of ethnological and social opposition to the union. The French Revolution and the Napoleonic Wars, together with the growing reform movement in Great Britain, left British statesmen with little leisure to contemplate Canadian problems. Those who did concern themselves with Canada were inclined to view the clash between the Executive and the Assembly in Lower Canada as a constitutional question rather than as the struggle of French Canada to survive as a separate entity. Consequently, little thought was given to whether assimilation was possible, or to the implications of the survival of two cultures in Canada if it were not. Before the rebellions occurred, only Roebuck and Glenelg seem to have sensed the potentialities of a federal solution.

The rebellions focused attention on the Canadian problem and at the same time fostered the conviction that the assimilation of French Canada was essential to the maintenance of the British connection. Against such a background, it is not surprising that few men caught a glimpse of the federal concept. One of the few was Edward Ellice, who had learned a great deal from the unsuccessful attempt at union in 1822. In 1860, as dualism asserted itself ever more strongly in Canada, Ellice reminded LaFontaine of his foresight: "All that has since occurred in Canada, confirms the advice, I gave in vain to the Govt. at the time of the Union Bill . . . I saw the difficulty that would sooner or later, arise, from the dissimilarity in habits & institutions, of the two Provinces, after the feelings that had been called into action, at the crisis . . . "[2]

Although Lord Howick and James Stephen shared Ellice's preference for a federal union, they were unable to exert any significant influence on the Government. Lord Durham saw the national possibilities in a federal union of British North America, but when this proved to be beyond his grasp, he could not bring himself to recommend a federal union of the Canadas alone. He believed that responsible government was the only solution for Canadian problems, but that it could not be safely conceded, nor could it function properly, unless French Canada was assimilated in a complete legislative union with Upper Canada. Of Durham's several recommendations, it is probable that the idea of assimilation was most in accord with the views of Melbourne and Russell. Some members of Parliament may have doubted that assimilation could be achieved by means of the Durham formula, but most admitted that, given the influence of the United States in

[2] LaFontaine Papers, vol. 17, pp. 3016-17, Ellice to LaFontaine, March 8, 1860.

North America and the state of public opinion in England, they could not suggest a better means.

The assimilation of French Canada would have been difficult, if not impossible, in 1791 – fifty years later it was an entirely unrealistic objective. Lord Sydenham was able to convey the impression that the union had been successfully inaugurated and that French Canada had no alternative but to submit to anglicization. Under Bagot and Metcalfe, however, it became clear that Canada was likely to remain a bi-cultural province, and the Imperial Government was forced, reluctantly, to abandon the union's primary objective.

Paradoxically, the union, which had been designed for precisely the opposite purpose, left considerable room for the development of federal characteristics. Once assimilation was rejected, equal representation assumed the guise of a political guarantee for the continued existence of two distinct cultures. It was soon discovered that the "harmony concept" could be subdivided to produce the fascinating, though impractical, theory of double harmony or double majority. The existence of duplicate law offices paved the way for the creation of hyphenated ministries which symbolized the dual character of the Canadian population. With the appointment of French Canadians to the Executive Council during Bagot's administration, the federal concept began to emerge and within a few years it gained wide recognition. The concept did not, however, become the all-pervading force within the union; there were some aspects of politics and many areas of administration which remained unaffected by the principle of dualism. Even Baldwin and LaFontaine, who were deeply committed to the principle, exerted pressure to replace the two separate provincial secretaries with a single one in the interest of economy. Nonetheless, there is ample evidence to support the claim that dualism did become a significant characteristic of the union.

When Lord Sydenham was making the administrative arrangements for the union, he was necessarily thinking in terms of a province in which cultural differences would eventually disappear. Consequently the continuation of separate administrative establishments in each section of the province for some departments was dictated primarily by the vast extent of territory involved. Assimilation was only prospective, however, and he could not entirely ignore the fact that, initially at least, each section would differ from the other in language, religion, civil code, judicial system, and the form of land tenure. These factors must have had some influence on Sydenham's decision that dual administrative establishments should be maintained by the law officers, the provincial secretaries, and the commissioner of Crown lands. In 1842, Bagot's decision to appoint two deputy superintendents of education was based entirely on the religious differences between the two sections of the province. As the federal concept developed, this administrative framework permitted the manifestation of dualism in the public service. Other departments maintained a single establishment, but, as J. E. Hodgetts has noted, some of these were "split right down the middle, starting at the top with the political head and going down to the subdivisions of the various branches."[3] One of the most striking applications of the principle of dualism was the rotation of the capital between Toronto and Quebec in the years after 1849.

If the Durham formula had functioned as its originator had anticipated, French Canadians would have joined the Government not to protect the particular interests of their compatriots, but rather to assist in the process of assimilation. When the continued existence of French Canada as a separate cultural entity was accepted as a recognized fact, however, French-Canadian politicians and public servants became the representatives of a separate unit of the population with its own rights and interests. It was in this context that dualism became a significant characteristic of the United Province of Canada.

Within the political arena, the union functioned well only when its federal aspects were dominant. This fact was recognized by John A. Macdonald during the Confederation debates:

> We, in Canada, already know something of the advantages and disadvantages of a Federal Union. Although we have nominally a Legislative Union in Canada – although we sit in one Parliament, supposed constitutionally to represent the people without regard to sections or localities, yet we know, as a matter of fact, that since the union in 1841, we have had a Federal Union; that in matters affecting Upper Canada solely, members from that section claimed and generally exercised the right of exclusive legislation, while members from Lower Canada legislated in matters affecting only their own section. We have had a Federal Union in fact, though a Legislative Union in name.[4]

Despite Macdonald's testimony, there were occasions when measures affecting only one half of the province were passed or rejected by a minority from that section with the aid of a majority from the other section. Equal representation proved to be an insufficient guarantee for the protection of sectional interests, and it was this fact which ultimately doomed the union. For more

[3] J. E. Hodgetts, *Pioneer Public Service*, (Toronto, 1955), p. 55.
[4] *Parliamentary Debates on the Subject of the Confederation of the British North American Provinces* (Quebec, 1865), p. 30.

than a quarter of a century the union managed to function as a quasi-federal system, but eventually the forces of dualism came into direct conflict with the unitary character of the constitution. During the early years of the union, it was Lower Canada that complained of interference; the LaFontaine Papers contain a list of seventeen votes taken during the years 1844 to 1846 in which Lower Canadian matters were decided by a majority from the upper province. Among the subjects listed are damages caused by the construction of the Beauharnois Canal, the Montreal election of 1844, the Lower Canada Election Bill, Lower Canadian rebellion losses, amendments to the Winter Roads Bill, land titles of naturalized persons, claims of the Chambly Canal contractors, the Lower Canada School Bill, and the Jesuits' estates.[5] The shoe began to pinch on the other foot in the 1850's and the charge was made that Upper Canada was suffering from French-Canadian domination. The suspicion grew that the secularization of the clergy reserves was being retarded by the influence of French-Canadian members of the Government. More positive evidence was presented when Upper Canadian school legislation was amended, by a Lower Canadian majority, to extend the provision for separate schools.

This situation, coupled with the fact that Upper Canada now had the larger population, produced the Clear Grit demand for representation by population which rapidly gained in popularity. G. F. G. Stanley has quite correctly observed that representation by population implied "the collapse of the federal concept."[6] However, it should be recognized that from another point of view, "Rep. by Pop." was a protest against the fact that the union could still assume a legislative character.

On the other hand, "Rep. by Pop." could never be acceptable to Lower Canada for it was a direct threat to French-Canadian interests. The necessity of finding some alternative led to a renewed interest in the "double majority" principle and the experiment of John Sandfield Macdonald from 1862 to 1864. The principle proved unacceptable in practice, however, because of the difficulty in securing a double majority for any contentious measure. Even John Sandfield Macdonald, the professed champion of the principle, could not resist the temptation in 1863 to carry Upper Canadian separate schools legislation by means of a Lower Canadian majority. With the failure of the "double majority" theory, the only alternative was a proper federal union and this was the solution adopted in 1867.

[5] LaFontaine Papers, pp. 5241-42.
[6] G. F. G. Stanley, "Act or Pact: Another Look at Confederation," *Canadian Historical Association Report*, 1956, p. 9.

Numerous factors, lying beyond the scope of this study, but familiar to every historian, determined that Confederation should embrace Nova Scotia and New Brunswick as well as the Canadas. There were also distinctive maritime factors which favoured a federal union, but the predominant federal influence was the dual character of the Canadas. Confederation was an impossibility without the concurrence of French Canada and that concurrence was forthcoming only when guarantees for its institutions, language, laws, and religion had been spelled out in the resolutions that were to form the basis for the British North America Act. If the union of 1841 had failed to fulfil the original expectations, it had, nonetheless, served as a useful experiment in federalism, and had produced both the concept and the experience upon which a larger and more satisfactory union could be built.

THE FEDERAL BARGAIN: THE CONTRACTARIAN BASIS OF CONFEDERATION

George F. G. Stanley

Source: G. F. G. Stanley, "Act or Pact: Another Look at Confederation," *Canadian Historical Association Report*, 1956, 1-25. The text given here is substantially abridged and is reprinted by permission of the author. The paper was originally presented, partly in English and partly in French, as the Presidential Address to the Canadian Historical Association at a joint meeting with the Canadian Political Science Association in Montreal on June 7, 1956.

To my mind the principal factor – I do not suggest it as the sole factor but as one of the most important – in determining the course of Canadian constitutional development, has been the existence, within Canada, of two competing ethnic, cultural groups. The Earl of Durham, in his famous *Report*, chose to refer to them as "two nations warring in the bosom of a single state."[1] Were he writing in today's idiom, he might have preferred to substitute the word "co-existing" for "warring." Certainly "warring" is too strong and too inaccurate a word to describe what has been simply the political struggle on the part of the English-speaking population for supremacy, and on the part of the French-speaking population for survival. This struggle has dominated the whole story of Canadian politics. It probably accounts for the prepossession of Canadian historians with political and constitutional history. The struggle is one which still continues, and the issues are still the same; supremacy as against survival, or to use the contemporary terms, centralization as against provincial autonomy.

And yet, perhaps, if the word "warring" is unsuitable as a general description of Anglo-French relations within the bosom of this country, Canada, at times it has not been without some aptness; for the bitterness and misunderstandings which have frequently accompanied our relations have cut, on occasions, close to the bone. That civil strife in Canada has never degenerated into civil war has been due, in part at least, to the recognition by both peoples of the necessity of some *modus vivendi* and the recognition by each of the rights of the other. The recognition and definition of these rights is the basis of the entente, understanding, pact, compact, call it what you will, which is the foundation of our political unity. Without such an entente there would have been, and would be no Canada as we know it today. Much

---

[1] Sir Reginald Coupland, *The Durham Report, an abridged version with an introduction and notes* (Oxford, 1945), p. 15.

has been written both in the French and English languages about this pact; some of it narrow and legalistic; more of it unhistorical; much of it purely polemical. If we attempt to look upon this pact or entente as a legal contract, freely entered into by two parties and intended by them to be legally enforceable in a court of law, our vision will be so limited as to be distorted; for a pact or compact is not a contract in the legal sense. It is a gentleman's agreement, an understanding based upon mutual consent, with a moral rather than a juridical sanction. The Anglo-French understanding which alone has made government possible within the boundaries of the larger Canada has become sanctified by time and continued acceptance, until today it is looked upon by many as a convention of our constitution. It is my immediate purpose, this evening, to trace for you the origin and growth of this convention, and to discuss some of its implications in the development of our constitution. . . .

There is no need for me to discuss the various factors leading to Confederation – the threat of American imperialism, the fear of the westward expansion of the United States, the necessity for improved railway communications, the political impasse in Canada; all of this is familiar ground to generations of Canadian students. Nor is it necessary for me to chronicle the erratic course of the ambulatory conference of 1864 or to follow its members, bottle by bottle, as they travelled through the Maritimes and Canada, dispensing good will and self-congratulatory speeches to all who were prepared to listen to them. However, I do wish to direct your attention, for a moment, to the fundamental problem which faced the delegates who met at Charlottetown and at Quebec, that of reconciling the conflicting interests of the two racial groups and of the conflicting principles of centralization and provincial autonomy. Broadly speaking – and there are, of course, exceptions to this general statement – the English-speaking representatives, pragmatists, suspicious of ideas and generalizations, preoccupied with economic and political interests and secure in their ever increasing majority over the French Canadians, were disposed to favour a strong central government, if not actually a legislative union; the French Canadians, empiricists, uneasy, apprehensive, and deeply concerned with the survival of their culture, were by religion and by history in favour of a constitution which would, at the very least, secure them such guarantees as they had already extracted from the British government during the hundred years which had gone before. No French Canadian, intent upon preserving his national identity or bettering his political future could ever agree to a legislative union. Only federalism would permit the two, distinct, and separate, cultures to co-exist side by side within the bosom of a single state. Federalism, not a half-way, hesitant, ill-defined, semi-unitary federalism like that which had evolved out of the Act of Union, but an honest, whole-hearted, clearly-stated, precise federalism was the only solution acceptable to the French Canadian leaders. Thus, the one group was, at heart, for unity and fusion; the other for diversity and co-operation; the one was dominated by economic fact and the other, philosophical principle.

The fundamental opposition of these two divergent points of view does not, unfortunately, appear in the documentary fragments of the conferences which we possess; it does, however, emerge clearly in a letter written by Sir Arthur Gordon, Lieutenant-Governor of New Brunswick, following his visit to Charlottetown and his conversations with Cartier, Brown and Galt. In a lengthy despatch to the Colonial Office outlining the details of the union scheme as the Canadians had put it up to the Maritimers, Gordon wrote:

> With regard to the important question of the attributes to be assigned to the respective Legislatures and Governments, there was a very great divergence of opinion. The aim of Lower Canada is a local independence as complete as circumstances will permit, and the peculiarities of race, religion and habits which distinguish its people render their desire respectable and natural.[2]

It was at Quebec that the new constitution took form and shape. To the old capital of New France came delegates from the six provinces, the four seaboard provinces of Nova Scotia, Newfoundland, Prince Edward Island and New Brunswick, and the two provinces of Canada, which, if they did not have a juridical basis, had, at least, as I have pointed out, a factual foundation. This gathering at Quebec was the first and only constituent body in the whole of our constitutional history. All previous constitutions had been drafted, considered, and passed, by an outside authority; in 1864 the thirty-three representatives of the British North American provinces met, with the blessing and approval of the British Government, to do what had hitherto always been done for them.

The constitution which they adopted in the form of seventy-two

---

[2] Public Archives of Canada, New Brunswick, C.O. 189, vol. 9: Gordon to Cardwell, confidential, Sept. 22, 1864. This letter is reproduced, in part, in W. F. O'Connor, *Report pursuant to Resolution of the Senate to the Honourable the Speaker by the Parliamentary Counsel* (Ottawa, 1939), Annex 2, pp. 84-6. Large sections of the original letter were, however, omitted in the printed version. The quotation given here is one of the omitted portions.

Resolutions had already been prepared in draft form before the Canadian delegates had ever disembarked at Charlottetown. In many respects it bore a striking resemblance to an outline plan which had appeared over the name of Joseph Charles Taché in *Le Courrier du Canada* in 1857, and which had been published as a book in the following year.[3] In summary form, what the Quebec Conference decided was that the new union should be federal in character; that its central parliament should comprise two houses, the upper based on representation by provinces, and the lower upon representation by population; that the powers of the central government should be of a general character and those of the provincial legislatures of a local nature. These powers were carefully enumerated, but the legislative residuum was given to the central parliament. The French and English languages were to enjoy equal status in the central parliament and courts and in the legislature and courts of the province of Lower Canada.

Georges Cartier, generally, was satisfied with what had been achieved. He felt that even though he had been obliged to yield much to the demands of Macdonald and Brown and other advocates of a strong central government, he had, nevertheless, succeeded in preserving the rights and privileges of his own people and of the province in which they lived.[4] He had, moreover,

---

[3] J. C. Taché, *Des provinces de l'Amérique du Nord et d'une union fédérale* (Québec, 1858).

[4] "Objection had been taken to the scheme now under consideration, because of the words, 'new nationality.' Now, when we were united together, if union were attained, we would form a political nationality with which neither the national origin, nor the religion of any individual would interfere. It was lamented by some that we had this diversity of races, and hopes were expressed that this distinctive feature would cease. The idea of unity of races was utopian – it was impossible. . . . We could not do away with the distinctions of race. We could not legislate for the disappearance of the French Canadians from American soil, but British and French Canadians alike could appreciate and understand their position relative to each other." (Cartier, Feb. 7, 1865, *Confederation Debates*, p. 60). Subsequently, in answer to the criticisms of A. A. Dorion, Cartier said, "I have always had the interests of Lower Canada at heart, and have guarded them more sedulously than the hon. member for Hochelaga and his partisans have ever done." (*Confederation Debates*, p. 714). Hector Langevin, the Solicitor-General, took the same view. He said, "We are considering the establishment of a Confederacy – with a Central Parliament and local parliaments. The Central or Federal Parliament will have the control of all measures of a general character . . . , but all matters of local interest, all that relates to the affairs and rights of the different sections of the Confederacy, will be reserved for the control of the local parliaments. . . . It will be the

succeeded in maintaining the fundamental principle of the entente between the two racial groups in Canada, equality of race, equality of religion, equality of language, equality of laws. Even George Brown, the old francophobe, had gone as far as to admit to the Canadian legislature "whether we ask for parliamentary reform for Canada alone, or in union with the Maritime Provinces, the French Canadians must have their views consulted as well as us (sic). This scheme can be carried and no scheme can be that has not the support of both sections of the province."[5] The new constitution might not be designed to be the most efficient, but it would, at least, be just.

The next step was as easy as it was logical. Since both races were equal, a decision taken, an agreement arrived at by the equal partners on the fundamental character of the new constitution, could not be changed without the consent of each. It was, in fact, a treaty, a compact binding upon both parties. This was a view which scarcely roused a dissenting voice in the Canada of 1865. Not one of the Canadians who fathered the resolutions at Quebec failed to stress the unalterable character of the agreement they had made. Macdonald said, "these resolutions were in the nature of a treaty, and if not adopted in their entirety, the proceedings would have to be commenced *de novo*."[6] McGee, in his high-pitched but not unmusical voice, cried:

> And that there may be no doubt about our position in regard to that document, we say, question it you may, reject it you may, or accept it you may, but alter it you may not. (Hear, hear.) It is beyond your power, or our power, to alter it. There is not a sentence – ay, or even a word – you can alter without desiring to throw out the document.... On this point, I repeat after all my hon. friends who have already spoken, for one party to alter a treaty is, of course, to destroy it.[7]

Taché, Cartier, McDougall, Brown, all of them described the Quebec Resolutions as a "treaty" or as a "pact," and argued for adoption without amendment.[8]

duty of the Central Government to see that the country prospers, but it will not be its duty to attack our religion, our institutions, or our nationality, which . . . will be amply protected." (*Confederation Debates*, pp. 367-8. See also pp. 373, 392.)

[5] *Confederation Debates*, p. 87.

[6] *Ibid.*, p. 16. Macdonald repeated this idea several times throughout his speech; see pp. 31-2.

[7] *Ibid.*, p. 136.

[8] *Ibid.*, pp. 83, 88, 714, 720. See also Chapter II in Sir George Ross,

It is easy for the lawyer or the political scientist, three generations later, to reply that in 1865 there was no treaty really made at all, that the Compromise of Quebec could not possess the attributes of a treaty or of a legal contract. Nevertheless the historical fact remains that the men who used these terms were the men who drafted the Resolutions; they chose their words with deliberation; many of them were lawyers, they knew what they were saying. They were not, every one of them, trying to becloud the issue before the legislature or to confuse the legislators. I have found no evidence which would lead me to question their sincerity or to believe that they disbelieved their own assertions. In strict law it is probably true that the terms they used to describe the Quebec Resolutions were not all that could be desired in the way of legalistic exactitude; but to my mind these terms adequately expressed the ideas which the Fathers of the Confederate Resolutions wished to convey to their listeners and to posterity, for they spoke to both. The idea of a compact between races was not a new one in 1865; it had already become a vital thing in our history. It influenced both the political thinking and the political vocabulary of the day; and it was already on the way to become a tradition and a convention of our constitution.

The idea of a compact as I have outlined it was essentially, in its origin, a racial concept. But the meeting of the maritime delegates with those of Canada at Charlottetown and at Quebec introduced a new interpretation which has had mighty impact upon the course of our later history, namely, the idea of a compact between the politico-geographic areas which go to make up Canada. Even before the conferences it had become the common practice to identify the racial groups with the areas from which they came. When thinking of French Canadians or of Anglo-Canadians, it was all too simple to speak of them in geographical terms, as Lower Canada and Upper Canada. It was a confusion of mind and speech of which we in our own day and generation are all too frequently guilty. Almost without thought "Quebec" and "French Canadians," or "Ontario" and "Anglo-Canadians," become synonymous terms in the mouths of Canadians of both tongues. It is, of course, a slipshod way of thinking as well as of speaking, for there are French Canadians in Ontario and English Canadians in Quebec; and in many ways it has been unfortunate, for it has limited to Quebec language rights which might, under happier circumstances, have been accorded French Canadians in other parts of the country. That English did

---

The Senate of Canada: its Constitution, Powers and Duties Historically Considered (Toronto, 1914).

not suffer the same fate in Quebec as did the French tongue in other provinces, was due in part to the effective role of English-speaking Quebeckers, like McGee and Galt, in the drafting of the federative act, as well as to a greater appreciation on the part of French Canadians of the need for toleration. However, the point which I really wish to make is this; once Canadians (as distinct from Maritimers) began to identify provinces with specific linguistic groups, the idea of a pact between races was transformed into the idea of a pact between provinces. And the Compromise of Quebec became a compact between the provinces which participated in the conference. I have no need to labour this point. It emerges in all clarity from a careful reading of the speeches to be found in the Confederation Debates of 1865.

However, the compact idea, was still, in 1865, peculiarly a Canadian one. It was not shared by the delegates of the several Maritime colonies who had journeyed to Quebec. From what I have seen of the debates in the legislatures and the speeches reported in the press of Nova Scotia and New Brunswick, the words so familiar in Canada, words like "pact", "treaty" or "compact" were rarely used in reference to what had been decided upon at Charlottetown or Quebec. There was never any idea in the minds of the Maritime representatives that the Seventy-Two Resolutions were sacrosanct. Thus, when Nova Scotia and New Brunswick resolved in 1866 to renew the negotiations for a federal union with Canada, they sent their representatives to London with full authority to make any changes and to conclude any new arrangement they might see fit. . . .

In the end, the terms of the agreement drafted and adopted at the Westminster Palace Hotel in London in December 1866 were substantially those which had previously been discussed and accepted at Quebec. A great deal has, I know, been made of the London Resolutions as a new departure and as an effective denial of the idea of a binding pact having been concluded at Quebec; but a detailed comparison of the two sets of resolutions reveals no really substantial points of difference. The outline is similar; the wording in many instances is unchanged. Such alterations as were made, appear to have been either of a minor nature intended to clarify an ambiguity or inserted to strengthen rather than to weaken the bi-racial, bi-cultural aspect of the pact. Certainly the people of the day who were most concerned viewed the revised resolutions after this fashion. On January 5th, 1867, the editor of *The Morning Freeman* of St. John, N.B., wrote, "If the Quebec Scheme has been modified in any important particulars they are profoundly ignorant of what the modifications are."[9] Two months

---

[9] *The Morning Freeman*, Saint John, N.B., Jan. 5, 1867.

later he wrote again while the British North America Bill was before Parliament:

> We ask any reasonable, intelligent man of any party to take up that Bill, compare it with the original Quebec Scheme, and discover, if he can, anything that could possibly have occupied honest, earnest men, for even a week, no matter what the particular objections to the few changes that have been made. . . . Could not all these matters have been settled as well and as much to the satisfaction of the public by letter, at an expense of a few shillings postage . . . as by this large and most costly delegation?[10]

The London Resolutions of 1866 were, in a word, little if anything more than an edited version of the Quebec Resolutions of 1864; the contractual nature of the pact remained unaffected.

The British seemed to like the idea of a provincial compact. Both the Colonial Secretary, Lord Carnarvon, and his undersecretary, the Honourable Charles Adderley, accepted it as an accurate description of what was intended and what was achieved. Mr. Adderley, who introduced the Bill based on the resolutions into the British House of Commons, urged upon the members, in words which might have come straight from the mouth of Macdonald or Cartier, that no change or alteration should be made in the terms of the Bill:

> The House may ask what occasion there can be for our interfering in a question of this description. It will, however, I think, be manifest, upon reflection, that, as the arrangement is a matter of mutual concession on the part of the Provinces, there must be some external authority to give sanction to the compact into which they have entered. . . . If, again, federation has in this case specially been a matter of most delicate mutual treaty and compact between the provinces – if it has been a matter of mutual concession and compromise – it is clearly necessary that there should be a third party *ab extra* to give sanction to the treaty made between them. Such seems to me to be the office we have to perform in regard to this Bill.[11]

Lord Carnarvon, in the House of Lords, said:

> the Quebec Resolutions, with some slight changes, form the basis of a measure that I have now the honour to submit to Parliament. To those resolutions all the British Provinces in North America were, as I have said, consenting parties, and

---

[10] *Ibid.*, March 7, 1867.
[11] Quoted in O'Connor, *Report*, Annex 4, p. 149.

the measure founded upon them must be accepted as a treaty of union.[12]

Later in the same speech Carnarvon, after pointing out that a legislative union was "impracticable," because of Lower Canada's jealousy and pride in "her ancestral customs and traditions" and her willingness to enter Confederation "only upon the distinct understanding that she retains them," stated emphatically that the terms of the British North America Bill were "of the nature of a treaty of union, every single clause in which had been debated over and over again, and had been submitted to the closest scrutiny, and, in fact each of them represented a compromise between the different interests involved." "There might be alterations where they are not material," he continued, "and do not go to the essence of the measure. . . . But it will be my duty to resist the alteration of anything which is in the nature of a compromise between the Provinces, as an amendment of that nature, if carried, would be fatal to the measure."[13]

The legalist will, of course, reply that the intervention of the Colonial Office and the passing of the Bill as an Act of the British Parliament in effect destroyed the compactual – I prefer to avoid the word "contractual" with its juridical connotation – basis of the historical process of confederation. Perhaps it does; to the lawyer. But to the historian the simple fact remains that the officers of the Colonial Office accepted without question the assessment of the situation given them by the colonial delegates. To them the Bill was in the nature of a colonial treaty, even if such a treaty were not to be found in the classifications usually given in the text books of international law. In consequence they were prepared to leave the colonial delegates alone, to let them make their own arrangements, thresh out their own differences, draft their own agreement. Neither Lord Carnarvon nor the members of his office entered the negotiations or took part in them until the Quebec Resolutions had undergone the revision or editing to which I have referred. When they did, it was at the specific request of the delegates, with the object of acting in an advisory capacity only. Perhaps the British role is best expressed in the suggestion that the Colonial Secretary acted in the capacity of a notary reducing to proper legal terms an understanding already arrived at by the parties concerned. That certainly was the role in which Carnarvon saw himself. The British North America Act was, therefore, not the work of the British authorities, nor the expression of ideas of the British Colonial Office; it was, in

[12] Sir R. Herbert, *Speeches on Canadian Affairs by Henry Howard Molyneux, fourth Earl of Carnarvon* (London, 1902) p. 92.
[13] *Ibid.*, pp. 110, 130.

essence, simply the recognition in law of the agreement arrived at originally in Quebec and clarified later in London, by the representatives of the provinces of Nova Scotia, New Brunswick, and Canada with its two divisions, Canada East and Canada West.

The British North America Act passed through its necessary readings in the House of Commons and in the House of Lords without change or alteration; on March 28, 1867, it received the Royal Assent. By royal proclamation it came into effect on the first day of July following. The new constitution was, without question, a statute of the British Parliament, and as such possessed the attributes of an ordinary statute. But it was a statute distinctly unlike any other previously passed by the Parliament at Westminster. The Quebec Act of 1774, the Constitutional Act of 1791, the Act of Union of 1840, all of them had been devised, drafted, and enacted, without reference to the people of the provinces concerned. Individuals and groups of individuals had been consulted, it is true; but the work was done and the responsibility was taken by the Imperial authorities. The British North America Act, however, was, to all intents and purposes, the work of the several self-governing, quasi-sovereign colonies themselves. The Colonial Office did no more than put the words into proper form and the British Parliament no more than give them legislative sanction. The British North America Act was, therefore, to use the words of an early Canadian jurist, "a simple ratification by the Mother Country of the agreement entered into by the provinces, which in confirming its provisions rendered them obligatory by giving them the authority of an Imperial Act."[14]

But the legal supplementing of the interprovincial pact, both by the Canadian and British governments, did not mean that the problems of the coexistence of the two contending races within the bosom of a single state had been solved. Agreement there could be on broad lines of how to divide authority between the central and provincial governments, but disagreement on the details of the division was inherent in the very nature of a federal constitution, and particularly in Canada where federal union in the mouth of a Lower Canadian usually meant "the independence of his Province from English and Protestant influences"[15] and in

---

[14] Hon. Justice T. J. J. Loranger, *Letters upon the Interpretation of the Federal Constitution known as the British North America Act 1867* (Quebec, 1884), p. 63.

[15] O'Connor, *Report*, Annex 2, p. 83: Gordon to Cardwell, Sep. 12, 1864. After visiting Charlottetown during the meeting of the provincial delegates and receiving daily reports from the New Brunswick delegation, Lieutenant-Governor Gordon wrote to the Colonial Secretary:

that of the Upper Canadian, a preference for a strong central government.[16] Ministers and Prime Ministers might pay lip service to the doctrine of a Pact;[17] they might honestly believe in its validity; they could shelve but could not shed their centralizing proclivities. There was never any underhand conspiracy to destroy the Anglo-French entente; but there was an open-handed effort to add to the powers of the central government at the expense of those of the provinces. I need only mention the names of Macdonald, Mowat and Mercier to recall to mind the early trials of strength of the two opposing points of view. Fortunately the arbiter was there, the courts: the controversies which opposing points of view engendered were resolvable by due process of law. The powers of the federal parliament and those of the provincial legislatures had, in 1867, been carefully tabulated. All that was necessary was to apply the tabulation to each specific dispute. . . .

But to return to the question of the Confederative pact. Despite the frequency with which Canadian political leaders have reiterated the existence of the pact, despite the legal support afforded the concept of the pact by the highest court of appeal – as late as the 1930's, the Privy Council referred to the British North America Act as a "contract," a "compact" and a "treaty" founded on the Quebec and London Resolutions[18] – the pact concept was never universally understood or wholly accepted by each and all of the provinces of Canada. Indeed the popularity of the pact idea seems to vary in some provinces in inverse ratio to their fiscal need. The concept of the pact was slow to be accepted in

---

A "Federal Union" in the mouth of a Lower Canadian usually means the independence of his Province from English and Protestant influences. In the mouth of an inhabitant of the Maritime Provinces it means the retention of the machinery of the existing local Executive Government, the expenditure within each Province of the revenue raised from it, except a quota to be paid towards Federal expenses, and the preservation of the existing Legislatures in their integrity, with the somewhat cumbrous addition of a central Parliament to which the consideration of some few topics of general interest is to be confided under restraints prompted by a jealous care for the maintenance of Provincial independence.

[16] *Confederation Debates*, p. 29.
[17] See, for instance, statements by Sir Wilfrid Laurier (*House of Commons Debates, Canada*, Jan. 28, 1907, p. 2199); Robert Borden (*Ibid.*, Jan. 28, 1907, p. 2199); Ernest Lapointe (*Ibid.*, Feb. 18, 1925, pp. 297-300); Arthur Meighen (*Ibid.*, Feb. 19, 1925, p. 335) and Richard B. Bennett (*Ibid.*, Feb. 24, 1930, p. 24).
[18] *Attorney-General for Australia v. Colonial Sugar Co.* (1914) A. C., p. 253; *In re the Regulation and Control of Aeronautics in Canada* (1932) A.C., p. 70; *Attorney-General for Canada v. Attorney-General for Ontario and others* (1937) A.C., p. 351.

the Maritimes. In the early years after Confederation, there was still strong opposition to the very fact of union, and the pact upon which it was based was never very popular. In 1869 the Saint John *Morning Freeman* criticized the idea of a pact of confederation, denying that there was any continuity between the pre- and post-confederation provinces.[19] From time to time, various provinces have supported the doctrine of the pact, including New Brunswick, Alberta and British Columbia; but their support has not been marked by unanimity or consistency. Only in Ontario and Quebec has the concept remained undiminished in strength and popularity, at least in political circles, if not always in legal and academic. The Ontario-Quebec axis has transcended both time and political parties. The original alliance of Mowat and Mercier has carried on through that of Whitney and Gouin, Ferguson and Taschereau, and Drew and Duplessis. It has always been the principal buttress of provincial autonomy.

The explanation why the pact idea has remained most vigorous in the two central provinces is to be found in their history. We need only recall . . . that the pact was, in its origin, an entente between the two racial groups of Old Canada, between the two provinces which were each the focus of a distinctive culture. Only in the two provinces of Old Canada did the racial struggle play any real part in our history; only in the two provinces of Old Canada did this struggle have any real meaning. The Maritimers of 1864 were not concerned with racial problems; their interest in federal union was largely financial, in the recovery of a passing age of sea-going prosperity. The western provinces, with the exception of British Columbia which found its own version of a compact in the terms of union in 1871, were the offspring of the federal loins; their interest in federal union was in their maintenance and subsistence. But in Upper and Lower Canada federation was the solution of the politico-racial contest for supremacy and survival, which had marked their joint history since the day Vaudreuil and Amherst signed the Capitulation of Montreal. The concept of a pact of federation was thus peculiarly a Canadian one (I use Canadian in the sense in which it was used in 1864, and in which it is still used in some parts of the Maritimes today); it still remains peculiarly Canadian. Duality of culture as the central feature of the constitutional problem has a meaning and a reality to the people of the two provinces of Old Canada which it cannot have to those of the other provinces. That is why neither Ontario nor Quebec has departed in its provincial policy from the strict interpretation of the federal basis of the constitution, or from the concept of a federative pact. The identification

[19] *The Morning Freeman,* Saint John, N.B., Nov. 25, 1869.

of the racial pact, which was a very real thing in the 1850's and 1860's, with the compromise arrived at by the several provinces in 1864 and 1866, has tended to obscure the racial aspect of the bargain and to deprive it of some of its strength. The Canadian delegates to Quebec and London were thoroughly convinced that their bargain was a treaty or a pact; however, this conviction was always weaker among the Maritimers than among the Canadians, and especially the French Canadians, whose principal concern as a vital minority has been and must be the survival of their culture and the pact which is the constitutional assurance of that survival.

It is the racial aspect of the pact of Confederation which gives the pact its historicity and confirms its continued usage. If the population of Canada were one in race, language, and religion, our federation would be marked by flexibility; amendment would be a comparatively easy matter where there was agreement upon fundamental issues. Since history had given us a dual culture, with its diversities of race and language, we must maintain a precarious balance between the two groups; and our constitution is rigid and inflexible. That is what I meant, when I said at the outset, that the historic pact of the Union has become, by acceptance and usage, a necessary convention of our constitution. It will continue to be such so long as the minority group retains its numbers and its will to survive.

CONSOCIATIONALISM AT PROVINCIAL LEVEL:
THE EROSION OF DUALISM IN MANITOBA,
1870-1890

Janice Staples

Manitoba was the first province to enter the Canadian Confederation after its inception in 1867. Its entry in 1869 and 1870 provides an interesting example of a federal bargain between a young, still fragile federation and a potential new member. Canadians – and particularly Upper Canadians – had been casting covetous glances at the sparsely settled lands of the Northwest since the 1850's, and with the annexation of the vast Hudson's Bay Company territory to Canada in 1869 their goal seemed within reach. In the Red River Settlement, however, with its distinctive combination of French-speaking and English-speaking half breeds, of Scottish Selkirk settlers and native Indians, insensitive Canadian expansionism had aroused a general distrust which quickly gave way to open resistance to Canadian rule and the formation of a Provisional Government under the *Métis* leader, Louis Riel, in December 1869.

There followed a period of *de facto* control by the Provisional Government and negotiation with Ottawa for several months with the aim of obtaining provincial status, minority guarantees, and the settlement of land claims in a society that was in full transition from a semi-nomadic hunting economy to prairie agriculture. The minority guarantees sought by the Red River representatives and incorporated in Riel's fourth "Bill of Rights" included the continuation of the existing confessional school system, official bilingualism, and a provincial second chamber like that of Quebec. All of these, together with the full provincial status, were conceded in the federal parliament's Manitoba Act of 1870, though on their side the Red River negotiators had to make concessions on other points including restricted provincial boundaries and federal control of Crown lands.

The central point, however, is clear. The Red River Settlement entered the Canadian federal system as a small but functioning consociational society, which after brief initial violence had been able to accommodate its remarkable cultural heterogeneity under the rule of the Hudson's Bay Company. Within two decades after 1870 this special blend of ethnic, religious, and cultural pluralism had been thrust aside by an emerging Anglo-Saxon Protestant hegemony. This paper examines the unfolding of these changes.

THE "EXTERNAL FACTORS" HYPOTHESIS
Most historians who have studied the Manitoba school question

have found the origins of the dispute principally outside the province of Manitoba. The basic differences among them arise as to the emphasis to be placed on outside agitation. Several historians find the origins of the agitation for a single public school system in Ontario, precipitated mainly by the issue of the Quebec Jesuit Estates Act of 1888 and by the action of Dalton McCarthy, an Ontario member of the House of Commons who acted as the leading spokesman against this legislation. John Dafoe notes that

> The Manitoba school question descended upon the public of Manitoba in the late summer of 1889 out of a clear sky. Indirectly, it may be said to have been derived from the controversy in the Dominion Parliament over the refusal of the Dominion Government to disallow the act passed by the Quebec Legislature, making compensation to the ecclesiastical authorities for the confiscation of the Jesuits Estates act early in the nineteenth century.[1]

O. D. Skelton also asserts that "the Manitoba school question was an echo of the storms which had raged over Riel and the Jesuits' Estates."[2] Lovell Clark specifically focuses on the part played by Dalton McCarthy when he writes:

> ...the controversy over schools in Manitoba in 1889 arose not from any necessities inherent in the local situation, but from the actions of a demagogue and bigot who succeeded in arousing the prejudices of the Anglo-Saxon Protestants of Manitoba.[3]

Contemporary comment for the most part reflected similar opinions. A *Manitoba Free Press* editorial of August 19, 1889, noted that "...Manitoba [was] being made the battleground of Ontario fanatics who dare not propose the abolition of separate schools in their own province". J. S. Ewart commented on Dalton McCarthy and the Jesuit Estates Act:

> What a magnificent record! From Ontario, the "sleepy Protestants of Quebec" (as Mr. McCarthy called them), on the one side, are stirred into sectarian strife, over an Act that passed the Legislature without a dissenting Protestant vote; and the dull, good natured Protestants of Manitoba, on the

[1] John Dafoe, *Sir Clifford Sifton in Relation to his Times* (Toronto: Macmillan, 1931), p. 36.
[2] O. D. Skelton, *The Life and Letters of Sir Wilfrid Laurier* (Toronto: Oxford University Press, 1921), Vol. 1, p. 440.
[3] Lovell Clark, *The Manitoba School Question: Majority Rule or Minority Rights?* (Toronto: Copp Clark, 1968) p. 4.

other side, are aroused into bitter attack upon a school system highly prized by their Catholic fellow-countrymen, and which *in no way interfered with their own methods of education*.[4]

W. L. Morton is the only writer, to my knowledge, who emphasizes the internal conditions of Manitoba at the time, the most important and basic of those conditions being the overwhelming presence of British and Ontario immigrants. However even he finds the main impetus outside the province: "The time was ripe for the raising of the School Question in Manitoba; yet the impulse to do so came not so much from within the province as from without."[5]

I have found it difficult to concur in these judgments. A review of the primary sources suggests that the changing internal conditions in Manitoba from 1870 to 1890 made the raising of both the school and language issues an inevitability by the late 1870's. If this is so, it follows that outside factors contributed very little to the Manitoba school crisis, and the search for an explanation of the causes must begin in Manitoba itself.

DEMOGRAPHIC CHANGES

The impact of immigration on the population in Manitoba can be seen in Table 1. At the provincial census of 1870, the vast majority of the population had been born in the Northwest; from 1881 onwards this element represented only about one third of the total population. There was considerable immigration from the British Isles, but settlers from Ontario formed the largest group by a considerable margin. Of the original population enumerated in 1870, approximately 82 per cent was of *Métis* or mixed Indian-European ancestry and only 14 per cent was recorded as white, the rest being recorded as Indian. The majority of this *Métis* population was French-speaking and Catholic. The bulk of the full-blooded Indian population does not seem to have been enumerated at this census.

Further evidence of demographic change may be seen in the data on the origins of the people, which in the Canadian census traces ancestry on the paternal side. Though comparable data are lacking for the provincial census of 1870, by 1881 some 59 per cent of the population was of British origin, 15 per cent of French origin, 13 per cent of German origin (including German Mennonites born in Russia and Poland) and 10 per cent of

[4] Quoted in *ibid.*, p. 5.
[5] W. L. Morton, *Manitoba: A History*. (Toronto: University of Toronto Press, 1957), p. 240.

Table 1   Population of Manitoba by Birthplace, 1870-1891.

	1870		1881		1886		1891	
	N	%	N	%	N	%	N	%
Manitoba & North-west Territories	11,298	92.4	24,442	37.0	34,644	31.9	51,433	33.7
Quebec	119	1.0	4,085	6.2	5,976	5.5	7,555	4.9
Ontario	118	1.0	19,125	29.0	34,121	31.4	46,620	30.6
Maritimes	n.a.	—	1,315	2.0	2,201	2.0	2,354	1.5
British Isles	422	3.4	8,161	12.4	19,925	18.3	28,014	18.4
U.S.A.	172	1.4	1,752	2.6	2,322	2.1	3,063	2.0
Others & not stated	99	0.8	7,049	10.7	9,451	8.7	13,467	8.8
Total	12,228	100	65,954	100	108,640	100	152,506	100

Source: Calculated from Census of Canada, 1871, 1881, 1891, and Census of Manitoba, 1886, as reported in *Statistical Abstracts*, 1887.

Indian extraction. The 1886 census of Manitoba gives more precise information as to the *Métis* population. By this time the population of British extraction accounted for 67 per cent of the total, and half breeds of British extraction counted for a further 3 per cent. The population of French origin was approximately 6 per cent, while the French *Métis* constituted a further 4 per cent. Other groups included 10 per cent of German origin, 5 per cent of Indian origin, and 2 per cent of Icelandic origin, for a total population of 108,640. Thus the population of French and mixed French-Indian origin accounted for approximately 10 per cent of the total population in 1886, and in the absence of figures by mother tongue during this period perhaps this is the most accurate indicator of linguistic-cultural affiliation.

The proportion of Roman Catholics and Protestants is shown in Table 2. In the 1870 census, the Roman Catholics were in a slight majority of those whose affiliation was reported, though religious data are almost entirely lacking for one of the five census districts. However, the more complete preliminary report submitted by Lieutenant-Governor Archibald on December 26, 1870, reveals an almost exact balance between Catholics and Protestants.[6] By 1881, the flow of immigration had created a strong Protestant majority, which increased marginally in succeed-

[6] Of the 6059 Catholics there were 5,568 French-speaking half breeds, 57 English-speaking half breeds and 360 whites. Of the 5,906 Protestants there were 126 French-speaking half breeds, 4,019 English-speaking half breeds and 1,254 whites. See Canada, Sessional Papers, v (20), 1871, p. 94.

Table 2 Population of Manitoba by Religious Denominations, 1870-1891

	1870		1881		1886		1891	
	N	%	N	%	N	%	N	%
Roman Catholics	5,452	44.6	12,246	18.6	14,651	13.5	20,571	13.5
Protestants	4,841	39.6	49,091	74.4	87,655	80.7	125,940	82.6
Others	–	–	2,290*	3.5	718	0.7	1,191	0.8
Not given	1,935†	15.8	2,327	3.5	5,616	5.2	4,824	3.2
Total	12,228	100	65,954	100	108,640	100	152,526	100

Source: Calculated from the Censuses of Canada, 1871, 1881, 1891, and the Census of Manitoba, 1886, as reported in *Statistical Abstracts*, 1887.

* includes 2,173 or 3.3 per cent listed as "pagans".

† The census return does not record religion satisfactorily, especially in the district of the boundary extension. However, the preliminary report lists 6,059 Catholics and 5,906 Protestants for a total of 11,965. See Canada, Sessional Papers, V (20), 1871, p. 94.

ing censuses. A corresponding progression may be seen in statistics on schools and pupils enrolled in the Catholic and Protestant school systems as can be seen in Table 3. Despite some anomalies in the form of reporting, enrolment statistics are available on a more or less continuous basis and thus reveal more closely, if indirectly, the demographic changes of the 1870's. As Table 3 shows, Protestant pupils outnumbered Catholic pupils by more than 2:1 in 1880, by 4:1 in 1882, and by almost 6:1 in 1890.

INSTITUTIONAL AND ATTITUDINAL CHANGES

The establishment of new provincial institutions after 1870 involved a certain persistence of conditions and attitudes that had been prevalent in the Red River settlement. The educational system had already been organized along denominational lines with schools being organized by Roman Catholics, Anglicans, and Presbyterians[7] and education grants to the Protestant and Catholic groups being apportioned equally. The old Council of Assiniboia, which acted in an advisory capacity to the Governor and which has been termed "fairly representative of all interests in the colony . . . ,"[8] exemplified a linguistic and ethnic diversity which reappeared in the Executive Council, the Legislative Council and

[7] The Presbyterians had organized only one school.

[8] F. A. Milligan, "The Establishment of Manitoba's First Provincial Government," *Historical and Scientific Society of Manitoba*, Series 3, no. 5, 1950, p. 7.

Table 3 Schools and Pupils by School System, Selected Years, 1873-1889

	Catholic			Protestant		
Year	No. of Schools	Pupils N	%	No. of Schools	Pupils N	%
1873	18	824	45.8	17	977	54.2
1874	20	945	48.2	18	1,014	51.8
1876	22	1,134	41.5	30	1,600	58.5
1880	27	1,658	31.4	99	3,614	68.6
1882	34	1,684	19.5	182	6,972	80.5
1889	73	3,236	15.0	545	18,358	85.0

Source: Reports of the Superintendent of Protestant Schools and Reports of the Superintendent of Education for Catholic Schools for the above years as found in the Appendixes of the *Journals of the Legislative Assembly.*

the Legislative Assembly after 1870. Further examples of earlier dualism include the appointment of two land surveyors in 1856, one English-speaking and one French-speaking, and the sharing of customs collection by four men, two English-speaking and two French-speaking. Further evidence could also be cited to show that both language groups had been given recognition in the colony prior to Confederation.

The first federally-appointed Lieutenant-Governor after Confederation, the Nova Scotian A. G. Archibald, seems to have been aware of these traditions while establishing embryonic political institutions for the new province.[9] His first appointed Executive and Legislative Councils deliberately balanced the *Métis* and the settlers of both language groups. The first electoral districts for the Legislative Assembly were evenly divided along racial lines into twelve English-speaking and twelve French-speaking constituencies.[10] The results of the first election in 1871 revealed the success of Archibald's attempt to maintain a balanced representation. Among the twenty-four elected members, there were twelve whites, twelve *Métis*, and within each group, half were Catholics and half Protestants.[11]

Evolution of political representation. The second provincial election in 1874 produced an increase in English-speaking representa-

[9] Archibald was active in the Confederation movement and attended the Charlottetown, Quebec, and London Conferences. At Quebec he introduced a motion to give residual legislative powers to the provinces.

[10] Morton, *op. cit.*, p. 146.

[11] Milligan, *op. cit.*, p. 14 note 57.

tion in the Assembly. Of 24 members returned, five were natives of the British Isles, two were from Ontario, one from the Maritimes, seven from Quebec (including one English-speaking Catholic) and eight were natives of Manitoba, seven being English-speaking and one a French-speaking *Métis*. French-speaking representation on the Executive Council decreased by one.[12]

The third Assembly returns in 1878 followed closely the pattern of the changing population mosaic of Manitoba. Eight of the members were natives of Ontario, three were from the British Isles and three from Quebec. Of the seven native-born members, five were English-speaking and two French-speaking. Only one member was a *Métis* (of French origin). The Executive Council of 1878, with two French-speaking members out of five, was more representative than the Assembly.[13]

In the Assembly elected in 1883, the number of French-speaking members declined from 6 to 4, and for the first time two members born in Europe of non-British origin were elected. The linguistic constitution of the Executive Council remained the same.[14]

At the 1886 election, the number of Ontario and British-born members increased further, while the Executive Council showed a decrease in French-speaking membership and also in the number of native Manitobans returned. By this time all but two of the Councillors originated from Ontario or Britain.[15]

The election of 1888 returned six French-speaking members of a total of 38 in the Assembly and only one French-speaking member was appointed to the Executive Council.[16] This was the ministry which two years later was the pass legislation to abolish the dual school system and the official status of the French language in Manitoba.

From this brief outline of the patterns of representation it is evident that as early as 1878 the influx of British and Ontario-born immigrants had severely disturbed the linguistic and ethnic balance of 1871. By 1888, the change in the legislative elite was complete. As Morton has commented, "This election of mid-1888 marked the triumph of Ontario over Quebec in Manitoba."[17] This triumph, however, had been in the making over the five preceding elections.

Another manifestation of change is the gradual development of party lines in Manitoba. Basically, there were three successive lines of cleavages within the Legislature: in the early 1870's, the

[12] *Parliamentary Companion*, 1875, p. 589-610.
[13] *Ibid.*, 1879, pp. 360-373.
[14] *Ibid.*, 1885, pp. 313-338.
[15] *Ibid.*, 1887, pp. 319-340.
[16] *Ibid.*, 1889, pp. 330-349.
[17] Morton, *op. cit.*, p. 233.

old versus the new settlers; from the mid-1870's to the early 1880's, the French-speaking versus the English-speaking population, and from the early 1880's, the Liberals versus the Conservatives. With the development of parties corresponding to those at the federal level in this third phase, the Manitoba Assembly ceased to be an effective vehicle for the expression of French-speaking political interests in the province.

Legislative Changes, 1870-1890. The change in the composition of the Legislative Assembly is not surprising since it corresponded roughly to ethnic changes in the population of Manitoba. The important factor to be studied is how the emerging English-speaking majority exercised its political power. That this power was used from an early date to erode dualism and to limit the political influence of the French-speaking minority may be seen in the bills introduced in the Assembly between 1871 and 1890. Many of the pertinent bills were technical and only a close look at their effects will indicate how they diminished the political position of the French-speaking Manitobans. A few, however, were direct frontal assaults on linguistic and cultural dualism.

One category of legislation provided Manitoba with an institutional framework shaped on British and Ontarian lines. It included three bills of 1871, 1873, and 1877 that gradually introduced a municipal system modelled after that of Ontario. This application of the Ontario municipal system is extremely important when seen in conjunction with certain school amendments of the later 1870's, which provided increased jurisdiction for municipalities over school districts within their area. As Morton remarks, " . . . the new municipal system was certain to assimilate to itself the district educational system of denominational schools and to raise religious and racial controversy in doing so."[18]

Another category of legislation that helped to decrease Franco-Manitoban political power was the periodic redistribution of electoral boundaries. Redistribution bills were passed in 1873, 1877, 1879, 1881, 1885 and 1888. Their combined effect was a steady decrease in the number of French-speaking electoral districts in Manitoba through the introduction of the principle of representation by population, as opposed to the original communal representation. It has been calculated that by 1888, only one of the original electoral districts of 1870 remained intact.[19] The French-speaking districts had been divided so as to decrease the influence of the Franco-Manitoban vote.

Another detrimental measure was the abolition of the Legisla-

[18] Morton, *op. cit.*, p. 189.
[19] *Ibid.*, p. 232.

tive Council, which was passed by both Houses in 1876 after being blocked by the upper house itself at the first attempt in 1875. The appointed Legislative Council, like its counterpart, the federal senate, had been conceived as a device for guaranteeing minority rights. The first Council appointed by Lieutenant-Governor Archibald consisted of one Scottish Catholic half breed, two French-speaking *Métis*, one Irish Catholic and three Protestant English-speaking settlers.[20] While Quebec had a similar upper house, Ontario did not, and a number of settlers from Ontario advocated its abolition. The Davis ministry had promised abolition as early as 1874, and when the federal government added its voice in the interest of economy, the fate of the Legislative Council was sealed.[21]

Two further bills, both rejected at this period, are indicators of changing public opinion in the later 1870's and portents of the final extinction of dualism in 1890. The first bill called for the abolition of both the official status of the French language and the dual school system but was twice defeated in the 1875 and 1876 parliamentary sessions. The second, the Public Printing Bill of 1879, provided for abolition of the printing in French of all public documents except provincial statutes. This measure was passed by the Assembly but was reserved for federal decision by the Lieutenant-Governor, Joseph Cauchon, a French Canadian. When, however, a more drastic bill to make English the sole official language was passed by the Assembly in 1890, the Lieutenant-Governor who gave assent to the bill was John Christian Schultz, the man who as leader of the Canadian party had led the opposition to Riel in 1869.

The member who introduced the bills of 1875 and 1876, William Luxton, was also the editor of the influential *Manitoba Free Press*. Many of the editorials of this period contained pointed attacks on both the dual school system and the official status of the French language. The premier and his cabinet were accused of being tools for the French-speaking element, and the official status of the French language was attacked as an unnecessary burden on the Manitoba taxpayers.[22]

Legislation on Schools. A further indicator that settler opinion was changing by the middle 1870's was a resolution passed by the Protestant Section of the Board of Education in 1875, that called upon the Manitoba government to enact new school legislation

---

[20] Milligan, *op. cit.*, p. 16.
[21] The correspondence between the federal government and the province concerning this issue can be found in the Appendix to the *Journals of the Legislative Assembly*, 1875.
[22] See, for example, the editorials of September 4, 7, 21, October 10 and 18, 1874, and March 11 and April 9, 1875.

providing for a single non-sectarian school system.[23] Though this was not acted upon, the various school amendments passed during the twenty-year period were frequent enough and of sufficient importance to be considered separately as further evidence of the decline of dualism.

The constitutional guarantee for the dual educational system in Section 22 of the Manitoba Act protected the denominational school system, as it existed prior to 1870, against provincial legislative encroachment and provided for appeal to the federal cabinet and remedial legislation by the federal parliament if such infringements occurred.

Under the first Education Act of 1871, existing local schools were taken over, classified as Catholic or Protestant, and placed under the superintendence of either the Protestant or Catholic section of the Provincial Board of Education. The Act also allowed for the establishment of new schools on the same principle.

The system soon underwent a series of amendments. Where the Act of 1871 provided that the educational grant was to be divided equally between the two sections,[24] an amendment of 1873 provided that the grant was to be divided in proportion to the yearly average attendance at all the schools under each section.[25] The same Act also laid down conditions for the establishment of separate schools when requested by the religious minority of any Catholic or Protestant school district. Another amendment of 1875, reorganized the Board of Education so as to upset the numerical equality between the Catholic and Protestant sections, which had existed since its establishment in 1871. Membership of the Board was increased from six Protestants and six Catholics to twelve Protestants and nine Catholics.

Other amendments in 1875 and 1876 had the effect of making the two sections of the Board more independent of each other, but the respective powers of the two sections were reduced to a certain extent by other legislation that gave municipalities increased authority over the school districts within their area. The first Act of this type granted virtual autonomy in educational matters to the city of Winnipeg in 1876. The main fear concerning the increased power of municipalities over the school districts involved the assumption that most municipalities were English-speaking and Protestant while the separate schools within those

[23] J. A. Jackson, *The Centennial History of Manitoba*. (Winnipeg, McClelland and Stewart, 1970), p. 138.

[24] *Statutes of Manitoba*, 1871, "An Act to Establish a System of Education", cap. 12, section 18.

[25] *Statutes of Manitoba*, 1873, "An Act to Amend the Act to Establish a System of Education in this Province," cap. 22, section 4.

districts were French-speaking and Catholic. The municipalities wielded potentially powerful instruments through taxation, appointment of personnel, and inspection, which could be employed to the disadvantage of the French minority. These amendments were of minor significance but they paved the way for the legislation of 1890, which gave municipalities even more control over the educational system.

The school acts of 1890 are two in number. The first, "An Act Respecting the Department of Education" abolished the Board of Education and created a Department of Education which was to consist of a committee of the Executive Council and an Advisory Board of seven members, with powers to authorize texts and prescribe the form of religious exercises. The second, "An Act Respecting Public Schools," repealed all former laws relating to education and established a system of non-denominational schools, instructing only in the religious exercises authorized by the Advisory Board. Any schools not adhering to the provisions of the Act were to be refused a provincial educational grant and the right to receive any funds raised by municipal taxation.

The various amendments of the school system from 1873 onward had the effect of undermining the principle of religious equality and breaking down linguistic and religious segmentation by providing for a closer linkage between the municipalities and the educational system. More generally, they eroded the structures of religious, linguistic and cultural dualism which had existed in the Manitoba of 1870. By 1890, the entrenchment of Ontario-based political attitudes was complete and the locus of political power in the province had shifted irrevocably. As Morton has noted of the redistribution of 1887:

> The old order, whether the dual school system in language and schools with all it meant to the French, or the influence the old settlers had exercised through their communal constituencies and their own representatives led by John Norquay, now existed only at the discretion of the new majority, largely Ontario-bred and Protestant by creed.[26]

And the new majority lost little time in exercising its political power to the detriment of the French-speaking minority.

CONCLUSION

The later phases of the story are better known than its beginnings, for after 1890 the schools question became a central issue in federal politics. Despite numerous appeals by the Catholic minority, the federal government did not disallow the Public

[26] Morton, *op. cit.*, p. 232.

Schools Act nor did it succeed in passing remedial legislation. All attempts at compromise failed until the Laurier-Greenway agreement of November 1896, which modified the public school system so as to allow limited periods of linguistic and religious teaching where numbers warranted.[27] Nevertheless, this was a political settlement, and one that left a lasting mark on the nature of Confederation, for it had shown the forces of provincial autonomy to be stronger than the claims of religious or ethnic minorities, stronger even than the rights incorporated and guaranteed constitutionally at Manitoba's creation as a province.

The politicisation of the Manitoba School Question has been linked by many writers to various issues outside the province: to the second Riel Rebellion and the sharp controversy over the fate of the *Métis* leader in 1885, to Quebec's Jesuit Estates Act of 1888 and the anti-Catholic extremism of Dalton McCarthy and the incongruously misnamed Equal Rights Association. But the seeds were sown within the province long before 1885 and had been germinating since the middle 1870's.

When McCarthy mounted the platform at Portage la Prairie on August 5, 1889 to launch his attack on the French language and the Catholic schools, all the ingredients for a conflagration were at hand save for the final spark to set it ablaze. By the time that the school question "descended upon the public of Manitoba in the late summer of 1889 out of a clear sky," as John Dafoe has remarked, its outcome was clearly prefigured by events already past. At this point only decisive intervention from outside the province could have saved the dual regime in Manitoba, and that intervention fell short both at the legal and political level.

[27] The clauses of the settlement were very general. It allowed not only French-language instruction but also German in German-speaking Mennonite areas, and later on other languages as immigration increased. However, all instruction in languages other than English was banned in 1917.

EPILOGUE

Most of this book so far has been concerned with descriptive and analytical approaches to consociationalism. In Part IV we have examined how far the consociational model can be used to explain the Canadian political system both now and in the past. Consociational democracy, however, may also be viewed prescriptively, as a normative model, a criterion for evaluating political systems and a guide to future policy and action. It is this normative aspect of consociationalism that gives great significance to the hitherto unresolved debate between Lijphart and Daalder:[1] just how far consociational systems are the product of earlier political tradition and how far they may be created through deliberate efforts by elites is crucial in deciding whether consociational patterns may be successfully transplanted to other settings.

In the Canadian case, as my own paper has indicated, the existing political system falls short of the consociational model and even of the other working consociational systems in several different ways.[2] Moreover the provinces, with the exception of Quebec, have functioned no better than the federal government in this respect, though the Manitoba example is perhaps an extreme case and some provinces have reflected a more accommodative atmosphere since the mid-1960's. Nevertheless the existing Canadian political system, even at its best, must be viewed as a very imperfect example of consociational democracy.

I suggest that the ultimate source of these shortcomings lies not so much in any specific institutional arrangements as in attitudes rooted deeply in the Canadian political culture, attitudes that fail to comprehend the meaning of a plural society. In the traditional political thought of the English-speaking world, minority status is a temporary phenomenon, and today's political minority becomes a nucleus for building tomorrow's majority. In the politics of segmented pluralism – whether based on religion, language, or race – minority status is far more likely to be a permanent fact of life, an ascribed characteristic, a burden to be carried perpetually by the smaller group or groups. In such a setting, appeals to the majority principle can be highly dangerous, and special accommodatory devices may be needed for resolving inter-group dif-

---

[1] See Daalder, above, 120-122; Lijphart, "Cultural Diversity and Theories of Political Integration," *Canadian Journal of Political Science*, Vol. 4 (1971), 13-14; and also Daalder, "The Consociational Democracy Theme: a review article," *World Politics* (forthcoming).

[2] See especially the summary above, pp. 260-261.

ferences. English Canadians collectively have never grasped this fundamental point, and because they have not done so French Canadians have reacted in the only effective way open to them, by an instinctive attempt to build – either by themselves or in concert with others – stable majorities of their own. As long as English Canadians remain majority-minded, many French Canadians will find their most effective response in an increasingly autonomous Quebec. This majoritarian attitude on both sides, I suggest, is the Achilles heel of the Canadian political system. It is the *damnosa hereditas* of Anglo-American democracy and Lockean political theory and liberal society, though in fairness one must note its all too frequent appearance in other political traditions also.

The point is that any genuinely pluralist society must learn to do better, and the consociational model offers some general guidelines as to how to do so. At first glance Canada may appear to offer a distinctly unpromising setting for a more explicitly consociational political system. The older political heritage is vastly different, and majoritarian attitudes are firmly rooted. The main linguistic groups are not closely balanced and majorities face minorities at both federal and provincial levels. There is no major external threat (except, perhaps, of an economic nature) to stimulate internal cooperation. However against these negative factors one must balance a very limited range of alternatives. The present political system is under considerable strain, and more integrative solutions appear to be ruled out for the foreseeable future. The one significant alternative is the separation or quasi-separation of Quebec. But this option, whatever its other consequences, would still leave substantial linguistic minorities in both Quebec and the rest of Canada because provincial boundaries do not follow linguistic ones. The paucity of alternatives is perhaps the best reason for considering seriously whether the Canadian system could not be improved by modifying its formal institutions along more consociational lines.

This is not the place to begin a comprehensive inventory of desirable or possible reforms. It is clear that the question is complex and that various approaches are possible. But among the more obvious topics for closer study one may readily select (1) the electoral system and its effects on the political representation of subcultural interests at both federal and provincial levels, (2) the party system and the problem of adequate articulation of subcultural interests within parties, and (3) the existing federal system and its overall impact on linguistic and ethnic relations. What is needed is a willingness to examine with an open mind certain well-established institutions and practices that appear to have become increasingly disfunctional as linguistic issues have become more salient. The four European democracies that we have examined all found it necessary to modify their political systems quite substantially in order to accommodate the new social forces that gave rise to their consociational systems, and Belgium has been doing so again since the early 1960's in order to accommodate linguistic diversity. It seems not impossible that Canada, through intensive discussion and negotiation among the subcultural elites, could do the same. The passing of the federal Official Languages Act in 1969 marked a significant step towards legal and administrative accommodation of Canada's linguistic and cultural diversity, but the accommodation of this diversity in the political process itself has lagged behind and must now be ranked high on any Canadian agenda for reform.

But the problems of segmented pluralism are by no means confined to Canada alone, and the consociational model may have some relevance wherever sharp and lasting cleavages occur. The political scientist or statesman would never build or perpetuate social segmentation unnecessarily, but he may be called upon, as Aristotle has observed, to do the best he can with the materials at hand.[3] Where segmentation is a *given*, the problem is to find the best political strategy for dealing with it. At this stage we know relatively little about the limiting conditions for consociational democracy, or about the possibilities of its successful adaptation to situations of linguistic or racial or communal pluralism. Until we do know these limits more precisely, we may take it as a working rule that accommodationist solutions are more civilized than forced integration, and that the inefficiencies of consociational politics are less costly than subcultural hostility and violence.

[3] *Politics*, 1288b.

SELECT BIBLIOGRAPHY

In addition to the studies printed or partially printed above, the following rather specialized bibliography may be helpful for those who wish to explore the consociational theme in greater detail. Section A contains mainly items of a more theoretical or analytical nature and also those dealing with more than one country; the rest are grouped by individual countries though many of these also have theoretical significance. Since explicit applications of the consociational model to Canada have so far been relatively few, I have included in section F a few studies on somewhat peripheral themes, in some cases themes that suggest avenues to be explored more fully from a consociational perspective.

A. THEORETICAL AND COMPARATIVE STUDIES

Almond, G. A. "Comparative Political Systems," *Journal of Politics*, Vol. 18 (1956), 391-409.

Daalder, H. "Parties, Elites, and Political Development in Western Europe," in J. La Palombara and M. Weiner, eds., *Political Parties and Political Development* (Princeton, 1966), pp. 43-77.

Daalder, H. "Cabinets and party systems in ten European democracies," *Acta Politica*, Vol. 6 (1971), 282-303.

Daalder, H. "The Consociational Democracy Theme: a review article," *World Politics* (forthcoming, July 1974).

Dunn, J. A. "Consociational Democracy and Language Conflict: A Comparison of the Belgian and Swiss Experience," *Comparative Political Studies*, Vol. 5 (1972), 3-39.

Fogarty, M. P. *Christian Democracy in Western Europe, 1820-1953* (London, 1957).

Hartz, L., et al. *The Founding of New Societies* (New York, 1964).

Hartz, L. "Violence and Legality in the Fragment Cultures," *Canadian Historical Review*, Vol. 50 (1969), 123-140.

Kirchheimer, O. "The Waning of Opposition in Parliamentary Regimes," *Social Research*, Vol. 24 (1957), 127-156.

Lehmbruch, G. *Proporzdemokratie: Politisches System und politische Kultur in der Schweiz und in Österreich* (Tübingen, 1967).

Lehmbruch, G. "The Ambiguous Coalition in West Germany," *Government and Opposition*, Vol. 3 (1968), 181-204.

Lehmbruch, G. "Konkordanzdemokratien im internationalen System," in E. O. Czempiel, ed., *Die anachronistische Souver-*

änität, special issue of the *Politische Vierteljahresschrift* (1969), 139-163.

Lehmbruch, G. "Segmented pluralism and political strategies in Continental Europe: internal and external conditions of 'Concordant Democracy' " (Paper presented at the Torino Round Table of the International Political Science Association, 1969).

Lehmbruch, G. "Strukturen ideologischer Konflikte bei Parteienwettbewerb," *Politische Vierteljahresschrift*, Vol. 10 (1969), 287-313.

Lijphart, A. "Typologies of Democratic Systems," *Comparative Political Studies*, Vol. 1 (1968), 3-44.

Lijphart, A. "Cultural Diversity and Theories of Political Integration," *Canadian Journal of Political Science*, Vol. 4 (1971), 1-14.

Lijphart, A. "Class voting and religious voting in the European democracies: a preliminary report," *Acta Politica*, Vol. 6 (1971), 158-171.

Lijphart, A. "Cleavages in Consociational Democracies: a four-country comparison" (Paper presented at the Symposium on Comparative Analysis of Highly Industrialized Societies, Bellagio, 1971).

Lijphart, A. "Linguistic Fragmentation and other Dimensions of Cleavage: a comparison of Belgium, Canada, and Switzerland" (Paper presented at the Ninth World Congress of the International Political Science Association, Montreal, 1973).

Moberg, D. O. "Religion and Society in the Netherlands and in America," *American Quarterly*, Vol. 13 (1961), 172-178, and reprinted in *Social Compass*, Vol. 9 (1962), 11-19.

Nordlinger, E. A. *Conflict Regulation in Divided Societies* (Occasional Papers in International Affairs, 29, Harvard University, Cambridge, Mass., 1972).

Social Compass, Vol. 9, nos. 1-2 (1962), 1-164. Special issue on "Vertical pluralism."

Steiner, J. "Conflict Resolution and Democratic Stability in Subculturally Segmented Political Systems," *Res Publica*, Vol. 11 (1969), 775-798.

Steiner, J. "Majorz und Proporz," *Politische Vierteljahresschrift*, 11 (1970), 139-146.

B. THE NETHERLANDS

Daalder, H. "Parties and Politics in the Netherlands," *Political Studies*, Vol. 3 (1955), 1-16.

Daalder, H. "The Netherlands: Opposition in a Segmented Society," in R. A. Dahl, ed., *Political Oppositions in Western Democracies* (New Haven, 1966), 188-236.

Daalder, H., "Leiding en lijdelijkheid in de nederlandse politiek," *Res Publica*, Vol. 9 (1967), 5-27.

De Boer, J. and Cameron, P. "Dutch Radio: the Third Way," *Journalism Quarterly,* Vol. 32 (1955), 62-69.

Gielen, J. J., et al., *Pacificatie en de Zuilen* (Meppel, 1965).

Goudsblom, J. *Dutch Society* (New York, 1967).

Heidenheimer, A. J. "Elite Responses to Ontzuiling: Reels within Wheels in Dutch Broadcasting Politics" (Paper presented to the Eighth World Congress of the International Political Science Association, Munich, 1970).

Kruijt, J. P. *Verzuiling* (2nd ed., Zaandijk, 1959).

Kruijt, J. P. and Goddijn, W. "Verzuiling en ontzuiling als sociologisch proces," in A. N. J. den Hollander et al, eds., *Drift en koers: Een halve eeuw sociale verandering in Nederland* (3rd ed., Assen, 1968), 227-263, translated into French as "Cloisonnement et décloisonnement culturels comme processus sociologiques," *Social Compass,* Vol. 9 (1962), 63-107.

Lijphart, A. *The Politics of Accommodation: Pluralism and Democracy in the Netherlands* (Berkeley and Los Angeles, 1968).

Lijphart, A. "Kentering in de Nederlandse politiek," *Acta Politica,* Vol. 4 (1969), 231-247, with English summary, 355.

Socialisme en Democratie, January 1957. Special issue on *verzuiling.*

De Sociologische Gids, Vol. 3, nos. 3-4 (March-April, 1956). Special issue on *verzuiling.*

C. AUSTRIA

Bluhm, W. T. "Nation-Building: The Case of Austria," *Polity,* Vol. 1 (1968), 149-177.

Bluhm, W. T. "Political Integration, Cultural Integration and Economic Development" (Paper presented to the Eighth World Congress of the International Political Science Association, Munich, 1970).

Bluhm, W. T. *Building an Austrian Nation: the Political Integration of a Western State* (New Haven and London, 1973).

Diamant, A. "The Group Basis of Austrian Politics," *Journal of Central European Affairs,* Vol. 18 (1958), 134-155.

Engelmann, F. C. "Haggling for the Equilibrium: the Renegotiation of the Austrian Coalition, 1959," *American Political Science Review,* Vol. 56 (1962), 651-662.

Engelmann, F. C. "Austria: The Pooling of Opposition," in R. A. Dahl, ed. *Political Oppositions in Western Democracies* (New Haven, 1966), 260-283.

Lehmbruch, G. "Das politische System Österreichs in vergleichender Perspektive," *Österreichische Zeitschrift fur öffentliches Recht,* Vol. 22 (1971), 35-56.

Powell, G. B. *Social Fragmentation and Political Hostility: an Austrian Case Study* (Stanford, 1970).

Secher, H. P. "Coalition Government: the case of the Austrian Second Republic," *American Political Science Review*, Vol. 52 (1958), 791-808.

Steiner, K. *Politics in Austria* (Boston, 1972).

Stiefbold, R. P. "Elite-Mass Opinion Structure and Communication Flow in a Consociational Democracy (Austria)" (Paper presented to the Annual Meeting of the American Political Science Association, Chicago, 1968).

Stiefbold, R. "Segmented Pluralism and Constitutional Democracy in Austria," in N. Vig and R. Stiefbold, eds., *Politics in Advanced Nations* (New York, Appleton-Century-Crofts, forthcoming).

D. BELGIUM

Claeys-van Haegendoren, M. "Recente tendenzen in de Belgische politiek," *Acta Politica*, Vol. 7 (1972), 323-341, with English summary, 400.

De Clercq, B. J. *Kritiek van de Verzuiling* (Lier, 1968).

De Meyer, J. "Verzuiling en doorbraak in de hedendaagse politiek" (Address to European Study and Information Centre, Brussels, April 3, 1967).

Huyse, L. *Passiviteit, pacificatie en verzuiling in de Belgische politiek* (Antwerp, 1970).

Lorwin, V. R. "Belgium: Religion, Class and Language in National Politics," in R. A. Dahl, ed., *Political Oppositions in Western Democracies* (New Haven, 1966), 147-187.

Lorwin, V. R. "Linguistic Pluralism and Political Tension in Modern Belgium," *Canadian Journal of History*, Vol. 5 (1970), 1-23, reprinted in J. Fishman, ed., *Advances in the Sociology of Language*, Vol. II, (Paris and The Hague, 1972), 386-412

Meynaud, J., Ladrière, J., and Perin, F. *La décision politique en Belgique: le pouvoir et les groupes* (Paris, 1965).

Urwin, D. "Social Cleavages and Political Parties in Belgium: problems of institutionalization," *Political Studies*, Vol. 18 (1970) 320-340.

Van den Brande, A. "Elements for a Sociological Analysis of the Impact of the Main Conflicts on Belgian Political Life," *Res Publica*, Vol. 9 (1967), 437-469.

E. SWITZERLAND

Gasser, A. "Der 'freiwillige Proporz' im kollegialen Regierungssystem der Schweiz," *Politische Studien*, Vol. 17 (1966), 269-276.

Girod, R. "Le système des partis en Suisse," *Revue française de science politique*, Vol. 14 (1964), 1114-1133.

Keech, W. R. "Linguistic Diversity and Political Conflict: Some Observations Based on Four Swiss Cantons," *Comparative Politics*, Vol. 4 (April 1972), 387-404.

Kerr, H. H. "Social Cleavages and Partisan Conflict in Switzerland" (Paper presented at the Ninth World Congress of the International Political Science Association, Montreal, 1973).

Lehmbruch, G. "Konkordanzdemokratie im politischen System der Schweiz: Ein Literaturbericht," *Politische Vierteljahresschrift,* Vol. 9 (1968), 443-459.

Mayer, K. B. "Migration, cultural tensions, and foreign relations: Switzerland," *Journal of Conflict Resolution*, Vol. 11 (1967), 139-152.

Mayer, K. B. "The Jura Problem: Ethnic Conflict in Switzerland," *Social Research*, Vol. 35 (1968), 707-741.

Meynaud, J. and Korff, A. *Les organisations professionnelles en Suisse* (Lausanne, 1963).

McRae, K. D. *Switzerland: Example of Cultural Coexistence* (Toronto, 1964).

Steiner, J. "Non-violent Conflict Resolution in Democratic Systems: Switzerland," *Journal of Conflict Resolution*, 13 (1969), 295-304.

Steiner, J. *Gewaltlose Politik und Kulturelle Vielfalt: Hypothesen entwickelt am Beispiel der Schweiz* (Bern, 1970).

Steiner J. *Amicable Agreement versus Majority Rule: Conflict Resolution in Switzerland* (Chapel Hill, forthcoming, 1974). Revised and expanded version of *Gewaltlose Politik und kulturelle Vielfalt.*

F. CANADA

Arès, R. *Dossier sur le pacte fédératif de 1867* (rev. ed., Montreal, 1967).

Cairns, A. C. "The Electoral System and the Party System in Canada, 1921-1965," *Canadian Journal of Political Science*, Vol. 1 (1968), 55-80. See also the comment by J. A. A. Lovink and rejoinder by Cairns, *ibid.*, Vol. 3 (1970), 497-521.

Clark, L., ed., *The Manitoba School Question: Majority Rule or Minority Rights?* (Toronto, 1968).

Cook, R. *Provincial Autonomy, Minority Rights and the Compact Theory, 1867-1921* (Studies of the Royal Commission on Bilingualism and Biculturalism, Vol. 4, Ottawa, 1969).

Cornell, P. G. "The Alignment of Political Groups in the United Province of Canada, 1854-1864," *Canadian Historical Review*, Vol. 30 (1949), 22-46, reprinted in R. C. Brown, ed., *Upper Canadian Politics in the 1850's* (Toronto, 1967), 64-88

Cornell, P. G. *The Alignment of Political Groups in Canada, 1841-1867* (Toronto, 1962).

Forsey, E. A. "The Problem of 'Minority' Government in Canada," *Canadian Journal of Economics and Political Science*, Vol. 30 (1964), 1-11.

Gibson, F. W. *Cabinet Formation and Bicultural Relations* (Studies of the Royal Commission on Bilingualism and Biculturalism, 6, Ottawa, 1970).

Irvine, W. P. *Cultural Conflict in Canada: The Erosion of Consociational Politics* (unpublished Ph. D. thesis, Yale University, 1971).

Kwavnick, D., ed., *The Tremblay Report: Report of the Royal Commission of Inquiry on Constitutional Problems* (abridged version, The Carleton Library, No. 64, Toronto, 1973).

Levitt, J., ed., *Henri Bourassa on Imperialism and Biculturalism, 1900-1918* (Toronto, 1970).

Lower, A. R. M. "Two Ways of Life: The Primary Antithesis of Canadian History," *Canadian Historical Association Report*, 1943, 5-18, reprinted in C. Berger, ed. *Approaches to Canadian History* (Toronto, 1967), 15-28.

Noel, S. J. R. "Political Parties and Elite Accommodation: Interpretations of Canadian Federalism," in J. P. Meekison, ed., *Canadian Federalism: Myth or Reality* (2nd ed., Toronto, London, etc., 1971), 121-140.

Noel, S. J. R. "The Prime Minister's Role in a Consociational Democracy," in T. A. Hockin, ed. *Apex of Power: The Prime Minister and Political Leadership in Canada* (Scarborough, 1971), 103-107.

Presthus, R. *Elite Accommodation in Canadian Politics* (Toronto, 1973).

Royal Commission on Bilingualism and Biculturalism, *Report* (6 vols., Ottawa, 1967-1970). In addition to the *Report* and the *Preliminary Report* (Ottawa, 1965), research findings appeared in two printed series, *Studies* and *Documents*, as well as in mimeographed form (distributed on microfilm by the Canadian Library Association, Ottawa). A full list and brief description of research projects appears in the *Report*, Book I, Appendix V, 201-212.

Senior, H. *Orangeism: The Canadian Phase* (Toronto, Montreal, etc., 1972).

Simeon, R. *Federal-Provincial Diplomacy: The making of recent policy in Canada* (Toronto, 1972).

Van Loon, R. *The Structure and Membership of the Canadian Cabinet* (mimeographed, Ottawa, 1966). A study prepared for the Royal Commission on Bilingualism and Biculturalism.

Wade, M. ed., *Canadian Dualism: Studies of French-English Relations* (Toronto and Quebec City, 1960).

NOTES ON AUTHORS

VAL R. LORWIN is professor of history at the University of Oregon. He is the author of *The French Labor Movement* (1954), co-author and editor of *Labor and Working Conditions in Modern Europe* (1967), and co-author and co-editor of *The Dimensions of the Past: Materials, Problems, and Opportunities for Quantitative Work in History* (1972). He has served as an adviser on United States delegations to the International Labour Organization, the Economic and Social Council, and the General Assembly of the United Nations.

AREND LIJPHART is professor of international relations at the University of Leiden and formerly taught at the University of California at Berkeley. His principal research interests are in comparative politics (especially western democratic systems) and international relations. In addition to the publications cited above he is author of *The Trauma of Decolonization: The Dutch and West New Guinea* (1966).

GERHARD LEHMBRUCH is professor of political science at the University of Tübingen. In addition to the works cited above he is co-author of *Einführung in die Politikwissenschaft* (3rd ed., 1970).

JÜRG STEINER is professor of political science at the University of North Carolina at Chapel Hill and also teaches at the Universities of Geneva and Zurich. His current research interest is the study of decision-making in subculturally segmented political systems; among other publications he is author of *Amicable Agreement Versus Majority Rule: Conflict Resolution in Switzerland* (forthcoming).

HANS DAALDER is professor of political science at the University of Leiden. His chief publications are in comparative European politics, British and Dutch government, Marxism, and the politics of the developing areas. He has published *Cabinet Reform in Britain (1914-1963)* and has contributed to a number of symposium volumes including S. C. Patterson and J. C. Wahlke, eds., *Comparative Legislative Behavior*, and those cited in the Bibliography above.

JACOB P. KRUIJT was professor of sociology at the University of Utrecht from 1947 to 1968, and is now retired. He has worked on the sociology of religion, work and leisure, the labour movement, class structure, family life and demography, and vertical ideological pluralism, as well as on the history of sociology with particular reference to Weber, Durkheim, Tönnies, and Steinmetz.

ALFRED DIAMANT is professor of political science at Indiana University. In addition to the work excerpted in this volume he has published articles and chapters in books in the field of comparative bureaucracy and administration. He is currently engaged in a study of the political role of the higher public bureaucracy in Western Europe.

PETER G. J. PULZER is University Lecturer in politics at Oxford and Student and Tutor of Christ Church. He is interested in the origins, composition, programmes, appeals, and followings of mass movements, chiefly in Western and Central Europe, and is currently working on modern Germany. His publications include *The Rise of Political Anti-Semitism in Germany and Austria* (1964) and *Political Representation and Elections in Britain* (2nd ed., 1972).

ROGER GIROD is professor of sociology in the University of Geneva and a former executive secretary of the International Sociological Association. His publications include *Attitudes collectives et relations humaines: tendances actuelles des sciences sociales américaines* (1952), *Ouvriers et employés* (1961), and *Mobilité sociale* (1971). His present research is on longitudinal and contextual factors of inequality, including inequality of access to political influence.

S. J. R. NOEL teaches political science at the University of Western Ontario. His main areas of interest are Canadian federalism and provincial politics. In addition to the articles already cited he is the author of *Politics in Newfoundland* (1971) and is currently engaged on a study of Ontario.

WILLIAM ORMSBY is professor of history at Brock University. In addition to the book drawn upon for this volume he has written many articles on Canadian history and has edited *Crisis in the Canadas, 1838-39: The Grey Journals and Letters*. His general area of research interest is French-English relations in British North America between 1760 and 1867.

GEORGE F. G. STANLEY is currently Director of Canadian Studies at Mount Allison University after a distinguished career as a historian at Royal Military College, at the University of British Columbia, and with the Canadian Army. He has published ten books and numerous articles, his special interests being the history of Western Canada, military history, and Canadian constitutional history.

JANICE STAPLES is a graduate student in political science at Carleton University.

The editor, KENNETH D. McRAE, is professor of political science at Carleton University and a former supervisor of research for the Royal Commission on Bilingualism and Biculturalism. His main areas of interest are the history of political ideas, Canadian and American thought, and the comparative study of plurilingual societies. His publications include a critical edition of Jean Bodin, *The Six Bookes of a Commonweale* (1962) and a Royal Commission study, *The Federal Capital: Government Institutions* (1969).

THE CARLETON LIBRARY